D1523085

Terrorism, Security, and Human Rights

TERRORISM, SECURITY, AND HUMAN RIGHTS

Harnessing the Rule of Law

Mahmood Monshipouri

LYNNE
RIENNER
PUBLISHERS

BOULDER
LONDON

In memory of my precious mother, Sarah,
who taught me about living right and cherishing life

Published in the United States of America in 2012 by
Lynne Rienner Publishers, Inc.
1800 30th Street, Boulder, Colorado 80301
www.rienner.com

and in the United Kingdom by
Lynne Rienner Publishers, Inc.
3 Henrietta Street, Covent Garden, London WC2E 8LU

Library of Congress Cataloging-in-Publication Data
Monshipouri, Mahmood, 1952–
  Terrorism, security, and human rights : harnessing the rule of law /
Mahmood Monshipouri.
  Includes bibliographical references.
  ISBN 978-1-58826-826-6 (alk. paper)
  1. Terrorism—Prevention. 2. Terrorism (International law) 3. Human
rights. 4. Security, International. 5. Rule of law. I. Title.
  HV6431.M657 2012
  363.325'17—dc23   2011027646

British Cataloguing in Publication Data
A Cataloguing in Publication record for this book
is available from the British Library.

Printed and bound in the United States of America

The paper used in this publication meets the requirements
of the American National Standard for Permanence of
Paper for Printed Library Materials Z39.48-1992.

5 4 3 2 1

Contents

Preface   vii

1 Introduction   1

2 Terrorism, Security, and Human Rights   17

3 Military Intervention: Risks and Costs   55

4 Democracy Promotion: Failed Efforts in the Middle East   95

5 Diplomacy: Seeking Long-Term Solutions   131

6 The Critical Importance of Human Rights   171

7 Immigration Politics and the Rise of Islamophobia   207

8 Toward Reframing the Debate   243

Bibliography   291
Index   303
About the Book   309

v

Preface

It is time to move past the days of bewailing the disastrous Iraq policies of the Bush era. Far better ways to combat terrorism than invasion and occupation are ever becoming evident. The 2011 uprisings in the Middle East and North Africa (MENA)—the Arab Spring—have demonstrated that the old US bargain with local Arab autocrats has unraveled, making it very difficult for the US and other Western governments to work with authoritarian, yet pro-West, regimes that fail to genuinely represent the will of their own people. It is also apt to note that these uprisings demonstrated that many in the MENA region are driven more by secular economic concerns (i.e., jobs, wages, and economic security), as well as political goals (i.e., achieving human dignity and participation in national affairs), than by grand ideological narratives. The Arab Spring has clearly provided a counternarrative of peaceful democratic change to the so-called "war on terror" strategy, which has provoked violent regime change and military intervention.

Arguably, there is a unique opportunity for the Western world to adjust itself to the outcomes of these uprisings, which might dovetail nicely with many long-term strategic interests of the West in general and the United States more particularly in the region. Fostering internal democratic processes and genuine enhancement of human rights in the Muslim world can be an effective strategy for combating terrorism. Foreign policy initiatives and operations must be rooted in a tone of reconciliation and cooperation with Muslim states. Replacing perennial proposals for military intervention and occupation, the most potent measures will be those that address the economic and political issues of Muslim people. But understanding terrorism and terrorists in terms of their goals, methods, and targets is a complicated task fraught with both conceptual and operational confusion. While much is at stake in analyzing the relationships between and among terrorism, security, and human rights, far more difficult and daunting is the challenge of responding to terrorism and containing or even deterring it. Moreover, in the campaign against terror it is not clear exactly how victory can be measured, neither logically nor from the conventional standpoint, given the nature of modern terrorist activities and operations. Terrorists sometimes constitute a shadowy organization and at other times a loose web of organizations. They are motivated by so many different sectarian, secular, and mundane causes that it is virtually impossible to apply consistently similar tactics in confronting them.

An effective campaign against terrorists, however, requires the coordination of law enforcement, intelligence, diplomatic, and military assets in a multilateral way. The limits of counterterrorism as a model of solving the problems of US foreign policy toward the Middle East and North Africa merit particular attention. In this book I seek to make three important contributions to the existing literature.

First, I move beyond a critique of the Bush administration's policies, especially in the Middle East, to offer three models for approaching key security concerns: (1) the security model, (2) the social model, and (3) the legal-diplomatic model. Second, I discuss new challenges that have emerged in the face of recent European counterterrorism policies.

Third, I pay special attention to the breakdown of the power dynamics into regional blocs—that is, a pro-Western bloc and a resistance bloc. The implications of Turkey's newly assertive foreign policy and that of Iran, especially in light of new uprisings in North Africa and the Middle East, deserve further scrutiny. Of particular relevance to this project are the 2011 uprisings in Tunisia and Egypt, which have been followed by the tidal wave of demands for democracy and human rights throughout the MENA region. These uprisings demonstrate both the inevitability of change in an age of a youth revolution and the failure of traditional party politics to generate democratic change. Additionally, the role of the powerful, foreign meddlers in upholding authoritarian but pro-Western regimes in the region has become practically obsolete given the homegrown nature of the uprisings. The implications of this radical shift are playing out across the region and rippling across the globe.

* * *

Like most books, this one benefited immensely from the contributions of colleagues, students, and friends. I owe a large debt of gratitude to San Francisco State University, which provided a faculty grant so that I could conduct research for the project in Turkey, Qatar, and the United Arab Emirates, where I met with a number of scholars, NGOs, and think-tank organizations. My colleague Sean Duffy, chair and professor of political science at Quinnipiac University, read the entire manuscript and offered his invaluable insights on the subject. I am pleased to offer my thanks to my former student, Jonathon Whooley, currently a Ph.D. candidate at the University of Florida, for his limitless help at various stages of the project. I am also especially grateful to Ali Assareh, of New York University, whose generous assistance made it possible for me to complete the book. I owe a special debt of gratitude to Burnet Davis, Jeffrey Deem, Erich Wieger, Timmy Shoenau, Kristina Salsman, Ace W. Wiseman, Soraya Okuda, Travis Trapp, and Kevin O'Donnell for their indefatigable assistance on the project.

I also would like to express my sincere gratitude to Ihsan Dagi, of the Middle East Technical University in Ankara, Turkey, who kindly invited me for several dialogues and exchanges with his colleagues and students in the Department of International Relations and put me in touch with several NGOs dealing with the issue of terrorism. I also extend my sincere thanks to James N. Sater, of the American University, Sharjeh, the UAE, for making possible a discussion with his students and the faculty on the subject of security and human rights in Iran. Finally, I am particularly indebted to two anonymous reviewers for their helpful comments and suggestions.

1

Introduction

Terrorism, an endemic feature of modern society, is one of the most difficult challenges facing the world today. This is especially true for the West in terms of its capacity to respond to this phenomenon without sacrificing its values. The key for Western democracies confronted with the threat of terrorism has always been to strike a proper balance between liberty and national security. Balancing, reconciling the relationship between liberty and security in the context of combating terrorism—even offering clarity on the issues—is an immensely complex, daunting, and evolving task. The so-called global war on terror has become intimately associated with such diverse features as detention without trial, torture, disappearance, rendition, and extrajudicial killings. Counterterrorism measures such as the preventive detention of enemy combatants have made it hugely difficult to extend certain freedoms to detainees tried under military commissions.

As much as terrorism blocks the way in which democratic systems normally operate, counterterrorism strategies pose formidable challenges and dilemmas to the protection of basic freedoms. Precisely because of this inherent dichotomy, the task of reconciling the protection of human rights with the promotion of security has proven even more difficult, and governments have typically used their coercive powers to stifle individual freedoms in the wake of emergency situations.

The increasing tensions between civil liberties and security after the attacks of September 11, 2001, have elicited a great deal of attention in both academic and policy circles. The ensuing debate over the limits and risks of balancing human rights and security has posed the most difficult and pressing political and ethical questions in the post-9/11 era. Renewed discourse regarding the existence or absence of trade-offs between freedom and security has undergone an important shift in focus. From being a paradigm exclusively centered on power politics and excessively concerned with defeating terrorism militarily, it has shifted to take a measured and pragmatic approach that effectively combats terrorism without undermining the unassailable protection of human rights.

The primary objective of this book is to underline the need to redefine security to include the protection of human rights, among other things, while examining alternative strategies for combating terrorism. Experts have noted that by evoking the war frame (i.e., the "war on terror") President George W. Bush was able to use certain tools against terrorism that undermined civil liberties. The war on terror justified torture, military tribunals, and the suspension of due process. This tendency both revealed the limits of power and made manifest the way antiterrorism measures can compromise fundamental democratic values. Seeking to debunk the narrative that security and human rights are intrinsically irreconcilable, I argue for reframing the human rights debate not merely in terms of "standards" but also in terms of "universality," "identity," and "enforceable commitment." Without universality, human rights are nothing but hollow rhetoric. The struggle against violent extremism should not change who we are and what values we hold dear. Ratification of international human rights instruments such as the Convention Against Torture (CAT) renders them the supreme law of the land, making their enforcement imperative. There can be no double standards in respecting internationally recognized human rights. All signatories to human rights instruments must comply with them, both nationally and internationally.

To better recalibrate the balance between security and civil liberties in the face of potential terrorism, Western policymakers must ask the right questions and think in terms of the human rights implications of their policies (armed conflict or negotiations). The present analysis focuses on the changing conceptions of security—from national or collective security to human security. The latter, which entails freedom from physical violence, poverty, hunger, and disease, places individuals and their moral worth at the core of its investigation. I argue that the provision of human security for citizens offers the strongest and most optimal antiterrorism strategy and that the effectiveness of any counterterrorism and counterinsurgency operation or policy must be gauged within the context of human security.

The Failure of Unilateralism and Military Intervention

Heavily influenced by neoconservative thinking, the Bush Doctrine described a set of unilateral policies based on the preemptive use of force against security threats—even before they clearly materialize. This doctrine was based on a grand strategy that envisioned a unipolar world that entirely asserted the right of the United States to act unilaterally in the face of perceived threats. As such, the United States was posited to be in a unique position to play a truly hegemonic role. President Bush portrayed Iraq as a threat to national and international security, arguing that Iraq possessed or had actively tried to possess chemical, biological, and nuclear weapons. Having linked Saddam Hussein's regime to the 9/11 terrorist attacks, this policy equated removing Saddam Hussein and his regime with eliminating the threat that his regime posed to international peace and stability. The post-9/11 wars in Afghanistan and Iraq served as clear illustrations of the Bush Doctrine in practice. As the war in Iraq fueled ethnic and sectarian conflicts inside that country and made any future reconciliation among the warring groups immensely complicated, the most visible backlash against the two military interventions emerged in Iraq in the form of an anti-American and antioccupation insurgency.

Theorists of international relations, by scrutinizing the utility of military force as well as the legal and diplomatic resources and strategies to counter terrorism, have both opened new possibilities for the human rights community and widened the divide within it. On one side are those who argue that security and human rights need not necessarily stand in a zero-sum relationship: through the regular application and protection of civil rights, substantial security improvements will manifest a spirit of respected dignity for all concerned. On the other side are those who argue that there is a need to reconcile human rights and security: achieving this goal, according to these scholars, requires a new theoretical discussion, acknowledging that certain rights must be subordinate to the urgent claims of security. The results of the debate between the two sides have been mixed. There is an unmistakable friction in the international community over measures and actions to protect and promote both security and human rights; at the same time, there is a growing consensus as to how the international community should constrain the exercise of power. Finally, many question the extent to which the use of force is an effective tool in the arsenal of counterterrorism.

There are no easy solutions to these contestable dilemmas. What is clear is that the effectiveness of any counterterrorism measure depends on several intersecting political, military, legal, and ethical dynamics, which in turn raise serious concerns and questions about the long-term effectiveness of such counterterrorist measures. In this regard, the most invasive and oft-cited example is the USA Patriot Act, passed by Congress in 2001, which authorizes the detention without due process—potentially indefinitely—of those labeled "suspected terrorists." In recent years, the uncertainty clouding the "war on terror" has resulted more from the frequent application of force, the practice of rendition, and the use of enhanced interrogation techniques (a euphemism for torture) than from reliance on law enforcement and international cooperation. In most cases, torture has produced false and fabricated information, undermined the legal and moral authority of the United States, and provided terrorist groups with a recruiting and motivational tool.

Furthermore, other negative consequences have followed the violations of humane treatment and due process—the hallmarks of the US Constitution and the Geneva Conventions. These antiterrorism programs have seriously damaged US relations with its allies in the West. Regardless of the short-term gains, violations of the Geneva Conventions have led to enormous losses in moral standing for the United States in the international community. There is reason to doubt that such counterterrorism measures have improved security in an age dominated by the need for international coordination and cooperation, as well as pragmatic solutions. Indeed, decisionmaking regarding the emerging global issues of the twenty-first century is increasingly informed by the concepts of legality, legitimacy, and pragmatism.

The promoters of the "power-trumps-justice" notion maintain that power can serve justice—specifically in the case of fighting terrorism through preemptive strikes, military interventions, and regime change, which all are held to be warranted under certain circumstances. This rationale is adamantly opposed by those who are reluctant to approve the politics of intervention without strong moral and legal sanction. Under such circumstances, the best that can be expected appears to be a two-pronged approach: supporting a move toward the creation of international law-enforcement mechanisms to hold individuals accountable under the standards of international justice while simultaneously promoting domestic laws to achieve local and national mechanisms of legal accountability vis-à-vis terrorism.

Counterterrorism Models and Their Limits

In this book, I offer three models of counterterrorism: (1) the security model, (2) the social model, and (3) the legal-diplomatic model.

The security model posits that sacrificing human rights in the interest of security is justified and provides the most effective means of countering terrorism. Security mechanisms, including military repression and preemptive strikes, are the hallmarks of this strategy. Some policymakers in the Bush administration underscored the importance of the security model, placing emphasis on security at the expense of human rights and the rule of law. The lead-up to the wars in Iraq and Afghanistan and the administration's disdain for the rule of law in conducting its counterterrorism activities were excellent examples of this precarious implementation and its pitfalls. In recent years, disagreements over the primacy of this approach and fears of much deeper entanglement in a protracted conflict have led to divisions among NATO members in their continued collaboration against the resurgent Taliban in Afghanistan. Notwithstanding the Bush administration's primary emphasis on security, there were others in that administration who claimed that the chief antidotes to terrorism were democracy and free market reforms. There is as of yet no empirical support for this contention.

The controversy surrounding preemptive strikes and military interventions has evoked varied responses. First, the proponents of intervention—humanitarian or otherwise—view any violations of human rights as legitimate grounds for invoking such an act. They also contend that it is morally imperative to "prevent or mitigate" human suffering and injustice when one has the capacity to do so. An alternative view holds that advocates of military intervention lack a secure theoretical home. Many holding this view argue that, to the extent that advocates of military intervention seek to revise, reform, or overturn the prevailing norm of nonintervention in international law, they challenge both realist and liberal notions of national security and international peace. They contend that the case for military intervention can be made on purely military and political grounds, often overriding the legal tradition of nonintervention by qualifying the "war on terror" and toppling "rogue states" as just cause for intervention.

A third perspective comes from the critics of military intervention, consensual or nonconsensual. These critics claim that the costs and consequences of such action—civilian suffering, regional instability, and the fueling of internal tribal, ethnic, and sectarian tensions—run counter to the stated objectives of military intervention: the ending of genocide, mass slaughter, and terrorism. Likewise, they argue that counterinsurgency and counterterrorism operations will encounter many difficulties since these measures often assume contradictory and competing approaches, involving trying to balance the security of the population under occupation with the objective of defeating terrorists or insurgents hiding among the local people. Under such circumstances, the use of military force achieves short-term tactical victories at the expense of the long-term goal: the winning of popular support that would form the backbone of an effective and sustainable strategy. Those who advocate this view emphasize how difficult it is to overcome the deeply ingrained perception of subjugation, occupation, and exploitation that has characterized the modern history of Western intervention in the Middle East.

At the core of my second model of counterterrorism, the social model, lies the protection of individuals from a wide range of threats—economic, environmental, criminal, military, and political. The social model postulates that targeting economic security and development assistance is a far more effective counterterrorism strategy than the one predicated on the number of tanks, ships, planes, and troops.

According to the social model, development aid for Afghanistan, for example, aimed at rebuilding the country, would be a crucial step toward winning the hearts and minds of village populations and tribes. This is a human-centered approach, focusing on the provision of security for individuals while promoting freedom from "fear" and "want." The advocates of this model argue that states cannot declare war on nonstate actors, such as al-Qaeda, and that the most effective counterterrorism strategy is one predicated on improving the lives of local people and gaining their support for the fight against terrorism. This is done simply by investing in the country's infrastructure, such as schools, hospitals, and water projects. On a broader level, this model attributes the cause of terrorism to the lack of social justice, making it crucial to bear in mind that economic opportunity is a more attractive alternative to people than supporting terrorism, and that this is especially true if that economic opportunity is actually available—regardless of winning "hearts and minds."

This model fosters the creation of an environment in which civil society organizations and prodemocracy Muslim organizations can flourish. The social approach deserves more attention, but it is not without its own complexities. When searching for the origins of terrorism, it is not simply the lack of socioeconomic development but also local political and cultural dynamics that need to be accounted for. The transatlantic rift over the Iraq war, as well as the experience of the European Union with its Muslim immigrants in the post-9/11 era, serve as good examples. US-European relations deteriorated markedly over the appropriate response to terrorism with the onset of the US invasion of Iraq in 2003. Growing support for the Iraqi resistance to US occupation throughout the Muslim world, along with the difficulties facing NATO forces in Afghanistan, drove a wedge between US leaders and their allies. This political and diplomatic dissonance exacerbates longstanding political divisions regarding the nature and terms of US–EU/NATO commitments.

The leaders of the European Union, having recently experienced terrorism motivated by radical Islamic movements on their own continent, and facing challenges similar to the ones faced by the US government, have become acutely aware of the difficulties and flaws of counterterrorism measures being promoted by the US-led "struggle against violent extremism." Significantly, these European leaders have realized that national security is far more contingent upon the inclusion of Muslim immigrants than their exclusion from European societies. The deep interconnection between security and integration has never been more apparent, yet in perilous times, integration policies tend to come under attack. As concerns over violent extremism grow in the West, European governments are rethinking their approaches to integration.

The third of the three models of counterterrorism, the legal-diplomatic model, employs the full panoply of law-enforcement instruments and justice system practices—not to mention international cooperation, intelligence sharing, and diplomacy. These tools are essential to both a successful response to acts of terrorism as well as to the prevention of future attacks.

The legal-diplomatic model offers a comprehensive definition of the "war on terror," stressing increased international cooperation and substantive cross-border participation. In the United States, this approach seems to have been widely embraced by the Obama administration. Many Europeans have castigated the United States for its unilateral occupation of Iraq. They have argued that the broad failures in Iraq have demonstrated that collective action, mobilization, cooperation, and support are indeed essential for combating terrorist organizations like al-

Qaeda. Significantly, proponents of the legal-diplomatic model argue that fighting terrorism should be a matter of law enforcement or the judiciary, rather than primarily a military affair.

What continuously emerges from this debate is that simply adapting to new political realities is woefully inadequate. A dynamic and original way of thinking is required to demonstrate that the commitment to liberty is resilient enough to withstand the brittle tyrannies of terrorism. If the campaign against terrorism fundamentally distorts the basic truths of Western existence, then the case can be made, however grudgingly, that the terrorists have been exceptionally successful. Proper moral weight must be given to both liberty and security because these two values are not irreconcilable or mutually exclusive. There is no easy remedy to the starkly apparent tensions between security needs and human rights. But to pursue a security template that invariably sacrifices civil liberties is not only morally debilitating but, over the longer term, also politically imprudent. More seriously, because terrorism is largely a modern political phenomenon, it is vitally important to address the grievances that fuel it in the first place.

To frame the tension between security and human rights in absolutist terms is fundamentally misleading. Although promoting and protecting deeply held legal and moral values is one way to enhance security, such basic values are better protected and advanced only within a stable and secure environment. The practices of torture and coercive interrogation techniques at Abu Ghraib and Guantanamo Bay are widely regarded as cruel, inhuman, and degrading. The real risk inherent in treating detainees inhumanely in the interest of national security, even under supreme emergencies, is that such a basis for action is outside the law—both moral law and statutory law. We should look for ways to tackle and overcome terrorism without putting our basic liberties and democratic ideals at risk.

The lessons for the West and the rest of the world beyond September 11 are varied and many. First, the responsibility for security and stability in the post-9/11 era, especially after the Afghanistan and Iraq wars, must be shared locally, regionally, and globally. The emergence of regional actors such as Turkey, capable of mediating conflicts and tensions in the region, has provided a unique opportunity that merits attention. Second, human rights may *not* provide a suitable vehicle for handling every political and legal issue. In times of crises, such as civil wars or acts of terrorism, stability and the preservation of international peace need to be balanced against—but not necessarily be detrimental to—the strict adherence to justice and human rights. In situations both before and after a crisis, however, the preservation of human rights is directly bound up not only with states' internal stability but also with international peace and tranquility. Under such circumstances, the dichotomy between human rights and security is an imprecise way of framing the debate. I argue rather that the notion of a reconstruction of security—collective and individual—can be more effectively employed to invoke debate over the consequences of military intervention or the use of force in the context of combating terrorism.

Iraq is perhaps the most telling example of counterinsurgency. Seven years after the US invasion, Iraq has become the epicenter of global terrorism, as the Bush Doctrine—manifested in unilateralist and interventionist policies—has contributed to greater levels of insecurity there. Experts caution that, for reasons ranging from ethnic conflict and sectarianism to military intervention, the invasion of Iraq has posed intractable challenges to US counterinsurgency efforts. The fact that Iraq has become a breeding ground for cultivating al-Qaeda's supporters for the global jihadist movement offers grim confirmation of such military misadventures.

The Bush administration's inconsistent and erratic position toward balancing the "war on terror" with the grandiose plan of democracy promotion proved inept and problematic, further compromising US foreign policy objectives. On balance, the longer-term cost of a military approach authorizing the use of force, torture, detention, and extraordinary rendition far outweighed its sporadic and unpredictable short-term benefits. The real question is: What is the most effective way to defeat terrorists? The answer is still up for debate. Some combination of the three approaches outlined above is perhaps the most effective way to mount a sustainable campaign against terrorism and hold together a coalition of support for that purpose.

One of the basic precepts of counterterrorism is that the fight against terror need not always be viewed in primarily military terms. Likewise, in counterinsurgency programs it is often said that "sometimes, the more force used, the less effective it is." Knowing when the use of force is effective and when it is counterproductive is essential. Exercising this choice prudently requires employing a comprehensive strategy that focuses on winning popular support, promoting reconstruction efforts, and establishing the rule of law. Military intervention and regime change, as we have come to see, did not work under the Bush administration. Driven by a culture of fear and crusade against jihadism, the US foreign policy agenda has proven self-defeating. The US presence in the pre-9/11 and post-9/11 periods, the latter under the rubric of a "war on terror," has given birth to terrorist movements with diverse, even contradictory, political agendas. It is reasonable to assume that an Arab-Israeli peace treaty that, among other things, promises a homeland for the Palestinians will prove the most effective antidote to counteract the poison of terrorism in the region. A reasonable and peaceful solution to the Arab-Israeli conflicts will provide the ultimate example of how diplomatic efforts to assuage feelings of resentment in the region may have far better results than a military approach.

In the post-9/11 period, we have to face the fact that both the Afghans and the Iraqis will determine their own fate. One can further argue that pragmatic and multilateral efforts, such as seeking the cooperation of allies on law enforcement and intelligence sharing, along with diplomatic campaigns, might offer the best way to balance human rights and security considerations. In a speech delivered at Cairo University on June 4, 2009, President Obama struck a fresh tone by asking for a "new beginning between the United States and Muslims around the world." President Obama went on to assert that "so long as our relationship is defined by our differences, we will empower those who sow hatred rather than peace, and who promote conflict rather than the cooperation that can help all of our people achieve justice and prosperity. This cycle of suspicion and discord must end." Obama's speech resonated strongly among moderate Muslims throughout the world, as he laid down crucial markers that signaled a new US approach to the Middle East and beyond.

After reviewing the US strategy in Afghanistan, Obama decided to send an additional thirty thousand US troops to Afghanistan as part of AfPak policy, setting 2011 as a drawdown date. His goal was twofold: (1) to prevent al-Qaeda from returning to Afghanistan (it was from Afghanistan that 9/11 was executed) and (2) to keep Taliban insurgents from overthrowing the Karzai government. The additional US troops were intended to secure several population centers and to assault Taliban strongholds such as Marjah and Kandahar. US forces were expected to collaborate with the Afghanis and create an independent, full-fledged army. Skepticism regarding this policy and exit strategy continued to grow as the nagging question persisted: Would sending more troops increase the difficulty of getting them out in an appropriate and timely manner? Beyond this and related operational questions, the vexing issue of human and material costs associated with security-oriented options, which often required the sacrifice of civil liberties and political free-doms in the name of combating terrorism, necessitated a rethinking of US counterterrorism strategies.

Equally contentious are growing divisions within NATO concern-ing Afghan policy. In Afghanistan, despite eight years of occupation, an enormous US leadership effort, and more than 150,000 troops on the ground, NATO has failed to achieve its objectives and is beginning a retreat without a clear victory. Given the existing trend in NATO away from real solidarity, some observers have cautioned that without US leadership, the alliance is likely to hollow out from within.[1] How President Obama will respond to this new challenge remains to be seen.

Moreover, the Obama administration's decision to withdraw US troops from Iraq by December 31, 2011, has resulted in mixed reactions from both Iraqi authorities and civilians. A broad consensus in Kirkuk, an area with a predominantly Kurdish population in northern Iraq, holds that a continued US military presence is integral to their region's stabili-ty. Because Kirkuk lacks a unified security force of its own, many Kurdish leaders warn against the possibility of terrorist groups concen-trating on places such as Kirkuk and Mosul, where they can exploit political differences among the groups. They argue that under such cir-cumstances the United States can play a key role as a broker among dif-ferent communities in Kirkuk and intervene in times of crisis.[2] It is worth noting that under intense US pressure, Iraqi prime minister Nouri al-Maliki has agreed to start negotiations on keeping some US soldiers in Iraq. Despite the opposition of the followers of Shiite cleric Muqtada al-Sadr, Prime Minister Maliki has enough support for such an agree-ment to be passed by parliament.

The Argument

In the chapters that follow I examine the limits of the use of force, tor-ture, rendition, and externally imposed democratization processes, while pressing the case for the continued relevance of international law and diplomacy as effective tools to sever the roots of terrorism in the Middle East. My point of departure lies in questioning the so-called "enhanced interrogation techniques" that the Bush administration authorized after the attacks of September 11, 2001. The involvement of US departments and agencies in detainee abuse in Iraq's Abu Ghraib,

Guantanamo Bay, Afghanistan's Bagram Air Base, and other locations has been well documented.[3] A recent study of the lives of former detainees once held in US custody in Afghanistan and Guantanamo Bay has revealed the prevalence and systematic nature of this abuse and the propriety of specific interrogation methods.[4]

Moreover, the 2011 democratic uprisings in North Africa and the Middle East demonstrate that maintaining order and stability can no longer be divorced from upholding human rights, human security, and social justice. The young generation of educated men and women throughout the Arab world and beyond appear to be more open and sympathetic to a liberal, constitutional order. Increasingly, their generation has shown more interest in addressing economic and political grievances, including governmental competence, corruption, and growth, rather than in making grand ideological statements.[5] The leaderless uprisings in Tunisia, Egypt, and the rest of the Arab world attest to the old order, built archaically around negotiation and collaboration with Arab autocrats, having fundamentally unraveled. It is no longer cost-effective to back dictators.[6] The time has come to underline the need for a more nuanced view of stability in the Middle East. The pursuit of a security template that suspends basic civil liberties not only is morally bankrupt but also has become increasingly imprudent politically.

In light of the 2011 uprisings, and given the complexity of the campaign against terrorism, this book's central argument is that peaceful, democratic change from within and from below offers an effective counternarrative to the so-called war on terror, illustrating the inevitability of change in an age of rebellious youth and failing traditional party politics. Increasingly, against the background of the homegrown uprisings, the role of powerful foreign meddlers in upholding authoritarian but pro-West regimes in the region has become practically obsolete.

In keeping with my core argument, I seek to reframe the debate on security and human rights while supporting legal and diplomatic counterterrorism tools. I subscribe to the notion that legal instruments—such as treaties, conventions, and covenants—and diplomatic means can bring about positive, lasting change.[7] Thus, this book is largely about the conditions under which such tools can be properly utilized. Its limitations notwithstanding, diplomacy has many principled advantages in facilitating new opportunities for the peaceful resolution of regional conflicts such as the Israeli-Palestinian one.

For instance, many experts argue that bringing a lasting end to the Israeli-Palestinian conflict through creating an independent, viable, and contiguous state for the Palestinians will minimize the threat of terrorism in the region more efficiently than a simple invasion (consider, for example, the dreadful consequences of the US invasion of Iraq). Because of its enormous resonance throughout the Muslim world, the Palestinian issue is one of the central issues fueling Islamic radicalism—the specific brand of militancy labeled most menacing to the United States.[8]

Although the examination of other counterterrorism tools (e.g., the interdiction of financial assets, the use of intelligence measures, reliance on the criminal justice system) are beyond the scope of this book, it is worth noting that effective intelligence gathering is critical for reducing the likelihood of terrorism and that prosecutions and the strict application of national law contain counterterrorism value far beyond simple emotional revenge. Some observers have noted that the creation by the US Department of Defense of a system of military tribunals to put captured people (alleged to be terrorists) on trial has demonstrated that the military and criminal justice systems are not entirely separate counterterrorism instruments.[9]

The arguments and examples cited in this introduction illustrate the need for reframing the debate over how best to deal with terrorism. I will also argue that there is a need for refining the conversation surrounding the notions of *universality, identity,* and *enforceable commitment* on the basis of legality and legitimacy, and not expediency alone. As such, terrorism is best dealt with as a crime, inside state borders, and through cooperative international law-enforcement efforts. This reframing offers a realistic and substantive opportunity to address a number of contemporary human rights problems in the context of the struggle against violent extremists, juxtaposed against the slogan "You are either with us or against us in the fight against terror."[10]

Such reframing goes to the heart of the challenge facing the global community in terms of "utilizing its advantages to win the war of ideas that motivates and sustains those responsible for the current wave of terrorist violence."[11] It is in this context that Western support for authoritarian yet friendly regimes in the Middle East and North Africa must be reevaluated. The popular uprisings that started in early 2011 have contributed to a new climate of political activism and change that is enormously receptive to ideas of peaceful democratic transformation and electoral democracies. These uprisings have provided a unique opportunity, for the Western world in general and the United States in particular, to exploit these internal political battles, because they can undermine the narrative of bringing about change through militancy and terrorism methods and tactics.

With the demise of Osama bin Laden, the debate over the withdrawal of US forces from Afghanistan has renewed opposing views. While the proponents of surgical strikes advocate attacking terrorist cells with special forces as they arise, supporters of counterinsurgency underscore the importance of relying on significant troop deployment.[12] Any fresh review of the post–bin Laden era must take into account both risks and benefits of counterterrorism measures. Failure to reframe and adequately alter the debate in this more refined direction will severely stunt and stymie the progress of the human rights project throughout the world, especially at a time when it seems to have gathered new and historic momentum in the Middle East and North Africa.

Organization of the Book

To open my review of the different strategies for combating terrorism within local, regional, and international contexts, Chapter 2 examines the roots of terrorism and revisits the competing ethical views on how to respond to it. Chapter 3 investigates the risks and costs of applying military solutions. Chapter 4 reveals the flaws of trying to export democracy to the Middle East by examining the Bush administration's democratization agenda in the region, and I also espouse embracing a new realism in US foreign policy toward the region. Chapter 5 critically examines the US-led war on terror as a campaign that has been largely fought based on US military prowess, a strategy devoid of utilizing diplomatic assets. In Chapter 6, I explore the issue of counterterrorism and human rights, arguing that the trade-off hypothesis (security over human rights) is far too crude to do justice to the human rights discourse. Chapter 7 offers an analysis of the costs and consequences of the current "war on terror" strategy for the West, including an examination of the socioeconomic and political conditions facing Muslim immigrants in the United States and Europe in the post-9/11 era. And in the concluding chapter, I assess alternative strategies for combating terrorism and discuss the US military misadventures in Iraq and Afghanistan and the failure of current counterterrorism measures. To overcome the legacy of the Bush administration and its flawed approach to the war on terror, it is crucial to seriously examine the components of the trade-off thesis: security over human rights.

Notes

1. Kurt Volker, "Afghanistan and Libya Point NATO to Five Lessons," *Christian Science Monitor*, August 1, 2011, p. 35

2. Mahammed A. Salih, "Why Oil-Rich Kirkuk Wants US to Stay," *Christian Science Monitor*, August 15 and 22, 2011, pp. 12–13; see esp. p. 12.

3. Shadi Mokhtari, *After the Abu Ghraib: Exploring Human Rights in America and the Middle East* (New York: Cambridge University Press, 2009).

4. Laurel E. Fletcher and Eric Stover, *The Guantanamo Effect: Exposing the Consequences of U.S. Detention and Interrogation Practices* (Berkeley: University of California Press, 2009), pp. 11–12.

5. Fareed Zakaria, "How Democracy Can Work in the Middle East," *Time*, Feb. 3, 2011; available at http://www.time.com/time/world/article/0,8599 ,2045888-4,00.html; accessed Feb. 14, 2011.

6. Fouad Ajami, "Demise of the Dictators," *Newsweek*, Feb. 14, 2011, pp. 18–27.

7. Beth A. Simmons, *Mobilizing for Human Rights: International Law in Domestic Politics* (New York: Cambridge University Press, 2009), pp. 12–13.

8. Paul R. Pillar, *Terrorism and U.S. Foreign Policy* (Washington, DC: Brookings Institution Press, 2001), p. xlv.

9. Ibid., pp. xxix–xxxiii.

10. President Bush made such remarks several times throughout the course of his presidency. On September 20, 2001, he said in his address to a joint session of Congress and the American people, "Either you are with us, or you are with the terrorists." See Address to a Joint Session of Congress and the American People, The White House, September 20, 2011, available at http://georgewbush-whitehouse.archives.gov/news/releases/2001/09/20010920-8.html. Again on November 6, 2001, during a joint news conference with French president Jacques Chirac, President Bush said, "You're either with us or against us in the fight against terror." See "Bush Says It Is Time for Action," CNN, November 6, 2001; available at http://edition.cnn.com/2001/US/11/06/ret .bush.coalition/index.html.

11. James D. Kiras, "Terrorism and Globalization," in John Baylis and Steve Smith, eds., *The Globalization of World Politics: An Introduction to International Relations*, 3rd ed. (New York: Oxford University Press, 2005), pp. 479–497; see esp. p. 495.

12. Anna Mulrine, "Bin Laden Raid: A New Template?" *Christian Science Monitor*, May 23, 2011, p. 20.

2

Terrorism, Security, and Human Rights

The relationship between terrorism, security, and human rights is widely regarded to be conflictive and contradictory. There has been considerable tension on how best to promulgate policies that promote security, protect human rights, advance international law, and combat terrorism effectively. A careful approach to concurrently advance these values and interests requires focusing on the underlying causes of terrorism as an essential first step in considering whether the campaign against terrorism can be effectively waged. Put simply, addressing the root causes of terrorism is an essential task of the campaign against terrorism.

During the Cold War, the United States supported unsavory governments and unpopular leaders in the Middle East, largely to protect its oil interests. In 1953, for instance, after Shah Mohammad Reza Pahlavi had been deposed and forced to leave Iran, he was restored to power in a coup carried out by the British secret intelligence service and the US Central Intelligence Agency (CIA). The United States continued to support the shah, even as a majority of the Iranian people staged a massive protest against his regime in 1979 that ultimately resulted in his downfall.[1]

Saddam Hussein, who came to power in 1979 through an internally orchestrated coup, was another protégé of the United States, a status that allowed him to get away with gruesome crimes, most notably the 1988 chemical attack against the Iraqi Kurdish population known as the Halabja massacre. It was only after the Iraqi invasion of Kuwait in 1990 that Hussein's actions were met with fierce resistance by the United States and its allies. Many Muslims resent the way the United States supports autocratic rulers such as the Saudi royal family. In fact, Osama bin Laden was himself a protégé of the United States, funding mujahidin freedom fighters to dislodge Soviet troops from Afghanistan during the 1980s. Nevertheless, after the Soviets had pulled out of

Afghanistan, no systematic assistance or aid was forthcoming for the war-torn country, whose chaotic political conditions made it possible for the Taliban to come to power.[2] The Taliban subsequently harbored al-Qaeda terrorists and their affiliated networks.

I begin by examining the roots of terrorism and then revisit the competing ethical views on how to respond to it before discussing counterinsurgency and counterterrorism and their tools, including torture, military measures, the promotion of democracy and human rights, good governance, the rule of law, criminal justice, and traditional diplomatic instruments. At the end of this chapter I examine the limits of counterterrorism and nation building as organizing principles for the actions of the United States and its NATO allies in both Iraq and Afghanistan.

The Roots of Terrorism

Why has the epidemic of terror reached a new height in the Middle East? This, despite the fact that Muslims all over the world condemn terrorism, outrightly rejecting the use of religious doctrine to commit terrorist acts. Radical and neofundamentalist Islamic groups have plunged some Muslim countries into civil war (Afghanistan, Sudan, Algeria), have threatened to disrupt life in others (Saudi Arabia, Indonesia), have resisted becoming marginalized in still others (Iran), and may have found a new home in another (Iraq). Terrorist incidents worldwide have increased threefold since the US-led invasion of Iraq in March 2003. Indiscriminate attacks against civilian targets seem to have been gaining momentum in recent years. These self-styled violent acts, especially against religious and nongovernmental organizations, defy logic and hardly win the support of the world's 1.2 billion Muslims. It is not clear whether these destructive operations are always committed by young disillusioned and disempowered members of Muslim societies left behind by modernity, as many have assumed. What is evident, however, is that such acts are part of well-coordinated, politically organized, and tactically selected operations to wreak havoc on political regimes that either do not share the terrorists' views or are seen as being in cahoots with the US and Israeli governments.

Terrorism perpetrated in the name of Islam is tantamount to hijacking the religion for a particular group's purpose or agenda. (Contrary to the politically and ideologically motivated violence advocated by terrorist groups to change existing regimes, the 2011 social unrest and peaceful democratic movements were spontaneous and had no ideological or political leaders.) Two blunt questions remain in the minds of many Muslims who denounce such acts: What religious rationale lies behind such acts of hatred and radicalism? And how could these heinous crimes be warranted in the name of jihad or self-defense? For Muslims all over the world, these radical Islamists do not represent the armies of God. Their acts cannot be justified by delusions of religious mandates. Attacking innocent civilians is a crime against humanity, committed by mercenaries of destruction.

Contrary to the naïve bravado of neoconservatives in the US Department of Defense and the White House under the Bush administration, it is unrealistic to believe that conventional military campaigns against al-Qaeda and similar groups will resolve the global problem of terrorism. The United States must work together with Muslim countries to debunk the myth of a "clash of civilizations"—a myth fueled by the perpetrators of radical Islamic terrorist attacks. To the contrary, what we are witnessing is a "collision of neoconservatives" on both sides, which appears to have stolen the stage from a more moderate and liberal approach. The mixing of political and religious ideologies poses a great menace to all civilizations.

Effective strategies to combat terrorism are those that foster internal democratic processes and bring genuine improvements in the area of human rights in the Muslim world. Foreign policy initiatives and operations must be rooted in a tone of reconciliation and cooperation with Muslim states. In place of perennial questions of military intervention and occupation, the most effective measures will be those that address the economic and political issues of Muslim people—such as addressing the needs of the Palestinian people. Only when such issues are properly addressed can we seriously hope to undermine the longevity of terrorist groups and networks. Recognizing the desirability of more diplomacy and increased integration into the fast-growing global economy, Muslims in the Middle East are striving to carve out their space in a modern world. Just as a commitment by political leaders to integration is critical to enhancing economic development and security, it is also crucial to bring about change from below in Middle Eastern countries. A new approach is needed to dispense with the overly ambitious and unrealistic aim of rapid democratic transformation. The poorly conceived, cookie-cutter strategy advocated by an earlier US administration—that of the Bush neoconservatives—clearly has fueled hostility and insecurity across the breadth of the Muslim world.[3]

The seemingly paradoxical nature of democracy promotion at gunpoint raises the question: Why cannot democracy be imported or exported? The short answer is that the requisite conditions of a functioning democracy, such as established parliamentary and judicial systems, security and economic institutions, a vibrant civil society, pluralistic cultural values, and the rule of law, are hard to come by in many countries. What is more difficult to achieve in nondemocratic countries—even beyond popular sovereignty—is the establishment of the institutions, skills, and values that a successful exercise of liberty requires, which can be neither imported nor exported.[4] Given the most widely accepted assumption that "the key to establishing working democracy, and in particular the institutions of liberty, has been the free-market economy," it may well be the case that questions of security, counterterrorism, and economic development must be addressed prior to the issue of democracy promotion in the Middle East.[5]

Apart from the obvious need to find a peaceful and conciliatory agenda, moving forward in eradicating terrorism will require overcoming a variety of hurdles, none more important than protecting and promoting human rights. This chapter proceeds from the assumption that, in combating terrorism, respect for the rule of law and human rights goes beyond the issues of fairness and tolerance and becomes also a question of security.[6] This assumption places our focus on the domestic policy environment by demonstrating how the interaction between state and society can minimize the terrorist threat within the Muslim world. While military options against terrorists have been widely implemented and discussed, sociopolitical and economic issues internal to the Muslim world have been less noticed. Local solutions for bringing about change and reform deserve equal attention.

For nearly half a century, the Muslim world has seen the resurgence of a political Islam and the rise of Islamists in a variety of contexts, as revolutionaries, radicals, and reformers.[7] Today, however, the mobilizing ideas in the Muslim world revolve around three key words: democracy, growth, and globalization. These democratically globalized concepts are bound to foster a new culture that defies terrorism and, when compared to previous generations, varies just as deeply. These ideas, which are not entirely unrelated, have engendered momentous changes in Muslim societies and communities, shaping in the process wide-ranging and dynamic debates about social changes and human rights. This trend has emerged even in the Middle East, albeit slowly. In 2005, democratic forces in Lebanon rose up to peacefully drive out Syrian troops. On May 16, 2005, Kuwaiti adult females (aged twenty-one and above) became eligible to participate in parliamentary elections, and in June 2006, they participated as voters and candidates in parliamentary elections for the first time. The 2011 Arab awakening throughout the Middle East and North Africa showed that the call for democratic participation, the rule of law, and the expansion of civil society were as much the driving force behind such upheavals as economic insecurity. The triumph of a peaceful popular movement to rid Egypt of its longtime autocrat, Hosni Mubarak, has been a nightmare for terrorist groups such as al-Qaeda.

This optimism has been undone, however, by the democratic recession caused by electoral fraud and endemic corruption throughout the world. In the developing and post-Communist worlds, experts argue, democracy has been a superficial phenomenon, manipulated by abusive police and security forces, and undermined by corrupt and incompetent local oligarchs, state bureaucracies and judiciaries, as well as contemptuous ruling elites that ignore the rule of law and their vested social responsibilities.[8] Alarmingly, in the Middle East, a growing rift has emerged between state and society, as aspirations for democratic progress have been thwarted, whether by terrorism and violence (as in Iraq), externally manipulated social divisions (as in Lebanon), or authoritarian regimes themselves (as in Egypt, Jordan, Iran, and some of the Persian Gulf monarchies, such as Bahrain).[9] Although many analysts place the rise of political Islam in the context of revolutionary and populist politics, a closer examination reveals that the conditions and issues that continue to inspire Islamists are also linked to the protection of human dignity and promotion of democratic values.

Proceeding from the assumption that democracy is not a culture-bound Western artifact, in this chapter I explain why democratic values—not terrorism—will drive Muslim societies for generations to come. To avoid political and religious violence, ruling elites in the Middle East must listen to their citizen's voices, foster their participation in the political process, protect and promote their rights, and respond to their socioeconomic needs. The contemporary political importance of Islamism can be best understood as a rational response not only to the failure of many governments in the Muslim world to rule wisely or well but also to the lack of democratic means and opportunities available to opposition groups to unseat them.[10] Islamist groups have articulated and expressed the concerns of society's underprivileged, especially the young, the unemployed, and the alienated. While it is true that the 2011 revolutionary movements were led by youth organizations, facilitated by social networking tools paired with information technology, Islamic groups still appear to be the most organized opposition and have very often functioned as important voices in civil society.[11] Islamist groups have grown over the last three decades in a context marked by economic strain, unemployment, repression, the fear of Westernization, and declining state legitimacy and authority. In these deteriorating political and economic environments, terrorists have been able to recruit beyond the young and the alienated, drawing also from the upper and middle classes.[12]

The Competing Ethical Views

What are the morally appropriate responses to terrorism? To assess and justify responses to terrorism, I articulate two contrasting rationales: the utilitarian model and the justice model. According to the utilitarian perspective, protecting innocent civilians against those who use violence is the ultimate goal—that is, to maximize the greater good of society—and must be pursued at any cost. To efficiently prosecute the tactical war on terror, a government must restrict certain civil rights and freedoms. These consequences are warranted by a "hard bargain," whereby the diminution of certain rights and liberties become imperative in exchange for providing the greatest good for the greatest number; such a bargain ensures that risks undertaken in such circumstances will bring tangible benefits to citizens in the long run. In this model, it is thus appropriate for the government to spy on citizens, rely on clandestine sources, hold secret detentions, disregard the sovereign rights of other nations, and subject terrorist suspects to torture. The logic behind these arguments is similar to that used to justify US support of authoritarian regimes in Latin America, Eastern Europe, Africa, and Asia during much of the Cold War period.

The justice perspective, in contrast, holds that commitment to the rule of law, human dignity, and social justice is humanity's greatest tool in the war on terror. This perspective embraces the idea that states ought to observe specific restrictions on the conduct of war that is assumed to be in self-defense. According to this view, states must avoid the mentality that says "the end justifies the means"—the view that underlies the utilitarian rationale. One significant problem with the utilitarian view is that it can legitimize certain acts, including excessive violence and retributive measures, in the name of self-defense. Terrorists use the same logic to justify the sacrificing of human lives in the name of the greater good. The real danger in adopting a utilitarian view is that if such abuses remain unquestioned or hidden, they are likely to become a common state practice. Western governments that used to express human rights concerns in their discussions with Middle Eastern regimes more often praised Egypt and Tunisia for their antiterror efforts and cozied up to the demands of authoritarian regimes such as Uzbekistan. Western pressure on China to honor human rights—though never consistent—has subsided considerably. Concrete common security and economic interests between China and the United States—on issues such as global economics, regional security, climate change, and fighting terrorism—still trump human rights concerns, even as Washington keeps human rights on its agenda. US policymakers have turned a blind eye to Moscow's war in Chechnya—a massive recruitment tool for terrorists. Likewise in East Africa, the United States has pursued the strategic goal of tracking al-Qaeda, which does much to explain why the Bush administration was reluctant to consistently push Sudan over the genocide in Darfur. In these states, the government's antiterrorism zeal has overwhelmed the need for political dissent, undermining a wide variety of human rights protections. To be sure, instrumental justifications are utterly immoral. The consequence of the utilitarian view may be an ever-increasing loss of liberties without making society any safer or freer in the long run. Similarly, resorting to the criminal justice system to prosecute human rights abusers may be neither prudent nor practical under some circumstances.[13] Political and diplomatic processes, for example, proved far more effective than strictly judicial solutions in the case of national reconciliation in South Africa. At a general level, it is also important to reflect on the possible practical and moral limits of Western attempts to advance its core values of human rights and democracy throughout the world.[14] And yet the question remains: would democratizing effects in such authoritarian systems undermine endemic corruption and terrorism?

Two major problems surround the strategy of promoting democracy as a way to weaken the motivation for terrorist acts. One is that it is hard to achieve "transitions to democracy" or "consolidation" of democracies in authoritarian systems. There is no template—often there is not even an identifiable point of departure—for a democratic evolution to unfold. The process is messy, unpredictable, and often faces a multitude of obstacles in existing policies and leadership.[15] Elections in societies with deep sectarian and ethnic divisions and identities entail grave risks and disastrous consequences. Economic welfare does not necessarily lead to democratization but is as crucial to stability as are elections.

A deeper issue is the extent to which the Western world's overriding interests are directly linked to energy resources in the Middle East. To those being "helped," the talk of democracy and self-determination is deceitful.[16] In some Middle Eastern countries, the democratic process is bound to bring to power Islamists who often hold unfavorable views toward the US presence in the region. In the past, democratic processes in Palestine have brought to power radical Islamic groups such as Hamas, and have consolidated the power of Hezbollah in Lebanon. In Yemen, if and when Saleh's regime collapses, a number of questions inevitably arise: Will the Socialist Party allow the Islah Party, which has played a crucial role in opposing Saleh, to rule the country? Will the Islah Party allow the Socialist Party to participate in the formation of the new government in the post-Saleh era, given that the Muslim Brotherhood considers it as an "atheist-communist party"? There is no easy answer to this dilemma.

The justice paradigm has its own drawbacks. Exporting democratic values and institutions to these countries is difficult. If anything, such attempts are widely seen in much of the world as manifestations of Western culture, economic exploitation, and imperialistic agendas.[17] That said, the central dilemma to the prevention of terrorism and democracy promotion is that countries with weak civil societies and authoritarian regimes—those perhaps in the greatest need of progress in democratization and perhaps least suited to the development of democratic institutions—have provided fertile ground for terrorism. The rise of anti-Americanism has also become inseparable from these trade-offs. It is worth noting that anti-American sentiments have increased significantly in reaction to the US invasion of Iraq, partly because there was no clear evidence of Iraq's logistical, financial, or tactical support for al-Qaeda, and partly because that military adventure has yet to establish the promised stable and democratic Iraq. In the past, the desire for a stable democracy has been overshadowed by the intensifying sectarian violence in Iraq, rendering any future compromises and bargaining immensely difficult. It remains to be seen if the 2011 uprisings in the Middle East and North Africa (MENA) region, which have shown enormous enthusiasm and demand for peaceful democratic change on the part of the Tunisian and Egyptian people, will have any major impact on the transition to democracy in Iraq. If anything, the 2011 uprisings in the MENA region demonstrated that the lack of a democratic history and democratic traditions in the Arab world presented no obstacle to the people's explicit demand for democratic change.

Additionally, one unintended consequence of the US invasion of Iraq has been to create the false impression among the Kurds that their cooperation with the United States is bound to lead to the fulfillment of their aspirations for autonomy and, ultimately, nationhood. No country in the region is concerned about this prospect more than Turkey, which has the largest Kurdish population in the region, more than the neighboring countries of Iran, Iraq, and Syria. Among Turks, feelings of alienation and bitterness toward the United States have grown dramatically, reaching a new height in 2010 after Israel's violent and deadly raid on the Gaza-bound flotilla that killed nine Turkish citizens.[18]

Counterinsurgency and Counterterrorism

The fear of terrorism has led to submissive attitudes toward increasing restrictions on civil liberties and political rights among some sectors of Western society. This fear has reinforced the idea that security is a right that trumps all others. It is also the case that, while the war on terrorism has replaced the Cold War, it employs the same concept of state security that undermines political rights. As the tension between a state's prerogative and individuals' rights intensifies, it highlights the question of whose security and whose rights are at stake in this political climate.

Politicians routinely play on real or perceived public fears of the chaos and disorder caused by terrorists, insisting that coercive interrogation and other tactics (that many would define as torture) are necessary in the face of a potential national security threat. Certainly, popular television shows like *24* have helped to play on this public sentiment as well. Although the "fear argument" is compelling in certain instances, it does not circumvent the problem that state security is not necessarily linked to individual human rights; nor is it always coincidental with individual security, if we conceive of individual security as a human right. Rather, it depends, first and foremost, on the character of the state being protected and the means applied to secure it.[19]

National security or state security is about protecting the state from its potential or real enemies. Those enemies may be citizens. But in cases where the enemies are primarily external, as one expert reminds us, the rights of citizens may be sacrificed in the interest of defensive measures.[20] The killing of the falsely accused Jean Charles de Menezes, a Brazilian national living in south London, by British authorities is an example of sacrificing an innocent person in pursuit of "national security" goals.

Many critics of current US policy support the view that terrorism cannot be defeated militarily. Aware of how unpopular this suggestion may be, they support engaging terrorists under certain circumstances. They insist that there is nothing to lose and much to gain by knowing one's enemies and that the task of counterterrorism will be made much easier if we are prepared to engage others. This also includes paying the necessary price to engage others with the ultimate goal of containing them: "Britain ended the Irish Republican Army's terrorism only through negotiating with the terrorists . . . the cease-fire currently enjoyed in Sri Lanka is a result of government talks with the hated Tamil Tigers."[21] Others warn against sacrificing principles of democracy in order to fight terrorism: "It is both unwise and unnecessary to sacrifice liberal democratic values to secure short-term security."[22]

An essential component of winning "ideological and political" wars around the world is winning the war of ideas—that is, the "hearts and minds" of the people. It is vitally significant to distinguish counterterrorism (fighting against a tactic or method) from counterinsurgency (fighting against those who primarily engage in organized violence aimed at overthrowing an existing state). It is crucial to know, as Michael J. Boyle warns, that these two models of warfare are not fully compatible or mutually reinforcing—that is, counterinsurgency is not a counterterrorist strategy. To treat every terrorist threat through the lens of counterinsurgency is to commit the United States to undertaking endless and costly—financially, militarily, and morally—state-building missions abroad, often with little or no prospects of success. Similarly, Boyle continues, "to treat every insurgency as the potential incubator of a future terrorist menace is a recipe for overextension, distraction and exhaustion."[23]

Counterterrorism refers to a combination of practices, tactics, techniques, and strategies that governments, armies, police departments, and military contractors adopt to prevent terrorism or respond to threats posed by the terrorists. Effective counterterrorism policies include two essential elements: (1) ensuring that citizens are safer from terrorist threats by taking multifaceted security measures—domestically as well as internationally, and (2) neutralizing terrorists through arrests, prosecutions, raids, and military actions. Questions remain about whether such policies have worked in the past. Counterterrorism strategies also enlist a reasonable degree of cooperation with other governments on matters ranging from international financial situations and strategic partnerships to intelligence sharing.[24]

Counterinsurgency, in contrast, is defined as the "military, paramilitary, political, economic, psychological, and civic actions taken by a government to defeat an insurgency."[25] Counterinsurgency entails wide-ranging measures that governments take to defeat insurgency. These measures, David Kilcullen notes, may be political, administrative, military, economic, psychological, or informational, and are almost always used in combination.[26] Counterinsurgency also involves protecting the local population from the fear of instability and chaos, building political legitimacy for the existing government, and generating good governance. These goals cannot be achieved without a local support base and close allies, as well as negotiations with the enemy at some point. The two most fundamental characteristics of this type of warfare are (1) the seeking of local solutions and (2) acting respectfully toward the local population and putting the well-being of noncombatant civilians ahead of any other considerations, even ahead of killing the enemy.[27]

A successful counterinsurgency operation relies on bottom-up tactical innovations and community-based approaches to mobilize support for leaders and governments faced with a crisis of legitimacy, especially in postconflict societies. Counterinsurgency, Kilcullen continues, mirrors the state that conducts it, and its success depends largely on the nature of the state.[28] If properly executed, counterinsurgency, rather than traditional counterterrorism, may offer the best approach to defeating global jihad.[29] The current Afghan government has been outperformed by the Taliban in parts of Afghanistan where mistrust of the Karzai administration runs particularly deep. With regard to respect for the rule of law, delivering justice, and enforcing rules and regulations that contribute to the country's stability and order, the Taliban have done a much better job than the present central government. For NATO forces, the real challenge is not reinterpreting counterinsurgency measures in light of contemporary affairs, but winning local and public support in Afghanistan. The latter appears—at least for now—far off. US foreign policy in the past decade, William R. Polk argues, has been rooted in the notion of applying an overwhelming force—that "all the king's horses and all the king's men" could, in fact, fix a broken social contract (as in Afghanistan) or give life to a new and improved one (as in Iraq). The results have been costly, interminable, and tragic.[30]

An interesting contrast with al-Qaeda in Iraq (AQI) and how it struck its relations with the local population is instructive here. While some argue that the Sunni tribes turned on AQI only when they saw that they could bandwagon with the United States, others state that AQI has had an obviously ambivalent relationship with the indigenous Sunni insurgents, who resented AQI, both because it relied heavily on foreign jihadists and indiscriminately assaulted civilian targets (hence the temporary alliance of convenience between some Sunni insurgents and US forces to oppose AQI).[31] If US forces were to withdraw from Iraq, the Sunni insurgents would most likely try to drive AQI out of the country, while also vying for political power and contesting the Shiites for supremacy. That explains why "most US intelligence officials and outside experts reject the argument that an American withdrawal could result in Iraq becoming a base for operations against the United States."[32] Although the killing of bin Laden has dealt a devastating blow to the core of al-Qaeda's leadership and organization, it is unlikely to spell the end of jihadist terrorism in Iraq. The focus of counterterrorism strategy should be not only on the actual perpetrators of the violence but also on the potential recruits of the terrorist groups and the communities from which they derive their support.[33] Winning in Iraq, experts argue, will require a new approach to counterinsurgency, one that aims at providing security to Iraqis rather than chasing insurgents. Both insurgents and the government seek to achieve legitimacy by protecting the local population. By providing the population with security and reforms, the counterinsurgency seeks to take from the guerrillas the very source of their support.[34] In Iraq, such a strategy has come to be known as the "oil-spot strategy," which is premised on the notion that rather than focusing on defeating and killing insurgents, US forces should concentrate on providing security and opportunity to the Iraqi people, thereby denying insurgents the popular support they need.[35] The key here is that the Iraqi people must believe that their government and US forces will prevail and that the insurgents' defeat is in their interest. In that case, they will be likely to share intelligence about the insurgents without fear of reprisals.[36]

Historically, the most oft-cited successful counterinsurgency operation took place in Malaya shortly after World War II. Not only did the ratio of British troops to insurgents favor the British military, many Malayans were openly hostile to insurgents, who were ethnic Chinese. Given the limits of US forces in Iraq, an oil-spot approach could be effective.[37] It is not clear, however, whether the US public is willing to pay the price to achieve such an eventuality. The long-term success of any counterterrorism strategy that overlooks basic democratic principles is much in doubt. Repression and the denial of human rights will only undermine the counterterrorism struggle. Democracy and democratic processes must be the core elements of an effective counterterrorism strategy and coalition.[38] Some experts correctly argue that there is reason to hope that the 2011 secular uprisings in the Arab world will benefit US counterterrorism efforts. To achieve this goal, the United States must make it clear to opposition figures at the initial stages of these uprisings that the United States will seriously consider offering foreign aid, recognition, and other forms of assistance to these movements provided that militants are kept out of the rebels' ranks. It is worth recalling that when jihadists set up shop in the Balkans in the 1990s, it was the US pressure that convinced Bosnia's mainstream Muslim leadership to purge them.[39]

Critics of the so-called war on terror counter by asserting that terrorism is a tactic, not a discrete enemy, and that one cannot wage a war against terror. It is a war that can never be won and that will have no end.[40] The struggle against al-Qaeda, however, can be won only if the United States straightens up its priorities and avoids entangling itself in an ever-growing number of distant conflicts.[41] Moreover, the war on terror is not intellectually, economically, or politically sustainable over the long run. "Winning" the war on terror is primarily a normative task, with its success hinging upon delegitimizing terrorism as a core foreign policy principle. The United States must push for establishing a global and institutional counterterrorism regime—a global compact of sorts—against terrorism that could take the form of a series of interlinked multilateral agreements. Such a strong and self-enforcing normative prohibition against killing noncombatants should facilitate antiterror cooperation (e.g., intelligence sharing and law enforcement) and allow for punitive measures for noncompliance.[42]

The problem with a declaration of war is that warfare invokes notions of victory and defeat. Yet "it is very difficult even to declare victory in a war on terrorism or terror, much less evil. We succeeded defeating the Taliban in Afghanistan, but that has not brought us victory in the war on terrorism."[43] We have succeeded in severely curtailing the freedom of operation of the al-Qaeda leadership. We have killed its head, Osama bin Laden, captured other of its leadership, and demolished its infrastructure, yet this has not brought us victory in the war on terrorism. If anything, the war in Afghanistan has taught us a familiar lesson: "winning battles does not necessarily equate with winning wars, especially when it comes to fighting terrorists."[44]

Reshaping a political, ideological, and economic system while simultaneously fighting in a conflict, as in Afghanistan and Iraq, presents a huge challenge to the United States and NATO forces.[45] The lesson learned is antique: "Big states repeatedly lose small wars because, in counter-insurgencies, the deck is stacked against occupying powers."[46] The fact remains that asymmetric wars tend to become immensely difficult to win for the metropolitan powers. The Boer War, the Algerian War, the Irish independence struggle, and the US war in Vietnam have all demonstrated that the costs of occupation—money and casualties, as well as political consequences—grow outrageously over time. The Vietnam War demonstrated not only that conventional military superiority fails to guarantee victory but also that, under certain conditions, the theater of war can extend well beyond the battlefield to encompass the social and political institutions of the imperial invader.[47]

The difficulties associated with counterinsurgency have led some observers to question whether the United States should still work with its regional allies, which are usually weak, corrupt, and antidemocratic. Is it better simply to devote resources to homeland defense and wage this fight without necessarily relying on unsavory partners? This is especially true in cases where US allies still face significant political opposition even where their counterinsurgency capabilities might be formidable. In such circumstances, US resources may be better utilized to improve national defense or increase domestic capabilities rather than to further assist allies facing intractable domestic problems or uncertain prospects.[48] If anything, the occupations of Afghanistan and Iraq have unified terrorists in their efforts to recruit more traditional insurgents that could have been won over through negotiation of grievances as opposed to continued armed conflict. In the case of Iraq, the difference between terrorists and insurgents has become somewhat murkier. It is also worth remembering that the United States and its Western allies realize that their values (i.e., liberal democracy) are not universally shared. One lesson learned from previous counterinsurgency operations in other places (such as Vietnam and Algeria) is what happens when the moral high ground is irrevocably lost.[49] The US occupation of Iraq risks the detrimental effects of such a loss.

Furthermore, any successful counterinsurgency program should emphasize "the ability to provide security for the populace, including protection from internal and external threats."[50] It is important to bear in mind that counterinsurgency operations present complex and often paradoxical considerations. A cardinal element is: "Sometimes, the more force is used, the less effective it is."[51] Counterinsurgency field manuals of the US Army and Marine Corps indicate that the key for counterinsurgency is knowing exactly when more force is needed and when it might be counterproductive. This judgment requires constant assessment of the environment, context, and a sense of timing regarding insurgents' actions. This is consistent with another principle of counterinsurgency that is grounded in the notion that "some of the best weapons for counterinsurgents do not shoot."[52] Counterinsurgency often achieves the most meaningful success in garnering public support and legitimacy for the host nation's government, with activities that often—if not always—do not involve killing insurgents. Having established basic order, lasting victory comes from a viable economy, political participation, and restored hope.[53]

I next turn to the negative fallout of torture used as a counterterrorism strategy.

The Torture Debate and International Law

There is strong agreement that we must confront terrorist groups such as al-Qaeda with a strong fist. But there is no consensus on how terrorism in general can be countered. In coming years, views will continue to clash on what constitutes an effective and just response to the new global terrorism: will it include the use of force, the legalization of torture, democracy promotion, or diplomacy? The war on terror, critics argue, has become a slogan, not a strategy to make the United States safe. If anything, it has bred even more terrorism and left the United States with fewer allies worldwide.[54]

In the West, disagreements over the US interventions in Afghanistan and Iraq have raised serious concerns about whether NATO can secure Afghanistan and build a functioning state there. The commitments and relationships that make up NATO, one observer cautions, are likely to fray publicly over just how much each member state wants to commit to produce a desirable outcome.[55] This concern reflects a broader problem within the alliance: the absence of consensus on NATO's proper role and mission. Some NATO members question whether transforming Afghanistan into a functioning democracy or fighting a war against terrorism are aspects of the organization's mission.

The Bush administration's invasions of Afghanistan and Iraq failed to make the world safer. Since the tragic events of September 11, 2001, two trends have dominated global politics. First, human rights concerns have been marginalized in favor of the crackdown on "terror." Now, more than in the past, Western democracies are opposing human rights protections and threatening to override human rights guarantees in the name of counterterrorism. The prevalence of indefinite detention, torture, and other abuses in the post-9/11 era pose a major threat to the existing system of human rights protections. The problematic treatment of detainees at Guantanamo Bay by the United States has prompted other governments to consider similar policies.

In the second post-9/11 trend, anti-American sentiments have drastically increased in reaction to the US invasion of Iraq. The intense level of Sunni opposition to the several elections held in Iraq in the immediate aftermath of Saddam's downfall, as well as the adoption of the new constitution, demonstrated that the prospects for building a stable democracy in Iraq are complicated. The failure to make much progress in this direction has undermined the credibility of US programs for the promotion of democracy. Confidence in US leadership and power has drastically declined, even among formerly staunch allies such as the United Kingdom and Poland, as well as among US allies in the Muslim world, such as Pakistan, Egypt, and Indonesia.[56] Perhaps the most dramatic decline in US prestige was with long-time US ally and fellow NATO member Turkey, where only 3 percent of the population expressed confidence in the Bush administration. Another US ally, South Korea, also has shown strong anti-Americanism, with 60 percent of the population holding negative views of the United States as a "colonial power."[57] In fact, anti-Americanism has increasingly become fashionable among young South Koreans.[58] Such views, which were emblematic of widespread opposition to US unilateral actions in global politics during the Bush administration, have changed in light of the Obama administration's attempt to promote multilateralism, in which the United States will count on other countries to assist and abet in the construction of a changing world order.

In addition to US unilateral policies and inclinations that have caused worldwide resentment, the difficulty in distinguishing between counterterrorism and torture has undermined the moral authority and credibility of the United States. The definition of torture found in the 1984 Convention Against Torture (CAT) signifies an act by which severe pain or suffering, whether physical or mental, is intentionally inflicted on a person for the purpose of obtaining information or confession. It is the element of purpose that typically distinguishes torture from other cruel, inhuman, or degrading treatment. In the Elements of Crime of the International Criminal Court (ICC), which identifies torture as a war crime, the only aspect that separates torture from cruel or inhuman treatment is that of purpose.[59] Universal and regional human rights treaties have uniformly prohibited torture. Even those treaties that envisage some of their provisions being suspended or derogated in times of war or public emergency clearly exclude the prohibition on torture from such suspension—the right to be free from torture is one of only a few rights that cannot be disparaged.[60]

While most states are parties to a treaty obligating them to refrain from torture or similar ill-treatment under all circumstances, the prohibition on torture may also be seen as a rule of general or customary international law.[61] Moreover, the prohibition against torture has become a rule of jus cogens—a preemptory rule of international law that cannot be circumvented even by a subsequent treaty. Many influential national and regional institutions, such as the British House of Lords, the European Court of Human Rights, and the American Law Institute's Restatement of US Foreign Relations Law, have taken the view that the prohibition against torture is a rule of *jus cogens*. The International Law Commission, the respected international law advisory to the UN General Assembly, has also recognized the prohibition of torture as a preemptory rule; so has the International Criminal Tribunal for the Former Yugoslavia (ICTY).[62] Similarly, a 1996 resolution by the UN Commission on Human Rights stated that "prolonged incommunicado detention may facilitate the perpetration of torture and can itself constitute a form of cruel, inhuman or degrading treatment."[63] The new Human Rights Council subsequently adopted the same position.

Beyond these legal restrictions placed on the use of torture, many argue that torture as a tactic in the name of security violates a nation's obligations under international law. "Torture still violates human rights," Ronald Dworkin notes, "even if information obtained through torture is needed to save American lives."[64] It is important to note, Dworkin continues, "torture's object is precisely not just to damage but to destroy a human being's power to decide for himself what his loyalty and convictions permit him to do."[65] Jailing suspected criminals without charge or trial, or jailing people who have not perpetrated a crime but whom our police judge to be dangerous, even on the word of another, would violate the US conception of the inherent and inalienable dignity of human beings.[66] From a practical point of view, the utility of torture has been questioned in cases where it is used in the name of saving lives, or under the so-called "ticking time bomb scenario." This is in large part because torture often fails to yield substantial information or leads to false information.

The abuse of prisoners both in Iraq and at Guantanamo Bay has significantly damaged the US image. Philip Zelikow, the executive director of the 9/11 Commission and later the State Department's top counselor under Secretary of State Condoleezza Rice, has argued that torture and the harsh interrogation of detention programs are immoral.[67] Some top CIA officials have acknowledged that much of the information that coercion produces is unreliable. Increasingly, government officials admit that secret interrogation programs have undermined the public's trust in US justice, both at home and abroad.[68] "Because of Bush's self-righteously unilateral conduct of US foreign policy after 9/11," Zbigniew Brzezinski observes, "the evocative symbol of America in the eyes of much of the world ceased to be the Statue of Liberty and instead became the Guantanamo prison camp."[69] The United States can regain and restore the world's trust and confidence, Brzezinski continues, only if it follows a truly post–Cold War globalist foreign policy, one in which US power is linked to the aspirations of millions of politically conscious people.[70]

In a broader context, most regional experts have found that there is little support for the thesis that anti-Americanism is rooted in essentialist cultural conflicts. Anti-Americanism in the Arab Middle East is manifestly political.[71] If the United States adopts policies such as genuinely promoting democratic reform and arranging an equitable settlement between Israel and the Palestinians, Arab attitudes of distrust and skepticism toward US intentions might change.[72]

I now turn to the discussion of other counterterrorism tools: the use of force, diplomacy, and democracy promotion.

Military Measures

Counterterrorism tactics that rely solely on coercive and military measures are questionable and often contested. Such coercive strategies typically do not address the root causes of terrorism. Although the temptation to use sticks, not carrots, in response to the threat of terrorism is irresistible for most governments, in most cases an overreliance on the use of military force is counterproductive. This happens because in many instances it has made "martyrs of terrorists, rallied recruits to the terrorist cause, and caused the uncommitted to lose confidence in the government."[73]

The rising violence between Hindus and Sikhs serves as a comparable example here. A spiral of violence that took place in both Punjab and Kashmir (1981–1994), as both terrorists and government forces in India engaged in the killing of innocent civilians, proved futile in winning over the terrorist support base. Human rights abuses by both the state and the militants failed to win the battle for the hearts and minds of the population. More specifically, the debacle of the first attack on the

Golden Temple (1984) by the Indian military, in which more than one thousand people died, led to further escalation of violence between Hindus and Sikhs.[74]

The US invasion of Iraq has also validated the widely held position that there is no generic, cookie-cutter military solution to countering terrorism in the long run. Under the control of the Bush administration, Iraq became a failed state of the sort that offered a new haven for terrorists.[75] During the critical weeks following the collapse of Saddam's regime, US policymakers initiated a de-Baathification process that led to the dissolution of the Iraqi army and national police force. This process substantially disrupted social stability and built opposition to the US presence, as hundreds of thousands were suddenly left without income and infrastructure systems were no longer supported or maintained.[76] Washington did not foresee the insurgency that took shape in Fallujah and Ramadi in the years that followed, as the Sunnis, not satisfied with a minority role in a governing democracy, challenged the Shiite-dominated regime. The US occupation has put in place a process for which the end result may not be fully acceptable to the Sunnis. An analogy to the US military adventure in Iraq, experts remind us, may be the case of the French in Algeria. Although there are many marked differences between the two, there are also striking similarities: "most notably, in both wars, a Western power found itself enmeshed in an Arab land fighting a primarily urban battle against a murky mix of nationalists and Islamists."[77]

The resulting turmoil in the Sunni-dominated areas provided an opportunity for foreign terrorists and jihadists to directly battle the United States.[78] At that time, Abu Musab al-Zarqawi, a Jordanian who set up al-Qaeda in Iraq, began his gruesome operations against both US troops and the Iraqi Shiites. Slowly but surely, the US military intervention led to the disintegration of the country into three constituent parts: a pro-Western Kurdistan in the north, a Shiite entity in the south influenced by Iran, and a restive and violent Sunni region in the center. In the north, Kurdish political parties filled the vacuum left by the collapse of Saddam Hussein's regime.

Following the December 2005 parliamentary elections, it became clear that Kirkuk would vote to join Kurdistan in secession. The situation in Kirkuk, with a minority of Arabs and Turkomans, was likely to draw Turkey into the vortex of chaotic Iraqi politics.[79] What the Kurds do in Kirkuk, Robin Wright aptly points out, will determine whether Iraq can discard the primordial instincts that have for centuries defined the Middle East and which ultimately hold Iraq together as a country.

"Iraq's fate," Wright asserts, "may ultimately be decided in Kirkuk. A multiethnic city of almost one million people, Kirkuk is claimed with equal vehemence by the Kurds, the Arabs, and minority Turkomans backed by Turkey. Kirkuk is the Jerusalem of Iraq."[80] The lack of any agreement among Kurds, Turkomans, and Arabs poses a major impediment to stability not only in Iraq but also throughout the region.

Turkey remains adamantly opposed to a fully independent Iraqi Kurdistan. Likewise, Iraq's other neighbors fear that Kirkuk's official recognition as part of the Iraqi Kurdistan will have profound ramifications for the rest of Iraq, prompting the Shiites in the south to demand a semiautonomous region of their own. These demands could culminate in the fragmentation of the country into three independent mini states.[81] The rise of Iranian influence in both southern Iraq and the wider region is yet another unintended consequence of the US invasion of Iraq and Afghanistan. In hindsight, it is obvious that US military involvement in Iraq has unleashed unprecedented dynamics in the regional political environment.

Evidence suggests that it is not possible to confront terrorism solely by force. Terrorism is a multifaceted problem requiring a multifaceted response. Democratic governments, according to one comparative study of counterterrorism, have sought simply to counter terrorism by force, but security measures have in fact led to a worsening of the problem. This study concludes that the use of force simply fanned the flames of discontent and added to the appeal and ranks of terrorist groups.[82] Another study demonstrated that the appeal of solidarist identities grew for many Muslims as the violence in Iraq intensified. This, coupled with the global proliferation of images from Guantanamo and Abu Ghraib, widened the appeal of solidarist identities. More specifically, the grand scale of the violence in Iraq allowed young Muslim men to view their lives as part of the ongoing "ancient cosmic struggles."[83]

In contrast, when governments attempted to address the underlying factors that gave rise to terrorism, in conjunction with the use of effective coercive policies, they were more likely to succeed. Put most simply, an approach that properly integrates both carrots and sticks offers the most effective way of campaigning against terrorism.[84] Most studies on counterterrorism underscore the importance of good intelligence and international cooperation in countering terrorist movements. Given the clear trend in which more terrorist groups will be operating outside the territory controlled by their enemies—translocally based terrorist groups—international cooperation will be even more crucial in the future. As a result, developing norms and procedures for international intelligence sharing will be an essential element of any successful counterterrorism strategy.[85] Increasingly, US officials are realizing that the best way to meet the key challenges of our times (terrorism and nonproliferation of nuclear weapons, the threat of pandemic disease, and global warming) is to join like-minded actors on the global scene. China and Russia are working closely with the United States on nonproliferation and other security issues in ways that suggest how the United States may benefit from an era of cooperative and balanced world power.[86]

Security and the Opportunity Cost

Every policy or strategy includes a trade-off of some sort. The opportunity cost associated with the ongoing war in Iraq is mind boggling. The cost of the occupation of Iraq, according to the Congressional Research Service, for the cumulative enacted fiscal year 2011 as of March 18, 2011, is estimated at $805.5 billion and is expected to reach to $823.2 for the fiscal year 2012.[87] The number of casualties of this war, as of July 18, 2011, has been unspeakable: 4,474 US soldiers dead and 33,125 seriously wounded.[88] According to a study by the Center for American Progress, a mere one-third of the amount spent in Iraq could have sufficiently safeguarded our ports, upgraded the Coast Guard fleet, improved cargo security, protected all US commercial airlines from shoulder-fired missiles, purchased state-of-the-art baggage-screening machines, equipped airports with walk-through explosive detectors, put one hundred thousand police officers on the nation's streets, secured from theft the world's entire weapons-grade nuclear material, and completed many other related projects. The total cost of such programs, according to the study, would not have exceeded $144.4 billion in 2004.[89]

Another study has suggested that just $1 billion in foreign aid, for instance, might have significantly altered the face of education in Pakistan and helped reduce or deplete the poisonous reservoir of anti-Western teachings in schools there.[90] A carefully crafted humanitarian assistance package to Afghanistan might have made the return of the Taliban to that country very difficult, if not impossible. Likewise, a similar investment could have prevented the impending Palestinian fiscal crisis and the collapse of the weak and cash-strapped Palestinian economy in both the West Bank and Gaza. In such ways, we could have won the hearts and minds of Muslims, while constraining the impetus of the tactics of terrorism.

We should also pursue the more modest and obtainable goal of containing terrorist recruitment. As we think about the shape of foreign policy in the years to come, it is important to consider that 84 percent of the US population do not believe that the United States is winning the war on terror. Nearly 92 percent of experts consulted in one study have said that the war in Iraq negatively affects US national security. According to a CNN/Opinion Research Corporation Poll, as of January 23, 2011, 66 percent of Americans opposed the US war in Iraq.[91] In June 2011, national security experts supported making significant troop reductions from Afghanistan starting in July 2011, reducing troops to one-third, one-quarter, or even a smaller fraction, of the previous levels over the next one to three years.[92] From a counterterrorism point of view, some experts argue, the war has been a costly mistake, for it enabled terrorists to portray the United States as using indiscriminate force. This reality has helped swell the ranks of local jihadist groups.[93]

It is clear that military force, as a strategy, is rarely effective against terrorism. No government alone can put an end to terrorism. Nor can a global war eternally terminate terrorist practices. Terrorism is a tactic, and war cannot be waged against a tactic. Even states with awesome military might have failed to prevail over small but adaptive terrorist groups. It is equally clear that terrorism itself has been a counterproductive strategy in the long run. The Irish Republican Army (IRA) became successful only after it abandoned terrorism. Counterterrorism, as has been shown repeatedly, has seldom, if ever, succeeded in fully eradicating the threat of terrorism. France learned that lesson in Algeria, as did the United States in Vietnam. Russia encountered harsh lessons in both Afghanistan and Chechnya. Israel may have reached the same conclusion in Lebanon and the occupied Palestinian territories. The key may be to pursue multilateral cooperation, such as intelligence sharing and law enforcement, to engage in more preventive actions. To do so, we need to strengthen international law and develop global institutions that better uphold such laws.

Democracy Promotion

The discernible shift in US foreign policy—the switch in Iraq from pursuing a war to destroy weapons of mass destruction to promoting democracy—has raised numerous concerns. Beleaguered by so many complex problems and issues, Iraq's civil society is not yet able to sustain the installation of democracy, and may not be for years to come. To begin with, the manner in which the US invasion of Iraq unfolded complicated peacebuilding in postconflict Iraq. The US approach to dealing with the Iraqi threat—including but not limited to bypassing UN-centered multilateral approaches—undoubtedly presented problems for the resolution of current tensions in Iraq. Moreover, differences in the European nations' conception of the terrorism threat and their reluctance to turn hastily to the ultimate option of the use of force illustrated sharp policy differences among long-standing allies in the West.

The framework for President Bush's democracy promotion was based on a flawed neoconservative ideology that envisioned a new way of looking at international politics, one that was heavily influenced by ideology rather than strategy. The Bush administration's inability to distinguish between ideology and strategy proved to be its Achilles' heel.[94] Domestically, framing the war on terror in terms of ideological and political fundamentalism, which presupposed US moral superiority, led to a shift away from open discussion and humility toward arrogance and disregard for international law. Under such circumstances, many politicians refrained from criticizing the campaign against terror on the grounds that they might be seen as disloyal or "un-American."[95]

A cursory look at Iraq's history is illuminating. From 750 AD to 1258 AD it was the seat of the Abbasid dynasty, during which time the Islamic civilization reached its peak. Then Iraq fell under the rule of the Ottoman Empire, until the defeat of the latter by Allied forces during World War I. With that defeat, Britain gained the mandate over Iraq. The country was artificially created in 1922 by the merger of three Ottoman regions: Mosul, Baghdad, and Basra. After a decade of encountering insurgency and violence, the British gave up their mandate and created a constitutional monarchy that was largely alien to local traditions and practices. This Iraq's first monarch, King Faisal I, came from a Hashemite family, a pro-British family with roots in modern-day Saudi Arabia. The British manipulation of the monarchical system intensified Iraq's lingering and deepening ethnic and religious divisions. To this day, such divisions have hindered the development of an Iraqi national identity—a key ingredient in promoting democratic change.

After 1958, Iraq witnessed several coups, the last of which brought Saddam Hussein to power in 1979. Iraq's domestic political instability, coupled with the political maneuvering and machinations of the region's key countries, has too often overshadowed internal ethnic tensions. Since Iran and Iraq signed the Algiers Agreement of 1975, in which Iran agreed not to provide assistance to the separatist Kurdish factions, the quest to find a solution to the plight of the Kurdish people has been consistently aborted. More to the point, the political culture of the Iraqi people has been heavily influenced by elements inhospitable to the installation of a sustainable democracy. These include Iraqis' strong distrust of foreigners, deep tribal loyalties, rival identities, and a contemporary history of political violence. The sense of common nationhood is still fragile and elusive.[96] Two decades of wars and economic sanctions have left the Iraqi state and society in disarray.

Free elections in Iraq after the fall of Saddam Hussein demonstrated voting patterns influenced largely by cultural identities and sectarian inclinations. Elections placed the Shiites, who made up 60 percent of the population, at the top, as the majority of Sunnis boycotted the election. The outcome reinforced existing identities and sectarian loyalties. The Shiite community as a whole was divided and held different views about the shape of things to come in postwar Iraq. Grand Ayatollah Sayyid Ali Husaini Sistani, the leader of one of the most dominant Shia political organizations, the Supreme Council for the Islamic Revolution in Iraq (ISCIRI), pressured the US occupation authorities into setting up early democratic elections, which established Shia political control. Sistani also issued fatwas urging Shiites to vote and to avoid responding to the violent attacks by radical Sunni groups.[97] The Badr Brigade, a military cadre associated with the ISCIRI, played an important role in intra-Shia power rivalries.

The Mahdi Army, named after a Shiite messianic figure, is a militia of several thousand members loyal to Muqtada al-Sadr. Most of its membership consists of unemployed, young Shiites from Sadr City and southern Iraqi cities such as Najaf. The group was responsible for two uprisings in 2004 against US forces, before agreeing to a cease-fire in October 2004. Some experts say the group is not an organized, disciplined unit with clear political objectives, but instead functions as a social movement. Mahdi followers have infiltrated Iraq's interior and defense ministries. Sadr holds no formal political post, but Sadr loyalists control as many as thirty seats in Iraq's parliament, giving him a powerful stake in Iraqi politics.[98] By 2008, Sadr's group had become one of the two most important Shia blocs in the country.

Sadr was not alone in vying for the popular support of Iraqi Shiites, however. His chief rivals—including the Islamic Supreme Council of Iraq (ISCI) and Prime Minister Nouri al-Maliki's Dawa Party—garnered support from the country's more conservative middle class. Some experts have argued that clashes between Mahdi fighters, Iraqi forces, and ISCIRI's Badr Brigade represent a class struggle of sorts.[99]

Similarly, the Sunni bloc is characterized by a growing fragmenta-tion. The emergence of groups opposed to al-Qaeda—known as Awak-ening Councils (Sons of Iraq, or *sahwas*)—among prominent shaikhs and Sunni tribes due to the sectarian violence associated with al-Qaeda demonstrated that local tribes were feeling threatened by the extent to which their communities were infiltrated by global jihadists associated with al-Qaeda. The Anbar Salvation Council, consisting of tribal leaders and former Sunni insurgents, continues to expand its base of support in Anbar province's Sunni community. Led by Shaikh Abdul Sattar Abu Rishawi, the council has turned at least one local tribe against al-Qaeda.[100] US support for the council in its fight against al-Qaeda, how-ever, complicates the broader democratization process in Iraq, and a practical compromise between Shiite and Sunni groups within the coun-try remains unlikely. The infiltration of the council by al-Qaeda adds yet another layer of complexity to this situation.

The important question continues to be whether the form of the future government—Islamic or secular—should be left to these rival factions. While some of these groups asserted that the formation of a theocratic government was no longer an option, others argued other-wise. These divisions were reflective of the nation's ethnic and sectarian diversity. Democracy promotion had clearly unleashed sectarian identi-ties, drawing political lines and determining regional alliances in a country that has historically lacked democratic values and political structures. "Greater democracy," Vali Nasr argues, "serves Shia interests across the region, and hence Shia revival is favorably disposed toward democratic change."[101] The rise of the Shiites to relative power in the region has injected a robust element of real pluralism into the too-often Sunni-dominated political life of the Muslim world. Many Shiites have found democracy appealing as an idea itself, and not simply as a useful vehicle for their power and ambitions.[102] But sectarian discord has become a major fault line in Iraq, as the euphoria of democracy promo-tion has vanished.

Just as importantly, democracy promotion at gunpoint has raised many questions regarding its legitimacy, its legality, and, most impor-tantly, its effectiveness. Many experts expect these efforts to promote democracy to fail. Aside from domestic impediments to democracy in both Iraq and Afghanistan, the strategic dilemmas appear intractable in the aftermath of military interventions. Military imperatives, combined with concern for the long-term stability of an ally, its government, or even friendly warlords may make it impossible to emphasize building a liberal democratic regime in Afghanistan or Iraq.[103] The promotion of democracy as a counterterrorism tool invites conflicting perspectives on the causes of and responses to terrorism. Those scholars who in the past have noted that the emphasis on electoral democracy, in light of the trends in the Arab world elections—with the exception of Morocco, Turkey, and Lebanon—cannot be said to serve US interests, either in combating terrorism or in other important policy areas such as the Arab-Israeli peace process, have confessed that many Middle Eastern studies have missed the Arab Spring. They argue that, while oil wealth remains a fairly reliable source and tool for ensuring regime stability, the way in which Arab regimes have achieved stability through oil riches has been entirely ignored. The destabilizing effects of poorly implemented liberal economic policies in the Arab world should not have come as a surprise to us.[104] Under such circumstances, these scholars have retreated from their previous positions that the United States has no reasonable alternative to working with authoritarian Arab governments that are willing to work with them.[105]

On the other hand, there are surely examples of former terrorist organizations growing more moderate after their inclusion in open political processes. For example, one can look to the IRA in Northern Ireland or the African National Congress (ANC) in South Africa.[106] It makes perfect sense, in the long run, to create the conditions under which advancing political and socioeconomic reforms abroad can contribute to reducing the militant extremism that fuels the recruitment efforts of such terrorist networks as al-Qaeda.[107]

In certain cases, however, it is very difficult to measure the effectiveness of social and economic reform policies in the campaign against terrorism. Such policies have to be evaluated over a long period of time, and too often they act in tandem with other societal influences.[108] It is equally difficult to find a direct link between social reform policies and success in counterterrorism. What is clear, however, is that social privation and political discontent are contributing factors to terrorism.[109] Although not entirely clear-cut, the evidence suggests that pursuing a coordinated strategy of undermining support for terrorism while also offering opportunities for political engagement is the most favorable option.[110]

The perception and hope that US military intervention in Afghanistan and Iraq would seriously undermine the activities of global terrorists have proved premature at best. There is a fundamental question as to whether the Bush administration and the neoconservatives surrounding him had a firm grasp of the limits of US military might. More problematic still was the Bush administration's decision to invade Iraq even in the face of stark opposition from the UN Security Council. Self-defense was invoked by the United States to justify the use of force. No other normative and legal frameworks, however, such as "humanitarian intervention," appear to have justified the Bush administration's unilateral policy in this case.

While it is important to defend one's values, it is morally untenable to impose them on other people and nations. Likewise, while it is essential to defend and further one's own interests, it is crucial that the pursuit of interests is not achieved at the expense of civil liberties and political rights in the long run.[111] Some suggest that the means used to conduct the global war on terror threaten two of the core principles they are supposed to be defending: liberal values and the unity of the West. The pursuit of the global war on terrorism invariably generates for liberal societies profoundly difficult choices between effective counterterrorism policies, on the one hand, and compromising elemental values and practices of the liberal order, on the other.[112] Many dilemmas arise out of the policy choices faced by liberal societies in responding to terrorism. The choices of insulation, repression, and military intervention require fundamental degradation of liberal economic and political values. Thus, the question becomes: Can the United States defend its core values without resorting to the excesses of securitization?

Rethinking what is feasible and desirable in the Middle East has perpetually brought paradoxical and contradictory policies into the open, compelling US foreign policy makers to face new challenges in the Middle Eastern region. By simultaneously promoting democracy and expanding its hegemonic powers in the region, the United States has damaged its "soft power"—that is, the power to influence others through persuasion and example. This is so, in part because democracy promotion is interpreted in the context of hegemonic expansion and in part because democracy promotion has been ineffective in the region. By invading Iraq on the pretext that the country's leaders had connections with al-Qaeda, followed by widespread prisoner abuses in Abu Ghraib and Guantanamo Bay, US foreign policy makers have compromised their ability to attain their goal of promoting both stability and democracy in the region.[113]

Arguably, both soft power and the power of encouraging economic reform and development are likely to benefit US foreign policy objectives in the region in the long run. Ultimately, however, internal security forces and policymakers are responsible for seeking the most effective counterterrorism strategies. Views differ on the extent to which local strategies offer the best solutions. Ihsan Bal, a senior research fellow at the International Strategic Research Organization, a think tank based in Ankara, Turkey, advocates promoting democracy in Turkey, arguing that the democratization experience in Turkey has proven to be the fastest and the most effective counterterrorism strategy. There has been, says Bal, a diminishing effect on terrorism in Turkey because of the democratization process. Likewise, the treatment of the war on terror as a criminal justice and legal issue—not as a military issue—has produced positive results in Turkey.[114]

Some legal observers in Turkey, such as Turgut Tarhanli, a faculty member at Istanbul Bilgi University's Law School, offer a contrasting view, arguing that the 2006 antiterrorist law in Turkey has further strengthened the heavy-handed policies of the Turkish government, making it possible for the Turkish army to recklessly fire into crowds of people and disrupt peaceful and civil protests guaranteed under the Turkish constitution.[115] Increasingly, these antiterror laws have led to the question of why, in the Turkish legal discourse, there is no specification as to Muslim minorities, including the Kurds, despite references made, however indirectly, to minority rights in the July 24, 1923, Lausanne Treaty. The treaty not only recognized Turkish sovereignty, but also provided for the protection of the ethnic Greek minority in Turkey, as well as the Turkish Muslim minority in Greece.[116] Similarly, Yildiz Imrek, a lawyer of criminal and family law in Turkey, who also represents the Emek Partisi (Labor Party), argues that there are no constitutional and legal guarantees to protect Kurdish human rights and that no provisions in the constitution refer directly to the Kurdish minority.[117]

Criminal Justice and Traditional Diplomacy

Two known but contradictory facts remain indisputable: (1) that the most commonly used weapon in the US arsenal of counterterrorism has been military force and (2) that the limits of the use of force have outweighed its benefits. The record of military intervention in the Middle East, however, raises important questions about the role of force in combating terrorism and promoting democratic change. It also raises relevant questions about the complex relationship between internal and external forces of political change.

Iraq presents an important case in which deep ethnic and sectarian divisions render the establishment of a democratic political order immensely difficult. It is in this context that the use of alternative counterterrorism tools must be examined. While military force has in some cases undermined the infrastructure and resources available to terrorists, it has often failed to contribute to the solution. In fact, prolonged military intervention and occupation, impacting broad sections of the population, is far less effective and has a significant negative impact.

Historically, the real challenge inherent in counterterrorism strategies has been how best to undercut terrorists' resources and recruits. In the past, states have relied primarily on military measures in their campaigns against terrorism. The post-9/11 period has shown that counterterrorism requires more than military might. More diplomacy is needed, with the Israeli-Palestinian issue continuing to be the principal fault line in the region.[118] The Iraqi case implies that counterterrorism strategies of coercion have failed to contain and deter terrorism. The unilateral policies and declarations of war of the United States have proven costly and counterproductive in the war on terror. The UN Security Council's tense deliberations over Iraq illustrated the lack of consensus in the international community on the utility and propriety of military intervention and the preemptive use of force. Clearly, a well-coordinated multilateral approach would have garnered broader, more desirable results.[119]

Diplomacy between governments aimed at undercutting terrorist resources and recruits can better serve counterterrorism strategies: there is no military solution to the fight against terrorism and no military deterrent to prevent it. Recognizing the difficulties involved in the use of force, Brigitte L. Nacos, a leading counterterrorism expert, asserts that over time, conventional criminal justice or policing has been far more successful in depleting and destroying terrorist groups than the use of military force. Italy's Red Brigade, Germany's Red Army Faction, the United States' Weather Underground, and similar groups all faded away largely because their leaders and many rank-and-file members were arrested, tried, and imprisoned.[120] In both Iraq and Afghanistan, Nacos argues, military actions against terrorists have been stopgap measures. In Iraq, massive military force resulted in a recruiting bonanza for terrorists. Similarly, as ground and air operations against al-Qaeda and Taliban forces in Pakistan's tribal region have demonstrated, such strikes in fact precipitate further terrorist attacks. In the long run, Nacos asserts, imposing economic and political sanctions against state sponsors and policing terrorist groups are the most effective approaches to ending terrorism and destroying terrorist groups and networks.[121]

A more promising course of action would concentrate on working toward a reasonable resolution of the Israeli-Palestinian conflict through diplomatic mechanisms. This opportunity should not be squandered by sole preoccupation with the military campaign against terror; rather, it should be seen as an effective approach to countering terrorism. Viewing Islamic terrorism as local phenomena in isolated pockets undermines effective strategy. In other words, it may not even be events concerning Iraq and Afghanistan that have the potential to address all the underlying political grievances that motivate political violence in those two places. Certainly, there are local issues (US presence being one of them), but they should not be seen in isolation, and the political approach to counterterrorism may necessitate approaches that take in the broad view that the resolution of larger regional issues must be given priority. Many Muslims believe that there has been a deliberate attempt in the West to paint Islam as a religion bent on violence, terrorism, and antimodernity, rather than one prone to progress, tolerance, and peaceful coexistence, values that have generally marked its historical trajectory. The invasions of Iraq and Afghanistan, and the ensuing mismanaged diplomacy toward both countries, have reinforced the prevailing view among many Muslims that the Bush administration was anti-Arab and anti-Muslim.[122] To disentangle itself from the Iraqi occupation, the Obama administration must seek diplomatic and regional solutions and strategies.

There are also international factors to consider, most notably the symbolic importance of the resolution of the Israeli-Palestinian conflict, especially after the 2009 Israeli attacks on the Gaza Strip, which led to many deaths and much destruction.[123] In a major speech delivered at the State Department on May 19, 2011, President Obama outlined his administration's policy in the Middle East and North Africa, endorsing the settlement of the Israel-Palestine conflict based on 1967 borders. This speech, which avoided mentioning the issues of settlements, refugees, and Jerusalem, underlined the extent to which any reasonable resolution of the Israeli-Palestinian conflict is crucial to the region's broader stability.

It is equally important to turn to Turkey's active role in effectively harnessing the tensions between competing blocs—the moderate Arab regimes and the resistance bloc, represented by countries such as Iran and Syria. Diplomatic solutions and negotiations stand a realistic chance to undermine terrorism in a region known for militancy. Democracy promotion, in contrast, must be viewed with some caution, as Iraq, following the US invasion, aptly demonstrates. The sharp ethnic and sectarian divisions in Iraq have proven to be major impediments to democratic change.

Another contentious area is that of the Middle East's ruling elites, most of whom have ruled or continue to rule either through outside help or privileged access to oil rent, or via some combination of the two.[124] Implanting democratic systems in environments characterized by ethnic and sectarian division and dominant state policies that are politically exclusionary is highly unlikely. Externally imposed democratization, especially through military intervention, can lead not only to failure but also to further intensification of existing internal conflicts. Acknowledging the limitations to power in the post-9/11 era, Shibley Telhami, an eminent US commentator on the Middle East, wrote:

> If the intent of a strategy of this sort is in part to exhibit America's overwhelming power and Washington's willingness to employ it so as to deter potential enemies, the result may be overextension—the Achilles' heel of many empires. America's ability to deter new threats to its interests would be undermined. This is the dilemma of power: It is most effective when it is least used; the more one uses it, the fewer the remaining resources and the less credible the threat of its use.[125]

Those words still ring true today.

* * *

The campaign against terrorism must begin with addressing the conditions conducive to the spread of terrorism. Failed states are breeding grounds for terrorism, as are repressive regimes, no matter how stable those regimes may be. Although there is no consensus on the best methods through which to curb the longer-term threats of terrorism, the struggle against terrorism cannot be left solely to military measures or military strategists. This campaign must be forged along several tracks simultaneously, including a systematic attempt to resolve prolonged unresolved wars (e.g., the Palestinian-Israeli conflict); establish the rule of law; prevent human rights abuses; eliminate ethnic, national, and religious discrimination; preclude political exclusion and socioeconomic marginalization; and promote good governance.

The impact of counterterrorism instruments and strategies can be measured in many ways. One gauge is to evaluate the level of compromise associated with the implementation of such strategies, and whether or not they might disrupt the viability of a democratic state. In the context of the war on terror, national security interests are often—and incorrectly—defined in terms that are detrimental to the rights and liberties guaranteed by a democratic state, resulting in the growth of new security systems, the militarization of power, and the rise of a new global order—consequences that are likely to compromise democratic governance. Some scholars and citizens question such counterterrorism strategies, arguing that US power must be made less threatening, more restrained, and more acutely attuned to the views and contexts of others.[126]

Another way to assess the effectiveness of counterterrorism tools is to ascertain which strategies can successfully reduce the capabilities of nonstate terrorist groups and actors to operate and recruit. The US invasion of Iraq demonstrated the illusion harbored by those who believed in the transformative nature of military measures. This may well be the case with the involvement of NATO forces in Afghanistan. The effectiveness of having more NATO troops in Afghanistan has spurred an intense debate among NATO members over the strategic merits of counterinsurgency, counterterrorism, and nation-building. In addition to helping US allies maintain support for the war in Afghanistan, one of the biggest challenges facing the Obama administration is its effort to instill good governance in a country in which corruption is widespread.[127] Some observers in the United States argue that after almost a decade of war, continued or increased US involvement in Afghanistan is unlikely to yield lasting improvements that would be commensurate in any way with the investment of US blood and treasure. With both nation-building plans and counterterrorism measures aimed at eradicating the Taliban forces failing, they argue, the time has come to scale back US objectives and drastically reduce US involvement on the ground.[128]

Whether Obama's current plan to fully withdraw from Afghanistan by 2014 will materialize remains to be seen. What is clear, however, is that the task of nation-building in Afghanistan presents its own panoply of problems. The prospects for delivering basic services, physical security, education, and minimal health care remain dim in Afghanistan, in large part because its central government has thus far failed to make progress toward building necessary institutions.

Notes

1. Karen Armstrong, "Ghosts of Our Past," in Thomas J. Badey, ed., *Violence and Terrorism, 05–06*, 8th ed. (Dubuque, IA: McGraw-Hill/Dushkin, 2005), pp. 14–17; see esp. p. 16.
2. Ibid.

3. Bassma Kodmani, "Clearing the Air in the Middle East," *Current History* 107, no. 709 (May 2008): 201–206; see esp. 202.

4. Michael Mandelbaum, "Democracy Without America: The Spontaneous Spread of Freedom," *Foreign Affairs* 86, no. 5 (September–October 2007): 119–130; see p. 123.

5. Ibid., pp. 123–124.

6. Giovanni Kessler, "Terrorism and War," in Jenny Hocking and Colleen Lewis, eds., *Counter-Terrorism and the Post-Democratic State* (Northampton, MA: Edward Elgar, 2007), pp. 20–27; see esp. p. 25.

7. For an interesting view on this, see John L. Esposito, ed., *Political Islam: Revolution, Radicalism, or Reform* (Boulder, CO: Lynne Rienner, 1997).

8. Larry Diamond, "The Democratic Rollback: The Resurgence of the Predatory State," *Foreign Affairs* 87, no. 2 (March–April 2008): 36–48; see p. 38.

9. Ibid., 37.

10. Jeff Haynes, *Democracy and Civil Society in the Third World: Politics and New Political Movements* (Cambridge, UK: Polity Press, 1997), p. 145.

11. Ibid., p. 147.

12. Ibid., p. 163.

13. David P. Forsythe, *Human Rights in International Relations*, 2nd ed. (Cambridge: Cambridge University Press, 2006).

14. Tonny Brems Knudsen, "The English School: Sovereignty and International Law," in Jennifer Sterling-Folker, ed., *Making Sense of International Relations Theory* (Boulder, CO: Lynne Rienner, 2006), pp. 311–325; see p. 312.

15. William Crotty, ed., *Democratic Development and Political Terrorism: The Global Perspective* (Boston: Northeastern University Press, 2005), p. 524.

16. Bergedorf Round Table, *Stability in the Persian Gulf: Regional and Transatlantic Perspectives*, December 2–4, 2005, Bergedorfer Gesprachskries, 2005, p. 44.

17. Crotty, *Democratic Development and Political Terrorism,* p. 525.

18. Jenny White, "The Ebbing Power of Turkey's Secularist Elite," *Current History* 106, no. 704 (December 2007): 427–433; see p. 428.

19. Jack Donnelly, *International Human Rights*, 3rd ed. (Boulder, CO: Westview, 2007), p. 216.

20. Ibid., p. 216.

21. Louise Richardson, *What Terrorists Want: Understanding the Enemy, Containing the Threat* (New York: Random House, 2006), pp. 212–213.

22. Louise Richardson, "The Roots of Terrorism: An Overview," in Louise Richardson, ed., *The Roots of Terrorism* (New York: Routledge, 2006), pp. 1–13; see p. 12.

23. Michael J. Boyle, "Do Counterterrorism and Counterinsurgency Go Together?" *International Affairs* 86, no. 2 (March 2010): 333–353; see esp. pp. 352–353.

24. Barry Kolodkin, "Combating Terrorism in 2010: Examining the Elements of the U.S. Counterterrorism Strategy," *About.com Guide: About U.S. Foreign Policy*; available at http://usforeignpolicy.about.com/od/defense/a/counterterrorism-strategy.htm; accessed June 22, 2010.

25. David Kilcullen, *Counterinsurgency* (New York: Oxford University Press, 2010), p. 1.

26. Ibid., pp. 1–2.

27. Ibid., p. 4.

28. Ibid., p. 10.

29. Ibid.

30. William R. Polk, "US Wars in Iraq and Afghanistan: Lessons from Humpty Dumpty," *Christian Science Monitor*, June 28, 2010, p. 33.

31. Christopher Layne, "Who Lost Iraq and Why It Matters," *World Policy Journal* 24, no. 3 (Fall 2007): 38–52; see p. 44.

32. Ibid., p. 44.

33. Richardson, *What Terrorists Want*, p. 215.

34. Andrea M. Lopez, "Engaging or Withdrawing, Winning or Losing? The Contradictions of Counterinsurgency Policy in Afghanistan and Iraq," *Third World Quarterly* 28, no. 2 (2007): 245–260; see 250.

35. Andrew F. Krepinevich Jr. "How to Win in Iraq," *Foreign Affairs* 84, no. 5 (September–October 2005): 87–104; see pp. 88–89.

36. Ibid., p. 93.

37. Ibid., p. 94.

38. Michael S. Stohl, "Counterterrorism and Repression," in Richardson, *The Roots of Terrorism*, pp. 57–68; see esp. p. 68.

39. Daniel Byman, "Terrorism after the Revolutions: How Secular Uprisings Could Help (or Hurt) Jihadists," *Foreign Affairs* 90, no. 3 (May–June 2011): 48–54; see esp. p. 54.

40. Virginia Held, "Military Intervention and Terrorism," paper at the 2007 annual meetings of the American Political Science Association, August 30–September 2, 2007, Chicago.

41. Boyle, "Do Counterterrorism and Counterinsurgency Go Together?" p. 353.

42. Michael J. Boyle, "The War on Terror in American Grand Strategy," *International Affairs* 84, no. 2 (March 2008): 191–209; see p. 203.

43. Richardson, *What Terrorists Want*, p. 172.

44. Ibid., p. 180.

45. Anthony H. Cordesman, "Iraq, Afghanistan, and Self-Inflicted Wounds: Strategic Lessons of Armed Nation Building," October 16, 2007; available at http://www.csis.org/index.php?option=com_csis_pubs&task=view&id=4116; accessed March 11, 2008.

46. Layne, "Who Lost Iraq and Why It Matters," p. 47.

47. Andrew Mack, "Why Big Nations Lose Small Wars: The Politics of Asymmetric Conflict," *World Politics* 27, no. 2 (January 1975): 175–200; see p. 177.

48. Daniel L. Byman, "Friends Like These: Counterinsurgency and the War on Terrorism," *International Security* 31, no. 2 (2006): 79–115; see p. 114.

49. Kristian William, "Counterinsurgency 101," March 5, 2007; available at http://www.inthesetimes.com/article/article/3956/counterinsurgency_101; accessed March 9, 2008.

50. US Army and Marine Corps, *Counterinsurgency Field Manual: U.S. Army*, Field Manual no. 3-24, Marine Corps Warfighting Publication no. 3-33.5 (Chicago: University of Chicago Press, 2007), p. 38.

51. Ibid., p. 48.

52. Ibid., p. 49.

53. Ibid.

54. John Edwards, "Reengaging with the World: A Return to Moral Leadership," *Foreign Affairs* 86, no. 5 (September–October 2007): 19–36; see p. 23.

55. Laura J. Winter, "NATO's Frayed Afghan Mission," *Christian Science Monitor*, February 6, 2008, pp. 1 and 11.

56. Oxford Analytica, "Anti-American Sentiment Grows Worldwide," Oxford Analytica, August 23, 2007; available at http://www.forbes.com /business/2007/08/22/bush-anti-americanism-cx_0823oxfordanalytica.html; accessed September 12, 2007.

57. Ibid.

58. Ibid.

59. Nigel S. Rodley, "Torture: International Law," in David P. Forsythe, ed., *Encyclopedia of Human Rights*, vol. 5 (New York: Oxford University Press, 2009), pp. 65–74; see esp. p. 67.

60. Ibid., p. 68.

61. Ibid., p. 68.

62. Ibid., p. 69.

63. Ibid., p. 69.

64. Ronald Dworkin, *Is Democracy Possible Here? Principles for a New Political Debate* (Princeton, NJ: Princeton University Press, 2006), p. 38.

65. Ibid.

66. Ibid., p. 44.

67. Jane Mayer, "The Black Sites: A Rare Look Inside the C.I.A.'s Secret Interrogation Program," *New Yorker*, August 13, 2007, pp. 47–57; see p. 57.

68. Ibid.

69. Zbigniew Brzezinski, *Second Chance: Three Presidents and the Crisis of American Superpower* (New York: Basic Books, 2007), p. 185.

70. Ibid., p. 216.

71. Marc Lynch, "Anti-Americanisms in the Arab World," in Peter J. Katzenstein and Robert O. Keohane, eds., *Anti-Americanisms in World Politics* (Ithaca, NY: Cornell University Press, 2007), pp. 196–224; see p. 198; see also Shibley Telhami, *Reflections of Hearts and Minds*, Washington, DC: Brookings Institution, 2005.

72. Lynch, "Anti-Americanisms in the Arab World," p. 223.

73. Robert J. Art and Louise Richardson, eds., *Democracy and Counterterrorism: Lessons From the Past* (Washington, DC: U.S. Institute for Peace, 2007), p. 571.

74. Paul Wallace, "Countering Terrorist Movements in India," in Art and Richardson, *Democracy and Counterterrorism*, pp. 425–481; see pp. 431 and 467.

75. Juan Cole made this observation. For more on this view, see Thomas E. Ricks, *Fiasco: The American Military Adventure in Iraq* (New York: Penguin Press, 2006), p. 431.

76. Ibid., p. 165.

77. Ibid., p. 435.

78. Peter W. Galbraith, *The End of Iraq: How American Incompetence Created a War Without End* (New York: Simon & Schuster, 2006), p. 180.

79. Ibid., p. 185.

80. Robin Wright, *Dreams and Shadows: The Future of the Middle East* (New York: Penguin Press, 2008), pp. 390–391.

81. Kerim Yildiz, *The Kurds in Iraq: Past, Present, and Future* (London: Pluto Press, 2007), p. 212.

82. Art and Richardson, *Democracy and Counterterrorism*, p. 564.

83. Ken Booth, *Theory of World Security* (Cambridge: Cambridge University Press, 2007), p. 358.

84. Art and Richardson, *Democracy and Counterterrorism*, p. 565.

85. Ibid., p. 568.

86. Howard LaFranchi, "Diplomacy Thriving, but Without U.S.," *Christian Science Monitor*, June 3, 2008, pp. 1 and 10–11; see esp. p. 11.

87. Amy Belasco, "The Cost of Iraq, Afghanistan, and Other Global Wars on Terror Operations Since 9/11," *Congressional Research Service*, March 29, 2011:1–55; see esp. p. 3.

88. Antiwar.com, http://antiwar.com/casualties. Last accessed on August 19, 2011.

89. Center for American Progress, "The Opportunity Costs of the Iraq War," National Security, August 2004; available at http://www.americanprogress.org/issues/2004/08/b171438.html; accessed September 3, 2007.

90. Ricks, *Fiasco*, p. 431.

91. PollingReport.com. http://www.pollingreport.com/iraq.htm; last accessed on August 19, 2011.

92. National Security Network. http://www.nsnetwork.org/node/2010; last accessed on August 19, 2011.

93. Robert J. Art and Louise Richardson, "Conclusion," in Art and Richardson, *Democracy and Counterterrorism*, p. 590.

94. For an illuminating essay on this point, see a review article by W. Andrew Terrill, "The Continuing Problem of Iraq," *Middle East Journal* 63, no. 4 (Autumn 2009): 661–667; see esp. p. 666.

95. Dirk Nabers and Robert G. Patman, "Bush's Political Fundamentalism and the War Against Militant Islam," in Jocelyne Cesari, ed., *Muslims in the West After 9/11: Religion, Politics, and Law* (New York: Routledge, 2010), pp. 67–87; see esp. p. 82.

96. Wright, *Dreams and Shadows*, p. 392.

97. Mark Juergensmeyer, "The Church, the Mosque, and Global Civil Society," in Mary Kaldor, Martin Albrow, Helmut Anheier, and Marlies Glasius, eds., *Global Civil Society, 2006–7* (London: Sage, 2007), pp. 144–158; see esp. p. 150.

98. Lionel Beehner, "Iraq's Militia Groups," *Council on Foreign Relations*, October 26, 2006; available at http://www.cfr.org/publication/11824/iraqs_militia_groups.html#4; accessed June 10, 2008.

99. Greg Bruno, "Muqtada al Sadr," *Council on Foreign Relations*, May 16, 2008; available at http://www.cfr.org/publication/7637; accessed June 10, 2008.

100. Bill Roggio, "The Sunni Awakening," *The Long War Journal*, May 3, 2007; available at http://www.longwarjournal.org/archives/2007/05/the_sunni_awakening.php; accessed June 10, 2008.

101. Vali Nasr, *The Shia Revival: How Conflicts Within Islam Will Shape the Future*" (New York: W. W. Norton, 2006), p. 179.

102. Ibid., p. 180.

103. Mark Peceny, "Democracy Promotion and American Foreign Policy: Afghanistan, Iraq, and the Future," in David P. Forsythe, Patrice C. McMahon,

and Andrew Wedeman, eds., *American Foreign Policy in a Globalized World* (New York: Routledge, 2006), pp. 215–239; see esp. pp. 222–223.

104. F. Gregory Gause III, "Why Middle East Studies Missed the Arab Spring," *Foreign Affairs*, 90, no. 4, July–August 2011, pp. 81–90; see esp. p. 87.

105. F. Gregory Gause III, "Democracy Promotion Is Problematic as a Counterterrorism Priority," in Stuart Gottlieb, ed., *Debating Terrorism and Counterterrorism: Conflicting Perspectives on Causes, Contexts, and Responses* (Washington, DC: Congressional Quarterly Press, 2010), pp. 238–251; see esp. pp. 250–251.

106. Stuart Gottlieb, ed., *Debating Terrorism and Counterterrorism: Conflicting Perspectives on Causes, Contexts, and Responses* (Washington, DC: Congressional Quarterly Press); see esp. p. 236.

107. Jennifer L. Windsor, "Promoting Democracy Can Combat Terrorism," in Gottlieb, *Debating Terrorism and Counterterrorism*, p. 263.

108. Art and Richardson, "Conclusion," p. 574.

109. Ibid., p. 577.

110. Ibid., p. 578.

111. Ian Lustick, Ivan Eland, Rand Beers, and Edward Luttwak, "Are We Trapped in the War on Terror?" *Middle East Policy* 13, no. 4 (Winter 2006): 1–27; see comments by Ambassador Freeman and Dr. Edward Luttwak, on p. 15.

112. Barry Buzan, "Will the 'Global War on Terrorism' Be the New Cold War?" *International Relations* 82, no. 6 (November 2006): 1101–1118; see esp. pp. 1115–1116.

113. Stanley Hoffmann, "The Foreign Policy the US Needs," *New York Review of Books* 53, no. 13 (August 10, 2006): 60–64.

114. I interviewed Dr. Ihsan Bal in his office in Ankara, on June 19, 2009.

115. I interviewed Dr. Turgut Tarhanli in his office at Istanbul Bilgi University, on June 24, 2009.

116. William L. Cleveland and Martin Bunton, *A History of the Modern Middle East*, 4th ed. (Boulder, CO: Westview Press, 2009), pp. 178–179.

117. I interviewed Ms. Yildiz Imrek on June 23, 2009, in Ankara. Ms. Sevda Karaca, of Hayat Televizyonu-Evrensel Gazeksi served as translator and also contributed to the discussion.

118. In the course of my trip to the United Arab Emirates and Turkey (June 12–July 6, 2009), I interviewed several groups, including local emirates in Dubai, such as Mr. Ahmed Al-Sharif of Master Development Company, UAE, as well as a group of Palestinian diaspora in Dubai, several Turkish journalists (Abdullah Bozkurt, Kadri Gürsel, and Kerim Balci), and several members of a well-known think tank in Ankara, Turkey, the International Strategic Research Organization—ISRO. In all these interviews there appeared to be a consensus that this line of thinking was crucial to the peace, stability, and counterterrorism efforts in the region.

119. Stephen J. Toope, "Human Rights and the Use of Force After September 11th, 2001," in Daniel J. Sherman and Terry Nardin, eds., *Terror, Culture, Politics: Rethinking 9/11*, Bloomington: Indiana University Press, 2006, pp. 236–258; see esp. p. 246.

120. Brigitte L. Nacos, "There Is a Need to Focus More on Building Bridges," in Gottlieb, *Debating Terrorism and Counterterrorism*, p. 213.

121. Ibid., p. 218.

122. Amin Saikal, "Radical Islamism and the 'War on Terror,'" in Shahram Akbarzadeh and Fethi Mansouri, eds., *Islam and Political Violence: Muslim Diaspora and Radicalism in the West* (London: Tauris Academic Studies, 2007), pp. 13–26; see esp. p. 22.

123. I interviewed Nicole Stracke and Christian Koch, both research fellows at the Gulf Research Center, Dubai, the United Arab Emirates, on July 2, 2009. While both underscored the importance of a holistic model to combat terrorism, they saw the resolution of the Israeli-Palestinian issue as the core issue in the region.

124. Fred Halliday, *The Middle East in International Relations: Power, Politics, and Ideology* (New York: Cambridge University Press, 2005), p. 291.

125. Shibley Telhami, *The Stakes; America and the Middle East: The Consequences of Power and the Choice for Peace* (Boulder, CO: Westview Press, 2002), p. 170.

126. John Keane, "Empire and Democracy," in Jenny Hocking and Colleen Lewis, eds., *Counter-terrorism and the Post-Democratic State* (Northampton, MA: Edward Elgar, 2007), pp. 200–211; see p. 210.

127. Thomas J. Billitteri, "Afghanistan Dilemma," in *Global Issues: Selections from CQ Researchers* (Washington, DC: CQ Press, 2011), pp. 1–24; see esp. pp. 18–20.

128. Richard N. Haass, "We're Not Winning. It's Not Worth It. Here Is How to Draw Down in Afghanistan," *Newsweek*, July 26, 2010, pp. 30–35.

3

Military Intervention:
Risks and Costs

During the last quarter of the twentieth century, humanitarian intervention—as seen, for example, in Somalia, Bosnia, Rwanda, Cambodia, Haiti, Sierra Leone, and East Timor—gradually and steadily came to be accepted as a normal response, but the unilateral use of force, as seen in Iraq from March 2003, raised central questions about the legitimacy of that kind of intervention.

Efforts to impose liberal internationalist ideals on non-Western countries through military intervention have invited worldwide criticism. While there is a vast and highly contentious literature devoted to understanding the consequences of military intervention, little attention has been paid to the fundamental question of whether security actually improves over time because of such unilateral interventions. In the case of Iraq, Lebanon, and the occupied Palestinian Territories, military intervention has proven counterproductive, futile, and costly in both human and economic terms. This chapter attempts to appraise such activities while systematically examining the appropriateness of military intervention. It calls into question the utility of military measures not only for combating terrorism and deterring future terrorist operations but also for establishing a democratic order. Military solutions are shown to be practically and politically tenuous in the long run.

Historically, US military intervention in the Middle East has typically revolved around countering Soviet influence, managing oil resources, preventing radical and anti-Western revolution, and supporting Israel. The awareness of this history has conditioned Middle Easterners to resist outside control and intervention. Such intervention has made (and will make) things worse, not better. The Soviet invasion of Afghanistan, Israel's iron-fist policies to suppress popular uprisings in the occupied Palestinian Territories and its invasion of Lebanon, and the

55

US invasion of Iraq all have proven that military responses are counter-productive and carry wider negative implications. The danger of terrorism has underlined the need to tackle the question of whether military interventions can contribute to the solution. After a brief discussion of the legacy of Western intervention, I turn to the Israeli invasion of Lebanon, the first and second intifada, the second Gulf War, and the US invasion of Iraq, highlighting US and Israeli use of military intervention to pursue US/Israeli interests. A final section attempts to assess the overall effect of outside intervention on the region as a whole.

The Legacy of Western Intervention in the Middle East

The modern history of Western intervention in the Middle East can be traced back to the French invasion of Egypt in 1798. This was followed by prolonged European subjugation and occupation of most Arab countries from the 1830s until the mid-twentieth century.[1] By the early twentieth century, Turkey, Egypt, and Iran had benefited from the spread of education and an increased mobility of people, goods, and ideas. Many among the elites and the growing professional, middle, and working classes in the region had become imbued with a desire to establish constitutional democracy, the rule of law, and modern governmental systems. They tended to use the liberal constitutional systems of Great Britain, France, and the United States as models. These empires, in turn, feared that constitutional reform in the Middle East would fortify the capability of southern Muslim states to block their imperial and expansionist objectives.[2]

The era of European colonialism marked the end of hopes for democratic reform in the region. France's invasion of Algeria and Britain's seizure of Aden on the southwestern corner of the Arabian Peninsula indicated colonial ambition. The expansion of the European powers into the Arab world was completed with Italy's invasion of Libya in 1911, France's establishment of a protectorate over Morocco in 1912, and, by the 1920s, the World War I Anglo-French partitions of the Ottoman Empire.[3] In the wake of World War I, the only Middle Eastern countries able to oppose these external interventions were Iran and the new Republic of Turkey. Until the end of World War II, Britain and France, together with Italy in Libya and Spain in the Western Sahara, maintained a political, economic, and strategic stranglehold over the Middle East. The British influence in domestic Egyptian politics—from 1922 until the military revolution of 1952—kept the overwhelmingly popular Wafd Party out of power.[4]

After the fall of the Ottoman Empire, the policies of many new states were determined by European occupiers. The League of Nations' mandate system treated these Middle Eastern countries as pseudo colonies, not independent countries, and their peoples had no rights of their own. They were regarded as subject peoples. The mandate system provided Britain and France with an opportunity to secure their interests in the Middle East while paying lip service to the widely known principle of self-determination. For most of the interwar period, Arab political activity was primarily aimed at achieving independence from foreign rule.[5] British colonial intervention in Iraq (1922–1932) contained the expansion of political participation there. When Iraq was created in the wake of World War I, the British rejected demands for participatory government by nationalist elites and instead installed Amir Abdullah's brother Faisal on the throne. Shortly thereafter, they used their air force against guerrilla insurgents in the Middle Euphrates region, the first ever attack of this kind.[6] That is the colonial legacy, and Rashid Khalidi finds its effects strongly relevant today, admonishing Westerners that they

> make a serious mistake in thinking that these events are buried in the distant past and thus are long forgotten by the younger generations that now dominate Middle Eastern societies. Leaving aside the fact that any citizen over fifty years old, including the majority of Middle Eastern elites, can recall vividly the waning days of the colonial era, the history of the struggle for liberation from foreign rule has for decades been amply conveyed to several generations of children by the national educational systems in Middle Eastern countries.[7]

During the Cold War, direct US military intervention would have risked provoking a severe backlash from the Soviet Union. Instead, the United States resorted to a more subtle technique of covert operations, such as the clandestine coup d'etat, to depose foreign governments. In Iran, Guatemala, South Vietnam, and Chile, diplomats and intelligence agents replaced generals as the instruments of US intervention.[8]

The removal of Iran's democratically elected prime minister, Mohammad Mossadeq, by a US-instigated and financed coup in 1953 put an end to the nationalistic and democratic aspirations of the Iranian people. With Mossadeq's oil-nationalization program threatening British interests, the United Kingdom imposed a blockade on the export and sale of Iranian oil, causing a drastic deterioration of the country's economy. As a result, the Iranian prime minister's popularity dramatically declined: the initial euphoria of nationalization gave way to progressively worsening economic conditions and reluctance by the conservative clergy to openly support him.[9] On August 19, 1953, a US-engineered coup overthrew Mossadeq. His removal led to an era of royal absolutism (1953–1977), which effectively ended the Iranian parliament's independence. Parliamentary elections became a charade, and parliament became the rubber stamp it had been during the earlier period of absolutism under Reza Shah. The shah practically controlled all levers of power, and his powers became synonymous with state powers. He ruled by mistrust, while relying on an elaborate and highly efficient police apparatus that permeated every aspect of life in Iran.[10] Not surprisingly, when the Islamic revolution occurred a quarter of a century later, Iran's revolutionary goals became diametrically opposed to those of US security interests in the Gulf region.

In the 1967 Arab-Israeli War (the Six-Day War), Israel attacked Egypt, Syria, Iraq, and Jordan, capturing Syria's Golan Heights, the Jordanian-controlled West Bank that included East Jerusalem, the Egyptian-administered Gaza Strip, and Egypt's Sinai Peninsula. Israel began colonizing the captured territories through the establishment of Jewish settlements. Ongoing intervention in the region by Western powers has continued, and Israel's actions have produced two main consequences: (1) the rise of transnational terrorism and (2) the emergence of Islam as a popular vehicle for pursuing the political and socioeconomic reforms that secular governments in the region have largely failed to provide.[11]

Arab nationalist leaders led authoritarian regimes during the 1950s and 1960s. The Western support for some of these authoritarian regimes created a credibility gap insofar as democratic change was concerned. Equally disturbing and disruptive was the Soviet invasion of Afghanistan in December 1979, prompted by the internal disintegration of the Afghani state. The Soviet penetration of the Afghan state apparatus included building or rebuilding the institutions that governed party, army and police, economy, and education.[12] By the time Mikhail Gorbachev gained power in the Soviet Union in March 1985, it was increasingly clear that both the Soviet regime and the Afghan government had failed to establish state control—or even state presence—in most of the countryside.[13] The Soviet withdrawal (1988–1989) and the subsequent loss of its military support, along with the increased availability of arms for the resistance, severely undermined the central authority of the state throughout much of the country. Afghani society, however, proved unable to organize itself to provide an alternative form of government. The political forces of society were too fragmented to replace it.[14]

The Soviet invasion of Afghanistan, which was wrongly perceived in Washington as a way for the Soviets to extend their influence into the Gulf area and perhaps beyond, led the United States to coordinate its response with Pakistan and Saudi Arabia in an effort to roll back Soviet forces in Afghanistan by mobilizing Islamic militants—the mujahidin. In 1989, after fifteen thousand Soviet soldiers were killed, thirty-five thousand were wounded, and nearly one million Afghans were killed, Soviet forces finally pulled out of Afghanistan. The equivalent of about a billion dollars had been spent during this time to support Soviet troops in Afghanistan. Unable to defeat the mujahidin and pressed by world opinion to leave Afghanistan, Soviet leaders were compelled to withdraw their troops.[15]

The defeat of the Soviets not only failed to bring lasting security and peace to Afghanistan and the Gulf region, it also left behind a tumultuous "failed state" of belligerent Islamist militants. Worse yet, with the Soviet withdrawal from Afghanistan, many of these militants left Afghanistan for their countries of origin in the hope of promoting puritanical Islamic reform by force of arms against the US presence or influence in their home countries.[16]

In the aftermath of the Soviet Union's dissolution in the early 1990s, the Afghan state collapsed and was replaced by hyperarmed power networks.[17] The international supporters of the resistance to the Soviet Union tried to reshape the mujahidin into a conventional military force led by a political alliance that would pose a genuine political alternative to the Soviet-installed government in Kabul. Seeking a political settlement, the Saudi and Pakistani governments agreed to promote orthodox Islamic factions and institutions in Afghanistan. Furthermore, with the end of the Cold War, Afghanistan lost the remainder of its foreign aid. The armed forces, its sole remaining national institution, dissolved and were absorbed into the country's regional-ethnic power networks.[18]

Both Pakistan and the United States were interested in stability in Afghanistan, albeit for different reasons. For both, gaining access to oil and establishing gas pipelines to the Caspian Sea and Central Asia through Afghanistan were long-term strategic goals. Seen from the US standpoint, this situation would help in maintaining economic sanctions on Iran. Additionally, Afghan and Pakistani traders and ultraconservative religious leaders supported the Taliban's attempts to reconstruct a centralized state.

Following the attacks on the United States of September 11, 2001, direct military intervention has become the preferred instrument for regime change in the region—a way of converting so-called rogue states into liberal, Western-style democracies. This has raised questions of legitimacy and practicality. In addition to the question of whether military intervention is legitimate, an issue of equal significance is whether such interventions are prudent and practical.

In the following section, I turn to the Israeli invasion of Lebanon, popular uprisings in the occupied Palestinian Territories, and the Gulf Wars of 1991 and 2003.

The Israeli Invasion of Lebanon

Israel invaded Lebanon on June 6, 1982, asserting the need to clear forces of the Palestine Liberation Organization (PLO) from an area north of its border with Lebanon. After an attack on Israel's ambassador in London, Shlomo Argov (carried out by the Abu Nidal group but blamed on the PLO), Israeli troops marched into southern Lebanon. The stated goals of the operation were to free northern Israel from PLO rocket attacks by creating a security zone, forty kilometers wide, in southern Lebanon and by signing a peace treaty with Lebanon.

The June 1982 invasion of Lebanon, called Operation Peace for Galilee, was the first war fought by the Israeli Defense Forces (IDF) without domestic consensus. Unlike the 1948, 1967, and 1973 wars, the Israeli public never viewed this operation as essential to the survival of the Jewish state. The architects of this invasion, Menachem Begin and Ariel Sharon, sought to use Israel's military strength to create a regional political environment conducive to Israel's security. This strategy included weakening the PLO and supporting the rise to power of Israel's Christian allies in Lebanon. The sustained, eleven-hour bombing of Beirut on August 12, 1982, evoked worldwide condemnation, including even that of the United States. In the end, all of West Beirut was destroyed, the PLO fighters left, and the IDF moved into Beirut.

The attempt to impose a military solution to the intractable Palestinian problem as well as to politically change the power balance in Lebanon failed. The PLO, although defeated militarily, remained an important political force, and Bashir Gemayel, Israel's major ally in Lebanon, was killed shortly after becoming president. Within Israel, a mounting death toll caused by ongoing skirmishes led to sharp criticism by a public weary of the war and the Likud government.[19] In 2000, Israeli forces withdrew from most of Lebanon, ending eighteen years of occupation. This left Hezbollah in firm control of southern Lebanon.

It was said that the reason for the Israeli invasion was the attempted assassination of Israeli ambassador Argov in London by Palestinian groups on June 3. This gave an excuse to Israeli prime minister Menachem Begin and his defense minister, Ariel Sharon, who had been waiting for an opportunity to get rid of the PLO raids emanating from Lebanon. Begin and Sharon, however, had secretly prepared a plan to expand their military forces all the way to Beirut, forcing both the PLO and Syrian forces entirely out of Lebanon and making it almost an Israeli client-state.[20] As the occupation continued, however, other Israeli goals emerged. Although the invasion appeared successful initially, it ultimately failed to secure Israel's objectives: namely, to drive out the PLO from Beirut and other parts of Lebanon, to help Bashir Gemayel to become Lebanon's president, and to sign an accord with the Lebanese government.

While the PLO forces were driven out, Gemayel was assassinated, and the agreement with the Lebanese government was abrogated, Gemayel's Phalangist paramilitary units, who were out for revenge, found an easy target in the Palestinian refugee camps. Between September 16 and 18, 1982, Lebanese Christian Phalangist militiamen were allowed to enter two Palestinian refugee camps—Sabra and Shatilla—in an area under Israeli army control. The militia massacred the civilians inside. These shocking events, which led to the loss of the lives of hundreds of men, women, and children, raised serious questions about the legal responsibility of the political and military leaders of the occupying forces. Israeli authorities or forces, a report concluded, were involved, directly or indirectly, in the massacres.[21] In fact, the Knesset-appointed Kahan Commission indicted Sharon for his "shared responsibility" in the massacres.[22]

In May 2000, when Israeli forces withdrew from most of Lebanon, they continued to occupy a ten-kilometer "security zone" on Lebanese territory, an occupation that mired it in a continuing war with Shiite forces in southern Lebanon. Perhaps the single most important ramification of the war, one expert pointed out, was the alienation of the Shia community in southern Lebanon, who initially welcomed the Israeli invasion because it liberated them from the perilous climate created by the PLO presence there. As the Israeli presence continued, however, the

Shia community increasingly saw Israelis as occupiers, and they responded with fierce resistance. The Shia became increasingly empowered through organizations such as Hezbollah and Amal. The Syrian-Iranian alliance that emerged following the Iran-Iraq War merged with Hezbollah's political agenda to render the Shia community and its power difficult to overlook.[23]

The report of the international commission of inquiry into reported violations of international law by Israel during its invasions of Lebanon concluded that the IDF's bombardment of Beirut during early August 1982 was a violation of the laws of war and was absolutely unwarranted by the principle of military necessity.[24] The commission found that the IDF bombings of population centers were, in many respects, disproportionate in their effects on civilians relative to military advantage gained;[25] the IDF was also held to have violated the principle of discrimination.[26]

Some Israeli citizens strongly reacted to the cruel and bloody invasion of Lebanon and its consequences. Dr. Shlomo Shmelzman, a survivor of the Holocaust, wrote a letter to the press in Israel during the bombing of West Beirut in August 1982. Announcing that he was going on a hunger strike, he wrote:

> In my childhood I suffered fear, hunger and humiliation when I passed from the Warsaw Ghetto, through labor camps, to Buchenwald. Today, as a citizen of Israel, I cannot accept the systematic destruction of cities, towns and refugee camps. I cannot accept the technocratic cruelty of the bombing, destroying and killing of human beings. I hear too many familiar sounds today, sounds which are being amplified by the war. I hear "dirty Arabs" and I remember "dirty Jews." I hear about "closed areas" and I remember ghettos and camps. I hear "two-legged beasts" and I remember "Untermenschen" (sub-humans). I hear about tightening the siege, clearing the area, pounding the city into submission and I remember suffering, destruction, death, blood and murder. . . . Too many things in Israel remind me of too many things from my childhood.[27]

In July 2006, another Israeli invasion of Lebanon fell generally into the same pattern as the earlier one. In 2006 the Israeli targets were Hezbollah and its infrastructure in southern Lebanon. Noam Chomsky wrote that the only viable support for Palestinians facing national destruction was from Hezbollah. The Israelis aimed at weakening or destroying Hezbollah, just as the PLO had had to be evicted from Lebanon in 1982. But Hezbollah was too deeply embedded within Lebanese society to be eradicated.[28] This invasion unified most Lebanese in their deep resentment over Israel's air strikes and restored Hezbollah as the main embodiment of the country's national resistance, well beyond the Shiite community.[29] Having shown unprecedented resilience in the face of gruesome Israeli attacks and destruction, Hezbollah grew stronger. Rami George Khouri, a veteran journalist and editor-at-large of the Beirut-based *Daily Star*, argued that "the Lebanese and Palestinians have responded to Israel's persistent and increasingly savage attacks against entire civilian populations by creating parallel or alternative leaderships that can protect them and deliver essential services."[30]

The First Intifada, 1987–1993

Israeli control and occupation of the Palestinian lands since 1967 had produced a spontaneous but dramatic resistance to Israel in the form of a popular uprising in the West Bank and Gaza. These events revived demands for active diplomatic intervention.

By the late 1980s, Palestinian living conditions had deteriorated, and it appeared that a deliberate Israeli policy was paving the way for eventual annexation of the occupied Palestinian Territories. The harsher measures adopted by Shamir's government, along with pent up frustrations at the relative impotence of the PLO, the leadership party of the territories, led to the outbreak of the intifada.[31] As the uprising permeated throughout the West Bank and Gaza Strip across sectional, religious, and class lines, an underground Palestinian leadership emerged to coordinate Palestinian activities and forge a common strategy. The Unified National Leadership of the Uprising (UNLU), made up of various leaders of Palestinian parties in the territories, was formed to guide protests and strikes. Shamir's heavy-handed tactics only emboldened the uprising and led to more and more Palestinian participation.[32]

Partly in response to the failure of governments in the region to bring about change and partly because of the growing inspiration for change in the form of nonstate groups and individuals, the Palestinians of the intifada emerged empowered. A new generation of Palestinians, born and raised under Israeli occupation, took to the streets in December 1987 to protest the continued Israeli occupation. This social upheaval was escalated by the Lebanon War of 1982–1985 in which an indigenous civilian population had compelled the IDF to withdraw from Lebanon.[33] These uprisings, which assumed a form of civil disobedience, had two goals: to oppose continued Israeli rule and to build an alternative system to it.[34] The impact of military and other tactics to quell these uprising proved futile. IDF countermeasures such as curfews and clampdowns; the use of riot batons, tear gas, and rubber and plastic bullets as well as live ammunition; and sanctions not only failed to suppress the intifada, they noticeably attenuated Israeli rule in the occupied territories.[35]

Although it can be said that the intifada gave the PLO a new political life (its leaders at that time were living in exile in Tunisia), it also made it clear that the PLO must operate and rule with the consent of those living within the territories. The uprising put the spotlight on the Palestinian crisis and generated tremendous international support for the Palestinian cause. International opinion came to regard as "legitimate" the response of the Palestinians to military occupation. In addition to rendering Palestinian self-determination inevitable, the most significant yet indirect effect of the uprising was the legitimization of the PLO.[36]

But the uprising was a youth movement driven by, among other things, the disenchantment of young Palestinians with their elders. Significantly, the intifada reflected the existence of a powerful internal nationalism largely immune to outside influences. For the first time in the history of the Palestinian struggle to recover land and gain self-rule, the Palestinian political community saw a shift in the balance of power between the Palestinians residing inside the occupied territories and the PLO leadership outside. This shift forced PLO leaders in Tunisia to accept the influence of West Bank and Gaza personalities, several of whom later represented the Palestinians at the 1991 Madrid Conference.[37]

Beyond the experiences of civil struggle and resistance, the Palestinians of the West Bank and Gaza underwent a far deeper educational transformation. Their involvement in the fight for political change reflected a process of self-regeneration in which a people traditionally cast as subjects transformed themselves into active citizens.[38] Intifada signaled a turning away from guerrilla strategies and warfare that had contributed so little to the solution. The Palestinian leaders, who had endorsed the idea of coexistence with Israel and had reached comity with the Islamic revivalists, should have been offered reinforcement rather than jail and deportation. Israeli policies, Mary Elizabeth King writes, instead undermined those who led the first intifada as well as the pursuit of a two-state solution.[39]

Immediately after the outbreak of the intifada, Palestinians in Israel expressed solidarity and identification with the Palestinian struggle in the occupied territories. The resolution of this conflict pushed the Palestinian Arab inhabitants of Israel to identify more wholeheartedly with Israel, while focusing on their internal campaign to achieve full equality with their Jewish fellow citizens. The prospects for this transformation dimmed, however, as the Israeli state and society became further entrenched in nationalistic identity.[40]

In 1987, in reaction to the intifada, Israel decided to establish the Landau Commission to investigate allegations of torture against the General Security Service (GSS). Its recommendations, however inadvertently, contributed to the systematic torture of hundreds of Palestinians in Israeli jails. The Landau Commission's report, which was issued on the eve of the first intifada, also confirmed that GSS personnel had lied under oath about their activities and that torture was used against 85 percent of Palestinian terror suspects. Some six years after the signing of the Oslo Declaration of Principles and Israel's withdrawal from Gaza, the threat posed by the Palestinian terrorists could no longer be defined as one against the "survival of Israel," and the Israeli supreme court moved to render the Landau report list of questionable interrogation techniques as illegal.[41] The court decision notwithstanding, the abuse of terror suspects and torture continued systematically. There may be no judicial action or remedy for abolishing torture. It is imperative, as one scholar notes, that we inquire about the conditions under which terrorism flourishes. Terrorism and torture are indeed "the cumulative result of war, occupation, colonialism, and colonization. Israel is a model for the licensing of torture when these conditions persist."[42]

The Gulf War II, 1991

Desperately in need of financial assistance after its eight-year war with Iran, Iraq invaded and occupied its much wealthier neighbor, Kuwait. An international coalition, led by the United States and including a number of Arab nations, launched an air and sea counterattack—Operation Desert Storm—in January 1991. In February, coalition group forces drove the Iraqi army from Kuwait and penetrated deep into Iraqi territory before a cease-fire took effect.

The future interests of the countries that forged an alliance against Iraq in the Gulf, especially those that are not situated in the Middle East, may arguably diverge or converge depending on the nature of future crises. For the United States, however, there was the continuing challenge of maintaining a consistent track record in the region as memories lingered of the Iran-Contra affair, which bolstered an Iraqi military buildup to contain the Iranian revolution, and of the failure of its policy to restore order in Lebanon in the 1980s. The aftermath of the Gulf crisis created a new era of both regional and international diplomacy, stressing workable collective security arrangements through the United Nations and regional structures. Although the crisis demonstrated the failure of diplomacy in preventing the war, it had the potential and dynamics for opening up new opportunities where diplomacy could be used as a catalyst for stability and peace in the area.

Mindful of exaggerated hopes for change, it seemed realistic to argue that new developments resulting from the Gulf crisis placed the United States in a historically rare position of carrying the dynamics of military victory in the Persian Gulf into subsequent diplomatic domains. It was not clear, however, whether the decisive defeat of Iraq served to encourage more pragmatism in some of the region's states—Iran, Syria, and Israel. Iranians had a reason to be concerned less with containing Iraq's hegemonic capability or self-proclaimed role as the regional power than with their own economic bottlenecks. Without in any way suggesting that the Iranians were any less interested in playing an active regional role, it can be argued that the war's outcome triggered the adoption of pragmatic policies by the Iranian government.

The longer the Arab-Israeli peace negotiations lasted, the slimmer the chances became for the religious fundamentalists to promote credible radical alternatives. At the time, this implied a strong correlation between the success of the peace talks and the triumph of pragmatism over ideology. The Iraqi invasion of Kuwait prompted new security concerns among the leaders of the small states of the Gulf. Having survived the aftershocks of the Iranian Revolution (1979) and nearly eight years of war between Iran and Iraq (1980–1988), the Persian Gulf crisis of August 1990 once again reminded these regimes of their domestic and foreign vulnerabilities. If these two events were among the principal catalysts for the creation of the Gulf Cooperation Council (the GCC, which had Kuwait as one of its six members), the Iraqi invasion of Kuwait inexorably led to the expansion of the defense and security aspects of the council's original constitutional documents. This invasion demonstrated the limitations of the "GCC's professed goal of self-reliance and of its capacity to insure regime security of a member confronting determined aggression from another state."[43]

Iraq's ethnic and civil war in the aftermath of Operation Desert Storm presented a problem. Saddam Hussein's cruel and savage treatment of Iraq's Kurdish population, for example, was simply another upsetting reality of the area. Having been driven out of Kuwait by coalition group forces, Saddam Hussein's survival was actually a victory of sorts, and, despite its weakened military state, the Iraqi government was able to wreak havoc on the Kurdish rebels in Iraq's north and the Shiite Muslims in the south. In fact, despite persistent calls by President Bush for Iraqis to topple the Hussein government, nothing short of covert action by the CIA and limited US military action appeared capable of wresting control of Iraq from Hussein and his coterie. The earlier George H. W. Bush administration (1988–1992) had seemed content with dislodging Iraqi troops from Kuwait. That military campaign—a "war of necessity"—had been focused on an obviously limited strategic objective of destroying Saddam's military capability and evicting Iraq from Kuwait.[44]

The Second Intifada

To provide a clear picture about the conditions leading to the second popular uprising (2000–2004), it is important to track down the divisions and disagreements that surfaced among Palestinians after the late 1990s. The future of state building and political sovereignty in the West Bank and Gaza Strip became far more problematic as ideological differences involved in reconciling their national aspirations further deepened divisions between the secular Palestinian nationalists and radical Islamists.

One of the most significant implications of the first intifada was the emergence of the Islamic Resistance Movement, Harakat al-maqawama al-islamiya, more popularly known as Hamas (the Arabic word for zeal, bravery, or ardor). Together with Islamic Jihad, the Hamas organizations established charitable services and carried out civil society functions for everyday Palestinians, who received no such support from either the Israelis or mainstream Palestinian organizations. For Hamas, this laid the foundation for the development of a political role within the Palestinian movements.[45]

The PLO's Yasser Arafat faced a choice: he could either accommodate Hamas or confront it. He either had to clamp down on extremists in the autonomous zones and confront them head-on or he had to control them by maintaining the balance of forces among various Palestinian factions. The growing popular support for radicalism among Palestinians, especially among the Gazans, and the importance of retaining broad-based Palestinian support presented a colossal challenge to Arafat. He had to incorporate Hamas into any future elections in order to unite Palestinians behind his rule, but at the same time he had to satisfy Israeli demands that he contain violent Hamas attacks without appearing an Israeli lackey. The PLO-Hamas rivalry had enormous implications for Palestinian self-rule.[46]

The Iraqi invasion of Kuwait and the ensuing Gulf crisis in 1990–1991 increased the world's awareness of the Palestinians' problem. Disillusioned by Israel's failure to respond to the PLO's peace initiative of 1988 and frustrated by the continued, massive immigration of Soviet Jews to Israel, Palestinians suffered many potentially serious demographic and political changes. They felt threatened as they saw themselves closer than ever before to expulsion.[47] Yet international attention once again pressed the Palestinian issue to the forefront of world politics. In the aftermath of the Gulf crisis, it became obvious that pressures for a peaceful resolution of the Palestinian-Israeli conflict were irresistible. In Israel, the June 1992 defeat of the Likud and the ascendancy to power of the Labor Party and Prime Minister Yitzhak Rabin ushered in a new era: peacemaking, not military occupation and suppression, became the main objective. Having participated in suppressing the intifada since 1987 and having witnessed Likud's inability to cope with Israel's growing social and economic problems, Rabin's government initiated its peace policies. Rabin's assassination on November 4, 1995, by a right-wing Israeli radical opposed to Rabin's signing of the Oslo Agreements, decimated these hopeful signs.

The second Palestinian intifada, which is often referred to as the al-Aqsa intifada, after the Jerusalem al-Aqsa mosque complex where the violence began, erupted at the end of September 2000. The collapse of the Camp David summit in July 2000 intensified the existing frustrations that years of negotiation had failed to deliver a Palestinian state. When the Palestinian-Israeli negotiations broke down, the paradigm of Pax Americana in the Middle East collapsed with it. A decade after the end of the Cold War that became synonymous with US dominance in the Middle East, economic development and political reform had stalled and the prospect of an Arab-Israeli peace agreement had severely diminished.[48] While the first intifada took the form of a militant but essentially unarmed civil insurrection, the second turned out to be violent. While Hamas emerged as a major force during the first intifada, the religious character of the uprising was relatively subdued. In comparison, religion played a central mobilizing and symbolic role in the second uprising, even as the participation of Hamas was largely confined to raising their flags at funeral processions. The enhancement of the confessional and sectarian aspects of the struggle at the cost of the diminution of the national and secular aspects of the second intifada proved to be deeply divisive.[49]

Ariel Sharon, then the leader of Israel's opposition party, paid a visit to the site in East Jerusalem known to Muslims as Haram al-Sharif and to Jews as the Temple Mount. The site houses the al-Aqsa mosque. Frustration resulted in violence and the second Palestinian uprising was born. In the early months of the al-Aqsa intifada, Israeli tanks rolled back into the West Bank. Israel's brutal treatment of refugees continued unabated and came to a head in early April 2002 with the invasion of the Jenin refugee camp. A deadly two-week Israeli assault left many Palestinians dead and hundreds wounded.[50]

The main negative economic consequences of widespread violence and movement restrictions in the aftermath of the start of the second intifada were the disruption of production and circulation of goods and services in the Palestinian territories and, thus, a swift curtailment of Palestinian national income. Gross National Income (GNI—a broad measure of national income) was estimated to have dropped from about $6.1 billion in 1999 to $5 billion in 2001—a 17 percent decline. Per capita income, when the effect of the population growth was taken into account, declined by about 23 percent in the first fifteen months of the crisis.[51] After twenty-seven months of severe movement restrictions, real GNI was estimated to have been more than 33 percent below the 1999 baseline, while population growth magnified the fall in per capita income to 40 percent.[52] The main effect of Israeli measures on the Palestinian population was unprecedented levels of unemployment, which increased from 11 percent in 2000 to more than 41 percent in the third quarter of 2002.[53] Moreover, by the end of 2002 some 1,970 Palestinians had been killed. Further impoverishment of the territories generated more resistance and violence.[54]

The death of Yasser Arafat in November 2004 marked the end of the second intifada and shifted the political pendulum in favor of Hamas. The ruling Fatah party's internal bickering and divisions fortified Hamas's repute among ordinary Palestinians, who overwhelmingly supported Hamas candidates in successive municipal elections.[55] Israel's proposed "disengagement" from Gaza—a process that started at the end of August 2005—and the Palestinian parliamentary elections led to drastic changes in the occupied territories. Israeli prime minister Ariel Sharon's unilateral disengagement plan, announced on June 6, 2004, called for the evacuation of settlements in the Gaza Strip. The withdrawal marked the first time since Israel's withdrawal from the Sinai Peninsula in 1982 that it had relinquished Jewish settlements to Arab control. The unilateral withdrawal from Gaza left the Palestinians in the tiny and nonviable economic and political entity isolated and strangled.

Jimmy Carter, the former US president, described the gravity of the situation, noting that Gaza maintained a population growth rate of 4.7 percent annually, one of the highest in the world. More than one-half of its people are under age fifteen. Controlled by Israeli checkpoints on the ground, the sole land access of the Palestinians in Gaza to the outside world was through Egypt's Sinai. Israelis blocked their transportation by sea and air. Fishermen were not permitted to leave the harbor; workers were prevented from going to outside jobs; the import and export of food and other goods was restricted. The police, teachers, nurses, and social workers were deprived of salaries. Per capita income decreased 40 percent during the period from 2002 to 2005, and the poverty rate reached 70 percent in 2005. UN officials warned about catastrophic humanitarian consequences ahead.

These were the impacts of Israel's unilateral withdrawal even prior to Israel's massive bombardment and reinvasion in July 2006—actions that were provoked by Hamas militants.[56] More recently, since the ouster in Egypt of President Hosni Mubarak, the Egyptian army lifted this Israeli-mandated Egyptian blockade on the Gaza Strip's main link to the outside world. That brought relief to nearly 1.5 million Palestinians.

But equally troublesome are the huge dividing wall in populated areas and an impenetrable fence in the West Bank's rural areas. This "security fence" was built within Palestinian territory. The International Court of Justice has said that the Israeli government's construction of the wall in the occupied Palestinian West Bank is illegal. In addition to cutting off about 200,000 Palestinians in Jerusalem from their relatives, property, schools, and businesses, the wall is designed to isolate and severely truncate parts of Palestine.[57] This illegal wall confiscates Palestinian land. It is not built along the pre-1967 line between the West Bank and Israel, and at some points it delves deep inside the West Bank. This is de facto annexation of Palestinian land—some 50 percent of the West Bank.[58]

The wall is constructed in various structural modes. In some areas, it consists of a high concrete edifice, eight meters tall (25 feet), with armed watchtowers hovering over residential areas. In other places it consists of layers of electric fences and buffer zones of trenches, patrol paths, sensors, and cameras. While nearly 10 percent of the West Bank has already been negatively affected by the wall's construction, it has also resulted in the confiscation and isolation of fifty-one villages.[59] If this system of apartheid, oppression, and structural violence continues, the consequences will be profound.

In the 2006 parliamentary elections, Hamas received a clear majority of parliamentary seats (74 of 132). A postelection public opinion poll indicated that 73 percent of Palestinians express their support for the two-state peace process with Israel, but most said that Hamas should refrain from recognizing Israel until some of the final status issues—refugees, borders, Jewish settlements in the West Bank, and East Jerusalem—are resolved. A mere 1 percent of the people were in favor of Hamas imposing Islamic law in Palestine. Equally heartening was the result of a March 2006 opinion poll by the Truman Research Institute at Hebrew University showing that 62 percent of Israelis favored direct talks with Hamas.[60] Palestinian prime minister Ismail Haniyeh announced that the Hamas government was "ready for dialogue" with the members of the Quartet—the UN, Russia, the European Union, and the United States. He expressed approval of the direct Olmert-Abbas peace talks and underlined the point that Hamas would change its rejectionist position if a satisfactory agreement could be reached and approved by the Palestinian people. This Palestinian approval of a final peace agreement was an essential element of the Camp David Accords.[61]

The expanding electronic fences and Israel's siege and blockade of Gaza following Hamas's victory in the 2006 parliamentary elections have trapped many Palestinians in the world's largest prison camp. This situation has raised a myriad of humanitarian concerns. A majority of Palestinians rely in part on handouts provided by the United Nations for nourishment. Nearly 80 percent of them rely on welfare to survive.[62] Supported by both the United States and the EU, the 2008 siege created great hardship for the 1.5 million Palestinians who live in the Gaza Strip. On December 27, 2008, Israeli forces launched a major air attack on Hamas political and military targets in Gaza. The UN investigation of the attack, led by South African judge and judicial investigator Richard Goldstone, found evidence that both Israeli and Palestinian forces had committed war crimes. Evidence indicates that during the three-week offensive mounted against Gaza (December 27 to January 18, 2009) Israeli forces committed, "serious violations of international human rights and humanitarian law," says the report; Israel "committed actions amounting to war crimes, and possibly crimes against humanity," and these operations "were carefully planned in all their phases as a deliberately disproportionate attack designed to punish, humiliate and terrorize a civilian population."[63] The report equally condemns rocket attacks by Palestinian groups. Israeli officials claimed it was the rocket attacks that precipitated their December 27 offensive.

The 574-page document, which reveals thirty-seven incidents where there was evidence that war crimes and crimes against humanity may have been committed, recommended that the authorities in both Gaza and Israel be required to investigate the allegations and report to the UN Security Council within six months. If Israel and Hamas failed to abide by this recommendation, the case would be referred to the International Criminal Court (ICC). The UN Human Rights Council adopted the report on October 16, 2009, with the possibility that it would reach the Security Council for a final decision. Both parties deny these charges. According to one report, 1,445 Palestinians were killed and 5,000 were wounded during the Israeli attacks. More than two-thirds of the fatalities were civilians.[64]

In response to the UN General Assembly, the Human Rights Council adopted a resolution that extended the mandate of the experts' committee to report on the progress of the domestic investigation undertaken by Israel and the Palestinian authorities. But it failed to call for the activation of the international accountability mechanisms as recommended in the Goldstone Report. The question of whether Israel can be held accountable for crimes committed against the occupied and blockaded Palestinian people of Gaza was revisited at the March 2011 meeting of the Human Rights Council, a body that still has the mandate to monitor and assess the investigations by both sides and to report back to the council. For the time being, no such legal accountability against Israeli officials has been determined and no punishment has been meted out.

Although Israeli officials say that the continued blockade of Gaza since January 2009 is aimed at undermining Hamas's leadership, relief agencies point out that it has in fact collectively punished the civilian population. Jimmy Carter called the Israeli siege of Gaza "one of the greatest human rights crimes on Earth. Most families in Gaza are eating only one meal per day. To see Europeans going along with this is embarrassing."[65]

Some observers think that Israel's goal has been to force Gazans to oust the de facto Hamas government and return to the Palestinian Authority fold. Bent on the "construction of a Jewish ethnocracy," Israel has denied housing to Palestinians by means of demolitions and withholding building permits in the occupied territories. Since 1967, Israel has demolished 18,000 Palestinian homes. Figures are not available on how many building permits have been denied.[66] Despite Israel's near total blockade, Hamas remains in control and shows no sign of losing its grip on Gaza.[67]

In a personal account, Jennifer Loewenstein describes Gaza as a floating island disconnected from the mainland while being drifted out to sea. She writes:

> And even as we dismiss Gaza as irrelevant, the bitterness against the worldview that permits and condones what is happening there, and to the Palestinians in general, deepens; the fault lines of the resistance to US and Israeli policies are crystallizing. Our denial and dismissal of the tragedy unfolding there will come back to haunt us; we ignore it at our peril.[68]

President Obama's speech on May 19, 2011, highlighted the return to the pre-1967 borders "with mutual swaps" between Israelis and Palestinians. While this was a good first step, the United States has still utterly failed to address or even express any concern over the humanitarian crisis in Gaza.

The US Invasion of Afghanistan, 2001

The George W. Bush administration's strategy of invading Afghanistan in the aftermath of 9/11 was aimed directly at capturing bin Laden and overthrowing the Taliban regime that had harbored terrorist networks. US policymakers made it abundantly clear that this was not a war against the entire Afghan people. Yet fighting the Taliban proved to be no easy task.

In recent years, the Taliban has made it very difficult for the UN and other aid agencies to deliver humanitarian relief in Afghanistan. The Bush administration insisted, however, that the invasion was the only way to prevent future terrorist attacks on the United States. Because of the Taliban's support for the global terrorist campaign of al-Qaeda, it was often argued that the stability of the whole Central Asian region depended largely on the establishment of a new, stable, and democratic government in Afghanistan. Thus the commitment to regional peace and stability was directly linked to the US interests in the region, a rationale that underlined the notion that such goals could only be achieved through an invasion of Afghanistan.

Although the Taliban were defeated and al-Qaeda's infrastructure dismantled in the early phase of this military intervention, the way the campaign was managed increased sympathy for the Afghan people caught in the crossfire. Some of the Taliban crossed the border and settled in Pakistan. This development not only increased the risk of future terrorist attacks against Afghanistan but also threatened the moderate government of Hamid Karzai. A report by the International Council on Security and Development revealed that the Taliban significantly increased its control over Afghan territory during 2008. Taliban groups controlled virtually three-fourths of Afghanistan in November 2008, up from slightly more than one-half of the country in November 2007. Afghanistan's neighbors viewed this development with trepidation as a potential catalyst for instability, both regionally and globally.[69]

Some elements of the Taliban are difficult to approach or maintain talks with, but tribal groups usually are less ideologically bent. They are more inclined toward maintaining autonomy and power. Rapprochement with these groups or other local insurgents, however, may also create friction with the Karzai government, making it less amenable to other US efforts.[70] Negotiations with Afghan insurgents would have a favorable outcome if Pakistan could be brought on board. Pakistan's intelligence sources in the past have provided training and logistical and financial support for these insurgents and can still manage to use their leverage effectively. If Pakistan continues to provide a sanctuary for the Taliban and Afghani militia fighters, the hope for improving security, boosting economic growth, and moving toward nation building in Afghanistan will be entirely dashed. Failure to get Pakistan's cooperation severely limits the incentives of various insurgent factions to talk. The unwillingness of these groups and their leaders to negotiate can perhaps be explained by the belief that they are unlikely to be defeated outright as long as they enjoy a sanctuary outside of Afghanistan.[71]

Some experts have emphasized that the urgent task before the international community is to help Pakistan understand that terminating the activities of all militant groups in its territory is in the best interest of its national security. To that end, they suggest that the United States and its partners reframe the problem as one of persuasion and negotiation. Rather than seeking to alter Pakistani behavior through enticements alone, "the United States must persuade Pakistan to abandon problematic policies by reconditioning Islamabad's cost-benefit assessment of those policies."[72] One suggestion is that the United States should be more proactive in engaging with states that Pakistan takes seriously, namely, China and Saudi Arabia. The United States, it is argued, should work more closely with these key states to forge some consensus on how best to nudge Pakistan along the path of contributing to regional security rather than undermining it.[73] Another suggestion, along the lines of positive inducements, would be for the United States to use military assistance to help Pakistan become a capable counterinsurgency and counterterrorism force.[74]

President Obama's decision to send an additional thirty thousand US troops to Afghanistan in mid-2010 was designed to wrest momentum away from insurgents. The Pentagon, which has begun to fulfill a promise made by President Obama to start bringing troops home in summer 2011, has also urged that the number of troops who will actually return home be relatively modest—somewhere in the vicinity of 10 to 15 percent of US surge forces. That said, there seems to be no clear answers to precisely how many US troops should remain on the ground. Defense department officials, however are aware that the country's patience for war is growing thin, particularly as Congress has expressed serious concern over the cost of the war—some $5.3 billion a month in Afghanistan—amid a lingering economic crisis. Adm. Mike Mullen has acknowledged that financial considerations will most likely affect the continuing debate over troop withdrawals in Afghanistan.[75]

It is also worth noting that while the surge has pushed back the Taliban in certain parts of the south, it remains an open question whether the Afghanistan security forces will be able to maintain security gains. Moreover, the gains that have been made on the battlefield are often undermined by a lack of similar efforts in the fields of aid, development, governance, and counternarcotics.[76] Meanwhile, several familiar questions about the nature of the mission persist: Will the surge culminate in nation building or will it be directed primarily at defeating and dismantling al-Qaeda terror networks? While it is clear that President Obama has sought to reassure NATO allies and the leaders of Afghanistan and Pakistan that he was not abandoning efforts to defeat the terrorists, it is not clear that this surge will successfully lead to the building of the Afghan army and police.

The huge increase in suicide attacks at Afghan and foreign military bases in Afghanistan illustrate the failure of US and NATO goals there. Critics have questioned the wisdom or rationale behind US/NATO strategy given rampant corruption in the Karzai government and, most importantly, given the Afghan government's weak capacity or readiness to take over political and security responsibilities within two years. Moreover, US preoccupation with Afghanistan has made it imperative to develop a policy for gaining the support of Pakistan, not only in denying the Taliban a sanctuary in Pakistan, but also in compelling the Taliban in Afghanistan to accommodate US policy.[77]

The US Invasion of Iraq, 2003

The September 11, 2001, attacks on the United States opened the door for the Bush administration to preemptively invade Afghanistan and Iraq. The invasion of Afghanistan was aimed at both defeating the Taliban regime and demolishing al-Qaeda's infrastructure there. The intervention in Iraq was justified on the grounds of preemption—that is, the Iraqi regime either possessed or would soon possess weapons of mass destruction. Iraq's program as such, it was argued, posed an imminent threat to the security of the United States and other countries, largely because Iraq would transfer these weapons to terrorist groups such as al-Qaeda. Other terrorist groups, it was thought, would target the United States at some point in the future.

While intervention in Afghanistan enjoyed a large measure of international legitimacy, this was not the case with Iraq. For military intervention to be considered legitimate, it is crucial that the member states of the United Nations adhere to a metadoctrine that emerged in the 1990s, stipulating the circumstances under which military intervention could be undertaken. During the 1990s, a majority of the international community came to regard legitimate military intervention as relief of human suffering and the safeguarding of human rights. A new consensus emerged that states should not be allowed to hide behind the shield of sovereignty when systematic and egregious abuses of human rights take place on their territory. Furthermore, the members of the international community largely acknowledged that military intervention often is a necessary tactic for halting the internal conflicts that are so harmful to achieving these goals.[78] The role of military forces justified their use in combat operations, including peacekeeping and peace-enforcement roles. It should be noted that military intervention also includes the use of military forces in a deterrent role by means of forward deployments and participation in regional training exercises.[79]

The war with Iraq and its aftermath have underscored the importance of UN authorization as a sign of legitimacy. With other nations increasingly suspicious of US motives and interests, the push for the legitimacy factor on the global scene has been accelerated. This reality also indicates the importance of obtaining UN authorization prior to future actions in two ways: (1) it validates the motives of the intervening powers and (2) ensures that some measure of burden-sharing will occur.[80] The US invasion has clearly done more to reinforce norms (that is, norms such as the relevance of institutions, the importance of taking into account public opinion, humanitarian concerns, and consensual government) than, by resisting international law, to demolish norms.[81]

Given that Iraq never posed an immediate threat to the United States, the 2003 military intervention in Iraq was clearly a war of choice rather than necessity. The invasion was caused, some experts argue, by three interrelated factors. The first was President George W. Bush's strategic vision of the US global role. Equally significant was the geostrategic importance of Iraq, in terms of both its location and its oil resources. Thirdly, the dynamics at work in domestic US politics were highly influential in shaping US foreign policy objectives before, during, and after the war.[82]

The invasion led to the disintegration of Iraq's central authority, plunging Baghdad into chaos. Looting and lawlessness prevailed. Clean water and electricity became scarce as elements loyal to the Hussein regime blew up power generators, water mains, and major oil pipelines. US forces soon faced a full-blown urban guerrilla war.[83] Evidently, no careful consideration had been given to postinvasion planning. Interagency disputes and policy inconsistencies added to the confusion that ensued.

The application of a rigorous sanctions regime during the 1991–2003 period, coupled with the imposition of a northern no-fly zone, had already severely weakened Hussein's regime. The UN Security Council had adopted an oil-for-food program in 1996 after growing criticisms of the humanitarian crisis in Iraq resulting from comprehensive economic sanctions. Under this program, the UN controlled all revenues from Iraq's oil sales, and the contracts within this program were subject to oversight. By 2001, it was evident that the program had become corrupted over contract prices and sales, drastically reducing funds available for humanitarian purposes. UN Security Council Resolution 1483 in May 2003 put an end to sanctions and monitored the termination of the program in subsequent months and the gradual transfer of its administration to US-UK authorities in Iraq. The oil-for-food program allowed Iraqis to sell more oil internationally and to pay for permitted imports after a 30 percent cut of oil production had been allocated, mainly for reparation payments to Kuwait. While some Iraqis blamed Saddam Hussein for the sanctions, many regarded the United States and the United Nations as responsible for their suffering.[84]

The invasion unleashed a gruesome sectarian conflict in a country with little experience in resource and power sharing. A Shiite revival following the Iraq War empowered the Shiite majority in Iraq, enhanced Iran's status as a regional power, and led to the empowerment of Shiites across Lebanon, Saudi Arabia, Kuwait, the UAE, and Pakistan. All this led to a drive toward a new distribution and balance of power in the Middle East, culminating in a momentum unprecedented in nearly fourteen centuries.[85] Some observers have warned, however, that the fear of an empowered "Shiite crescent" in the Middle East is overstated. They argue that a number of factors—nationalism, domestic courts, and local clerics—prevent such a dramatic development.[86]

Nevertheless, the Shiites' rise to power in Iraq and the country's troubles today, as Vali Nasr reminds us, have offered Washington and Tehran another chance not only to normalize their relations but also to set the stage for curbing future potential tensions between Shiites and Sunnis. Such cooperation would certainly require the United States to address broader security issues in its relationship with Iran.[87]

Washington and Tehran worked closely together to bring the Northern Alliance and its Shiite affiliate into the mainstream political process during the Bonn Conference. Although a similar diplomatic possibility is worth exploring, the fact remains that the powerful centrifugal forces at work in Iraq undermine such prospects without serious diplomatic processes. Despite the view that deepening ethnosectarian rifts make it difficult to visualize the future of Iraq as a truly unified political entity, it appears that the Maliki government can keep the country stable enough to maintain the Iraqi coalition government now in place and for the development of its oil resources to proceed for the foreseeable future.[88]

Iraqi popular support for defeating the insurgency is as critical to the long-term prospects in Iraq as the prospects for continuing US support for the war–whether among US servicemen and servicewomen or the US public. Some observers have noted that US forces have failed to defeat the insurgency or improve security. They have warned that insurgency could very well turn into a bloody civil war, with the unforeseen consequences of involving Saudi Arabia, Turkey, Syria, and Iran. Additionally, Islamic nationalists and particularly Islamic radicals would see the US departure as a victory, and the subsequent chaos would drive up oil prices.[89] While the withdrawal of the US forces has already begun, and virtually all combat troops have been removed from Iraq, volatility in the region as well as troubling boundary disputes between the Kurdish-controlled north and central Iraq has the Obama administration and some leaders in Iraq rethinking full troop withdrawal. Adm. Mike Mullen, chairman of the Joint Chiefs of Staff, has expressed Washington's willingness to keep a US military presence in Iraq beyond December 2011.[90]

More recently, in relation to Washington's approval of a deal to allow 10,000 US troops to stay in Iraq to continue training Iraqi forces on various military equipment, Mullen noted that any agreement to keep US troops in Iraq beyond 2011 must provide immunity from prosecution for those troops, and that such a deal must be approved by Iraq's parliament.[91]

The looming power struggle has been almost inevitable given how little money the southern region has received from Baghdad and how poor government-related services have been, even in Shiite areas. This illustrates that "incompetence and corruption are not sectarian."[92] It is not clear whether these tensions will disrupt the cause of political accommodation or lead to a compromise facilitating the creation of legitimate local and provincial governments. For its part, the US government has pursued a policy of divide-and-rule that has pitted Iraqis of different ethnic and sectarian loyalties against each other. Washington's aim, one expert notes, was in fact to play off one community against another in order to preclude the emergence of an Iraqi national liberation organization such as the Shiite-Sunni movement formed to resist British occupation in 1920.[93]

The rising violence pointed to an intra-Shiite blood feud waged between the Mahdi Army and the Iraqi government. Shiite cleric Moqtada al-Sadr, the Iraqi religious leader of the Mahdi Army, continues to present a serious challenge to the Iraqi central government, as Iraq's rival Shiite parties are all vying for power and political supremacy in southern and central parts of the country. The government, meanwhile, is allied with Abdul Aziz al-Hakim and his militia, known as the Badr organization. The conflict has brought US forces into direct confrontation with the Madhi Army—a new situation that belies the complexity of what has up until now been attributed to the Shiite-Sunni divide. As one journalist reminds us: "Sadr and his militia—the ones that fought British forces the most until their retreat from the city [Basra] center in September [2007]—feel their perceived sacrifice has earned them the right to be a mover and shaker."[94]

At the urging of the US government, the Shiite-dominated central government recently passed a law to give provincial governors wide-ranging powers over security forces and public works. Furthermore, the narrow victory of the secular Iraqiya bloc over Maliki's sectarian-influenced government in the March 7, 2010, parliamentary elections could have spelled instability if no party could form a viable government. The Iraqiya bloc, headed by former premier Iyad Allawi, took 91 seats in the new 325-member national assembly. Maliki's State of Law faction got 89 seats. The Iraqi National Alliance (INA), a Shiite bloc dominated by the Supreme Iraqi Islamic Council (SIIC) and the followers of radical cleric Muqtada Al-Sadr, won 17 seats.[95]

Since Prime Minister Nouri Al-Maliki has formed his second government, he has appointed new members to the cabinet to consolidate his position within the country's power structure and better safeguard his governing method. In July 2011, Maliki appointed the former culture minister, Sadun al-Dulaymi, as acting minister of defense. Dulaymi held the same position in the Ibrahim al-Jaafari government in 2005–2006. This appointment was significant in two ways. First, in terms of the architecture of the second Maliki government, it means Maliki could be seen as moving toward consolidating his situation whereby no regular parliament appointments may take place for the near future with respect to the security ministries. In early June 2011, he appointed Falih al-Fayyad of the Jaafari wing of the Daawa movement as acting minister of state for national security, whereas Maliki himself continues as acting interior minister. Secondly, at the political level, this move is clearly directed against the secular Iraqiya, which has expressed concerns about the direction in which the second Maliki government is moving.[96]

These uncertainties have complicated the stabilization process in Iraq. The United States, experts concur, is in a global struggle for winning the hearts and minds of people around the world, but it is losing in the face of mounting anti-Americanism. US power is now much more feared than welcomed around the world. "If anti-Americanism continues to grow," Stephen M. Walt writes, "Washington will face greater resistance and find it harder to attract support. Americans will feel increasingly threatened in such a world, but trying to counter these threats alone will merely exacerbate the fear of US power and isolate the United States even more."[97]

The net result of the war in Iraq has been a distraction from the campaign against terror. The world's sympathy and support for the United States after 9/11 fractured when Washington turned its attention to Iraq, whose links to the 9/11 attacks were tenuous at best. The war also gave real urgency to the debate over reforming the system of multilateral governance with the aim of defining real threats to international peace and security through collective endeavors.[98] The gain of removing Saddam Hussein from power was offset by fallout from the lingering crisis in Iraq as sectarian tensions and instability spread. Richard N. Haass, who served on the senior National Security Council staff for the Middle East and as an assistant to then National Security Advisor Brent Scowcroft, admits frankly that while the first Gulf War against Saddam

Hussein was a "war of necessity" in which the United States reacted to the Iraqi invasion of Kuwait (1990), an aggression that threatened vital US interests, the US invasion of Iraq (2003) was manifestly a "war of choice" in which the United States sought to change the character of Iraq and justified going to war with ambitious ideological and moral aims. The ideologically motivated and ambitious goals of the second Iraq war, in contrast with the limited geopolitical ones of the first, proved to have disastrous consequences.[99]

The Libya No-Fly Zone and the Politics of "Responsibility to Protect"

Following the February 17, 2011, uprisings in Libya, the prodemocracy forces and rebels in Benghazi met a fierce military response by Col. Muammar Qaddafi. The dangers and fear of a vindictive bloodbath by Qaddafi forces were apparent enough to prompt international intervention to protect Libyan civilians. It was in this context that the UN Security Council passed two resolutions. Resolution 1970 on February 26, 2011, froze Libyan assets, banned travel, and imposed an arms embargo on the country and its leaders. Less than a month later, on March 17, the Security Council adopted Resolution 1973. A vote of ten in favor to none against, with five abstentions (Brazil, China, Germany, India, and Russia), extended a no-fly zone over Libya and authorized the international community to take "whatever additional measures necessary" to protect civilians under threat of attack in the country, including Benghazi, while excluding a foreign occupation force of any form on any part of Libyan territory.[100] The phrase "whatever additional measures necessary" became open to various interpretations.

Resolution 1973 supported the establishment of a ban on all flights in Libya's airspace, considering it to be an important element in protecting civilians and facilitating delivery of humanitarian assistance. It was seen as a crucial step toward the cessation of hostilities in Libya.[101] One obvious point to make is that the responsibility to protect civilians—a practice approved and utilized by the United Nations since 2005—reinforced the notion that the protection of those who have been subject to grave human suffering and mass killings clearly supersedes state sovereignty. If invoked, this practice would almost certainly help prevent genocide and mass atrocities and fortify the international community's response. However, the debates surrounding the responsibility to protect tend to hinge not on *whether* international actors should engage, but *how*.[102]

Moreover, some scholars argue that upholding the "responsibility to protect" norm may be exceedingly costly and can lead to unforeseen consequences. Although such an intervention may save lives, it irreversibly changes the dynamics of the local political situation by privileging some actors at the expense of others. Under such circumstances, maintaining neutrality is untenable, given that intervention requires the use of force on behalf of one party in a dispute against another.[103]

To effectively deal with such humanitarian emergencies, as Richard Falk aptly notes, it is imperative to erode objections grounded in claims of sovereign rights by emphasizing an ethos of international responsibility and human solidarity.[104] It is equally essential to promote the establishment of some capability at the regional and global levels that would not renew the "South" countries' anxieties about the revival of intervention methods or gunboat diplomacy by the North. The actions of the Arab League seem to confirm this position, despite their subsequent criticism of air strikes against Tripoli. To minimize the controversial nature or status of humanitarian intervention, the responsibility to protect the "other" must be accorded legitimacy on the basis of human rights, rather than geopolitical factors.[105]

While the debate concerning the motives behind imposing a no-fly zone continues—whether those motives be oil markets, geopolitics, or preventing human rights violations or massive flows of refugees, or something else—it is crucial to bear in mind that such interventions are justified as long as the primary, though not necessarily the only, motive for intervention is achieving a humanitarian outcome.[106] At the same time it is worth noting that reliance on air power alone in previous Western interventions aimed at promoting humanitarian values have failed to bring about a positive humanitarian outcome. Air power, as one observer notes, failed to stop the atrocities and mass expulsion of civilians in both Bosnia (1992–1995) and Kosovo (1999). NATO's problematic outcome of the bombing of Kosovo in March 1999, for example, became evident in the face of increasing civilian casualties, raising the question (as in another case, Somalia) of whether violent means can ever properly serve humanitarian ends.[107] In striking contrast, the no-fly zone in Iraq maintained during 1992–2001 to preserve and protect potentially vulnerable Kurds proved to be a fairly successful application of this method.

Although creating a no-fly zone to protect civilians under threat of attack and to conduct humanitarian missions to safeguard refugees was the most effective short-term strategy, disagreements within NATO emerged on the issue of how to enforce a UN arms embargo against Libya. Germany and Turkey raised questions about the mission and the scope of NATO operations. Recep Tayyip Erdogan, Turkey's prime minister, voiced concerns that the mission might become an occupation and not be the brief intervention that Western European powers and the United States claimed it would be.[108] Eventually, however, all twenty-eight NATO allies authorized military authorities to enforce a no-fly zone and develop an operation plan for NATO to take on the broader civilian protection mission under Resolution 1973.[109]

It was crucial that there be support for the no-fly zone from the Arab League and the rest of the Arab countries (Qatar and the United Arab Emirates)—that they participate in establishing such a zone and offer humanitarian missions. With the collapse of the Libyan regime, the opposition movement, headed by the Libyan National Transitional Council (NTC), will be charged with the responsibility to serve as provisional government. Mahmoud Gebril, the de facto prime minister and a leader of the NTC, who is beholden to the NATO powers for its political victory, cannot claim sole ownership of revolution. There are more than 140 tribes and clans in Libya, some of them with deep-seated enmities. There is also an old ethnic and linguistic division between the Berber minority and the Arab population. Qaddafi kept them all in line by employing a mixture of patronage and social control. Matching that— but without resorting to repressive measures—may very well be the NTC's toughest challenge.[110] While some in the NTC insisted on putting Qaddafi and his family members on trial, others have suggested establishing a Libyan version of the South African Truth and Reconciliation Commission.[111] The International Criminal Court has issued arrest warrants for Gadhafi, his son Seif al-Islam, and al-Senoussi, accusing them of killing civilians to try to crush the uprising. As of this writing, all three remain at large. Because Qaddafi decided to use foreign mercenaries and commit large-scale forces against his own people, the international community was left with no choice but to act in the hope of ending the violence.

With the consequences of NATO operations in Libya remaining uncertain at best, some analysts raised serious doubts about the effectiveness of NATO's role in the Middle East and North Africa. They argued that "NATO is of limited help in Afghanistan, was irrelevant in Iraq and simply does not matter in the larger Middle East. The defense budgets of member states in Western Europe are generally below the NATO standard of 2 percent of GDP, even as these same countries now brace for the steepest cuts in military spending since the end of the Cold War."[112] By midsummer, NATO was facing a stalemate in Libya and seemed likely to intensify attacks on government forces to break the military logjam. The United Nations was pushing for a humanitarian presence to help civilians trapped in the conflict. Some experts noted that while NATO bombing had damaged Qaddafi's military power it had not been enough to break the stalemate, leaving the alliance with little choice but to use helicopters.[113]

A Call for a New Paradigm

Experts concur that the Palestine crisis is a prime example of the way the colonial powers shaped the emergence of the modern Middle East. It has also been a harbinger of the problems that will trouble the region for decades to come.[114]

Iraq's claim to territories formerly under the control of the Ottoman province of Basra in the modern state of Kuwait (1937, 1961, and 1990) provoked the greatest destabilizing conflicts in the region. Saddam Hussein's invasion of Kuwait on August 2, 1990, divided the Arab world and led to war in 1991, instigated twelve years of brutal sanctions that devastated the country's economy, and ushered in a second war in 2003. This has had negative consequences for the entire region.[115] It should be noted, however, that in the case of the second Gulf War, US intervention changed nothing substantial with regard to arms sales to the Middle East, beyond dealing a military blow to Iraq.

The persistence of arms transfers to Arabs and Israelis as a tool of US foreign policy and influence peddling has shown no sign of ending; nor of creating stability in the area. The Bush plan—emphasizing a ban on chemical weapons, plutonium production and enrichment, and surface-to-surface missiles—appeared to be nothing more than political oratory—an unrealistic overture to the Middle East. In the end, the post–Gulf War era provides mixed illusions and opportunities: illusions that Arab cooperation will provide another opportunity for Pan-Arabism (the idea that a quick defeat of Iraq and resultant UN sanctions would create an opportunity to overthrow Saddam Hussein and an opportunity for Pax Americana to prosper in the Middle East).[116] Although many opportunities for new Middle East diplomatic initiatives have surfaced, Israel's continued occupation of the Palestinian Territories, coupled with settlement construction, proves to be a major obstacle to any diplomatic breakthrough. Recurrent Arab-Israeli peace conferences have failed to generate grand-scale changes in the US agenda, despite shakeups in the region.[117]

At the same time, Israeli military interventions in the occupied Palestinian Territories and Lebanon have proven tenuous. If anything, they have mobilized Islamic radicalism and provoked nationalistic sentiments among many Arabs in the region. Continued Israeli occupation and the US failure to break the roadmap impasse pitted Fatah against Hamas in Palestine. In the wake of the 2011 Arab awakening, however, the two rival Palestinian factions signed reconciliation agreements in Egypt on April 27, forming a national unity government and fixing a date for a general election within a year.

The attack on Iraq, according to Richard Falk, was widely regarded as illegal, wrong, and imprudent in the extreme. War and excessive force have been ineffective in achieving their objectives and dangerously corrosive of world order. Rather than reducing threat, the Iraq experience has substantially invoked violent anti-American extremism in the region.[118] The mistake of military intervention, says Falk, was further compounded by extending the perimeter of the war far beyond al-Qaeda; under the operative definition of "terrorist" threat, all forms of nonstate violence are included. This extension of the conflict by the US government emboldened Israel, Russia, and China to treat self-determination movements within and near their borders as belonging to the global war on terror. Falk calls this logic flawed and its consequences perverse:

> Both the futility and injustice of treating the Palestinians, the Chechens, and the people of Xingiang as part of the same struggle that unleashed the 9/11 attacks was to distort and deflect a more genuine and focused pursuit of security for the United States, as well as give governments around the world an unconditional mandate to engage in uncontrolled violence and oppression against non-state movements seeking human rights and self-determination.[119]

The reckless and deadly Israeli raid on a Turkish-flagged ship in the Gaza flotilla on May 31, 2010, in which nine Turkish activists were killed, sparked international condemnation of the Netanyahu administration. Growing anger and resentment over the acts of Israeli naval commandos, who stormed the ship in international waters some 80 miles from Gaza's coast, also demonstrated in some respects the difficulty of Turkey's effort to bridge the East–West divide.[120] Significantly, however, the violent Israeli reaction to the aid flotilla illustrated the futility of military means in dealing with such political situations. The Israeli blockade of more than a million and a half Palestinians in Gaza for more than four years has led to suffering, malnutrition, lack of housing, and substandard medical care. Ankara's support for the Turkish-led aid flotilla to Gaza was understandable, given that the Palestinians' plight has won the sympathy of the Turks.[121]

Faced with such issues as demography (rising Arab birth rates in Israel and the occupied territories), ideology (resurgent militant Islam), and technology (rockets that can travel long distances and globe-spanning information technology that mobilizes sympathy for the Palestinian cause), Israeli leaders and the general Israeli public are under increasing pressure to come to terms with emerging trends and new realities in the region.[122] The use of force and blockades has invited nothing but widespread global opposition to the way in which Israeli leaders have dealt with the Palestinian issue.

Military solutions are ineffective as the sole means to confront terrorism. As we have seen in this chapter, if pursued wantonly, such measures alone are certain to fail. "There is," some experts insist, "only one way to win the global war on terrorism—by supporting the moderate Muslims around the world, and by asking for their help."[123] And as the Israeli-Palestinian conflicts have demonstrated, wars have failed to provide longer-term solutions. Equally contentious have been diplomatic processes without tangible progress. The two-state solution will most likely become discredited among Palestinians if there is no serious diplomatic breakthrough.[124]

Six decades of occupation and the failure of secular Middle Eastern regimes to address the Palestinian plight and the lingering Arab-Israeli conflicts have marginalized the significance of nationalist movements and instead have pushed Islamic movements to the forefront of the region's politics. Many people have turned to Islamic movements in large part because corrupt regimes and governments have no consideration or plan for the welfare of their people. Hezbollah in Lebanon, Hamas in Palestine, and the Muslim Brotherhood in Egypt attract grassroots support because state bureaucracies are either indifferent or inept.[125] Moreover, the 2011 Arab revolts in the Middle East and North Africa demonstrated that the real inspiration for change came in the form of peaceful protests across the region by disaffected and disillusioned people who did not demand an extremist Islamic government but instead sought fundamental human rights and political freedoms.[126]

The Iraq War has reinforced the lesson that, absent global consensus, military interventions could have deadly and long-term consequences. The history of the rise of Islamic militancy in the Middle East demonstrates that as countries experience large-scale devastation—such as defeat in a war, exposure to political suppression, and other related crises—Islamic forces have been strengthened. Military invasions have done little to delegitimize terrorism. To eliminate transnational terrorism, it is important to isolate terrorist groups by neutralizing their claims to relevance in the lives of Arab and Muslim people.[127]

The use of force to compel another country's cooperation or bring about its capitulation rarely, if ever, works in a globalized world.[128] Because terror is a political challenge—not a military challenge—defeating it thus requires defeating its claims and values, not the terrorists themselves.[129] Recognizing this reality calls for a new paradigm that places counterterrorism in the broader framework of addressing the longstanding disputes in the region. There are real incentives for using diplomacy. As former US National Security Advisor Zbigniew Brzezinski said in advocating US talks with the Palestinian and Hamas leadership: "I think we have to talk to everyone that is involved in this conflict, directly or indirectly. One does not gain anything by ostracism; it is a self-defeating posture."[130] The countries experiencing terrorism should not adopt a stringent policy of "no talk" or "no concessions."

* * *

Diplomatic malpractice and mismanaged diplomacy in the post-9/11 foreign policy pursued by the Bush administration has severely undermined US diplomatic soft power in the fight against terrorism. A series of military confrontations and nationalist upheavals and revolutions—cultural uprisings extending from the 1956 Suez crisis to the first Gulf War and then the US invasion of Iraq in 2003—profoundly altered the political landscape of the Middle East. Yet, US orientalism has persisted—the tendency to overestimate the ability of the United States to change things for the better and to underestimate local solutions and peoples' capacity to bring about real change.[131] Most people in the United States have assumed that US wealth and power would provide the moral authority necessary to control the Middle East.[132] Perhaps the most visible lesson learned from the outcome of military intervention in Iraq thus far has been to see that such an assumption is spurious.

A lesson to be learned from the NATO intervention in Libya's 2011 civil war is that air strikes alone cannot substantially alter the political situation on the ground. While a quick intervention is imperative for preventing massacre, military interventions may lead to messy civil wars with ensuing disturbances, complexities, and unintended consequences. One such consequence might be that the removal of the targeted regime may not bring an end to the conflict and bloodshed. A new outlook is required in order to support democratic change short of military intervention.

The challenge now is to consider ways in which peaceful democratic change can be promoted throughout the region. The Bush administration's policy of democracy promotion in Iraq and Afghanistan by way of external pressures and intervention, which abruptly elevated democratization as a panacea for the ills of these societies, came to define political discourse in Washington in the post-9/11 era. In both cases, military intervention has failed to produce a stable, predictable, and sustainable democratic system. The democracy-promotion agenda has faced a myriad of challenges. The next chapter sheds light on these difficulties.

Notes

1. Rashid Khalidi, *Resurrecting Empire: Western Footprints and America's Perilous Path in the Middle East* (Boston: Beacon Press, 2004), pp. 10–11.

2. Ibid., p. 15.

3. Ibid., p. 19.

4. Ibid., pp. 20–21.

5. William L. Cleveland, *A History of the Modern Middle East*, 3rd ed. (Boulder, CO: Westview Press, 2004), p. 172.

6. James A. Bill and Robert Springborg, *Politics in the Middle East*, 5th ed. (New York: Longman, 2000), p. 169.

7. Khalidi, *Resurrecting Empire*, pp. 29–30.

8. Stephen Kinzer, *Overthrow: America's Century of Regime Change from Hawaii to Iraq* (New York: Times Books, 2006), p. 5.

9. Mehran Kamrava, *The Modern Middle East: A Political History since the First World War* (Berkeley: University of California Press, 2005), p. 143.

10. Ibid., p. 144.

11. Michael Heazle and Iyanatul Islam, "New Interventionism but Same Old Promises and Perils?" in Michael Heazle and Iyanatul Islam, eds., *Beyond the Iraq War: The Promises, Pitfalls, and Perils of External Intervention* (Northampton, MA: Edward Elgar, 2006), pp. 1–15; see p. 5.

12. Barnett R. Rubin, *The Fragmentation of Afghanistan: State Formation and Collapse in the International System*, 2nd ed. (New Haven, CT: Yale University Press, 2002), pp. 121–126.

13. Ibid., p. 145.

14. Ibid., pp. 165–175.

15. "The Soviet Invasion of Afghanistan, 1979–1989"; available at http://nhs.needham.k12.ma.us/cur/baker_00/2002-p4/baker_p4_12-01_mj_sz; accessed June 24, 2008.

16. Michael C. Hudson, "The United States in the Middle East," in Louise Fawcett, ed., *International Relations of the Middle East* (New York: Oxford University Press, 2005), pp. 283–305; see p. 292.

17. Ibid., p. 264.

18. Ibid., p. 265.

19. "Israel in Lebanon," available at http://www.country-studies.com /israel/israel-in-lebanon.html; accessed June 15, 2008.

20. David W. Lesch, *The Arab-Israeli Conflict: A History* (New York: Oxford University Press, 2008), pp. 292–293.

21. Ibid., pp. 182 and 192.

22. Ramzy Baroud, *The Second Palestinian Intifada: A Chronicle of a People's Struggle* (London: Pluto Press, 2006), p. 29.

23. Lesch, *The Arab-Israeli Conflict*, p. 297.

24. Sean S. C. MacBride, *Israel in Lebanon: The Report of International Commission* (Ithaca, NY: Ithaca Press, 1983), p. 35.

25. Ibid., p. 83.

26. Ibid., p. 91.

27. John Rose, "The Israeli Invasion of Lebanon 1982," *Double Standards*, 1986; available at http://sss.doublestandards.org/rose1.html; accessed June 17, 2008.

28. Noam Chomsky, "On the U.S.-Israeli Invasion of Lebanon," *Al-Adab*, August 19, 2006; available at www.chomsky.info/articles/20060819.htm; accessed June 18, 2008.

29. Noam Chomsky and Gilbert Achcar, *Perilous Power: The Middle East and U.S. Foreign Policy: Dialogues on Terror, Democracy, War, and Justice* (Boulder, CO: Paradigm, 2007), p. 227.

30. Ibid., p. 236.

31. Lesch, *The Arab-Israeli Conflict*, pp. 301–302.

32. Ibid., pp. 302–303.

33. Aryeh Shalev, *The Intifada: Causes and Effects* (Boulder, CO: Westview Press, 1991), p. 43.

34. Ibid., p. 97.

35. Ibid., p. 122.

36. Mahmood Monshipouri and Wallace L. Rigsbee, "Intifadah: Prospects and Obstacles in the Aftermath of the Gulf Crisis," *Journal of South Asian and Middle Eastern Studies* 15, no. 2 (Winter 1991): 46–67.

37. Joshua Teitelbaum, "The Palestinian Liberalization Organization," in Ami Ayalon, ed., *Middle East Contemporary Survey* (Boulder, CO: Westview Press, 1992), pp. 211–243; see esp. p. 214.

38. Andrew Rigby, *Living the Intifada* (London: Zed Books, 1991), p. 202.

39. Mary Elizabeth King, *A Quiet Revolution: The First Palestinian Intifada and Nonviolent Resistance* (New York: Nation Books, 2007), pp. 343–344.

40. Rigby, *Living the Intifada*, p. 217.

41. Gershon Shafir, "Torturing Democracies: The Curious Debate over the Israeli Model," in Alison Brysk and Gershon Sahfir, eds., *National Insecurity and Human Rights: Democracies Debate Counterterrorism* (Berkeley: University of California Press, 2007), pp. 92–117; see p. 113.

42. Ibid., p. 117.

43. See Amitav Acharya, "Regionalism and Regime Security in the Third World: Comparing the Origins of the ASEAN and the GCC," in Brian L. Job, ed., *The Insecurity Dilemma: National Security of Third World States* (Boulder, CO: Lynne Rienner, 1992), pp. 143–164; see esp. p. 160.

44. Zbigniew Brzezinski, "A Tale of Two Wars: The Right War in Iraq, and the Wrong One," review essay of the book by Richard N. Haass, *War of Necessity, War of Choice: A Memoir of Two Iraq Wars* (New York: Simon & Schuster, 2009), *Foreign Affairs* 88, no. 3 (May–June 2009): 148–152; see esp. p. 149.

45. Lesch, *The Arab-Israeli Conflict*, pp. 306–307.

46. Mahmood Monshipouri, "The PLO Rivalry with Hamas: The Challenge of Peace, Democratization and Islamic Radicalism," *Middle East Policy* 4, no. 3 (March 1996): 84–105; see p. 86.

47. Monshipouri and Rigsbee, "Intifadah," pp. 57–58.

48. Shibley Telhami, *The Stakes: America in the Middle East: The Consequences of Power and the Choice for Peace* (Boulder, CO: Westview Press, 2004), p. 59.

49. Rema Hammami and Salim Tamari, "The Second Uprising: End of New Beginning?" *Journal of Palestine Studies* 30, no. 2 (Winter 2001), pp. 5–25.

50. Baroud, *The Second Palestinian Intifada*, p. 39 and 112.

51. Salem Ajluni, "Report: The Palestinian Economy and the Second Intifada," *Journal of Palestinian Studies* 32, no. 3 (Spring 2003): 64–73; see p. 67.

52. Ibid., p. 68.

53. Ibid., p. 69.

54. Ibid., pp. 70–72.

55. Baroud, *The Second Palestinian Intifada*, pp. 139–140.

56. Jimmy Carter, *Palestine Peace Not Apartheid* (New York: Simon & Schuster, 2006), pp. 175–176.

57. Ibid., p. 195.

58. "Bad Fences Make Bad Neighbors"; available at http://www.tomjoad.org/wall.htm; accessed June 18, 2008.

59. Jamal Juma, "The Wall in Palestine," August 18, 2003; available at http://www.zmag.org/content/showarticle.cfm?ItemID=4059; accessed June 18, 2008.

60. Ibid., p. 185.

61. Ibid., p. 186.

62. Rafael D. Frankel, "For a Few Gazans, Wealth Eases Pain of Year-Long Siege," *Christian Science Monitor*, June 24, 2008, p. 4.

63. BBC News, "UN Condemns 'War Crimes' in Gaza, September 16, 2009; available at http://news.bbc.co.uk/2/hi/8257301.stm; accessed March 4, 2010.

64. Michael Jansen, "Horrors of War," *Panorama: The Gulf Today*, February 5, 2010, pp. 54–55.

65. Michael Jansen, "EU Going along with Bush's Fictions," *Panorama: The Gulf Today*, May 30–June 5, 2008, pp. 52–53.

66. Michael Jansen, "Hidden Agenda," *Panorama: The Gulf Today*, April 18–24, 2008, pp. 54–55.

67. Michael Jansen, "Living in Hell," *Panorama: The Gulf Today*, May 23–29, 2008, pp. 56–57; see esp. p. 57.

68. Jennifer Loewenstein, "Notes from the Field: Return to the Ruin That Is Gaza," *Journal of Palestinian Studies* 36, no. 3 (Spring 2007): 23–35; see esp. p. 35.

69. The International Council on Security and Development, "Struggle for Kabul: The Taliban Advance," available at http//www.icosgroup.net/documents/Struggle_for_Kabul_ICOS.pdf.

70. Daniel Byman, "Talking with Insurgents: A Guide for the Perplexed," *Washington Quarterly* 32, no. 2 (April 2009): 125–137; see esp. p. 134.

71. Ibid., p. 135.

72. C. Christine Fair, "Time for Sober Realism: Renegotiating U.S. Relations with Pakistan," *Washington Quarterly* 32, no. 2 (April 2009): 149–172; see esp. pp. 163–164.

73. Ibid., p. 165.

74. Ibid., p. 165.

75. Anna Mulrine and Tom A. Peter, "Is the Afghan Surge Working?" *Christian Science Monitor*, June 13, 2011, pp. 26–27, 31; see esp. p. 26.

76. Ibid., p. 31.

77. Zbigniew Brzezinski, "From Hope to Audacity: Appraising Obama's Foreign Policy," *Foreign Affairs* 89, no. 1 (January–February 2010): 16–30; see esp. p. 25.

78. William J. Lahneman, "Military Intervention: Lessons for the Twenty-First Century," in William J. Lahneman, ed., *Military Intervention: Cases in Context for the Twenty-First Century* (New York: Rowman & Littlefiled 2004), pp. 165–199; see pp. 173–174.

79. Ibid., p. 174.

80. Ibid., p. 195.

81. Andrea Kathryn Talentino, *Military Intervention after the Cold War: The Evolution of Theory and Practice* (Athens: Ohio University Press, 2005), p. 300.

82. Mehran Kamrava, *The Modern Middle East: A Political History since the First World War* (Berkeley: University of California Press, 2005), p. 205.

83. Ibid., p. 209.

84. John Gee, "From Sanctions to Occupation: The U.S. Impact on Iraq," in Rick Fawn and Raymond Hinnebusch, eds., *The Iraq War: Causes and Consequences* (Boulder, CO: Lynne Rienner, 2006), pp. 225–234; see p. 227.

85. Vali Nasr, *The Shia Revival: How Conflicts within Islam Will Shape the Future* (New York: W. W. Norton, 2006), p. 184.

86. Maximilian Terhalle, "Are the Shia Rising?" *Middle East Policy* 14, no. 2 (Summer 2007): 69–83.

87. Vali Nasr, "When the Shiites Rise," *Foreign Affairs* 85, no. 4 (July–August 2006): 58–74; see p. 73.

88. Adeeb Dawisha, "The Unraveling of Iraq: Ethnosectarian Preferences and State Performance in Historical Perspectives," *Middle East Journal* 62, no. 2 (Spring 2008): 219–230; see p. 230.

89. Andrew F. Krepinevich Jr., "How to Win in Iraq," *Foreign Affairs* 84, no. 5 (September-October 2005): 87–104; see p. 88.

90. Jane Arraf, "Iraq: Why the US May Pause on the Pullout," *Christian Science Monitor*, May 23, 2011, p. 12.

91. *National Institute of Military Justice*, August 5, 2011, http://www
.nimjblog.org/2011/08/immunity-from-prosecution-for-american.html. Last
accessed on August 20, 2011.

92. Anthony H. Cordesman, "A Civil War Iraq Can't Win," *New York
Times*, March 30, 2008, p. 13.

93. Michael Jensen, "Iraq's Trials and Tribulations," *Panorama: The Gulf
Today*, April 9, 2010, pp. 58–59.

94. Sam Dahger, "Sadr Sends Mixed Signals," *Christian Science Monitor*,
March 31, 2008, pp. 1 and 11; see esp. p. 11.

95. Michael Jansen, "An Uphill Task," *Panorama: The Gulf Today*, April
23, 2010, pp. 54–55; see esp. p. 54.

96. Reidar Visser, "The Last Straw? Malike Appoints Dulaymi as Acting
Minister of Defense," *Iraq and Gulf Analysis*, August 17, 2011, available at
http://gulfanalysis.wordpress.com/category/iraqs-2010-parliamentary
-election. Last accessed on September 7, 2011.

97. Stephen M. Walt, "Taming American Power," *Foreign Affairs* 84, no. 5
(September–October 2005):105–120; see p. 117.

98. "The Iraq War in Retrospect," *Japan Times*, March 28, 2004, in
Ramesh Thakur, ed., *War in Our Time: Reflections on Iraq, Terrorism and
Weapons of Mass Destruction* (New York: United Nations University Press,
2007), pp. 101–103; see p. 103.

99. Brzezinski, "From Hope to Audacity," p. 150.

100. UN Security Council, 6498th Meeting, March 17, 2011; available at
http://www.un.org/News/Press/docs/2011/sc10200.doc.htm; accessed March
20, 2011.

101. Ibid.

102. Alex J. Bellamy, *Global Politics and the Responsibility to Protect:
From Words to Deeds* (New York: Routledge, 2011); see pp. 49 and 69.

103. Robert Farley, "Over the Horizon: Initial Lessons Learned from
Libyan Intervention," *World Politics Review*, April 20, 2011; available at
http://www.worldpoliticsreview.com/articles/8581/over-the-horizon-initial
-lessons-learned-from-libyan-intervention; accessed April 20, 2011.

104. Richard Falk, *Achieving Human Rights* (New York: Routledge, 2009),
p. 177.

105. Ibid., p. 177.

106. Eric A. Heinze, "Humanitarian Intervention: Overview," in David P.
Forsythe, ed., *Encyclopedia of Human Rights*, vol. 2 (New York: Oxford University Press, 2009), pp. 443–455; see esp. p. 444.

107. Nicholas J. Wheeler, *Saving Strangers: Humanitarian Intervention in
International Society* (New York: Oxford University Press, 2000), p. 243.

108. Elizabeth Bumiller and Kareem Fahim, "U.S.-Led Assault Nears Goal
in Libya," *New York Times*, March 21, 2011; available at http://www.nytimes
.com/2011/03/22/world/africa/22libya.html; accessed March 21, 2011.

109. US Department of State, "Update on Implementing UN Security Council Resolutions 1970 and 1973 on Libya," Remarks by Hillary Rodham Clinton, March 24, 2011; available at http://www.state.gov/secretary/rm/2011/03
/159097.htm; accessed April 20, 2011.

110. Bobby Ghosh, "The Qaddafi Regime is Broken: What Will Take Its Place," *Time*, September 5, 2011, pp. 34–37.

111. Dirk Vandewalle, "To the Shores of Tripoli: Why Operation Odyssey Dawn Should Not Stop at Benghazi," *Foreign Affairs*, March 21, 2011; available at http://www.foreignaffairs.com/articles/67669/dirkvandewalle/to-the-shores-of-tripoli?page=2; accessed March 22, 2011.

112. Robert D. Kaplan and Stephen S. Kaplan, "America Primed," *The National Interest*, no. 112 (March–April 2011): 42–54; see esp. p. 45.

113. Michael Georgy, "Stalemate May Force NATO to Expand Its Libya Offensive," *Mail and Guardian Online*, April 19, 2011; available at http://mg.co.za/article/2011-04-19-stalemate-may-force-nato-to-expand-libya-offensive; accessed April 20, 2011.

114. Eugene L. Rogan, "The Emergence of the Middle East into the Modern State System," in Louise Fawcett, ed., *International Relations of the Middle East* (New York: Oxford University Press, 2005), pp. 17–39; see p. 37.

115. Ibid., p. 38.

116. For further information on this issue, see William B. Quandt, "The Middle East in 1990," *Foreign Affairs* 70, no. 1 (1990–1991): 46–69.

117. Mahmood Monshipouri and Thaddeus Zolty, "Shaping the New World Order: America's Post-Gulf War Agenda in the Middle East," *Armed Forces and Society* 19, no. 4 (Summer 1993): 551–577.

118. Richard Falk, "The Middle East and the World Five Years after 9/11," September 13, 2006, Nuclear Age Peace Foundation; available at http://www.wagingpeace.org/articles/2006/09/13_falk_after911.htm; accessed June 22, 2008.

119. Ibid.

120. Yigal Schleifer, "Why Turkey Is Taking a Bolder Role," *Christian Science Monitor*, June 21, 2010, p. 10.

121. Ibid.

122. Walter Rodgers, "Rift Between Israel and the United States: It's Personal," *Christian Science Monitor,* June 14, 2010, p. 35.

123. Maria A. Ressa, *Seeds of Terror: An Eyewitness Account of Al-Qaeda's Newest Center of Operations in Southeast Asia* (New York: Free Press, 2003), p. 220.

124. Gary Sussman, "The Challenge to the Two-State Solution," *Middle East Report* 34, no. 231 (Summer 2004).

125. Stephen C. Pelletiere, *Losing Iraq: Insurgency and Politics* (Westport, CT: Praeger, 2006), p. 110.

126. Kurt Volker, "America's Journey from 9/11 to 5/1," *Christian Science Monitor*, May 15, 2011, p. 33.

127. Michael Heazle, "Covering (up) Islam, Part III: Terrorism and the US Intervention in Iraq," in Michael Heazle and Iyanatul Islam, eds., *Beyond the Iraq War: The Promises, Pitfalls, and Perils of External Intervention* (Northampton, MA: Edward Elgar, 2006), pp. 120–137; see p. 134.

128. Mel Gurtov, *Global Politics in the Human Interest*, 5th ed. (Boulder, CO: Lynne Rienner, 2007), p. 317.

129. Sedat Laçiner, "Combat Against Religionist Terrorism: Lessons from the Turkish Case," in *USAK Yearbook of International Politics and Law*, vol. 1 (Ankara: International Strategic Research Organization, 2008), pp. 449–472; see esp. p. 472.

130. Quoted in Gurtov, *Global Politics*, p. 318.

131. Douglas Little, *American Orientalism: The United States and the Middle East since 1945* (Chapel Hill: University of North Carolina Press, 2002); see pp. 311–314.

132. Ibid., pp. 317–318.

4

Democracy Promotion: Failed Efforts in the Middle East

Since the attacks of September 11, 2001, domestic conditions in the Middle East region have come to be seen as a major source of violence, both domestically and internationally. Thus, the US government increased its pressure for political and economic reform in the Middle East as a way to confront the growing terrorist threat.[1] This policy, which represented a shift from maintaining the status quo to supporting reformist regimes, soon proved to be a daunting task. Opinions differ on the prospects of promoting democracy in the Middle East and the complexity and enormity of the challenge facing the region.

A skeptical view holds that many rulers around the world, including in the Middle East, have mastered the art of a democratic rhetoric that only remotely resembles their practice of governing. Many of these autocrats stage elections and put on a charade of democracy. To name only some of them, these leaders have included Islam Karimov of Uzbekistan, Robert Mugabe of Zimbabwe, Pervez Musharraf of Pakistan, Hosni Mubarak of Egypt, Meles Zenawi of Ethiopia, Mwai Kibaki of Kenya, Than Shwe of Burma, and Vladimir Putin of Russia.[2] Some of these leaders have been replaced; others have stayed the course. The problem presented by this charade is accentuated by the world's consolidated democracies who, under the influence of commercial and strategic interests, often turn a blind eye to electoral manipulation, and thus these sham democrats get away with calling themselves democrats.[3]

From a hard-nosed realist standpoint, some have argued that the Middle East region presents some of the world's most perplexing obstacles to democracy promotion. To begin with, regional stability is tenuous. Supporters of the process of promoting democracy are undermined by internal instability and regional fissions; to cite two examples: in

95

Iraq, the cooperation of democracy-promotion allies is crucial in the drive to stabilize the country; similarly they are needed in jumpstarting the Israeli-Palestinian peace process.

Secondly, democratic elections held under conditions of political turmoil, foreign occupation, or economic adversity often lead to outcomes that are inconsistent with long-term US interests. Examples are numerous: Hamas's victory in the Palestinian elections; the resurgence of Hezbollah and the ensuing political turmoil in Lebanon; the success of the Muslim Brotherhood in Egyptian elections in 2006; the Iranian elections in 2005 that replaced a moderate clergy with a populist and hard-line figure; again in Iran, after the rigged 2009 elections, the crackdown on the Green Movement; and the intensifying sectarian violence and divide in Iraq—all these cast a shadow of doubt on the wisdom of rapid democratization as a panacea for the region's ills.[4]

An optimistic outlook, in contrast, tends to emphasize the existence of an audience for such reformist views, underlining the desire of Middle Easterners for economic reform, accountability, transparency, and anticorruption policies. And the 2011 Arab revolts have added support to the optimistic point of view. Adhering to the old order while simultaneously claiming a belief in democracy will not serve US interests.[5] In Indonesia, the United States encouraged Suharto to resign, and similar situations will doubtless confront future US presidents in the Middle East. It is crucial to understand that economic and social security, viable political institutions, and protecting and promoting civil rights and civil society are the key to pursuing a sustainable strategy of democracy promotion in the long term.

Some experts have underscored the importance of informal institutions and social networks—based on kinship rather than class—as the key to understanding the participation of the urban poor and lower-income classes.[6] They note that serious Western commitments to promoting democracy in the Middle East should entail sustainable support for institutions, with tools that will enable effective political participation, thus challenging the structural bases of authoritarian governments.[7]

It is also important to bear in mind that the main threat to US security is no longer rogue states but rather substate or transnational actors who engage in terrorist activities.[8] The Bush administration's inability to target substate or transnational actors led to a linking of terrorism to rogue states. Hence a policy developed of acting preemptively against rogue states possessing—or believed to possess—weapons of mass destruction. Allegations of torture and detention of terrorist suspects without charge or trial in Abu Ghraib and Guantanamo Bay deepened the credibility deficit of US policies in the eyes of the public throughout the Middle East. As a result, US influence and reputation plummeted to new depths. Significantly, Washington's attempt to fight al-Qaeda in Iraq was seen by many Muslims throughout the Middle East as part of a larger US strategy to maintain new strategic and logistical bases in Iraq in the hope of effectively projecting its power in the region.

I want to examine the effectiveness of a US strategy built around a democratization agenda in the Middle East. In the first section below, I examine the vision of the Bush doctrine for the greater Middle East and then go on to investigate the process by which democracy will be promoted as a way of combating the terrorist epidemic and containing the proliferation of weapons of mass destruction. Finally, this chapter analyzes the practical implications of a democracy-based approach to US foreign policy in the region, arguing that US foreign policy interests comport with the ideals and principles of democracy.

The Bush Doctrine

US involvement in the region's internal affairs and conflicts since the 1940s has been based on promoting stability, but it has ignored human rights abuses and undemocratic systems of government from which the United States has stood to benefit. This policy, marked by inconsistencies and paradoxes, has won the United States few friends in the Middle East.[9]

The inconsistencies explain why today there is—at least in some parts of the region—widespread skepticism regarding the greater Middle East initiative of the United States. Feelings of impotence, humiliation, and frustration have continued to pervade much of the Middle East, especially since the invasion and occupation of Iraq. These feelings are compounded by traditions and authoritarian governments in the region that give people little opportunity to participate in their own governance. There can be no doubt that terrorism thrives in an atmosphere where opportunities for democratic participation are lacking.[10] Defeating terror entails attenuating the rage that fuels it, and hence the argument for democratic transformation of these societies.[11]

The US "democracy promotion doctrine" in the Middle East was articulated in President Bush's speech on the twentieth anniversary of the National Endowment for Democracy, November 6, 2003, in Washington, DC. The president noted:

Sixty years of Western nations excusing and accommodating the lack of freedom in the Middle East did nothing to make us safe—because in the long run, stability cannot be purchased at the expense of liberty. As long as the Middle East remains a place where freedom does not flourish, it will remain a place of stagnation, resentment, and violence ready for export. And with the spread of weapons that can bring catastrophic harm to our country and to our friends, it would be reckless to accept the status quo.[12]

In another speech, before the American Enterprise Institute in February 2003, President Bush suggested that the Allied occupation and reconstruction of Germany and Japan provided good models for the greater Middle East initiative. "After defeating enemies," the president asserted, "we did not leave behind the occupying armies, we left constitutions and parliaments . . . we established an atmosphere of safety, in which responsible, reform-minded local leaders could build lasting institutions of freedom. In societies that once bred fascism and militarism, liberty found a home."[13] US-style liberty, President Bush implied, could find a home via similar large-scale occupations in the Middle East.[14]

The Bush administration pushed for democracy promotion through wholesale occupation, arguing that the historical experience of Germany and Japan in the postwar period showed that military occupation may increase the likelihood of democratization and that wise policy choices could certainly improve its chances. Critics claim, however, that the US experience in Germany and Japan was unique and not easily replicable today. The outcome of such interventions, Eva Bellin finds, "is largely shaped by factors, both domestic and international, that cannot be controlled by military engineers operating within the confines of current cultural norms and conventional limits of time and treasure."[15]

It bears noting here that the process of the emergence of democracy in Germany and Japan in the eighty years or so before US troops occupied them after World War II was a complex one. This should serve as a warning against the simplistic notion that US military occupation alone could lead to democratization in other countries.[16] Michel Gobat argues that US occupations of countries like Nicaragua at the first part of the twentieth century offer a better parallel. In Nicaragua, the United States intended to establish institutions to undergird a modern democracy and replace the existing clientelist social/political structure. Instead the US occupation created the institutions that would be used to oppress the Nicaraguan people under a US-supported dictatorship for nearly fifty years.[17]

Prior to the outbreak of World War II, both Germany and Japan were highly industrialized countries with advanced levels of economic development that generated an impressive GNP per capita. They were both relatively homogenous ethnically, with a significant consensus about their sense of social solidarity and national identity. After World War II, both Germany and Japan retained an effective police force, judicial system, and civil service with which to govern.[18] Both also had extensive experience with democratic rule prior to World War II and had committed leaders whose embrace of the democratic project helped anchor democratic projects at home. Additionally, context-specific factors such as the experience of total devastation and defeat, the fear of Communist threat and takeover, and the imposed freedom of occupation bestowed by contemporary cultural norms made it possible for democracy to endure in those countries.[19] These endowments crucial to democratic outcomes—levels of economic development, ethnic homogeneity, strength of state institutions, historical experience, and elite leadership—are factors conspicuously lacking in many Middle Eastern countries.

Especially problematic is the way in which the region's political economy presents obstacles to a transition to democracy. In the post-colonial era, Alan Richards notes, Arab governments emphasized their military strength to protect their often hard-won independence. Their struggle for independence—often violent, and followed by a half-century of conflict with Israel within the context of the Cold War—in turn greatly fostered authoritarianism.[20] Another key barrier to a transition to democracy has been the "low dependence of states on citizens."[21] This is indeed in the nature of the region's rentier states—states that live off "rents"; that is, income from oil.

In many Arab countries, Richards continues, the most viable and best-organized opposition forces are those of political Islam. Islamists now participate in elections in countries as diverse as Bahrain, Iraq, Jordan, Lebanon, Kuwait, Morocco, Palestine, and Yemen, as well as Bangladesh, Malaysia, Pakistan, and Indonesia. There exist strong democratic trends within the movements of "political Islam."[22] The main barriers to a transition to democracy in the Arab world, Richards insists, are "fundamentally political."[23] External interventions leading to occupation exacerbate the situation of Middle Eastern countries. The US invasion of Iraq, for instance, has strengthened the popular appeal of antidemocratic extremists such as al-Qaeda and other Salafi jihadists.[24] The endemic interstate and intrastate conflicts and the massive infusions of military aid into the region are major barriers to democratization and political development.[25]

There is not a single "free" country among the Arab states of the Middle East and North Africa—a region with a population of almost 350 million people. Free elections are not allowed in most of the Arab world. The region's well-entrenched and nondemocratic—but especially oil rich—regimes have survived numerous political upheavals. Some observers caution against the idea of instant democratic transformation in the Middle East, describing it as a mirage. What reform programs exist in the region, they contend, represent mostly top-down liberalization agendas designed more to protect against the possibility of far-reaching political change than to foster it. The United States can hardly afford to use its coercive foreign policy tools (sanctions and aid) as a way to foster political reform in the rich monarchies of the Gulf without jeopardizing other interests. It cannot afford to antagonize the very regimes whose cooperation it seeks—the regimes whose aid it seeks to combat terrorism, find a solution to the Israeli-Palestinian conflict, and gain continued access to military bases to wage war on countries such as Iraq and Afghanistan. The United States has no meaningful or practical alternative to working with existing regimes toward gradual change.[26]

There are contrasting views regarding the link between democracy and economic growth. While some observers emphasize good governance and accountability as a necessary precondition for economic growth, others argue that an independent judiciary "would allow people to invest more freely" and that without democratization, economic changes will still occur, although at a much slower pace.[27]

Despite parliamentarian dispute over the country's economic growth, Kuwaiti deputies have increased their call for political reforms and placing more curbs on the power of the ruling families, especially in the aftermath of the 2011 democratic uprisings in the MENA region. Kuwait's parliament, while weak by global standards, one study finds, is the most powerful elected body on the Arabian Peninsula and one of the strongest in the Middle East region. All of Kuwait's neighbors have assemblies, but some are appointed by the ruler and lack a clear legislative mandate or authority. Throughout the region, parliaments are granted independent authority in theory, but they are closely controlled or manipulated by the executive or the ruling party in practice. Kuwait's parliament is not only fully elected but, in a legal or constitutional sense, possesses impressive law-making abilities as well as considerable oversight powers over cabinet ministers and the budget. Furthermore, it plays a key role in the approval of the crown prince and thus in the selection of the ruler. Thus, one can plausibly argue that Kuwait is the only Arab country in the region with a parliament that could effectively check decisions by the executive branch of government.[28]

Democratic movements have, however, made some strides in the Middle East. In Turkey, the Justice and Development Party (Adalet ve Kalkinma Partisi—AKP), with Islamic roots and ideological orientation, has been in power since 2002. Restricted democracy in Iran has led to an insatiable public desire for a more open, tolerant, and democratic political system. The Gulf monarchies, such as Bahrain, Kuwait, and Qatar, have taken meaningful if rudimentary steps toward more constitutional rule. But US officials have criticized Kuwait, Qatar, the United Arab Emirates, and Saudi Arabia for doing little to stop forced labor and other forms of "modern slavery," such as labor and sex trafficking (importing workers and people who are forced into prostitution) within their borders.[29] There are, however, hopeful signs of democratic struggles in both Iraq and the Palestinian occupied territories.

According to one study, since 9/11 fifty-one countries have made democratic gains as opposed to twenty-seven countries where there have been setbacks.[30] The evidence suggests that democracy now enjoys enormous support in non-Western countries and cultures. Although there is a less liberal attitude in Muslim societies than in the West toward such social issues as gender equality and gay rights, there exists no difference at all when it comes to support for democratic institutions. One empirical study concludes that nearly 90 percent of the respondents in Muslim societies favor democracy, the same level of support as in the West.[31]

Women's empowerment is in critical deficit in the region. Arab women's participation, both political and economic, remains the lowest in the world. This is evidenced by the very low proportion of women in government, at the ministerial level and in parliament. Gender inequality in education and economic activity is rampant throughout the Middle East. It should be noted, however, that Arab countries have made great strides in girls' education. Female literacy rates have increased threefold since 1970, and female primary and secondary enrollment rates have more than doubled. But despite this progress, female enrollment rates remain lower than those for males.[32] Arab women remain marginalized and underutilized in all sectors of the economy and society in terms of their economic, intellectual, and leadership potential.[33] The unemployment rate is high among women, who are the most likely to be deprived of access to health and educational services because of financial pressures on families.[34]

It is important to underscore the significance of the Middle East region and why it figures prominently in the strategic calculation of the United States, the European Union (the EU), and East Asia. The Gulf region and the Caspian Basin together have by far the world's largest reserves of oil and natural gas. Reliable access to energy is vitally significant to the world's great powers, Zbigniew Brzezinski notes, explaining why "strategic domination over the area, even if cloaked by cooperative arrangements, would be a globally decisive hegemonic asset."[35]

The September 11, 2001, terrorist attacks in the United States have laid bare the fact that the Middle East cannot be left to its own devices. To ignore this region's problems and underestimate its potential for global disruption, Zbigniew Brzezinski writes, would be "tantamount to declaring an open season for intensifying regional violence, region-wide contamination by terrorist groups and the competitive proliferation of weaponry of mass destruction."[36]

These realities have pushed Europe and the United States toward a convergence of new interest: confronting the threat of Islamic extremists. Unlike during the Cold War era, the menace of Islamic fundamentalism is not restricted to a certain border; it is global.[37] The mounting threat of Islamic fundamentalism in Europe is directly linked to the increasing flow of Muslim immigrants to Europe; their attempts to promote their own cultural traditions and religious beliefs have prompted an intense debate over such issues as the wearing of the headscarf and veil. Similarly, Muslims warn of Western cultural invasion, fearing the loss of their identity.[38] Muslim immigrants' participation in (or their absence from) the politics and economy of the country in which they reside has also caused numerous reactions throughout Europe.

The real question is: Did the Bush administration bring the EU and the United States closer or did it drive a wedge in the transatlantic alliance? Prior to the US-led invasion of Iraq, the United States and Europe disagreed over how to fight the global war on terrorism. In the aftermath of invasion, however, talk of international cooperation has permeated diplomatic forums. Increasingly, the United States and EU member states have tacitly reached an agreement on oil distribution and their active role in the Middle East peace process. The upshot has been the US emphasis on a sustained effort to delegitimate terrorism and to promote forces within the Muslim world that are intent on building and preserving modern, moderate, and democratic political institutions.[39] This may mean different things in different countries of the region. In some cases, it may only require a minimal degree of democratization so that the stability of friendly and pro-Western countries would not be jeopardized. A shift of approach toward countries such as Iran must be seen in this context. For now, at least, US diplomatic pressure on Iran has supplanted a threat of the use of force or a preemptive strike.

Bush's new foreign policy entailed three elements. First, the administration sought a broader engagement with the world than that seen in his first term. This greater willingness to listen and engage the rest of the world, especially the rapprochement with the EU, indicated the drawbacks of its unilateral foreign policy toward Iraq. Secondly, a shift in rhetoric from fighting terrorism to a discussion of freedom and democracy shaped this new foreign policy. The administration was no longer preoccupied with a preemptive use of force to the extent it was in the preceding term. Thirdly, Bush's "forward strategy of freedom," which was based on applying external pressures for internal political reform, gradually morphed into what came to be known as democratic development. Ultimately, US Secretary of State Condoleezza Rice argued that one of the best ways to support the growth of democratic institutions and civil society was to expand free and fair trade and investment. Emphasizing democratic development, Secretary Rice prescribed the use of several tools of foreign assistance, both security cooperation and trade, making a familiar case for the interrelated nature of economic and political liberalization:

> The very process of implementing a trade agreement or a bilateral investment treaty helps to hasten and consolidate democratic development. Legal and political institutions that can enforce property rights are better able to protect human rights and the rule of law. Independent courts that can resolve commercial disputes can better resolve civil and political disputes. The transparency needed to fight corporate corruption makes it harder for political corruption to go unnoticed and unpunished. A rising middle class also creates new centers of social power for political movements and parties.[40]

Focusing on a common policy, however, overlooks the diversity of the area. The region's diversity requires a differentiated and nuanced policy. There is no uniform plan and there cannot be a coherent strategy vis-à-vis such widely different countries. In fact, the absence of policy cohesion has caused a fundamental difference of opinion among Middle Eastern governments and scholars concerning the definition, goals, and implications of a preemptive strike or unilateral action in the region.

The Democracy Conundrum in the Middle East

The invocation of democracy as a visionary complement to the war on terrorism has drawn mixed reactions in the Middle East. Varying groups tend to interpret the reforms associated with the Bush doctrine differently. Increasingly, the battle lines over reform within the Middle East are drawn between the pessimists and optimists. On the one hand, lopsided support by the United States for Israel, the US invasion of Iraq, and the abuse of prisoners in Abu Ghraib and Guantanamo Bay have intensified the national sentiments of many Arabs. They dismiss the democracy rhetoric as yet another ploy to control the region's vast oil supplies. On the other hand, Middle Eastern people have welcomed the democracy initiative, given the repressive atmosphere under which they have lived for so many years. The ordinary people of the Middle East have never been more ready than now for such a serious engagement with reform.[41] These varying perspectives notwithstanding, no one should underestimate the importance of an immediate and just resolution of the Israeli-Palestinian conflict as the most effective way to mitigate terrorist activity in the region. The unwillingness of the United States to use its leverage on Israel to resolve the Israeli-Palestinian conflict weakens its own legitimacy as well as that of its Arab allies, while strengthening the hands of radical Islamic groups throughout the region. The major beneficiaries of such double standards have always been and will be Islamic extremist groups.

The skeptics also call our attention both to the exceptional and common causes preventing democratic reform in the Middle East. The uniqueness of the Middle East and North Africa, they note, lies not so much in the absent prerequisite of democracy as in the present conditions, which strengthen the tenacity of governments' coercive apparatus. Abundant oil rent subsidizes much of the cost of these overdeveloped coercive institutions. A multitude of Western security considerations in the region guarantees outside support to authoritarian regimes. Contributing to the prevention of democratic reform in the region are other factors: the prevalence of clientelism and patrimonialism in state structures and the low level of popular mobilization—factors that are by no means unique to the area.

The sudden and pervasive turn toward democracy in Latin America during the 1980s discredited socioeconomic determination in theories of democratic transition, highlighting the key role that elite choice and voluntarism play in establishing democracy. Similarly, the dramatic transition to democracy that swept sub-Saharan Africa and Eastern Europe in the 1990s drew attention to the centrality of popular mobilization in bringing down authoritarian regimes.[42] Given the international support and financing of these authoritarian regimes and given the patrimonial institutions' embrace of coercive capacity, authoritarianism is likely to endure. Rapid regime change is unlikely.[43]

Furthermore, many of these regimes have practiced arbitrary detention and unfair trials in the name of the war on terror. The Saudi authorities are one example. According to the Cairo Institute for Human Rights Studies (CIHRS), the Saudis have often justified extended detention by claiming that they expose detainees to "religious guidance" programs that will ensure their rehabilitation and social integration.[44] Trials of some detainees have been conducted semisecretly, the presence of international observers and the media at trials being blocked. By the beginning of July 2009, CIHRS reports, secret trials convicted 330 detainees, many of whom suffered cruel treatment; they were kept in shackles, beaten, and in some cases deprived of sleep, as well as being denied contact with family members.[45] The report claims that arbitrary detentions without charges or trials have also targeted non-Saudi Arabs. Some Yemeni, Kuwaiti, and Egyptian citizens, for instance, have been detained for more than a year in Saudi Arabia, the Saudi government failing to disclose the charges made against them.[46]

Iran's Green Movement

In his Cairo speech on June 4, 2009, US President Barack Obama really struck a positive cord with many in the Muslim world. The speech put the issue of democratic reform back on the agenda. While many experts point to the huge significance of Obama's challenge, others insist that his idealism must not be summarily dismissed.[47] With respect to Iran, for instance, Obama's reversal of prior US positions—that is, dialogue and negotiation, not intervention under the rubric of democracy promotion—gave the Iranian people tremendous hope that the June 12, 2009, presidential election there was their rendezvous with history.[48]

Evidence suggests that, via texting, Twitter feeds, blogging, and Facebook pages, Obama's strategies and tools have shaped overseas campaigns. Web outreach has spread all over the world, becoming critical in elections in many countries such as South Africa, Israel, India, Ecuador, and Iran, to name only a few.[49] In the case of Iran, there can be no doubt that the revolution in online campaigning played an instrumental role in shaping presidential candidate Mir-Hossein Mousavi's "green movement." Crystallized in Mousavi's slogan "Every person is a campaign office," the so-called green wave of the pre- and post-June 12 election days made it very difficult for the Islamic Republic to stuff the genie back into the bottle. More importantly, the homegrown, popular green movement in Iran revealed the Islamic Republic's hand and made it immensely difficult, if not impossible, for the regime to hide behind the mask of enemy construction.

Far from buying into the state-sanctioned narrative of Western interference in the election, and relying on the reach of online communication and social networking sites, the Iranian population constructed an alternative narrative that accused Russia, not the United States and EU member states, of interfering in the Iranian election. In the early days following the election and the declaration of Mahmoud Ahmadinejad's victory, rumors were rampant on Iranian Web sites and in the blogosphere condemning Russia—and to some degree, China—of assisting the Islamic Republic in orchestrating a military coup against the true winner, Mir-Hossein Mousavi. The rumors eventually evolved into a coherent popular narrative accusing Iran of providing energy and security concessions to Russia and China in exchange for their practical and diplomatic support for the military coup in Iran. That Mahmoud Ahmadinejad visited Russia only hours after being declared the winner of the presidential election, while canceling all other foreign trips and receptions, put the stamp of validity on claims of Russian interference in the eyes of many Iranians.

The Iranian public's passionate response to the conduct and outcome of the election revived the age-old accusation of foreign interference. This time, however, the public had constructed its own, unique narrative, one that stood diametrically opposed to the one espoused and promoted by the state. A quick examination of Iran's contemporary history reveals the historical significance of this break from the state and shift in public attitude. In 1953, the state's narrative of the Soviet Union's interference in Iranian affairs through manipulating the communist Tudeh Party in Iran seriously weakened Prime Minister Mohammad Mossadeq's base of popular support, especially among the clerical establishment, which led a significant portion of the population.

In 1979, Ayatollah Ruhollah Khomeini's endorsement of the takeover of the US embassy proved to be hugely popular, despite opposition by members of the provisional government, who argued that the act would isolate Iran and severely damage the country's international standing. During the 1980s, the state's narrative of a global attack on the Iranian revolution united even the most disparate elements of the population. Even as recently as 1999 and 2003, the state's narrative of foreign intervention played a role in preventing student protests from spilling outside university campuses. Most significantly, Ahmadinejad himself had managed to prop up his popular support during the 2005 presidential election and throughout his first term by portraying himself as a nationalist hero willing to stand up to the United States and its

Western allies, which he said seek to deprive Iran of its inherent rights as well as deserved privileges.

What separated the 2009 "green movement" from the previous protests was that, this time, a significant portion of the populace rejected the state's sanctioned narrative of enemy construction and replaced it with its own, unique version. That the Islamic Republic, with its hardened monopoly over the means of mass communication—including all six nationally televised channels, dozens of radio networks, and all but a few newspapers and magazines—is unable to sell its narrative to the public is a testament to the reach and penetration of digital communication networks in Iran. According to the Central Intelligence Agency, Iran (which is twentieth on the list of the world's largest populations) ranked fourteenth globally in number of Internet users in its population in 2008. More than 23 percent of Iranians use the Internet.[50] Iran boasts even more impressive statistics for mobile-phone penetration. By the first quarter of 2009, nearly 50 million Iranians owned mobile phones—a penetration rate of more than 70 percent.[51] Not surprisingly, the Iranian government shut down short message service (SMS, commonly known as text messaging) communication networks for several weeks beginning on June 12, the election day. In fact, immediately after the election, the Iranian government stepped up its cybercensorship efforts, unleashing a massive campaign to prevent online access by filtering opposition Web sites, reducing Internet bandwidth to the lowest possible levels, and setting up fake opposition Web sites.

Nevertheless, the 2009 green movement in Iran will be remembered around the world by the varied images transmitted amid the protests. These images documented not only the oppression and violence the Iranian protesters faced but also the Iranian people's yearning for democracy and human rights.[52] Further, as Robin Wright notes, these uprisings are not a passing phenomenon, like the student protests of 1999 that were quickly and forcibly squashed. This time, Iranians' resolve is firm and reminiscent of civil disobedience in colonial India before its independence in 1947 or in the Deep South of the United States in the 1960s. Although the current uprising is not as widespread as that of 1979 that ushered in the Islamic Republic, the activism is creating a new political space in Iran. What is original in this movement is that opposition figures, such as Mehdi Karoubi and Mir-Hossein Mousavi, are in fact responding to sentiment on the street, rather than directing it.[53]

The green wave that engulfed Iran during the 2009 election highlighted the political and social energies of the resistance and suggested a new movement that will not settle for anything short of a just and democratic order. The continuing images of the show of resistance that now emerge daily in Iran are in fact powerful symbols for the strength of the green wave. Facilitated by constant digital interaction via instant messaging and social networking services such as Twitter and YouTube, the green wave drew immediate attention to human rights violations and political violence in Iran. Many observers have cautioned that on their own, digital technologies and devices cannot produce revolutions. "To generate fundamental change," Darrell West argues, "it still takes strong leadership, powerful ideas, and people willing to risk arrest and imprisonment."[54]

If there is a teachable moment in this episode, it is that the days of so-called enemy construction that used to confer legitimacy on the Islamic Republic are over. Under the watchful eyes of the international community and the Iranian people, it has become obvious that the train of the Islamic Republic has been set off track. The Ahmadinejad administration must recognize that without internal legitimacy and credibility, Iran will not remain a dominant regional power. Although one should not underestimate the resilience of the Islamic Republic in leading proxy powers in the region, it would be immensely difficult for Iran's ruling elite to pursue formidable foreign policies in the region and beyond at a time when their credibility is questioned internally. There is poetic justice—if not irony—here. The Islamic Republic that came to power with a platform to fight against the decay, corruption, and suffocation that resulted from decades of autocratic policies under the shah now finds itself embroiled in decadence. Political history has a way of coming full circle. It has caught up with Iran.

When Iran's supreme leader, Ayatollah Ali Khamenei, declared the election of Ahmadinejad a "divine assessment," he clearly chose the state over the people. Whereas Ayatollah Khomeini chose to be on the side of the Iranian people to topple the shah, Khamenei has opted for the reverse course. The idea of *velayate-e faqih*, rule by the supreme jurist, has now assumed a different meaning, but it cannot escape the reality that the struggle between secular and religious faiths and ideologies is far from over. This accounts for how insecure the ruling elite of Iran have become. One observer notes that a totalitarian regime can be overthrown by war, as Hitler's Germany was—in the case of Iran, an option that is almost inconceivable. A more realistic alternative is collapse from within, as happened in the Soviet Union.[55] It is this uprising from within that poses the greatest danger to the regime. That explains why the government restricted the alternative media and shut down other means of communication shortly after the election.

Mass Uprisings in the Middle East and North Africa

The 2011 leaderless uprisings in Tunisia, Egypt, Libya, and the rest of the Arab world attest to the fact that the time has come to end the bargain with autocrats.[56] These uprisings have also demonstrated that maintaining order and stability can no longer be divorced from upholding human rights, human security, and social justice.[57] The young generation of educated men and women throughout the Arab world and beyond appear to be more open and sympathetic to a liberal, constitutional order. Increasingly, this generation has shown more interest in addressing economic and political grievances, including the issues of governmental competence, corruption, and growth, than grand ideological statements.[58]

The sudden eruption of these revolutionary movements has made it difficult to contain or deter such uprisings. The old order, built archaically around negotiation and collaboration with local autocrats, has fundamentally broken down. It is no longer cost-effective to back dictators. The time has come to underline the need for a more nuanced view of stability in the Middle East. The pursuit of a security template that suspends basic civil liberties is not only morally bankrupt, it also has become increasingly politically imprudent. The key issue is how not to be naive about the much-touted stability maintained by these autocratic but pro-West regimes while, at the same time, not isolating the masses on the Arab street.

A strategy of pressuring nondemocratic Arab regimes to introduce reforms will produce positive results. Although, from the US foreign policy standpoint, there are risks if the United States promotes reforms, those risks are far more manageable than the risks that will be run if Washington continues to support autocrats—the posture that has become an unfortunate staple of US foreign policy.

A US position of supporting political reforms will serve a dual purpose: it will (1) contain further unrest and uprisings in the region, and (2), more importantly, it will successfully reduce the capabilities of terrorist organizations—both financially and socially—to operate and recruit. The triumph by a peaceful popular movement in Egypt, getting rid of long-time autocrat Hosni Mubarak, has been a nightmare for groups such as al-Qaeda. For the United States, this may be a time of great promise for the much-vaunted, ongoing "campaign against terror," but only through diplomacy and promotion of human rights can the goal of a safer world be reached.

Throughout much of the post–World War II era, and especially since 9/11 and the war on terror, US foreign policy was fixated on refraining from direct interference with the way in which regional autocrats fashioned a ruling bargain with their people. With demonstrations flaring around the region, we are beginning to understand the depth of the political and socioeconomic crises that have been long brewing beneath that relatively placid surface. After Tunisia and Egypt now come Libya, Jordan, Bahrain, Morocco, Kuwait, Algeria, Iraq, Iran, the Palestinian Occupied Territories, and Yemen; there is a distinct possibility of even more daunting challenges ahead.

Not long ago, former US president Bill Clinton expressed deep regret to the people of Guatemala and El Salvador for US support for right-wing military regimes during the Cold War. In 1999, Clinton was remarkably forthcoming: The United States must not repeat the mistake of backing repressive forces. Contrast that with the Obama administration's response to protests in Libya: The White House's initial silence was deafening. At least in the initial stages of the Libyan uprising, US foreign policy continued to be beleaguered by ambiguities and incoherent propositions. As we face a transformative moment in the lives of many people who have lived under tyrannical rule for too long, there is a persistent need for new policies to take advantage of this unique opportunity—policies that reconcile US strategic interests with democratic reforms. Certainly, government transparency and a more effective distribution of oil and aid money toward infrastructure and education are the right places to start reform. Without such policies, the US government will be locked into supporting autocratic regimes while disingenuously voicing support for the democratic aspirations of their people—a policy already tried for far too long. If we are to defeat the threat of further unrest and instability in the region, this is the time to turn the page on the failed policies of the past.

The Obama Doctrine

The Obama administration's approach toward the Middle East region has relied more on dialogue and persuasion than unilateral and preemptive military measures reminiscent of Bush-era interventionist politics. The newly enunciated US position under the Obama administration, including stating that Israel is occupying "Palestine" and demanding that Israel halt the construction of settlements, were both emblematic of a new US policy toward the region. Equally salient has been the emphasis on diplomacy and development, as opposed to military adventures in the region.

Similarly, Obama's restrained reaction to events in Iran in the aftermath of that country's June 12, 2009, rigged presidential elections demonstrated that the new president supported Iran's civil society without undermining the country's sovereignty. Many experts have argued that explicit support by Obama for the opposition leader Mir-Hossein Mousavi would have jeopardized the internal legitimacy of the so-called green movement as well as Mousavi himself. It would have provided the Iranian clerical establishment with a pretext for imprisoning Mousavi as a traitor.[59]

Negotiating with Iran makes sense given Iran's new role as a major regional power. For its part, the Obama administration must understand the logic behind Iran's regional power and assets. The challenge for the US government is to give Iran incentives to reassess its strategy toward the United States. Neither a carrot-and-stick approach designed to halt progress on Iran's nuclear program nor democracy promotion will work. A better approach is a strategy of full engagement that addresses first and foremost common interests (defeating al-Qaeda and stabilizing Afghanistan and Iraq). Engagement could then move on to substantial areas of disagreement.[60]

Further economic pressure on Iran's economy will not bring about a solution. Employing diplomatic means and ways must not be equated with appeasement, thus antagonizing Iran's Arab neighbors, who might suspect that such US diplomatic concessions to Iran could ultimately help enhance Tehran's hegemonic ambitions in the region. In the aftermath of two regional wars, the main lesson to draw is that without the cooperation of central players such as Iran, the United States may utterly fail to stop terrorism. In the long run, the war against terror is a war without military solutions. Similarly, the US policy of selling arms to regional players, strengthening Sunnis or Shiites to the detriment of both and pitting one group against the other, is no solution. The old and familiar strategies of balancing power to maintain the status quo or using ethnic minorities to undermine a particular regime have backfired. Such strategies have proven dangerous and have been adeptly manipulated in various ways by the extremists on all sides. The only way to allay the fears of Iran's Arab neighbors regarding the former's rising power and to address Arab concerns about emerging sectarian tensions is to end regional ideological and power competition between Iran and its Arab neighbors. That could be managed, as President Obama has noted, by "tough and principled diplomacy."[61]

Blending idealism and pragmatism, the Obama vision of the US role in the emerging global political landscape is premised on a world of increasingly diffuse power where multilateral action is elevated to a "prerequisite status" for US international involvement.[62] US leadership, according to the Obama doctrine, though still often indispensable, must stand back in a world of emerging new powers. The use of US military power in the world's troubled spots must not be a first impulse but a last resort. Unless there is multilateralism, the United States cannot and will not act.[63] While the Obama administration supported, however hesitantly and belatedly, the departure of Tunisia's long-ruling authoritarian president Zine El Abidine Ben Ali on January 14, 2011, and subsequently facilitated the exit of Egyptian president Hosni Mubarak following the popular uprisings in Egypt, its reluctance to assume a lead role in NATO operations in Libya in relation to establishing a no-fly zone demonstrated that the doctrine of humanitarian intervention has not been fully embraced by this administration.

In much the same vein, the Obama administration refrained from opposing Saudi intervention in Bahrain to suppress the Shia's unarmed and democratic uprisings there. As a result, the sectarian divide between the Shia majority and the Sunni minority has deepened in Bahrain. The Arab states of the Gulf, experts concur, have amplified sectarian divisions in order to resist moves toward democratic reforms.[64] The Obama administration has returned to the all-too-familiar approach of supporting stability over democracy. While Arab awakening was welcomed and even encouraged in some situations, it was stifled in others. This continuing support for pro-American but authoritarian regimes has fostered resentment and more anti-US opposition in the region.

The Skeptics' Views

On a broader level, skeptics point to the history of US intervention in other parts of the world in the name of promoting democracy or fighting communist aggression in the postwar period: they see it as a dubious history at best. Consider, for example, the US interventions in the twentieth and early twenty-first centuries: Iran, Korea, Guatemala, Cuba, Laos, Vietnam, Cambodia, Grenada, Libya, El Salvador, Nicaragua, Panama, Somalia, Sudan, Yugoslavia, Afghanistan, and Iraq.[65] Differences persist over what kinds of reform must be implemented and how extensive they should be. What is clear is that the rhetorical appeal to democracy alone is unlikely to lead to a sustainable democratic transformation. A wide variety of questions have emerged regarding the method and content of reform, given the Middle East region's intricate historical and political milieu. There is also major disagreement over the issue of whether ending the long-running Israeli-Palestinian dispute is directly linked with pressing for more freedoms.

Throughout the Middle East, Muslims saw no virtue in the preemptive US attack against Iraq. Although they despised Saddam Hussein, as one observer notes, they perceived the goal of the US-led invasion in more sinister terms, as one that was driven by the motive of weakening the Arabs and Muslims and strengthening Israel. They accused the Bush administration of dealing with the consequences—not the causes—of terrorism. Arabs and Muslims more generally argued that terrorism was a response to US policies that have empowered autocratic regimes as well as Israeli and Zionist policies that have been harmful to Arabs and Muslims. These policies have generated violence and hatred. They noted that, instead of reexamining its own policies, the US government has blamed others for such violent outcomes.[66]

An examination of the views of different Islamic groups elucidates pervasive perceptions in the region. Conservative Islamists viewed the Bush doctrine with skepticism. They argued that the doctrine was bound to fail to resonate deeply with the Arab street, largely because of the widely held perception in the region that the Bush doctrine was a euphemism for war on Islam. They asserted that the United States was not the appropriate agent to initiate reform in a region where the US government has routinely supported authoritarian, pro-West regimes for both political and economic reasons since the mid-twentieth century. Protecting US access to oil and political regimes friendly to the United States, Islamic conservatives note, has long been the central premise around which US Middle East policy has taken shape. Highly suspicious of this democratic initiative, conservative Islamists take the view that the relationship between democracy and economic growth is an unproven one and that the United States is the wrong agent for promoting democracy in the region. The wave of protests and democratic change sweeping the MENA region has provided a unique opportunity for the Obama administration to recast US–Middle East relations in a new light. Aware of the fact that the status quo is unsustainable in the MENA region after the 2011 uprisings, Obama has proposed to realign US policy on the Middle East, considering a shift from decades of support for autocratic but pro-West regimes to backing for pro-democracy movements and pushing for an Israeli-Palestinian peace deal.

Some observers, Islamists as well as others, assert that it is the Arab-Israeli conflict—not internal reforms in the Arab world—that lies at the heart of the Arabs' lack of freedom. There is, in any case, widespread recognition that resolution of the Arab-Israeli conflict is at least as relevant as progress toward reform. The Palestinian issue has arguably become a matter of identity for the region's Arabs and non-Arab Muslims. "The contemporary political consciousness of the region," Shibley Telhami writes, "has been largely defined in relation to Israel and Palestine."[67]

Radical Islamic groups, such as the Wahhabis and Salafis, consider liberal democracy contrary to Islam, arguing that this type of democracy is an alien intrusion—part of the larger pernicious influence of the Great Satan and his cohorts.[68] These neocons advocate *ijtihad*—that is, Islamic reasoning in matters relating to Islamic law. Extremely devout and often puritanical, this group's goal is to "establish an Islamic state based on the comprehensive and rigorous application of the Shari'a."[69] Such radicals are not drawn exclusively from the ranks of the *ulama* (Islamic scholars). They regard the conservative approach, as represented by the orthodox ulama, as unrealistic, and they oppose modernist Islamic groups that emulate Western ideas, practices, and institutions that neoconservatives regard as alien to Islam.[70]

Islamic neoconservatives see the principal causes of the Muslim world's decline as colonialism, neocolonialism, and disunity within the Muslim world. They emphasize a constitution that is Islamic. Most of them view with skepticism the imposition of liberal democracy from outside. They argue that the greater Middle East initiative is a new ploy to gain access to oil—a pursuit that has figured prominently in US foreign policy toward the Middle East since the mid-twentieth century.

It is a fact that a major goal of US foreign policy has been to maintain access to foreign oil supplies, especially since 1971, when domestic oil production began its gradual decline. By 1996, the United States imported one-half of its oil.[71] By 2007, US oil imports hovered around roughly the same percentage. The Gulf countries supplied 21.19 percent of total US oil imports.[72]

Despite the very real differences between ideological positions in the Muslim world, what they all hold in common is a distrust for externally sponsored democratic reform movements. Hence, a direct approach in this direction from US foreign policy is problematic at best, and more likely doomed to elicit resistance from indigenous prodemocracy trends.

The Case for Peaceful Democratic Change

The pessimists' arguments are contested by the view, shared by some Muslims, that with the end of the Cold War, Western powers seem more committed to advancing a democratic order in the Arab world—at least in the hope that more inclusive governance could serve as an antidote to both religious extremism and terrorism. Today, there are more chances for sustainable democratic systems in the Arab world than ever before.[73] A worldwide commitment to democracy in the Muslim world, optimists argue, would doubtless empower Muslim democrats; whereas local and global pressures will render the cost of repression incredibly high.[74]

One observer notes that the Arab monarchies that committed themselves to reform and prepared the ground for gradual change—whether for pragmatic reasons or otherwise—tended to be more successful and were generally perceived in a better light.[75] The liberalization process in Arab monarchies has undoubtedly threatened to destabilize regimes in the short and medium terms. And yet, whenever ruling families recognized that their legitimacy was jeopardized, they quickly adopted such measures to preserve and protect their regimes. Where social issues such as women's rights, workers' rights, or general human rights strained a ruling family's abilities to govern a traditional society effectively, appropriate measures have quickly been taken to address them.[76]

A growing number of Muslims argue that the construction of civil society and democratic institutions should be seen as global and legitimizing efforts. Turkey's dominant party, the Party of Justice and Development (Adalet ve Kalkinma Partisi—AKP), although not the only party to criticize the US invasion of Iraq, is in fact an example of liberal Islam. Ali Bulaç, a Turkish Islamic thinker, argues that the superiority of Western principles and institutions such as human rights, democracy, the market economy, and the rule of law have gained near universal consensus. The debate is no longer over these principles and institutions; rather, it is about the unfair distribution of benefits derived from universal principles and institutions.[77]

The AKP has attempted to reconcile itself to the give-and-take nature of secular democracy. The courts' attempt to close down the democratically elected AKP on the grounds that the party has lifted a controversial ban on wearing headscarves in universities has raised serious questions about the future of democracy not only in Turkey but also in the entire Muslim world. The case for the censure of the AKP appeared to be based on a purely political maneuver with no grounding in law. The AKP has never sought an alternative to Kemalist secularism in

Islam; it seeks modern standards and institutions such as democracy, human rights, and the rule of law.[78] By seeking integration into the European Union, the AKP leadership seems to have practically abandoned the ideal of establishing an Islamic government in Turkey, as EU membership is certain to eliminate such a possibility.

On balance, liberal Islamists tend to appeal to women and more generally to the young in order to reconcile calls for reform with efforts to widen democratic participation. This may be, they suggest, an accident, but nevertheless it is a move that is consistent with a desire for democracy and the fulfillment of human rights among the masses. Seeking accommodation and engagement—not isolation—is in fact an effective way to construct democratic institutions and promote a democratic political culture. It should be noted that mounting US pressure for reform is widely appreciated by dissenting voices in the Arab world. While arguing that free, fair, and competitive elections are central to all types of reform, they also insist that a separation of state and religion is unacceptable and that laws made by elected parliaments must be compatible with Islamic law.[79] Many Islamic reformists question the US detention practices in Guantanamo Bay as well as human rights abuses of the prisoners at Abu Gharib prison in Iraq. They also question the US refusal to re-sign the convention for the International Criminal Court (ICC). They see US pressure for domestic reform in their countries contradictory to what US foreign policy dictates.

Secular Arab intellectuals and political leaders, who tend to embrace Western values and institutions, welcome the emphasis on liberty and freedom but warn against trying to impose Western models on Arab societies. In the past, secularists—divided between socialists and nationalists—have always spearheaded riots, peaceful antigovernment protests, strikes, revolution, and guerrilla warfare. Today, secularists are among the groups and factions who tend to support reform. Ironically, however, the leaders of many Middle Eastern countries fit this description. As ardent proponents of modernizing programs, they have fiercely resisted democratization programs, in part because such an agenda would jeopardize their political survival and in part because of Western powers' unwillingness to push for such changes given their interests in maintaining the status quo.

Consider, for example, the case of the Gulf monarchies, where there is abundant evidence that the rulers do intend to control any change and limit its extent. In Saudi Arabia, the 2005 municipal elections did not grant any real power to those elected beyond some functional matters of local importance, and for the most part their authority was counterbalanced by appointed members who composed the other half of the councils. The royal family exercises immense sway over key positions in the government.[80]

In Bahrain, a tiny island kingdom and new boiling pot, rhetoric and reality have clashed head-on. The government does not enjoy the same natural resources as its neighbors, thus it has been unable to buy off its opposition. It should come as no surprise that revealing details have come out about pockets of poverty in Bahrain—a country of fewer than a million people, known for being the center of banking in the Gulf region, that is in fact a generally wealthy country in terms of GNP per capita ($14,187). The Bahrain Centre for Human Rights has frequently reported that one-half of Bahraini citizens are suffering from poverty and poor living conditions. Many are unemployed.[81] While some beneficiaries of social aid are unable to work, others are employees with low income. Poverty is pervasive among the majority Shia population, which harbors deep socioeconomic and political grievances against a Sunni minority that rules with a tight grip.

Since 1783, Shiite Arabs in Bahrain have continuously lost their land and legal rights to Sunni Arabs. The Al-Khalifa family, which has ruled Bahrain for more than two hundred years, has conquered the land and seems to have no sense of sharing identities with local populations. The Al-Khalifa family has averted public demands for more participatory and accountable government since the 1950s. Constitutional reforms promised since the 1970s have not been kept. Hamad ibn Isa Al-Khalifa, the present ruler, promised reforms when he came to power in 2002, but nothing came of it. Bahraini officials offer citizenship to anyone who is willing to serve in the army and police department. This is done both as an attempt to reduce the Shia demographic preponderance and to repress the majority Shia—with the latter motive being the more significant.[82] Standing between Bahrain and the rest of the Gulf region since 1995 has been the US Navy's Fifth Fleet and a naval base in Manama, the country's capital. This security insurance has allowed the rulers of this archipelago to avoid the need to share the country's wealth with a poor majority.

Absent local reforms, such tensions are certain to have broader regional implications, intensifying Bahrain's existing Shia-Sunni divide. The United States and the United Kingdom have supported Bahrain's ruling family because it has allowed the United States to operate naval bases, assisting in preserving the status quo. Today's rising public frustrations, as manifested by new waves of unrest and protests, are fueled largely by young Shia groups. Crying out for dignity and a decent life, the protests are rarely, if ever, motivated by sectarian and religious factors, although the escalation of the security crisis in Bahrain could transform the nature of the protests along more sectarian lines. The deployment of forces from Saudi Arabia and the United Arab Emirates to help secure the country for the Sunni ruling family only further radicalizes the more religious segments within the Shia majority. Thus far, with the enforcement of several coercive measures, including the imprisonment of Shiite activists and members of civil society, as well as the suppression of assembly, Bahrain's Sunni rulers have launched a calculated campaign to intimidate supporters of the prodemocracy protest movement into submission. These measures, which have quashed uprisings for the time being, are likely to prove ineffective in the long term as sectarian tensions are bound to resurface again.

In Kuwait, on March 31, 2011, the cabinet resigned en masse when disputes erupted in the country's parliament, the Majlis Al-Umma, over the political unrest in neighboring Bahrain and the political turmoil sweeping the Middle East. Three cabinet ministers, members of the ruling Al Sabah family, resigned to avoid being questioned over why Kuwait did not send troops to the Saudi-led Gulf force that was sent to Bahrain. Such resignations are common in Kuwait, where despite the rising power of parliament, the Al Sabahs remain the ultimate arbiters and continue to eclipse successive cabinets. Political parties are banned.

It is similar in Qatar. One-third of the forty-five-member parliament is appointed by the emir; a two-thirds majority is needed to vote out ministers or to override decrees issued by the emir when parliament is not in session. Parliamentary power remains significantly hemmed in.[83] In Oman, the elected consultative council (the Majlis al-Shura) is balanced by the appointed state council (the Majlis al-Dawlah) and the confined scope of members' power. Key decisions are ultimately contingent upon the sultan's word.[84] In most of these monarchies, economic liberalization is unlikely to lead to democratization. If anything, liberalized autocracies often tend to resort to mechanisms of political decompression, cooptation, and divide-and-rule more generally.[85]

Can Democracy and Security Be Reconciled?

The relationship between democracy promotion and security enhancement is crucial to understanding the complexities of implementing democracy in the region today. Historically, as Rashid Khalidi writes, Western powers have never rendered the promotion of democracy integral to their Middle East policies. In fact, British and French policies were contingent on the negation of meaningful self-determination throughout the region—for example, in Palestine, Egypt, Algeria, Iraq, and Syria.[86]

Since the 1930s, the Western world has gained access to the region's oil resources more by working with dictators than with accountable democratic regimes. The 1953 coup in Iran is a notable case in point. The CIA and British agents, in collaboration with Iranian army generals, engineered a coup against the nationalist and constitutionally elected prime minister of Iran, Mohammad Mossadeq, who nationalized the Anglo-Iranian Oil Company. He was deposed and the shah was restored to power shortly afterward. US foreign policy between 1953 and 1978 stressed a special relationship with the shah and his inner circle, while largely disregarding the needs and demands of the Iranian masses. When, in the late 1970s, President Carter's concern for human rights had to be balanced against US support for the shah's repressive regime, the policy of having it both ways led to contradictory policies, causing the fall of the monarchy in the process.[87]

After 9/11 the Bush administration sent mixed signals to the Saudis. On the one hand, they argued that Saudi Arabia had done little to crack down on Islamic extremists. On the other hand, the then US secretary of state, Condoleezza Rice, praised Saudi officials for taking "some first step toward openness" in the holding of municipal elections. She however condemned denying women the right to vote and the arrest of nonviolent dissidents.[88] But Washington was reluctant to push the Saudi royal family beyond a certain point, fearing that the Saudi government was susceptible to Islamist opposition movements. Moreover, the Saudis played, and continue to play, a constructive role in determining oil production and prices, in advancing the Arab-Israeli peace process, and in supporting the reconstruction of Iraq.

The Bush administration permitted its war on terrorism to dilute its democracy-promotion efforts in such key countries as Pakistan, Saudi Arabia, and Kuwait.[89] Many countries around the world were using the US-led campaign against terror as a pretense to justify the repression of dissenting voices and activities, including nonviolent ones. The United States lifted restrictions on military aid for countries that expressed support for the "war on terrorism," particularly those with large Muslim populations.[90]

The United States adopted an approach toward Egypt that was similar to its approach to Saudi Arabia. Secretary Rice also praised Egyptian president Hosni Mubarak for taking "encouraging" first steps toward democracy promotion, but she insisted that "Egypt's elections, including Parliamentary elections, must meet objective standards that define every free election, including freedom of assembly, speech and press."[91] She nevertheless refused to meet with the leaders of the outlawed Islamist organization the Muslim Brotherhood (Ikhwan-ul-Muslemeen), even though it was believed to be the most popular opposition group.[92]

Given Egypt's critical roles in the Egyptian-Israeli peace treaty and in working to resolve the Israeli-Palestinian conflict, the Bush administration was very cautious about pushing Mubarak to democratize Egypt's political system. While the Bush administration urged the Egyptian and Saudi governments to press for democracy, it continued to provide them with arms and funds because they were generally regarded as allies in the war on terror and crucial to the region's stability.[93]

The United States is often resented for propping up dictatorial and corrupt regimes rather than prodding them to change their ways.[94] Osama bin Laden was the price of a US victory over the Soviet Union in Afghanistan.[95] With the active encouragement of the CIA and Pakistan's Inter-Services Intelligence (ISI), the mujahidin played a significant part in dislodging Soviet troops from Afghanistan in the 1980s. The Taliban's rise to power in Afghanistan by the mid-1990s was made possible by Pakistan's ISI, which in turn was influenced by the CIA. The actions of the Taliban at that time largely served US geopolitical interests.[96]

The task of reconciling democracy with security is generally seen as the weakest link of US foreign policy. Skeptical analysts argue that embarking on democratic experiments in the context of deep ethnic divisions and sectarian cleavages fraught with social division and insecurity is a fundamentally flawed strategy.[97] Take the example of Lebanon. Far from the democracy promotion that the Bush administration had claimed the elections would effect, elections there have revealed the underlying sectarian divisions that have characterized Lebanese politics under Syrian occupation for a long time.[98] Syrians continue to wield considerable clout in Lebanon. They could indeed make things difficult for Lebanon if the new government moves to further sever the decades-old bonds with Damascus.[99] The agreement reached in Qatar in May 2008 ended an eighteen-month chaos hovering over that nation's politics.

Many Lebanese fear that uprisings and religious tensions in Syria could spill over into Lebanon. The escalating violence against Syria's Sunni community might contribute to instability in Lebanon, especially in northern Lebanon where there is a delicate balance between the Sunni and Alawite communities. The flow of Syrian refugees across the border also means economic trouble for Lebanon, as the country can barely deal with existing Palestinian and Iraqi refugees. A change in the Syrian regime—or even its weakening—would bear negative consequences for the Syria-Hezbollah alliance and disrupt its arms trade route to Iran, leaving the coalition in a vulnerable position.[100]

Of the Lebanese cabinet's thirty ministers, sixteen of them supported the prime minister, Fouad Siniora; eleven were supporters of the opposition grouping, which included Hezbollah. This gave Hezbollah and the opposition allies of the Shiite militants more than one-third of the cabinet seats, affording the opposition parties enough control in the government to have veto power over legislation. Shortly after the Doha accord, Lebanon's parliament elected as president the army chief, General Michel Suleiman, who was the declared consensus candidate of both the country's major parties. Under Lebanon's complex power-sharing system, the president is always a Maronite Christian, the prime minister a Sunni Muslim, and the speaker of parliament a Shiite Muslim. Caught between major international and regional forces—with the West and Saudi Arabia on one side and Syria and Iran on the other—Lebanese politics remain in the grip of complicated and uncertain political challenges in the coming years.[101]

How significant is electoral politics in stalled transitions in Yemen and Jordan? One expert argues that elections typically are not important, given that in Jordan, for instance, the electoral system is structured so as to generate particular results. In the early 1990s, new legislation was introduced whereby anything passed by the lower house has to be approved by the appointed upper house. This ensured that nothing can be approved by the legislators without the king's approval. In short, the king may never need to use the veto.[102] In Yemen, one has to be either in the ruling party or be out of power. There is one ruling party, and the Islamist party, Islah (Reform), has to either ally with the ruling party or become a loyal opposition.[103] Outside the sphere of electoral politics, Islamists and leftists engage in cooperative activity on a number of specific issues.[104]

In the Palestine territories, the unintended consequences of a sudden opening of the political system made the Bush doctrine inconsistent and less cohesive. The victory of the Islamic militant group Hamas in the January 2006 parliamentary elections delivered a mortal blow to Mahmoud Abbas's powers as the Palestinian president. The rift between Hamas and Fatah clearly fueled tensions between moderate secular and Islamist nationalist movements in the territories.

Western sanctions imposed on Hamas after its victory, including ending funding for the Palestinians in the occupied territories, coupled with Israel's halting of tax revenues, further spawned the interfactional dispute among Palestinians. Equally contentious was Abbas's refusal to surrender control of security to Hamas. In the ensuing tensions between Israel and Gaza residents, the Israelis created a humanitarian crisis by closing the borders. The United Nations and the International Committee of the Red Cross warned of an impending humanitarian disaster, caused by closed border crossings with Israel and Egypt, a shortage of basic food and commodities, and poor water supplies and sanitation. More than 80 percent of Gaza's population relies on humanitarian assistance, with UN food aid reaching approximately 1.1 million people. A high proportion of these people are children.[105] Gaza has a young population, with almost 48 percent of the population below age fourteen.[106]

With revolutionary fervor sweeping the Middle East and North Africa, Israel faces a UN vote in September 2011, welcoming the state of Palestine as a member whose territory includes all of the West Bank, Gaza, and East Jerusalem. This will have various legal and political consequences for Israel in the years to come. The Palestinians see Israel as more isolated than ever before, and they believe that this move can strengthen their hand in future negotiations with Israel. This may turn out to be effective diplomatic maneuvering on the part of the Palestinian leadership if Fatah and Hamas can close the gap between their differing political and ideological positions vis-à-vis Israel and maintain some semblance of unity through the process.

* * *

The Bush administration policy of democracy promotion as part of a new regional transformation was eventually employed as a justification for the invasion of Iraq. This policy proved fraught with risk and difficulty. Western supporters of democracy promotion, who abruptly elevated democratization as a panacea for the ills of Muslim societies, have since arrived at a modest conclusion: democratization is a complicated and difficult process that entails numerous uncertain consequences.

In the post-9/11 era, a neoconservative idea of unilateral preemptive attack and military intervention was justified as a global moralism of sorts. But throughout the Middle East, the neoconservatives' idea of reshaping the Middle East in their own image was viewed with outright and widespread skepticism, in large part because it reinforced perceptions of imperialism and orientalism.[107] Today, this Western moral crusade continues to face countervailing challenges by daily television coverage of the US-led occupations of Afghanistan and Iraq, US support of authoritarian regimes in the region, and the suppression of popular political movements such as Hezbollah and Hamas.[108]

Increasingly, however, the promotion of democracy risks being discredited especially when it is naively equated with regime change through military force.[109] Throughout the Middle East, political inclusion is seemingly the key to any meaningful dialogue between Islamists and secularists. In many cases, a process of political opening and inclusion, properly calibrated, would bolster stability and moderation in the long run, even as it empowers Islamic groups.[110] The 2011 popular uprisings in the Middle East and North Africa have shown that the road to building a secure and stable region is through peaceful democratic change and economic development. Democracies are likely to grow in a climate of socioeconomic security. While it is too early to interpret the meaning of these uprisings, it is even more difficult to foretell whether the current ferment could fundamentally reshape the region by bringing real and lasting democratic change. This is largely due to the fact that revolutionary changes are not only slow to emerge but usually take many years to become fully operative, and even then modest gains may be incremental and fractious—if not reversed. Whether these revolutionary movements, led by youth organizations and facilitated by social networking tools paired with information technology, will prevail over well-entrenched institutions (such as the army and old bureaucracies and power structures), vested interests of privileged classes, and traditional Islamist groups remains to be seen.

Although a visionary pathway for democracy promotion can be mapped, it is a mistake to exaggerate its priority in view of other competing interests. There exists no uniform model toward democracy promotion in the region. Success in confronting terrorism will depend on the ability of policymakers to understand its deeper roots. It may be practical to demand a higher standard of respect for human rights in Middle Eastern countries, especially in relation to the rights of women, minorities, and children. It is clear that the old bargain with the Arab autocracies is no longer operative. Externally enforced democratization is likely to evoke resistance and reaction, both from the political regimes and adherents of cultural and Islamic traditions. There are both sound diplomatic and analytic reasons to believe that democracy is most likely to last, not because of US intervention, but when it is the outcome of a long process of internal political and socioeconomic change.[111]

For change to be sustainable, the pace of democratic transformation must be gradual, systematic, and directly linked to homegrown movements. While President Obama has embraced the notion of democracy promotion in the Middle East and North Africa, as evidenced in the cases of Tunisia and Egypt, he has adopted an inconsistent approach toward that idea. The policy is still to give primacy to geostrategic considerations over moral principles and commitments. The president's Afghanistan strategy, which entails a more limited view of the global war on terrorism and a much narrower definition of US national interests, stands in stark contrast to that of his predecessor. He has narrowed the scope of the mission: it is now limited to defeating and dismantling al-Qaeda in Afghanistan.[112]

I now turn to demonstrating how the US invasion of Iraq has strengthened the position of some authoritarian regimes in the region. The next chapter centers on how Iran and Syria have become the major beneficiaries of the instability in Iraq. Arguably, for reasons of both regional stability and the requirement to defeat al-Qaeda, it may be warranted to seek regional diplomatic cooperation.

Notes

1. This chapter is a substantially modified version of the earlier Mahmood Monshipouri, "The Bush Doctrine and Democracy Promotion in the Middle East," in David P. Forsythe, Patrice C. McMahon, and Andrew Wedeman, eds., *American Foreign Policy in a Globalized World* (New York: Routledge, 2006), pp. 313–334.

2. Kenneth Roth, "Despots Masquerading as Democrats," *Journal of Human Rights Practice* 1, no. 1 (March 2009): 140–155; see esp. pp. 140–141.

3. Ibid., p. 155.

4. William B. Quandt, "New US Policies for a New Middle East," in David W. Lesch, ed., *The Middle East and the United States: A Historical and Political Assessment*, 4th ed., (Boulder, CO: Westview Press, 2007), pp. 493–503; see p. 503.

5. Ibid., p. 502.

6. Ellen Lust-Okar and Saloua Zerhouni, eds., *Political Participation in the Middle East* (Boulder, CO: Lynne Rienner, 2008).

7. Saloua Zerhouni, "Looking Forward," in Lust-Okar and Zerhouni, *Political Participation*, pp. 259–266; see p. 265.

8. Daniel Neep, "Dilemmas of Democratization in the Middle East: The Forward Strategy of Freedom," *Middle East Policy* 11, no. 3 (Fall 2004): 73–84; see esp. pp. 74–75.

9. Rashid Khalidi, *Resurrecting Empire: Western Footprints and America's Perilous Path in the Middle East* (Boston: Beacon Press, 2004), p. 43.

10. Carol C. Gould, *Globalizing Democracy and Human Rights* (Cambridge: Cambridge University Press, 2004), p. 259.

11. Henry Munson, "Lifting the Veil: Understanding the Roots of Islamic Militancy," in Helen E. Purkitt, ed., *World Politics*, Annual Editions, 26th ed. (Dubuque, IA: McGraw-Hill/Dushkin, 2006), pp. 179–181.

12. President Bush's speech at the 20th anniversary, National Endowment for Democracy, US Chamber of Commerce, Washington, DC, November 6, 2003; available at http://www.cdhr.info/aquote 11060301.asp; accessed June 2, 2005.

13. Quoted in Julie A. Mertus, *Bait and Switch: Human Rights and US Foreign Policy* (New York: Routledge, 2004), p. 63.

14. Ibid.

15. Eva Bellin, "The Iraqi Intervention and Democracy in Comparative Historical Perspective," *Political Science Quarterly* 119, no. 4 (Winter 2004–05): 595–608; see p. 595.

16. Khalidi, *Resurrecting Empire*, p. 39.

17. Michel Gobat, *Confronting the American Dream: Nicaragua under US Imperial Rule* (Duke, NC: Duke University Press, 2005).

18. Bellin, "The Iraqi Intervention," p. 599.

19. Ibid., pp. 601–603.

20. Alan Richards, "Democracy in the Arab Region: Getting There from Here," *Middle East Policy* 12, no. 2 (Summer 2005): 28–35; see esp. p. 30.

21. Ibid., p. 30.

22. Ibid., p. 31.

23. Ibid., p. 33.

24. Ibid.

25. James A. Bill and Robert Springborg, *Politics in the Middle East*, 4th ed. (New York: HarperCollins College, 1994), p. 27. See also Khalidi, *Resurrecting Empire*, p. 71.

26. Marina Ottaway et al., "Democratic Mirage in the Middle East, 2002," in Thomas Carothers, *Critical Mission: Essays on Democracy Promotion* (Washington, DC: Carnegie Endowment for International Peace, 2004), pp. 229–236; see p. 236.

27. Kenneth Jost and Benton Ives-Halperin, "Democracy in the Arab World," in CQ Researchers, *Global Issues*, 2005 ed. (Washington, DC: CQ Press, 2005), p. 190.

28. Nathan J. Brown and Dina Bishara, "Kuwaitis Vote for a New Parliament . . . and Maybe a New Electoral System," Carnegie Endowment for International Peace, pp. 1–5; see esp. p. 4; available at http://www.carnegie endowment.org/files/Kuwait_final.pdf; accessed March 5, 2010.

29. Joel Brinkley, "US Faults 4 Allies over Forced Labor," *New York Times*, June 4, 2005, p. A5.

30. Cited in Carl Gershman, "Democracy as Policy Goal and Universal Value," *Whitehead Journal of Diplomacy and International Relations* 6, no. 1 (Winter–Spring 2005): 19–38; see esp. p. 22.

31. Ibid., p. 22.

32. United Nations Development Programme, *The Arab Human Development Report, 2002: Creating Opportunities for Future Generations* (New York: UNDP, 2002), p. 52. Also see UNDP, *Human Development Report, 2004: Cultural Liberty in Today's Diverse World* (New York: UNDP, 2004); see esp. pp. 225–237.

33. Ibid., p. 98.

34. See the report by the Canadian International Development Agency (CIDA), "Support to Gender Equality in the Middle East Region: Jordan, Lebanon, West Bank and Gaza, and Yemen"; available at http://www.acdicida.gc.ca/cidaweb/webcountry.nsf/VLUDocEn/NorthAfricana ndMiddleEast; accessed June 6, 2005.

35. Zbigniew Brzezinski, "Hegemonic Quicksand," *The National Interest* 74 (Winter 2003–2004): 5–16; see esp. p. 13.

36. Ibid., p. 6.

37. Mustafa Zahrani, "September 11, Globalization, and the US Hegemony," in Mohammad Javad Zarif and Mustafa Zahrani, eds., *The New International Trends* (Tehran: Office of Political and International Studies, 2005), pp. 1–61; see esp. p. 48.

38. "A Roundtable on 'The European Union and Islamic Fundamentalism: Challenges and Policies,'" *Discourse: An Iranian Quarterly* 5, no. 4 (Spring 2004): 1–16; see esp. p. 3.

39. Douglas J. Feith, "On the Global War on Terrorism," in John T. Rourke, *Clashing Views on Controversial Issues in World Politics*, 12th ed. (Guilford, CT: McGraw Hills/Dushkin, 2006), pp. 232–236.

40. Condoleezza Rice, "Rethinking the National Interest: American Realism for a New World," *Foreign Affairs* 87, no. 4 (July–August 2008): 2–26; see esp. 12.

41. Marina Ottaway and Thomas Carothers, "The Greater Middle East Initiative: Off to a False Start," *Policy Brief*, Carnegie Endowment for International Peace, no. 29 (March 2004): 1–8; see esp. p. 2.

42. Eva Bellin, "Coercive Institutions and Coercive Leaders," in Marsha Pripstein Posusney and Michelle Penner Angrist, eds., *Authoritarianism in the Middle East: Regimes and Resistance* (Boulder, CO: Lynne Rienner, 2005), pp. 21–41; see pp. 36–38.

43. Ibid.

44. Cairo Institute for Human Rights Studies, *Bastion of Impunity, Mirage of Reform*, Human Rights in the Arab Region, annual report, 2009, Cairo, 2009, pp. 178–179.

45. Ibid., p. 179.

46. Ibid.

47. Richard Youngs, "Dicing with Democracy," *World Today*, July 2009, pp. 7–9; see esp. p. 9.

48. This section is based on Mahmood Monshipouri and Ali Assareh, "The Islamic Republic and the 'Green Movement': Coming Full Circle," *Middle East Policy* 16, no. 4 (Winter 2009): 27–46; see esp. pp. 39–40.

49. Shane D'Aprile, "Operation New Media," *Politics* (April 2009), pp. 26–37; see esp. pp. 28–37.

50. Central Intelligence Agency, *World Factbook*; available at https://www.cia.gov/library/publications/the-world-factbook/geos/ir.html; accessed August 3, 2009.

51. "ICT Statistics Newslog—Iran Subscriber Growth Still Going Strong but Signs of a Slowdown," International Telecommunications Union, July 27, 2009; available at http://www.itu.int/ITU-D/ict/newslog/Iran+Subscriber +Growth+Still+Going+Strong+But+Signs+Of+A+Slowdown.aspx; accessed August 12, 2009.

52. See the reactions to Darrell West, "The Two Faces of Twitter: Revolution in a Digital Age," *Huffington Post*, June 22, 2009; reactions by Nicola Colbran, "Twitter and YouTube: Positive Developments for Human Rights Protection?" Shareen Hertel, "Protest, Iranian Style: A Two-Way Conversation?" and Anja Mihr, "Iran: Who Is Quicker—the Hacker or the Twitter?" *Human Rights and Human Welfare*, August 2009; available at http://www.du.edu/korbel /hrhw/news/index.html. accessed August 3, 2009.

53. Robin Wright, "Fighting Back," *Time*, August 10, 2009, p. 43.

54. Darrell West, "The Two Faces of Twitter: Revolution in a Digital Age," *Huffington Post*, June 22, 2009; available at http://www.huffingtonpost.com /darrell-west/the-two-faces-of-twitter_b_218734.htm; accessed August 3, 2009.

55. David Pryce-Jones, "Green Flags and Brown Shirts," *National Review*, July 6, 2009, pp. 16–17.

56. Fouad Ajami, "Demise of the Dictators," *Newsweek*, February 14, 2011, pp. 18–27.

57. For an excellent analysis, see, "The Arab Revolutions and Human Rights," *Human Rights and Human Welfare*; available at http://www.du.edu /korbel/hrhw/roundtable/2011/panel-a/01-2011/arabrevolution.html; accessed February 21, 2011.

58. Fareed Zakaria, "How Democracy Can Work in the Middle East," *Time*, Feb. 3, 2011; available at http://www.time.com/time/world/article /0,8599,2045888-4,00.html; accessed Feb. 14, 2011.

59. Mariano Aguirre, "Democracy-Promotion: Doctrine vs. Dialogue," *Open Democracy*, July 14, 2009; available at http://www.opendemocracy.net/article /idea/democracy-promotion-doctrine-vs-dialogue; accessed July 28, 2009.

60. Mohsen M. Milani, "Tehran's Take: Understanding Iran's US Policy," *Foreign Affairs* 88, no. 4 (July–August, 2009): 46–62; see esp. pp. 60–62.

61. Mahmood Monshipouri, *US-Iran Relations: Embracing a New Realism*, 77 Emirates Lecture Series, Emirates Center for Strategic Studies and Research, Abu Dhabi, UAE, 2009; see esp. pp. 34–35.

62. Howard Lafranchi, "Obama: Dawn of a Doctrine?" *Christian Science Monitor,* April 11, 2011, pp. 16–18; see esp. p. 18.

63. Ibid., p. 17.

64. Kristin Smith Diwan, "The Failed Revolution," Middle East Policy Council, March 31, 2011; available at http://mepc.org/articles-commentary /commentary/failed-revolution; accessed April 21, 2011.

65. Joseph P. Lawrence, "Some Questions about Freedom," *Zaman Daily News*, Zaman Online; available at http://www.zaman.com/include/yazdir .php?b1=commentary&trh=2005050&hn=16706; accessed May 2, 2005.

66. Yvonne Yazbeck Hadda, "Islamist Perceptions of US Policy in the Middle East," in Lesch, *The Middle East and the United States*, p. 525.

67. Shibley Telhami, *The Stakes: American and the Middle East: The Consequences of Power and the Choice for Peace* (Boulder, CO: Westview Press, 2002), p. 101.

68. Bernard Lewis, "Freedom and Justice in the Modern Middle East," *Foreign Affairs* 84, no. 3 (May–June 2005): 36–51; see esp. p. 48.

69. Ottaway and Carothers, "The Greater Middle East Initiative," pp. 125–130.

70. Ibid., p. 93.

71. Mary H. Cooper, "Oil Production in the Twenty-first Century," in *Global Issues: Selections from the CQ Researcher* (Washington, DC: CQ Press/Congressional Quarterly, 2001), pp. 113–131; see p. 117.

72. This information is based on http://dunner99.blogspot.com/2008/06/update-how-much-oil-does-america-import.html; accessed February 28, 2010.

73. Saad Eddin Ibrahim, "Arab Liberal Legacies Full Circle," in Shireen T. Hunter and Huma Malik, eds., *Modernization, Democracy, and Islam* (Westport, CT: Praeger, 2005), pp. 205–220; see p. 219.

74. Moataz A. Fattah, *Democratic Values in the Muslim World* (Boulder, CO: Lynne Rienner, 2006), pp. 135–144.

75. Joseph A. Kechichian, *Power and Succession in Arab Monarchies: A Reference Guide* (Boulder, CO: Lynne Rienner, 2008), p. 419.

76. Ibid., p. 420.

77. For further perspective on Ali Bulac's ideas, see Wendy Kristianasen, "New Faces of Islam," *Le Monde Diplomatique*; available at http://mondediplo.com/1997/07/turkey; accessed June 23, 2005.

78. Ihsan Dagi, "Turkey's AKP in Power," *Journal of Democracy* 19, no. 3 (July 2008): 25–30; see esp. p. 28.

79. Ottaway and Carothers, "The Greater Middle East Initiative," p. 2.

80. Gerd Nonneman, "Political Reform in the Gulf Monarchies: From Liberalization to Democratization? A Comparative Perspective," in Anoushiravan Ehteshami and Steven M. Wright, eds., *Reform in the Middle East Oil Monarchies* (Reading, Berkshire, UK: Ithaca Press, 2008), pp. 3–45; see p. 28.

81. See, for example, "Half of Bahraini Citizens Are Suffering from Poverty and Poor Living Conditions," Bahrain Center for Human Rights, September 24, 2004; available at http://www.bahrainrights.org/node/199.

82. Michael Hudson, "Crackdown in Bahrain: Notes from the Field," *Al-Jazeera*, March 21, 2011; available at http://english.aljazeera.net/indepth/opinion/2011/03/201132111471720661.html; accessed March 22, 2011.

83. Ibid., p. 29.

84. Ibid.

85. Ibid., p. 30. In this context a reference is made to Daniel Brumburg's notion of "liberalized autocracy" in rentier states of the Persian Gulf region.

86. Khalidi, *Resurrecting Empire*, pp. 16–25.

87. For further analysis of the contradictory policies of the United States toward the Middle East, see Mahmood Monshipouri, "The Paradoxes of US Foreign Policy in the Middle East," *Middle East Policy* 9, no. 3 (September 2002): 65–84; see esp. p. 72.

88. Steven R. Weisman, "Rice Challenges Saudi Arabia and Egypt on Democracy Issues," *New York Times*, June 20, 2005; available at http://www.nytimes.com/2005/06/20/international/middleeast/20cnd-diplo.html; accessed June 20, 2005.

89. This point is particularly emphasized by Harold Hongju Koh, the former assistant secretary of state for human rights in the Clinton administration. See

Julie A. Mertus, *Bait and Switch: Human Rights and US Foreign Policy* (New York: Routledge, 2004), p. 64.

90. Ibid., p. 67.

91. Weisman, "Rice Challenges Saudi Arabia."

92. Ibid.

93. Benjamin R. Barber, "Democracy Cannot Coexist with Bush's Failed Doctrine of Preventive War," *Los Angeles Times*, December 3, 2003; available at http://www.globalpolicy.org/empire/analysis/2003/1203democracy.htm; accessed June 9, 2005.

94. Augustus Richard Norton, "America's Approach to the Middle East: Legacies, Questions, and Possibilities, *Current History*, January 2002, pp. 3–7; see esp. p. 4.

95. Noam Chomsky, "United States, Global Bully: Terrorism, Weapon of the Powerful"; available at http://www.matrixmasters.com/wtc/chomsky/bolly/bolly.htm—an edited extract of a talk Chomsky gave at the Massachusetts Institute of Technology on October 18, 2001.

96. Michel Chossudovsky, "Who Is Osama Bin Laden?" *Global Dialogue* 3, no. 4 (Autumn 2001): 1–7; see p. 5.

97. Eva Bellin, "Democratization and Its Discontents: Should America Push Political Reform in the Middle East?" *Foreign Affairs* 87, no. 4 (July–August 2008): 112–119; see esp. p. 115.

98. Chris Talbot, "Swing to Right-Wing Christian Leader Aoun in Lebanese Elections," *World Socialist Web Site*, June 17, 2005; available at http://www.wsws.org/articles/2005/jun2005/leb-j17.shtml; accessed June 29, 2005.

99. P. V. Vivekanand, "Lebanese Elections: An American Roulette," *Panorama: Gulf Today*, June 3–9, 2005, pp. 18–23; see esp. p. 23.

100. Michelle Bouchebel, "Syria's Uprisings Deepens Lebanon's Instability," *Policymic: New Generation News and Politics*, available at http://www.policymic.com/articles/syria-s-uprising-deepens-lebanon-s-instability; accessed on August 21, 2011.

101. Crispin Thorold, "Divided Lebanon Forges New Future," *BBC News*, July 11, 2008' available at http://news.bbc.co.uk/2/hi/middle_east/7503008.stm; accessed July 31, 2008.

102. Ottaway et al., "Democratic Mirage"; see comments by Jillian Schwedler, p. 5.

103. Ibid., p. 6.

104. Ibid.

105. "Fuel Crisis Halts Food Aid," *BBC News*, April 24, 2008; available at http://news.bbc.co.uk/2/hi/middle_east/7364172.stm; accessed July 31, 2008.

106. "Gaza Strip Demographics Profile 2007," *Index Mundi*; available at http://www.indexmundi.com/gaza_strip/demographics_profile.htm; accessed July 31, 2008.

107. Steven M. Wright, "US Foreign Policy and the Changed Definition of Gulf Security," in Anoushiravan Esteshami and Steven M. Wright, eds., *Reform in the Middle East Oil Monarchies* (Reading, Berkshire, UK: Ithaca Press, 2008), pp. 229–245; see p. 244.

108. Iason Athanasaidis, "How the Best and the Brightest Plan to Fight Terrorism," *Christian Science Monitor*, July 29, 2008, p. 9.

109. Kenneth Roth, "Filling the Leadership Void: Where Is the European Union?" Human Rights Watch, *World Report 2007: Events of 2006* (New York: Human Rights Watch, 2007), pp. 1–32; see esp. p. 4.

110. Bellin, "Democratization and Its Discontents," p. 119.

111. Gideon Rachman, "Democracy: The Case for Opportunistic Idealism," *Washington Quarterly* 32, no. 1 (2009): 119–127; see esp. p. 126.

112. Howard LaFranchi and Robert Marquand, "The New Realism," *Christian Science Monitor*, January 17, 2010, pp. 26–31; see esp. p. 27.

5

Diplomacy:
Seeking Long-Term Solutions

What is the appropriate response to terrorism? What are the elements of a proper strategy to fight terrorism? It is difficult to determine what is the most important ingredient in dealing with this scourge. Confronting terrorism, violent extremism, and similar asymmetric threats will require, in the long term, a range of diplomatic skills and resources, including international cooperation and law enforcement, in addition to military capabilities. The long-range goal of the Western world should be to promote diplomatic tools and cooperative law enforcement. Whether such a path is chosen depends largely on the international community and its commitment to enforcing the rule of law.

The answer to the question of whether to resort to force or diplomacy is virtually always linked to the issue of capabilities, appropriateness, effectiveness, and consequences. We have already examined the limits of military action against terrorists. No military intervention in the Middle East is feasible for bringing about the resolution of the problems there, although such intervention has established US dominance in the area.

The challenge for the future will be to combine military power with diplomacy in a region that can no longer be divorced from the broader issues of the Middle East, international politics, and the global economy.[1] William B. Quandt, one of the architects of the first Camp David negotiations, writes that while in the past the justification for US diplomatic efforts was often that they would promote stability, enhance pro-American regimes, and help to avoid conflicts that could prove costly to the United States, today the rationale may be that Israeli-Palestinian peace could be one effective means of reversing the rising tide of anti-American sentiment in the Muslim world, that it might reduce the number of recruits for extremist political groups and organizations, and that it might expedite the spread of democracy and political reforms.[2]

Many years of war and uncertainty in Palestine, Lebanon, Afghanistan, and Iraq have proven that pursuing diplomacy is inevitable. The wisest path to peace—politically and legally—is diplomacy and engagement. Bringing to justice those responsible for perpetrating acts of violence against innocent civilians is the most desirable method within the broader context of seeking international peace. But relying on diplomatic means and strategies to defuse political tensions is just as desirable. Multilateral diplomacy and cooperation will optimize the opportunity to combat terror. Counterterrorism measures also require international cooperation and resolve.[3]

Gareth Evans, president of the independent Brussels-based International Crisis Group, nicely captures the ineffectiveness of the so-called war on terror: "The most visible product of the war on terrorism so far has been more war and more terrorism."[4] The resolution of the Israeli-Palestinian conflict, rather than the occupation and democratization of Iraq, would help democratization in the region. Western governments must be seen as willing to address the legitimate political grievances— the occupation of Palestine and Iraq—of the people who live in the Middle East.[5] Some observers have directly linked the failure of the Iraq War to a failure in use of the war to facilitate progress on the Israeli-Palestinian front.[6] Before launching the war in Iraq, the United States failed to undertake the necessary diplomatic and coalition-building measures and grossly miscalculated its capacity to perform nation-building tasks in parts of the world it does not understand very well.[7]

What is more, excluding Iran and Syria, key regional players, from negotiations over the future of Iraq brings to the forefront, yet again, serious doubts about the capabilities of US policymakers to carry on a sustainable campaign against terror. Discussion with states such as Syria and Iran can resolve ongoing tensions in the region. Sanctions on these two countries have failed to undermine their ruling regimes. Ironically, but understandably, the US invasion of Iraq has strengthened the position of these regimes. Emerging as a dominant regional power, Iran has solidified its powers internally, whereas Syrian leadership has invariably become the major beneficiary of the instability in Iraq. Whatever the outcomes in Syria and Iran, they both could serve as a conduit for intelligence sharing, thereby becoming pragmatic partners along the way.

US Hegemony and the Failure of Unilateralism

As is evident by uncertainties and tensions surrounding the invasions of Iraq and Afghanistan, Washington's effort to remake the politics of the region has met with fierce resistance. Although the United States has succeeded in pushing Saudi Arabia to cooperate more actively in the war on terror, it has not been equally effective in pressuring Iran for major changes in its regional state behavior. The multipolar world of the post–Cold War era has in fact necessitated an entirely different US foreign policy—one that is in line with the emergence of a complex form of power-sharing at both the global and regional levels. A decade-long sanctions regime on Iraq following the US-led eviction of Iraqi forces from Kuwait in 1991 wreaked devastating effects on the Iraqi civilian population without undermining the regime. This crisis, along with the continued Israeli occupation of the Palestinian territories and the US policy of "dual containment" of Iraq and Iran, contributed to the growing hostility toward the United States in Arab and Muslim public opinion.[8]

The euphoric unilateralism of the early 1990s, embraced shortly after the downfall of the Soviet Union by a small but influential group of hawkish US officials known as neoconservatives, led to a weakening of the long-standing transatlantic alliance. The most hawkish of the neocons were intent on creating a new security architecture by using force and, more importantly, imposing their moral vision. In addition to running counter to historical evidence that previous efforts by Western powers to dominate this region had proved both costly and temporary, this view entirely ignored indigenous ideas of regional experiments in collective security such as the League of Arab States and the Gulf Cooperation Council (GCC). Further, it rejected Iran's perennial position that Gulf security should be the sole concern of the littoral countries of the Gulf on both the Arab and Iranian sides.[9]

The trouble with US intervention in the affairs of lesser states, as historians remind us, was seemingly twofold: (1) it allocated insufficient resources to the nonmilitary aspects of the project, and (2) it attempted economic and political transformation in an unrealistically short time frame. The worst failures—in Haiti, Cuba, and Vietnam—were due in part to this disastrous blend of inadequate resources for nonmilitary purposes and a truncated time horizon. It should have come as no surprise when potentially the same tragedy began to repeat itself in the Balkans, Afghanistan, and Iraq.[10] The fact remains that moral appeals have become inextricably intertwined with power considerations on the global scene. Power is dispersed, and real power for the United States may come to depend on having credibility in the eyes of other powers and legitimacy in the eyes of its own people. Lasting global supremacy may hinge on the competent deployment of an increasingly elusive resource: moral authority.[11]

Diplomacy and the Israeli-Palestinian Conflict

Critics of US foreign policy toward Israel point out that the limits to US power vis-à-vis the Israeli-Palestinian conflict are illustrative of failed US policies. John Mearsheimer and Stephen Walt argue that while a case can be made—albeit not emphatically—that subsidizing and protecting Israel may have been a net plus for the United States at the height of the Cold War, that rationale dissolved when the Soviet Union collapsed and the superpower competition in the Middle East terminated. Today, uncritical US support of Israel is neither defensible on strategic grounds nor is it making the United States safer or more prosperous.[12] To the contrary, unconditional support by the United States for Israel is weakening relations with its allies, rendering doubtful US wisdom and moral vision, helping to bring about a generation of anti-American extremists, and complicating US attempts to deal with a volatile but crucial area of the world.[13]

As for US leverage over the Israelis, domestic constraints are a key factor. Where US influence over Palestinians is concerned, the troubling issue has often been, given the US strategic alliance with Israel, a credibility gap with regard to impartiality. As to why the United States has never been an honest broker in the resolution of the Arab-Israeli dispute, Mearsheimer and Walt point to the impact of the Israeli lobby on US foreign policy. According to Congressional Research Service data, since 1951 direct US economic and military assistance to Israel is estimated to be over $190 billion.[14] Technically the assistance is defined as loans, but as a practical matter, the military aid has grant status. As Mearsheimer and Walt have pointed out:

> Israel now receives on average about $3 billion in direct foreign assistance each year, an amount that is roughly one-sixth of America's direct foreign assistance budget and equal to about 2 percent of Israel's GDP. In recent years, about 75 percent of US assistance has been military aid, with the remainder broken down into various forms of economic aid. In per capita terms, this level of direct foreign assistance amounts to a direct subsidy of more than $500 per year for each Israeli. By comparison, the number two recipient of American foreign aid, Egypt, receives only $20 per person, and impoverished countries such as Pakistan and Haiti receive roughly $5 per person and $27 per person, respectively.[15]

A consistent failing of US presidents has been their inability to get Israeli governments to stop settlement activities in the occupied territories or to limit military incursions into the West Bank and the Gaza Strip. This in part has been due to the US power of persuasion having been circumscribed.[16] Hence, continued Israeli intransigence in the occupied lands has demonstrated the limits to US power. President George W. Bush proved impotent to convince Israeli Prime Minister Ariel Sharon to leave Gaza after Israeli retaliation against Palestinian suicide bombings in Israel. Likewise, both President Clinton and President Bush, were unable to persuade militant Palestinian elements to accept a negotiated peace or to restrain their extremist conduct—further clear evidence of the limit to US power.[17]

The issue of the legitimacy and legality of US intervention in Iraq has become a subject of further scrutiny as the failure of the occupation has shown the limitations of US military power. Although the Bush administration insisted that regime change in Iraq would better deliver a resolution of the Israeli-Palestinian dispute, the connection between the two has never been systematically made obvious. Richard A. Clarke, a terrorist expert who served under both Clinton and Bush, reveals the lack of wisdom of the unprovoked US invasion of an oil-rich Arab country. Clarke points to the inability of the Clinton and Bush administrations to see the "big picture" in the Middle East. More critically, he is scathing about President Bush's obsessive focus on Iraq when in fact there was no proof of a connection between Saddam Hussein and 9/11. Far from challenging the popular appeal of al-Qaeda, Clarke notes, Bush handed the enemy precisely what it wanted: a United States at war with Islam and the image of new crusaders occupying Muslim land.[18] According to Clarke, by invading and occupying Iraq, while paying scant time and attention to the Israeli-Palestinian problem, US policymakers delivered to al-Qaeda the greatest recruitment propaganda imaginable and made it immensely difficult for friendly Islamic governments to work with the United States.[19]

In 2002, the Bush administration developed a so-called roadmap for ending violence, rejuvenating negotiations, and establishing a viable and sovereign Palestinian state. Crucial to the sustainability of the roadmap was the involvement of the Quartet (the United States, Russia, the European Union, and the United Nations) and the role it could play in this framework. The attempt to advance the roadmap with a view toward creating a two-state solution of the conflict was overshadowed by the US invasion of Iraq in March 2003 and led many in the Arab world to doubt the sincerity of the Bush administration's purpose.[20] Some observers described the war in Iraq as "the stupidest and most recklessly undertaken war in modern times."[21] Others, such as Senator Robert Byrd (D-West Virginia) raised a key question: "How can we abandon diplomacy when the turmoil in the world cries out for diplomacy?"[22]

Diplomacy: What Works and What Doesn't

The 1991 Madrid conference on the Arab-Israeli conflict was designed to start a process with an outcome to be determined by the parties' negotiations through confidence-building stages. The US obsession with protecting and preserving the process meant that the talks failed to answer basic questions about Jerusalem, refugees, and the nature of any future Palestinian entity dotted with Israeli settlements.[23] Despite the lack of progress in multilateral negotiations, the bilateral conduit produced a peace treaty in October 1994 between Israel and Jordan, which provided an appropriate setting for the attainment of a negotiated settlement of the Arab-Israel dispute.[24] Yet no significant accommodation between Israeli and the Palestinians was reached. The exclusion of Iran from the peace process undermined US efforts to nudge the peace process along.

The Oslo Accords, also known as a Declaration of Principles (DOP), signed on September 13, 1993, provided for the creation of a Palestinian Authority and the phased withdrawal of Israeli forces from the occupied territories. The major difficulty with the Oslo Accords was that the issue of settlements had been left out of the accords because it had been generally agreed that neither party would have taken steps to alter the status of the Occupied Territories before final negotiations. In 1994, Baruch Goldstein, a settler in Hebron, killed twenty-nine Palestinians in a mosque, revealing the gravity of the situation and rendering the Oslo Accords effectively irrelevant.[25] The Goldstein massacre led to the advent of suicide bombings against Israeli targets. More than one hundred Israelis died in attacks between 1994 and 2000 and a climate of fear dominated the lives of the Israeli public.[26] The Oslo process, which was amended in a series of subsequent meetings in Cairo (1994), Taba (1995), and at the Wye River (1998), gradually saw the waning of the optimistic climate that surrounded its early years.

During the second Clinton administration, secretary of state Madeline Albright suggested that instead of using the gradual confidence-building approach of the Oslo Accords, it might be helpful if negotiations could be moved quickly into the final-status stage—that is, getting the parties to focus on their ultimate goal.[27] After a long hiatus, President Clinton brought Israeli and Palestinian leaders to the negotiating table at the Wye River Plantation. This US-convened summit (May 15–23, 1998) produced a memorandum of agreement between Yasser Arafat and Benjamin Netanyahu. This provided for the transfer of land under full Israeli control to Palestinian control in two tranches: 13 percent in the first tranche and 14.2 percent in the second—and the establishment of a committee to consider any subsequent transfer.[28] Netanyahu's government was divided between those who wanted a peace settlement and those who desired a West Bank incorporated into Greater Israel (*Eretz Yisrael*).[29] On the Palestinian side, the negotiations secured annulment of Palestinian charter provisions calling for the destruction of Israel.

Internal political dynamics in Israel, especially the rise of the Labor Party in May 1999, which put Ehud Barak at the helm, offered the prospect of movement toward the peace objective. The Camp David Summit in July 2000 failed to produce a resolution of issues on borders, refugees, or Jerusalem. The Oslo Accords, according to Lawrence Davidson, were doomed from the start because the United States refused to consistently pressure Israel to stop settlement activities in the occupied territories.[30]

On February 6, 2001, Ariel Sharon and his Likud Party won the Israeli election, causing more fear and uncertainty among the Palestinians. As we saw earlier (Chapter 3), the outbreak of the second intifada in 2000, caused by the provocative visit made by Sharon to the al-Aqsa mosque complex, followed by the 9/11 attacks in the United States, placed Israeli-Palestinian negotiations on hold. Sharon conflated the Palestinian insurgency with the larger, global terrorist menace and found a receptive audience in Washington. Positioning the Israeli-Palestinian conflict within the broader paradigm of fighting terrorism served only to confuse the central differences between the need for political resolution of legitimate Palestinian grievances, on the one hand, and the agenda of fighting transnational terrorist groups, such as al-Qaeda, on the other.[31]

In February 2002, a peace proposal outlined by Crown Prince Abdullah of Saudi Arabia called for Israel to withdraw to its 1967 borders in exchange for a normalization of relations with Arab states. This proposal was, in effect, a restatement of UN Resolution 242, which guided the Oslo peace process. Many experts reacted to this proposal positively, arguing that the Saudi plan offered something new and bold. More importantly, they noted that the entire Arab world signed onto the plan, including even Iraq and Libya. This represented a concrete offer from a nationalist Arab leader that was relatively devoid of ideological elements. It showed a serious commitment from an important Arab leader seeking a real solution.[32] Ensuing violence in the occupied territories marginalized the Saudi plan.

The cycle of violence and retribution, as manifest in increasingly frequent Palestinian suicide bombings and ensuing Israeli retaliations, led to growing international condemnation. President George W. Bush, whose high level of attention to the war on terror—and later the war in Iraq—distracted him from the Middle East peace process, felt compelled to intervene, demanding Israel's withdrawal from Arafat's compound and other areas previously transferred to the Palestinian Authority.[33] The Israelis also began to build a wall—or security fence, as it is called—to protect themselves from Palestinian suicide bombers. Both the International Court of Justice and the UN General Assembly have condemned its construction, and an Israeli court has demanded that its intended route be altered. But the United States has yet to challenge the validity of the barrier.[34] It became clear, as one observer notes, that "the US policy of leaving matters to Israel and the Palestinians had achieved little."[35]

Growing divisions among Palestinians, combined with US preoccupation with the war on terror and Sharon's policy of unilateral disengagement from the Gaza Strip, left Israeli-Palestinian negotiations going nowhere. The Quartet's negotiations over the roadmap, which began under George W. Bush's presidency in April 2003, were set aside in deference to Israel's disengagement initiative. Mahmoud Abbas's accession to power in 2005 produced no change in the US approach and policy.[36] Four years of intense international diplomacy in the Middle East by the world's most powerful negotiating team bent on creating a new Arab state between Israel and Jordan in 6 percent of historic Palestine had finally been declared a failure.[37] The failure of the Oslo process and the demise of the roadmap dashed the hopes for incrementalism and interim agreements in favor of an approach aimed at endgame solutions or an endgame diplomacy, helping the parties make the necessary concessions to reach agreement on core issues.[38]

The Hamas victory in the elections for the Palestinian Legislative Council (PLC) on January 25, 2006, placed Mahmoud Abbas in a difficult situation as the United States and Israel found themselves faced with new challenges. Under pressure from the United States, other members of the Quartet refused to deal with Hamas. Russia soon broke ranks with its Quartet colleagues by receiving a Hamas delegation in Moscow and offering the Palestinian Authority economic assistance. US policy toward the Arab-Israeli conflict appeared to be in a state of total disarray.[39]

In response to the question of why the peace process failed, some experts argue that the claim that the Palestinians and Israelis did not want peace is the least persuasive idea. The procedural explanation is more persuasive: the initial terms of the 1993 Declaration of Principles made no explicit mention of a Palestinian state or a settlement freeze. The process was woefully slow, and this left opponents in both camps many opportunities to thwart the drive toward peace. Moreover, the process was elitist and left out the Israeli and Palestinian publics.[40] Perhaps only a resilient and well-managed process, spearheaded by robust US leadership, could have succeeded.[41]

Dealing with Iran: Launching a Diplomatic Offensive

The bipartisan Iraq Study Group (ISG) was spearheaded under the leadership of two distinguished co-chairs: James A. Baker III, former secretary of state and honorary chairman of the Baker Institute, and Lee H. Hamilton, former congressman and director of the Woodrow Wilson International Center for Scholars. The balance of the bipartisan group was comprised of Americans who have distinguished themselves in service to their nation: Robert M. Gates, Vernon E. Jordan Jr., Edwin Meese III, Sandra Day O'Connor, Leon E. Panetta, William J. Perry, Charles S. Robb, and Alan K. Simpson. The members of the study group consulted with members of Congress and others, including four working groups of experts and a group of retired military officers. The four working groups were comprised of experts from private industry and leading policy and academic institutions. On December 6, 2006, ISG published its report.

The ISG report underlined building an international consensus as a way to break the deadlock over Iraq. In fact, the ISG made it abundantly clear that any resolution of the Iraq crisis depended on the involvement of Iran and Syria. Dealing with Iran and Syria is polemical, the ISG report concluded, but at the same time, "in diplomacy, a nation should engage its adversaries and enemies to try to resolve conflicts and differences consistent with its own interests."[42] The recommendation was thus that the United States "should actively engage Iran and Syria in its diplomatic dialogue, without preconditions."[43]

The Bush adminstration argument that the confrontation with Iran would lead to the region's stabilization and the defeat of Islamic militancy was fundamentally misguided and dangerously naïve. The decision to label Iran's Revolutionary Guard Corps as a "terrorist" group, coupled with emphasizing regional deterrence strategies such as new arms sales to Israel, Saudi Arabia, and some Gulf countries, sent confusing messages to Iran.

Clandestine operations against Iran, Seymour M. Hersh wrote at the time, were not new in 2008. US Special Operations Forces had conducted cross-border operations from southern Iraq, with presidential authorization, since 2007. These included capturing members of Al Quds, the commando arm of the Iranian Revolutionary Guard, and taking them to Iraq for interrogation, as well as the pursuit of "high-value targets" in the campaign against terror, who could be captured or killed. During 2007–2008, the scale and the scope of the operations in Iran, which involved the CIA and the Joint Special Operations Command (JSOC), were significantly expanded.[44]

The strategy followed in Iran by the United States of using ethnic divisions among non-Persian ethnic factions, notably Arabs, Azerbaijanis, Kurds, and Baluchis, to bring down the central government of the Islamic Republic of Iran was flawed. Such a strategy would likely backfire, alienating the majority of the Iranian population.[45] Similarly, the United States has encouraged Arab countries to fund right-wing Sunni terrorist groups in Lebanon. Ironically, this new strategy of allying with conservative Sunnis against Shiite Iran put the United States on the side of political movements sympathetic to al-Qaeda. The United States promoted a similar alliance in the 1980s with fundamentalist Sunnis to evict Soviet forces in Afghanistan. Some mujahidin freedom fighters, such as Osama bin Laden, who were trained, equipped, and mobilized by the United States, wound up forming al-Qaeda.[46] Continued violence caused by an intra-mujahidin civil war in Afghanistan during the post–Cold War era deepened the country's fragmentation—a situation that frustrated Pakistan because it prevented that country from having trade and influence in Central Asia. In the summer of 1994, some elements within Pakistan and Saudi Arabia began to support what was then a new movement—the Taliban ("religious students"). The Taliban were Afghani refugees and fighters based in rural Pakistani and Afghan madrassas—Islamic religious schools. Their control of a great portion of Afghanistan in 1994 marked the end of mujahidin infighting.[47] The Taliban ruled over a weak government and a fragmented society overwhelmed by seemingly intractable problems until they were removed by the US invasion in October 2001.

In the case of Iran, caution must be exercised not to overestimate the gravity of the security threat it poses, thus justifying support for covert operations of the sort espoused by the Bush administration. The December 2007 release of the US National Intelligence Estimate (NIE) concerning Iran's nuclear status contradicted President Bush and his team, who were beating the drums of war, arguing that Iran's (nonexistent) weapons program threatened World War III. The NIE said that Iran had given up its effort to develop nuclear weapons in 2003 and that there was no Iranian nuclear threat. The debate on Iran has been systematically distorted by political considerations having nothing or little to do with the perceived threat.[48]

Historically, the Iranian threat has been exaggerated. The last time Iran started a war was in 1850 in an effort to win back territory it had lost to the Afghans. Its last invasion of another country was in 1738.[49] Were Iran to become a nuclear power, it would likely act pragmatically. It is unlikely to become "the new Pakistan, selling nuclear fuel and materials to other states."[50] Even if this were to become the case, a well-calculated US containment strategy could deter Iran and undermine its influence in the region. The idea of air strikes against Iran has been and continues to be open to skepticism on several accounts. Military strikes alone may disrupt Iran's nuclear program but it would still be difficult to isolate Iran, not to mention change the regime. Sanctions against Iran are not effective in large part because of Iran's geography and vast oil reserves. There are reasons to seriously negotiate with Iran. While the Bush administration's basic position held that talks between the two countries could not take place until Iran halted its enrichment of uranium, the Iranians consistently rejected that precondition.

Diplomatic solutions to US-Iran relations might represent a win-win scenario for both countries, and a more positive dialogue could represent an investment in long-term peace and stability throughout the Middle East. Iran is a Shiite-majority country that could cultivate close ties with Iraq's US-backed Maliki government. Moreover, by most accounts, Iran is about five to ten years away from manufacturing the key ingredients for a nuclear weapon. Iranians have always felt insecure in a neighborhood where they are surrounded by nuclear-armed powers—Pakistan, India, Israel, and Russia.

Two central factors reinforce this insecurity. First, Iran is not a member of any regional security pact. While Iran does not threaten Gulf countries, it wants its legitimate regional interests to be recognized by its neighbors. Second, the US presence in the region has increased Iran's sense of urgency over acquiring some form of strategic deterrence. The utility of nuclear force in cases where there are regional disputes or conflicts is highly questionable. It would be foolish for Iran, as some experts argue, to threaten the use of force, including nuclear weapons, as long as the United States has the capacity to defeat any Iranian adventure against its neighbors. It is clear that the overwhelming retaliatory capability of the United States serves as the major deterrent to Iran from contemplating any use of nuclear weapons against its Gulf neighbors.[51] Under such circumstances, it is only natural to assume, as do many experts, that the primary reason Iran would consider a nuclear option is for reasons of national survival, not as an instrument for regional aggression.[52] That explains why the most obvious threat perception shaping Iranian security doctrine is US opposition to the Islamic Republic of Iran.[53] The talk of "regime change" through military force has invariably exacerbated this perception of threat and alienated Iran's ruling elites.

Since the 1990s, Iran's relations with all GCC members have noticeably improved. Perhaps the single most important reason for the rapprochement between Iran and Saudi Arabia during the 1990s was Iran's distancing of itself from the revolutionary zeal that had characterized it in the 1980s.[54] Despite 2011 unrests in Bahrain that are mostly rooted in the mundane demands of its Shiite majority for basic rights, jobs, and a fair share of economic prosperity, the Iranian government has shown persistent interest in an evolving rapprochement with GCC members, an engagement that will surely have a stabilizing impact on the entire area.[55]

Following the US invasions of Afghanistan and Iraq, Iran's foreign policy behavior can be characterized as having a status quo orientation, not a revisionist one. Since 2007, Iranian experts point out, Iran has begun to diversify its foreign policy by opening up to Egypt, seeking observer status at the Arab League, and displaying more flexibility toward the European Union. Iran was the first country in the region to accept the legitimacy of Iraq's governing council, set up by the United States.[56] Moreover, some experts remind us, Iran is likely to move in the direction of economic development, further engagement in the global economy, and political stability. At the regional level, Iran's security policies will be increasingly based on trade, economic interdependence, and cultural exchange.[57]

Iran holds the key to many problems in the region. Iranians have many incentives to continue working toward establishing a dialogue with the United States. Iranians can play a constructive role in rebuilding Afghanistan and Iraq. If they demonstrate transparency in their nuclear programs, they may even convince the United States of their long-term interests in maintaining regional stability. The fact remains, however, that the more the US military presence in the region increases, the more it reinforces Iran's underlying threat perception. Unless the United States pursues negotiations that address Iran's security concerns, the tensions between the two will linger on. An attack on Iran would likely send the Gulf region into chaos and oil prices through the roof. A military strike would also inflame Iranians' nationalistic sentiments and cause them to rally around the current clerical regime. Furthermore, an attack, like the Osiraq strike carried out in 1981 against Iraq, stands little chance of success in a huge country like Iran that has dispersed its nuclear power installations across the country.

In the past, Iran has identified to the UN Security Council a list of more than two hundred suspected al-Qaeda members, formerly based in Iran, who had been extradited to their countries of origin. Washington has pushed Tehran to hand over suspected al-Qaeda members still in Iran and has suggested that doing so would further improve relations. Iran's approval of the formation of the governing council in Iraq and its proposal to form a trilateral commission to consult about the stabilization of Iraq could be crucial to that country's stability. The mutual security interests of the United States and Iran in restoring stability to Iraq and Afghanistan have unexpectedly merged. Hamid Karzai, Afghanistan's president, sees a positive role for Iran that could be vitally significant to his country's stability. Moreover, there is a growing consensus in Iran—in spite of its polarized politics—that dialogue with its neighbors, such as Iraq, Pakistan, Turkey, and Afghanistan, is the only way to enhance peace in the region.

A strategy centered on sanctions is unlikely to alter Iran's behavior. On the other hand, future cooperation with Iran could enhance the possibility of addressing the issues regarding Palestinians in the occupied territories and Hezbollah in Lebanon, two thorny security issues for the region. At a time when the occupation of Iraq has alienated some key US allies, a turn toward multilateral diplomacy could prove to be prudential. Without the cooperation of key countries in the region, the United States may utterly fail to stop terrorism. In the long run, the campaign against terrorism is a campaign without military solutions. As he should have done with North Korea, the Bush administration should have pursued a diplomatic track with Iran. US-Iran cooperation could work to abort al-Qaeda plans, promote stability in the region, fight drug trafficking from Afghanistan, and advance regional détente.

It bears noting that any long-term US military presence in Iraq will attenuate the legitimacy of Iraqi governments and will be challenged by the Iranian and Syrian governments. The solution to this dilemma can be reached only through negotiations with these governments to establish a long-term Gulf security arrangement and to bolster chances for an ultimate resolution of the Israeli-Palestinian and Syrian-Lebanese conflicts.[58] Increasingly, experts argue that no single factor would more boost the US capacity to redress the power balance in the Middle East than US-Iran cooperation.[59] It is time to pursue serious, direct negotiations that address Iran's security concerns, bearing in mind that bargaining is not appeasement.

It is important to embrace the notion that the postconflict nation building in Iraq need not be achieved at the expense of deepening Shia-Sunni rifts. The emergence of an Arab Shia government, Ali M. Ansari points out, has always been unsettling for US traditional allies in the region, some of whom have sizable Shia minorities struggling to secure concessions from their own governments. To placate their Arab allies, Western leaders warn of a Shia empowerment, ignoring the fact that it was the US invasion of Iraq that propelled it. This notion belies the complexity of regional politics by simply assuming that the menace of rising Shia will likely strengthen the alliance between the United States and its allies, while simultaneously offering Israel a sense of solidarity with moderate Arab regimes.[60] What is more, Ansari notes, it allows the United States to blame the crisis in Iraq on the Shia, conveniently collapsing the two narratives of confrontation— the nuclear issue and the Iraqi debacle—into one major reason for the use of force against Iran.[61]

Regarding Gulf security, the view from Iran is that extremist movements are a by-product of intervention by powers from outside the region. Outside intervention has facilitated the recruitment of fundamentalist Salafi groups and hard-line trends.[62] Increasingly, the region's observers argue, enduring Gulf security has become inseparable from finding a role for Iran. "Iran ought to be part of a regional security order," one expert observes, "simply because there cannot be a comprehensive regional security arrangement without Iran."[63]

For the Obama administration, the fundamental challenge persists: how to alter Iran's foreign policy behavior. In her speech on July 15, 2009, to the Council on Foreign Relations, US Secretary of State Hillary Rodham Clinton noted that engagement is aimed at both problematic regimes and the international community. Leading with diplomacy, Secretary Clinton pointed out, advances US interests and values, while placing US diplomats and policymakers in a far better position to lead with its other partners. "Negotiations," Secretary Clinton emphasized, "can provide insight into regimes' calculations and the possibility— even if it seems remote—that a regime will eventually alter its behavior in exchange for the benefits of acceptance into the international community." [64]

A Triangle of Diplomacy

As Islamic militancy permeates the region, it may be useful to turn to yet another regional diplomatic initiative. At the heart of Middle East tensions lies a triangle of diplomacy and complex state-to-state relations that requires a nuanced and subtle understanding of three groupings: the resistance bloc, the pro-West Arab bloc, and the Turkey-US-Israel bloc. Understanding each bloc and how their interactions and diplomatic relations could reduce regional tensions is particularly significant in the context of the campaign against terrorism.

The Resistance Bloc

On one side, there is Iran, Syria, Hezbollah in Lebanon, and Hamas in Palestine. These have formed a resistance alliance—a group with majority Shiite membership. Although this is not a sectarian alliance, it has been perceived by many Sunni ruling elites as fanning the flames of sectarianism across the region.

This camp is emblematic of resistance to the US presence in the region. It argues that US policy aims in the region are twofold: (1) to strengthen Israel as an instrument of US influence and (2) to preserve control over the region's oil.[65] For the Iranians, the history of external manipulation—in the form of the 1941 Anglo-Russian invasion and the covert intervention in the case of the military coup organized in 1953 by the US and British secret services—continues to be a source of resentment.[66] The rise of Islamism in the 1970s was also a response to and rejection of Western modernizing pressures in the region more generally.

After the shah's fall in Iran, the convergence of regional interests and foreign policies gave further impetus to the Syrian-Iranian rapprochement. The clerical regime drew closer to the radical Arab grouping at a time when the Arab world was becoming more polarized and divided over issues like the Camp David Accords and the Iranian Revolution. Likewise, Syria's relations with many pro-Western Arab states deteriorated. The growing tensions with Iraq facilitated the emergent Syrian-Iranian alliance. The Iran-Iraq War (1980–1988) was the single most important parameter since the early 1980s in formalizing the Tehran-Damascus alliance.[67] The Israeli invasion of Lebanon further strengthened the alliance. The prolonged Israeli occupation of southern Lebanon (1982–2000) radicalized the Shiites, who eventually forced Israel to withdraw its forces.

The Iraqi invasion of Kuwait and the subsequent US attack against Iraq were a mixed blessing for the Syrian-Iranian axis. These events reinforced the notion that Saddam Hussein was the aggressor. Both Damascus and Tehran attempted to mend fences with key Arab and Western governments in order to break out of their regional and international isolation. The collapse of the USSR, Damascus's ally, in the early 1990s pushed Syria in the direction of strengthening its regional alliance with Iran. Washington's pro-Israeli stance in the Arab-Israeli negotiations, its espousal of the emergence of a Turkish-Israeli alliance to isolate Iran and force Syria into accommodation, Washington's presence in the Gulf, and its huge arms sales to its regional allies rejuvenated Syrian-Iranian cooperation in the post–Cold War era. Both countries viewed the US toppling of the Iraqi regime with ambivalence, while trying to coordinate their policies in order to display Arab-Iranian solidarity in the face of the Arab-Israeli conflicts and the US neoconservatives' agenda of regime change.[68]

Resistance to these external pressures has become a cause around which the members of this camp have consistently rallied. International law experts have argued that although the Israeli government and the US media insist on portraying Palestinian resistance as a theater of combat in the global war on terror, under international law Palestinian resistance to occupation is a legally protected right.[69] Since the 9/11 tragedy, these experts have noted, Israel has intensified its illegal and coercive occupation by linking its actions against the Palestinians with the US-led war against global terror. Israeli operations in the occupied territories under the guise of antiterrorism have not only resulted in greater hardship and suffering for the Palestinians, they have also tended to underline the legality of the Palestinians' claims and resistance. The basic calculus in this current context of the war on terror is to criminalize Palestinian terrorism while simultaneously categorizing the state aggression associated with Israeli military operations as "security" or "antiterrorism."[70]

Similarly, although Hezbollah has engaged in acts that generally constitute terrorism, it has been fully within its rights to resist the Israeli occupation of southern Lebanon.[71] The Israeli attack on southern Lebanon in July 2006 further bolstered Hezbollah's stature and popularity in the wider Arab world. Strong support for Hezbollah—both during and after the war—was apparent within Iraq's Shia community.[72] In short, as experts concur, the Shia emerged from the war "as a mobilized, assertive, more militant community."[73] The resurgence of Iran, the resilience of Hezbollah in Lebanon in its war with Israel, and the perception of shifts in the regional balance of power have all contributed to unleashing the forces of sectarian strife.[74]

With Lebanon becoming a central arena for regional power struggles, Iran and Saudi Arabia are bound to compete with one another to establish spheres of regional influence. Under such circumstances, Syria will reemerge as a central power broker. Precisely because of the significance of such role, US pressures on Syria have been inconsistently applied over the years. Consider, for example, the US-imposed sanctions on Syria in an attempt to increase the pressure on Bashar al-Assad's regime to forego its brutal crackdown on prodemocracy protesters. These sanctions are basically symbolic, in large part because Assad and his top advisers have few assets in the United States. Given that the United States fears the prospects of an Islamic alternative to Assad's regime, President Obama initially refused to directly call for Assad to step down. The fact remains that the resolution of some of the regional problems is not possible without the cooperation of Iran and Syria, suggesting that the West should actively engage these regional powers in diplomatic dialogue without preconditions.[75] These countries are unlikely to profit from regional wars and instability. Some of the possible incentives for both countries include bilateral negotiations with the United States (which result in discarding the rhetoric of regime change) and gaining access to international organizations, such as the World Trade Organization.

In the case of Syria, prospects for a real secure and lasting peace to be negotiated between Israel and Syria, with US involvement, is worth contemplating.[76] Most experts take the view that no single factor would more elevate US capacity to restore the balance of power in the Middle East than US-Iran cooperation.[77] It is time to pursue bilateral and direct negotiations with Iran and Syria that address issues of mutual concern, taking the perspective that bargaining is not appeasement.[78]

Equally important is Iranian influence in Afghanistan. Iran's cooperation with the United States during negotiations in the Bonn discussion (December 2001) and The Hague Conference (April 1, 2009) on the future of Afghanistan has been critical. Under the Bonn Agreement, a commission was established to draft a new constitution. The agreement called for a grand national assembly—*loya jirga*—to be convened within eighteen months of the establishment of a transitional authority and for the use of the 1964 constitution as the basis for a new constitution. This constitution, which was later accepted by the loya jirga, remains today as the basis of Afghanistan's democratically grounded legal system. The Hague Conference underscored the importance of finding a regional solution to the insurgency in Afghanistan and Pakistan, and general agreements on drugs, development issues, and elections in Afghanistan.[79]

The friendly and diplomatic language emerging from The Hague indicated the Obama administration's initial approach toward Iran, which emphasized the search for common ground rather than confrontation. This diplomatic approach was in stark contrast to President Bush's perspective, reflected in his 2002 state of the union address in which he described Iran, along with Iraq and North Korea, as part of an "axis of evil." This rhetorical device put Iran's reformists on the defensive, as hard-liners urged an end to the reform process. For the hard-liners, tough posturing rather than negotiation was the only alternative.[80] The Bush administration appeared to be intensely preoccupied with Iraq, and its strategy was almost exclusively one of force.[81]

As one scholar has asserted, the Iraq invasion was pursued because it was militarily possible; Iran was ignored because it was politically too difficult. The most effective policy—support for the reform movement—received the least attention: "Rather than pursue the military solution in Iraq, the United States should have taken the opportunity to pursue the political solution in Iran. The democratic architecture, for all of its flaws, was in place, and the audience was receptive. The events of 9/11 and subsequent polling throughout 2002 had shown an Iranian population eager for dialogue. They were ignored."[82]

On the contrary, the Bush administration's rhetoric of regime change, which signaled a possible willingness to use force to topple Iran's Islamic Republic, did much to reinforce Iranians' nationalist sentiments. These sentiments were especially reinforced after the US invasion of Iraq. But more to the point, the fragile and fractured reform movement opened the way for the rise of populism and religious nationalism. Moderation gave way to such revolutionary beliefs and ideologies. Pragmatic and traditionally conservative clerics lost ground to radicals and neoconservatives. Mahmoud Ahmadinejad's ascendancy to the presidency in 2005 and his disputed reelection in 2009 demonstrated not only the collapse of the reform movement but also the rising intensity of power struggles within the clerical establishment.

Iran's June 12, 2009, presidential elections—overshadowed by accusations of cheating and vote rigging, which were raised as hundreds of thousands of supporters of reformist candidate Mir-Hossein Mousavi poured into the streets and confronted riot police, charging massive fraud—illustrated a confluence of identity, authority, and legitimacy crises that are likely to besiege the Islamic Republic for years to come.

The conflict over the legitimacy of elections lingers.[83] Increasingly, a new power struggle grinds on behind-the-scenes that reveals the very nature of the Islamic Republic and the extent to which the system should represent the republican form of government as well as its theocratic aspects.[84] The old consensus forged by Iran's revolutionary leader Ayatollah Khomeini has clearly been broken, as many influential religious leaders have refused to support the beleaguered president, Ahmadinejad, or the supreme leader, Ayatollah Ali Khamenei. Many clerics who traditionally supported the government have remained quiet or have even offered weak but open criticism.[85]

How these internal developments will influence Iran's foreign policy in the region remains to be seen. Iran's rising clout at the regional level has put the country's leaders in a position to promote the policies needed to stabilize the entire region. Iran, for example, hosted its first three-way summit meeting on May 24, 2009, with the leaders of Pakistan and Afghanistan to discuss cooperation on regional issues. The summit served as a clear sign that Iran is increasingly seen as less of a threat to the West, and the region, than the prospect of the Taliban's rising power in Pakistan and Afghanistan. An equally important consequence of the meeting was the notion that Western efforts to isolate Iran over its nuclear program have given way to more pragmatic regional concerns.[86] Particularly ineffective has been the lack of a policy toward Iran that could have represented its complexities and not merely overstated the totalitarian aspects of its system.

It is vitally important to recognize that Iran-US relations in the twentieth as well as twenty-first centuries have been defined as much by collaboration as by confrontation and that the room for compromise still exists.[87] Iran's acceptance of a nuclear-fuel swap in Turkey demonstrates a new signal of willingness to work with the West. Iran-Turkey relations have evolved in recent years. The unprecedented surge in anti-American sentiment in Turkey following the US military interventions in Afghanistan and Iraq has placed Turkey's ruling party, the AKP, in a unique position to take a somewhat innovative foreign policy approach toward certain issues in the region. That development, along with the growth in Turkey's dependency on natural gas and oil from Iran, has led to further improvement in Iran-Turkey relations. Additionally, the two countries have a common stake in the stability of the region at a time when the rise in both Islamic militancy and ethnonationalist movements pose crucial challenges to their rule.

More specifically, Turkey's leaders have consistently said that imposing more nuclear-issue sanctions on Iran is not the best option and that Iran's nuclear self-sufficiency and its right to produce peaceful energy is legally warranted within the bounds of the NPT agreements. To defuse the tensions, Turkish prime minister Recep Tayyib Erdogan has offered his good office to serve as a conduit for diplomatic solutions. While appearing keen on averting yet another round of sanctions, Iran's ruling elites have come to consider the Erdogan administration an honest broker. Recent communications between the EU and Iran's diplomats via Turkey point to a safe bet: a diplomatic breakthrough cannot be ruled out.

The Moderate Arab Bloc

The "moderate Arab countries" form the pro-Western camp: Egypt, Jordan, Saudi Arabia, and the Gulf monarchies. This group argues that Israel will never be secure until a viable Palestinian state is created that gives the Palestinians dignity and justice. They link the creation of a Palestinian state to the decisive resolution of some of the regional tensions. A negotiated agreement that leads to a viable and contiguous independent Palestinian state on Palestinian territory will help establish a just, comprehensive peace that provides security and stability to every Arab and Israeli. Increasingly, the preference for the two-state solution has been widely embraced by both civil groups and NGOs.[88] The September 2011 vote at the UN for recognition of the statehood and independence of Palestine is likely to strengthen the Palestinians' hand.

Several developments, however, have pushed public opinion away from the peace process, including the collapse of the Oslo negotiations, the outbreak of the second intifada, and the ensuing deterioration of Israeli-Palestinian relations into widespread violence, including the Israeli air strikes and invasion against Gaza residents and Hamas camps during December–January 2008–2009. On May 31, 2010, a deadly Israeli attack on a humanitarian aid flotilla—a Turkish ship in international waters—en route to the Gaza Strip, in which nine activists were killed and at least thirty people were wounded, invited worldwide condemnation of these violations of international law. The Obama administration failed to condemn this blatant Israeli act of aggression.[89] This incident has strained Israel-Turkey relations. Turkish opposition to the Israeli blockade on and war against Gaza has been at the heart of the dispute between the two countries since 2008.

Moderate Arab states have supported the two-state solution to the Israel-Palestine conflict. In 2002, Saudi King Abdullah's proposal for a two-state solution garnered the unanimous support of the Arab League.

The proposal offered the support of moderate Arab countries to Israel in return for the creation of a Palestinian state. Jordan's King Abdullah has defended the viability of a two-state solution by arguing that "we envisage the future of Israel not just having borders with Jordan, Syria or Egypt. The future of Israelis . . . is to be welcomed from Morocco on the Atlantic to Oman on the Indian Ocean. I think that is the prize for the Israelis. But that comes at a price and that is the future of the Palestinians."[90]

Weary of Iran's ascendance as a regional power in the Gulf region, ruling elites in Saudi Arabia appear resolute in their attempts to resolve this issue, neutralizing or diminishing Iranian political influence in the region in the process. Now, however, in the aftermath of the removal of Egypt's Hosni Mubarak, and especially given the prominence of the public opinion factor in Egyptian foreign policy, a rapprochement between Iran and Egypt has emerged, creating a rift of sorts in this bloc.

Egypt's efforts to reconcile rival Palestinians factions—Fatah and Hamas—have been received warmly by Iran. It is worth recalling that the Saudi decision to send troops to Bahrain to stifle Shia uprisings there demonstrated the extent to which they seek to contain Iran's rising influence in the region—not to mention the Saudis' burgeoning concerns over their own vocal Shia minority in eastern provinces in close proximity to Bahrain.

The situation in Lebanon throws further light on relationships within the moderate Arab bloc. The assassination of the former Lebanese prime minister, Rafiq Hariri, on February 14, 2005, led to Syria's withdrawal from Lebanon. Subsequently, however, the Shia community, led by Hezbollah's leader Hassan Nasrallah, began wider political activities in Lebanon. Hezbollah has developed autonomously from the state, while, like other Lebanese parties, forming alliances across sectarian boundaries for mutual strategic and political advantages.

Hezbollah has become a success story of the Lebanese confessional system—a system that was based on an unwritten agreement that allocated political power determined in the 1932 census. Seats in parliament were divided on an equal ratio of Christians to Muslims. Accordingly, the country's president was required to be a Maronite Christian, the prime minister a Sunni Muslim, and the speaker of the parliament a Shia Muslim. As of its decision to run in 1992 elections, Hezbollah's resistance movement and party became "Lebanonized."[91] Since the Israeli attack on southern Lebanon in the summer of 2006, Nasrallah's reputation has risen throughout the Arab and non-Arab Muslim world, in large part because Hezbollah successfully withstood the destruction of Israeli

air strikes. It is clear, however, that absent Syrian and Iranian cooperation, instability in Lebanon would persist, making it a fertile ground for
resistance movements. These groups' operations would complicate and
likely defeat the purpose of Washington's war on terrorism.[92]

It should come as no surprise that the Arab League's intervention in
Lebanon in 2006 was primarily aimed at precluding Lebanon from
becoming an Iranian base and only secondarily intended to rescue Syria
from its regional problems.[93] The moderate Arab regimes have turned
toward resolving regional problems without Iranian or US mediation.

Qatar's emir, Shaykh Hamad bin Khalifa Al Thani, brokered a deal
in May 2008 in which various factions in Lebanon reconciled their differences and reached a political accord—an agreement that ended an
eighteen-month political deadlock between the Hezbollah-led opposition and the Western-backed government. The deal was regarded in the
Middle East as a major victory for Hezbollah and its allies, who
received their much-touted demand for veto power over all government
decisions. Most Lebanese, however, were jubilant in large part because
the specter of war, at least for a while, was lifted.[94] While the election of
the army chief, Michel Suleiman, as president ended a prolonged political crisis, the underlying issues and questionable implications for
democracy remained unresolved.

Elections on June 7, 2009, represented a turning point in the country's politics, as a majority, pro-West group was brought back to power
thanks to broad popular support. The leader of the largest bloc in the
pro-Western coalition, Saad Hariri, expressed hope for a national unity
government to be formed that would include Hezbollah and its supporters, enhancing the prospect that both sides are willing to cooperate. In
early 2011, however, Lebanon's government collapsed after Hezbollah
and its allies resigned from the cabinet in a dispute with Western-backed
factions over upcoming indictments in the 2005 assassination of former
prime minister Rafik Hariri. A new prime minister, Najib Mikati, was
appointed after the government's collapse. In June 2011, Mikati
announced a new government dominated by members and allies of
Hezbollah. The politics of bickering over posts in the cabinet and their
distribution among different sects and political powers are emblematic
of divisive ideological and political currents that continue to character-
ize Lebanon's political landscape. Some experts on Middle Eastern politics have advocated parallel tracks. Parallel to the rightful rejection of
terrorism, they have argued, engagement provides an opportunity to test
the ground for possible change, to discover whether the objectives of
such groups as Hezbollah and Hamas can be reconciled with those of
the United States.[95]

The Turkey Connection

As an important regional player with the potential to become an even more significant force in the changing politics of the Middle East, Turkey can increase its role in the region by serving as a bridge between the two blocs described above. In recent years, Turkey has been revamping its ties with countries that border it, such as Iran, Iraq, and Syria. It has also planned to launch its own Arabic-language satellite TV station as an outreach to the Arab world.

This new approach has been vividly accelerated by the opposition of some European countries to Turkey's admission to the European Union. To a large extent, the major architect of this new realignment is Turkey's new foreign minister, Ahmet Davutoglu, who has pushed for a policy of "zero problems with neighbors."[96] Having almost gone to war in the late 1990s over Syria's harboring of Kurdish militants, the friendship between Turkey and Syria became a virtual poster child for Ankara's new regional foreign policy. In recent times, however, Davutoglu has sharply criticized the Syrian regime's violent response to prodemocracy protesters in Syria, warning that Bashar al-Assad could face isolation similar to that of Libya's Muammar Qaddafi, if he does not halt his brutal crackdown on protesters. Davutoglu has made it clear, however, that a military operation similar to that in Libya is unlikely to resolve the crisis in Syria. Turkey's first reaction to the spiraling violence in Syria has been to consider ways in which the crisis can be contained.[97] By maintaining ongoing diplomatic relations with all three camps, and most notably with the United States and Israel, Turkey can play a pivotal role in this triangle.

Today, some experts describe Turkish foreign policy as a new activism, which is a marked departure from its foreign policy since the end of World War II. The new activism is largely a response to structural changes in its security environment since the end of the Cold War. Turkey's growing concern over the rise of Kurdish ethnonationalism/separatism, sectarian violence in Iraq, the resurgence of Iran, and the fragmentation of Lebanon have brought Ankara closer to the governments of Iran and Syria, which not only face a major escalation of the Kurdish problem at home but which also influence developments in both Iraq and Lebanon.

Of the several roles that Turkey has played in the Middle East in the post–Cold War era, the most significant one is in relation to Iran, Iraq, and Syria, and the issues of water, oil and gas, power rivalries, religion, boundaries, and the Kurdish Workers' Party—commonly known as the PKK—a Kurdish political organization that has fought an armed struggle against the Turkish state since the mid-1980s.[98] In recent years, Turkey has established close ties with Iran and Syria, with whom it had tense relations during the 1980s and 1990s. It has also adopted a more active approach toward the Palestinians' grievances and improved relations with the Arab world more generally.[99]

Today, Iran provides nearly one-third of Turkey's natural gas, making it Turkey's second largest supplier of gas after the Russia.[100] Turkey and Iran signed a security cooperation agreement in 2004 that branded the PKK a terrorist organization. In 2007, Turkey and Iran signed a memorandum of understanding for the construction of a new pipeline between the two countries as part of the Nabucco project. The idea of Iranian-Turkish gas exports via the Nabucco pipeline to Europe continues to face formidable challenges from the US government. The volume of trade between Iran and Turkey has increased from $1.3 billion in 2002 to $10 billion in 2008.[101] Iran is also seen as a natural stepping-stone by Turkish ruling elites who want to reach into the markets of Central Asia and Pakistan. Given such long-term and strategic mutual interests, Turkish-Iranian relations are likely to stay stable.[102] Turkey's relations with Saudi Arabia and Egypt have also been strengthened under the Erdogan administration.

At the same time, Turkey's ties with the West have weakened. Turkey's chance at membership in the European Union has been complicated by disagreements with Brussels over Cyprus and the growing concern among Europeans about immigration, unemployment, Greece's economic collapse, and EU enlargement. Additionally, Turkey's relations with the United States deteriorated over the US invasion of Iraq. According to a poll conducted by the German Marshall Fund in September 2006, 81 percent of Turks disapproved of President Bush's handling of international policies.[103] These trends have been reinforced by the construction of a new Turkish identity, one influenced by both conservative and globalist forces simultaneously. In this new identity, the Islamists have found the EU to be a natural ally in curtailing the influence of the army, demanding democratic governance, and pursuing further guarantees for civil-political rights in Turkey. Increasingly, Turkey's traditional stance as a Kemalist state guarded by the army has become unsustainable.[104]

Since 1999, domestic dynamics for change, along with the failure of antidemocratic, anti-Western, and antiglobalization forces to reestablish their hegemony in the country, a new Turkey has gradually replaced the old Turkey.[105] Turkish politicians have pushed for more substantial internal reform and the opening up of political spaces for Islamic and ethnonationalistic groups, despite Turkey's EU accession push having yet to come to fruition.[106] The Turkish elites have many incentives to play a constructive role in bringing stability to the region. Turkish membership in the EU, experts argue, would significantly enhance the Middle Eastern profile of European foreign policy, which in turn would have a positive impact on Turkish foreign policies on the Middle East, the Muslim world, human rights, and the promotion of democracy. The Justice and Development Party (AKP) has led the Europeanization of center-right conservative, Islamic voters in recent years with its human rights and prodemocracy agenda.[107] Turkey's EU membership would validate both the compatibility of liberal democracy with Islam and the multireligious inclusiveness of the EU, thus deflating the notion of cultural or civilizational clashes between the Muslim and Western worlds.[108]

In the Turkey–United States–Israel bloc, Israelis as well as pro-West Arab regimes, have long been trying to drive a wedge between Syria and Iran in an effort to stymie Iranian influence in Lebanon.[109] The most important development in this camp is that Syria and Israel have resumed negotiation through Turkish mediators. In 2000, negotiations between Israel and Syria broke down over details of Israel's proposed withdrawal from the Golan Heights, the strategic plateau it has occupied since the 1967 War. Turkey's role as a go-between in the region was welcomed by both the United States and the EU.[110] Prime Minister Erdogan's repeated position that Turkey is willing to play a constructive role in the resolution of the Israeli-Palestinian conflict by promoting confidence-building measures has been in line with both EU interests and also the preferred EU approach to the conflict.[111] It is worth noting that Turkish-Israeli relations have not fully recovered from the flotilla episode (May 31, 2010), and there is no prospect of improvement any time soon. The two sides show no sign of reconciliation, as Turkey has begun to assert a new foreign policy identity by playing a more active role in the Middle East and North Africa.

It is important, however, to realize the limits that Turkey encounters. Turkey's failure to persuade Hamas leaders, following their victory in the Gaza elections, to recognize Israel and to act according to the Oslo agreements demonstrated that Turkey's Middle Eastern policy has its limitations.[112] The AKP government's unprecedented openings to the Hamas-controlled government since January 2005, however, pointed to a balanced approach toward the Israeli-Palestinian conflict. The visit of a Hamas delegation, led by Khaled Meshaal and Omar al-Bashir, to Ankara in February 2005 alienated Israel and major Jewish associations, such as the Anti-Defamation League (ADL), which subsequently announced a change in their stance on the Armenian genocide. The ADL decided to support the Armenian position.[113] Some experts have called upon the AKP leadership to explain its motivations and goals behind such foreign policy changes. Nonetheless, they admit that such transformation of foreign policy signifies changes in decisionmaking processes, diversification of issue areas, and democratization dynamics in Turkey rather than an ideological reconfiguration, de-Westernization, or "Middle Easternization" of Turkish foreign policy.[114]

Having improved its democratic image and its economy, Turkey has aimed to play a more active, independent role in the region. Unlike the 1990s, Ankara has dismissed some suspicions about its pro-Israel rhetoric and Western-inclined policies. Turkey's antiwar attitudes and position are favorably viewed in the Middle East. In this regard, the inevitable question is: how can Ankara balance its role and interests as the promoter of regional peace yet at the same time continue its policy of rapprochement with neighboring Syria and Iran, which belong to the resistance bloc?

Turkey's changing security perceptions are better understood in the context of both the post–US invasion of Iraq and the country's broader democratic consolidation process, a move that rendered government more responsive to public opinion on foreign policy issues. It is in this context that the rise of Turkish anti-Americanism also can be linked to the incremental reconfiguration of US-Turkey strategic relations. The resurgence of the PKK issue in the aftermath of the 2003 US invasion of Iraq is a major reason for the deterioration of the US image in Turkey and the burgeoning distrust between the two countries. With the effective control of northern Iraq under the president of the Kurdish Regional Government (KRG) in Iraq, Massud Barzani, the PKK was able to develop its own facilities, such as the Kandil mountain camp, and gain access to crucial military supplies. Meanwhile, in Turkey, the Democratic Society Party (DTP), a Kurdish minority party in parliament, failed to deter the PKK from escalating its operations.[115]

Turkey's rapprochement with Iran was arguably a reaction to the increasing presence of the PKK in northern Iraq and Washington's tilt toward Kurdish groups and organizations.[116] Ongoing military cooperation with Israel, especially in the areas of military technology and intelligence, has further bolstered Turkey's military power.[117] For their part, Israeli officials appear more interested in splitting Syria-Iran relations, Syria-Hezbollah ties, and Syria-Hamas connections as part of the bargaining for the return of the Golan Heights to Syria. Reluctant to weaken its alliance with Iran, Syria moved to sign a new defense agreement with Tehran.[118] The Syrians are clearly interested in getting back the Golan Heights, but they have other legitimate regional concerns. Of the many windfalls that rapprochement with Syria has brought Israel, the most significant one is that Israelis could use Syrian influence to their liking in Lebanon. For all this to work, subtle, nuanced diplomacy is needed.

Lessons of History

The argument that, absent political and diplomatic approaches, no solution would emerge to counter terrorism needs careful parsing. Military intervention and occupation tend to fuel resentment and resistance. Although initially welcomed by the Shia community, the US occupation of Iraq has given Iraq's Islamists, both Sunnis and Shiites, a major boost in their pride and nationalism. It is now evident that hatred for Saddam Hussein did not produce automatic support for occupation.[119] The open-ended US presence in Iraq gave rise to armed nationalist resistance and the influx of al-Qaeda. From the very start, occupation was doomed to failure.[120]

If the lessons of history are worth anything, they should have taught us that the pervasive sense of despair and humiliation that helps fuel terrorism cannot be diminished, much less eradicated, by military force. Neither democracy promotion from outside nor military intervention presents a real way out of the current impasse. The Palestinian cause, analysts and scholars of terrorism concur, is the central feature of al-Qaeda's narrative of Western Crusader aggression against the Muslim community, or umma.[121] Political, diplomatic, law-enforcement, and intelligence efforts against terrorism require great energy, focus, and, not least, commitment. If there is to be a long-term and realistic chance of countering terrorism in the Middle East, coming to grips with the current standoff over the Israeli-Palestinian dispute might be a good place to start. Perhaps most importantly, it can be said that a regional system of security and cooperation in the Middle East cannot be established without a reasonable resolution of this conflict.[122]

Encouraging democratic reform from within might be one of the most promising long-term solutions to the terrorism problem. Security scholar Daniel Byman, having reviewed most elements of counterterrorism strategy, including disruption of terrorist groups and their operations as well as changing the overall environment to defuse the groups' anger or make it harder for them to raise money or attract recruits, examines the case for internal democratic reform:

> Killing and capturing al-Qaeda leaders, building defenses or encouraging jihadist groups to attack elsewhere all push back the problem, at best. But if some of the grievances that lead to terrorism can be addressed, the supply of money and recruits might dry up. Northern Ireland offers perhaps the best example. Credible British offers of political power to Irish nationalists made the use of violence seem increasingly unnecessary. Over time, and it took decades, the IRA leadership recognized that they had more to gain by working with a democratic system.[123]

Byman concludes that this option in Iraq is very expensive and probably not feasible. A more effective approach would be to encourage allies' cooperation in an attempt to contain and, in the long term, expose terrorists' divisions and disrupt them.[124] In this regard, the US strategy of ceding Anbar Province to the Sunni tribes to counterbalance the rising Shia power in Iraq may be successful and could provide some security gains in at least some areas. There is little guarantee that these gains will persist in the long term, however. Even Saddam Hussein had difficulty managing Iraq's tribes, despite ruling as a totalitarian and profusely disbursing patronage.[125]

The right strategy and the right war, as Philip H. Gordon so aptly notes, requires that we take seriously the views of our potential allies, recognize their legitimate interests, and secure their support and cooperation in confronting the common threat: terrorism. Islamic extremism will end up where Communism was laid to rest—on the same ash heap of history. "Ultimately," Gordon writes, "violent Islamism is not likely to win enduring support."[126]

The fallout from the US invasion of Iraq can be best summarized as "winning the war and losing the peace." Herein lies a lesson: military intervention is not the most effective way for the United States to remake the world in its own image. The revelations that the US military forces abused Iraqi detainees at Abu Ghraib prison strengthened the prevalent image in the Arab world of the United States as a neocolonial and imperialist power whose human rights rhetoric was little more than a cover for its broader geopolitical agenda in the region.[127] Yet, the great irony of Abu Ghraib was that most Arab governments allowed treatment of their own citizens that was just as bad or even worse. Arab human rights activists and journalists professed that what happened in their countries was not much different from what happened in Iraq's prisons.[128]

Nevertheless, many analysts and experts assert that for the peace process to move forward, US leadership will be essential. "Nothing in the historical record suggests that the parties will be able to reach agreement on peace by themselves," William B. Quandt writes, "and without a comprehensive Arab-Israeli peace, the hopes for stability, moderation, and democracy in the region will remain dim."[129] Diplomacy will go the distance should the United States and its partners make a serious commitment to the implementation of a two-state solution. Provision of security for Israel and sovereignty for the Palestinians, backed by strong regional and international support—these are the necessary guarantees for the conflicting parties, and they are not remedies beyond the purview of diplomatic solutions. These commitments can be linked to a major development plan for the entire eastern Mediterranean area, a sort of Marshall Plan for the Middle East, which could be achieved at a small percentage of the cost of war in Iraq.[130]

Freedom from foreign domination in Palestine and Iraq has become equated with peace for many Muslims in the Middle East. Military interventions have failed to deliver peace and stability in the region. At the heart of any sustainable solution should be a diplomatic resolution of the Israeli-Palestinian dispute. Although military interventions are appropriate on humanitarian grounds, there are many negative consequences involved in such interventions. Military interventions are an indefensible strategy for stabilizing, nation building, and democracy promotion. There are many ways to contain terrorism, but the most effective way to defuse the terrorist impulse is through multilateral diplomacy and international cooperation. The notion that the Iraq venture will lead to a democratic regime there—thus warranting its consequences—is dubious at best. Terrorism will continue to be a problem in the Middle East.

Looking to the Future

The Middle East is fraught with risks but also ripe with opportunities. Either good use is made of these opportunities or the United States could find itself constantly entangled in countering the risks. Diplomacy may not be feasible under all circumstances, but it is a step in the right direction that could save the region from accelerated, internecine violence. The commonly made claim that the use of force is the ultimate weapon for confronting terrorism is simply false. In fact, the concerns shown throughout the Middle East—by both governments and the public—suggest how seriously diplomatic measures are taken, even if some of their most ardent advocates admit they may not deter terrorism in the short term.

Among the points made in the foregoing analysis was that, just as the military intervention in the interest of combating terrorism has produced a greater obstacle to success, so has foreign presence led to a panoply of insecurities. The prospect of maintaining permanent US military bases in the Gulf region is a troubling one, posing a question: What are the threats that Arab countries of the Gulf face that requires permanent US military presence there? The new leaders of Iraq seek constructive engagement with their neighbors, and Iranians, for their part, have grown more pragmatic, while sharing with the Gulf countries several common interests, including safeguarding regional stability and the free flow of oil in the area. By contrast, the US military presence in the region, along with the formalization of the US security relationship with the Gulf monarchies, has led to the delegitimization of these governments.[131] As one Middle Eastern scholar notes, political Islam has often been a reaction to foreign rule or intervention, providing the Muslim clerics with a basis to challenge monarchies with European or US backing.[132] What needs to be kept in mind is that political reforms are the key to creating true opportunities for building effective security systems and bringing about change in the region.

* * *

This book addresses one central question: Will terrorism be contained or controlled in the Middle East? Three scenarios seem possible.

Scenario 1

Continuation of the occupation of Iraq by the United States and of the Palestinian territories by Israel presents the possibility that Iran and Turkey will be dragged into Iraq's internal tensions. These interventions could also lead to repercussions, such as US attacks on Syria and Iran, deepening even further the perimeter of US military involvement in the area.

The demonstration of US military might and coercive diplomacy to tame so-called rogue states is counterproductive. The risks and costs of such an approach have made it very difficult for the United States to pursue a sustainable policy in the campaign against terror. What is more, the Iraq War showed that NATO's centrality for US foreign policy toward Iraq has profoundly diminished, as has the once-characteristic unity within that organization.[133] Evidence of a rupture in NATO, which emerged largely when France and Germany opposed the Iraq invasion and Turkey's parliament denied the US military use of its bases, mounted even after the removal of Saddam Hussein's regime. Germany and France joined Russia to openly express opposition to the war. Key European members of NATO also expressed their discomfort about a unipolar world in which US power was predominant.[134] These divisions within NATO raised a question about whether military pacts of the past would work for solving future problems, calling into question US unilateral policies. NATO's operations in Libya beyond the creation of a no-fly zone in March 2011 were yet another indication of the ongoing divisions in the organization and the limits to achieving political goals.

Scenario 2

The second scenario—the one supported by the transatlantic alliance—would be cooperation and coordination of policies to counter terrorism and foster political reform and change in the Middle East while quickly moving toward US handover in Iraq. This option suggests that diplomatic and political measures are particularly suited to defuse regional tensions.

Foremost among diplomatic measures would be an effort to seek a reasonable solution to the Israeli-Palestinian dispute. For many Muslims, the key touchstone is the resolution of that conflict. There is a broad consensus that the creation of a Palestinian state, which would also enable Israel to live in security, is likely to seriously undercut the arguments of those who seek to exploit the plight of Palestinians in their effort to recruit terrorists.[135] On September 20, 2011, Palestinians will put this request for nationhood to a vote in the UN General Assembly, officially asking the international community to recognize them as a sovereign state. If the vote goes through successfully, Palestine will become the UN's 194th member state. Having seen no progress in peace process in recent years and having witnessed ongoing Israeli settlement construction in the West Bank, the Palestinian have decided to turn directly to the world's public opinion and the global community.

This raises the question of what happens if diplomacy fails. Skeptics will present the all-too-familiar argument that the animosity between Arabs and Israelis is so deeply seated that it simply defies diplomatic remedies. Psychological and social research has shown that, even were it hard to reach a political and diplomatic solution, we can increase dialogue by casting off zero-sum negotiating tactics in favor of a cooperative problem-solving approach. This tactic may not give us the certainty of peace, but it will surely take us closer.[136]

After Saddam Hussein's ouster, the Bush administration accused Syria of interfering in both Lebanon and Iraq by allowing Islamic militants to control southern Lebanon and infiltrate Iraq to fight US forces. In 2004, the US government imposed economic sanctions on Syria to isolate it. That policy intensified after the 2005 assassination of Rafik Hariri, the former Lebanese prime minister, which a UN investigation found to have implicated high-ranking Syrian officials. But these sanctions have proven harmful, as Mohamad Bazzi, a fellow at the Council on Foreign Relations, explained: "The more the West cut Syria off, the more Assad's regime turned to Iran, which helped bolster the Syrian economy with construction investments and cheap oil."[137]

Scenario 3

In a third scenario, solutions would grow out of a regional context that defined new relations among the countries involved. This would require sensitivity to the complexity and fluidity of national and international politics and recognition of these countries' geopolitical, economic, and cultural interests. This approach would require a multipronged strategy. It would stand a good chance of isolating Islamic militants and terrorists by undercutting their breeding grounds and denying them recruiting sources.

In such a context, US foreign policy toward Iran would have to be be based on engaging Iran, with respect for Iran's genuine and legitimate interests, while giving Iranian leaders the incentive to choose a different path.[138] The policy of containment toward Iran has been problematic at best.

The Lebanon war of 2006, in which Israelis bombed Beirut for several weeks, not only failed to strengthen the image of Israel's invincible deterrence, it also made Israel itself more vulnerable.[139] Hezbollah's strategic capability, in contrast, was not substantially damaged; if anything, its political strength was bolstered significantly. In fact, as one analyst argued, Israel faced as much threat after the war as before.[140]

The US invasion and occupation of Afghanistan and Iraq led to Iran's emergence as a key power in the Gulf, making accommodation with Tehran prudent. Increasingly, recognition of Iran's legitimate security considerations would make the region more stable and less costly for the United States.[141] To fight the right war in the Middle East, therefore, the United States must prevent Afghanistan from returning to the chaos that led to Taliban rule and sanctuary for al-Qaeda.[142] Given that Pakistani elements, in the army and the wider population, support the Taliban, US foreign policy faces a huge challenge in coming years.

It is equally crucial to understand why most Turks are skeptical of US intentions in Iraq. Turkish politicians are wary, knowing that the Iraq crisis could potentially lead to the creation of a loose confederation, further enhancing the prospects of the formation of an autonomous Kurdistan in northern Iraq in the near future. This possibility carries great importance for the region and would prove decisive in shaping future Turkey-US relations.[143]

The resolution of all these problems requires close collaboration among regional players and great powers. The plain truth is that terrorism has complex origins and that US-led military intervention and democracy promotion—that is, democracy instigated from outside—cannot fully eradicate its roots. More and more it appears that the neoconservative agenda of transformation and regime change throughout the Middle East to pave the way for US hegemony in the region has lost credibility. Although the nature of the diplomatic enterprise is changing, multilateralism, when it comes to defusing tensions, is the name of the game.

Diplomacy and negotiation, especially when compared with other alternatives, are less costly and more promising in the long term. Whether we treat terrorism as a war or a crime, separate or competitive approaches to confronting this threat will prove woefully inadequate.[144] "The Iraq War," Joseph Nye wrote, "was a dazzling display of America's hard military power. It removed a tyrant, but did little to reduce our vulnerability to terrorism. At the same time, it was costly in terms of our 'soft power' to attract others."[145] One of the many lessons of the conflict in Iraq is that reconstruction, negotiation, and international cooperation are far more likely to succeed, and surely less costly.

Notes

1. Gary Sick, "The United States in the Persian Gulf: From Twin Pillars to Dual Containment," in David W. Lesch, ed., *The Middle East and the United States: A Historical and Political Reassessment*, 4th ed. (Boulder, CO: Westview Press, 2007), pp. 315–331; see esp. p. 327.

2. William B. Quandt, *Peace Process: American Diplomacy and the Arab-Israeli Conflict Since 1967* (Washington, DC: Brookings Institute Press, 2005), p. 416.

3. Douglas Sturkey, *The Limits of American Power: Prosecuting a Middle East Peace*, (Northampton, MA: Edward Elgar, 2007), p. 194.

4. Gareth Evans, "Responding to Terrorism: A Global Stocktake," Daniel S. Hamilton, ed., in *Terrorism and International Relations* (Washington, DC: Center for Transatalantic Relations, Johns Hopkins, 2006), pp. 147–158; see p. 147.

5. Ibid., p. 155.

6. This point is made by Francis Fukuyama, cited in Simon Lee, "The Politics of Globalization and the War on Terror," in Maurice Mullard and Bankole A. Cole, eds., *Globalization, Citizenship, and the War on Terror* (Northampton, MA: Edward Elgar, 2007), pp. 145–167; see p. 157.

7. Ibid.

8. Michael C. Hudson, "The United States in the Middle East," in Louise Fawcett, ed., *International Relations of the Middle East* (New York: Oxford University Press, 2005), pp. 283–305; see p. 294.

9. Ibid., p. 303.

10. Niall Ferguson, *Colossus: The Price of America's Empire* (New York: Penguin Press, 2004), pp. 294–295.

11. Niall Ferguson, "Power," *Foreign Policy*, no. 134 (January–February 2003):18–24.

12. John J. Mearsheimer and Stephen M. Walt, *The Israel Lobby and US Foreign Policy* (New York: Farrar, Straus & Giroux, 2007), p. 77.

13. Ibid., p. 77.

14. Jeremy M. Sharp, "US Foreign Aid to Israel," *Congressional Research Service*, September 16, 2010, available at http://www.fas.org/sgp/crs/mideast/RL33222.pdf; accessed on September 7, 2011.

15. Mearsheimer and Walt, *The Israel Lobby and US Foreign Policy,* p. 26.

16. Sturkey, *The Limits of American Power*, p. 183.

17. Ibid., p. 173.

18. Richard A. Clarke, *Against All Enemies: Inside the War on Terror* (New York: Free Press, 2004), p. 246.

19. Ibid., p. 264.

20. Sturkey, *The Limits of American Power*, p. 184.

21. Edward W. Said, *From Oslo to Iraq and the Road Map* (New York: Pantheon, 2004), p. 266.

22. Quoted in ibid., p. 267.

23. Sturkey, *The Limits of American Power*, p. 65.

24. Ibid., p. 79.

25. Kylie Baxter and Shahram Akbarzadeh, *US Foreign Policy in the Middle East: The Roots of Anti-Americanism* (New York: Routledge, 2008), pp. 145–146.

26. Ibid., p. 146.

27. Sturkey, *The Limits of American Power*, p. 114.

28. Ibid., p. 116.

29. Ibid., p. 133.

30. Arthur Goldschmidt Jr. and Lawrence Davidson, *A Concise History of the Middle East*, 8th ed. (Boulder, CO: Westview Press, 2006), p. 439; see specifically Lawrence Davidson's argument.

31. Baxter and Akbarzadeh, *US Foreign Policy in the Middle East*, p. 150.

32. Graham E. Fuller, "Saudi Peace Plan: How Serious?" *Middle East Policy,* June 2002; available at http://findarticles.com/p/articles/mi_qa5400/is_200206/ai_n21313474; accessed June 27, 2008.

33. Sturkey, *The Limits of American Power*, p. 158.

34. Ibid., p. 173.

35. Ibid., p. 158

36. Daniel C. Kurtzer and Scott B. Lasensky, *Negotiating Arab-Israeli Peace: The American Leadership in the Middle East* (Washington, DC: US Institute of Peace Press, 2008), p. 36.

37. "Quartet Quartered, Road Map Thwarted, and Palestine Aborted," April 11, 2008; available at http://jordanispalestine.blogspot.com/2008/04/quartet-quartered-road-map-thwarted.html; accessed June 26, 2008.

38. Kurtzer and Lasensky, *Negotiating Arab Peace*, pp. 39–40.

39. Robert O. Freedman, "The Bush Administration and the Arab-Israeli Conflict: The First Term and Beyond," in Lesch, *The Middle East and the United States*, pp. 275–311; see esp. p. 306.

40. Jeremy Pressman, "From Madrid and Oslo to Camp David: The United States and the Arab-Israeli Conflict, 1991–2001," in Lesch, *The Middle East and the United States*, pp. 257–274; see esp. p. 269.

41. Ibid., p. 271.

42. James A. Baker III and Lee H. Hamilton, *The Iraq Study Group Report: The Way Forward—A New Approach* (New York: Vintage, 2006), p. 50.

43. Ibid.

44. Seymour M. Hersh, "Preparing the Battlefield: The Bush Administration Steps Up Its Moves Against Iran," *New Yorker*, July 7, 2008; available at http://www.truthout.org/article/preparing battlefield; accessed June 30, 2008.

45. Vali Nasr quoted in Hersh, "Preparing the Battlefield."

46. Reese Erlich, *The Iran Agenda: The Real Story of US Policy and the Middle East Crisis* (Sausalito, CA: PoliPoint Press, 2007), pp. 174–175.

47. Larry P. Goodson, *Afghanistan's Endless War: State Failure, Regional Politics, and the Rise of the Taliban* (Seattle: University of Washington Press, 2001), p. 76.

48. William Pfaff, "The Iran National Intelligence Estimate and the Eight-Year Carnival of Lies," *Washington Report on Middle East Affairs* 27, no. 1 (January-February 2008): 12.

49. Sir Eldon Griffiths, *Turbulent Iran: Recollections, Revelations, and a Plan for Peace* (Santa Ana, CA: Seven Locks Press, 2006), p. 231.

50. James M. Lindsay and Ray Takeyh, "After Iran Gets the Bomb," *Foreign Affairs* 89, no. 2, (April–May 2010): 33–49; esp. p. 37.

51. Geoffrey Kemp, "The Impact of Iran's Nuclear Program on Gulf Security," in Emirates Center for Strategic Studies and Research (ECSSR), *The Gulf Challenges of the Future* (Abu Dhabi, UAE: ECSSR, 2005), pp. 209–232; see p. 231.

52. Ibid.

53. Mahmood Sariolghalam, "Iran's Emerging Regional Security Doctrine: Domestic Sources and the Role of International Constraints," in ECSSR, *The Gulf Challenges of the Future*, p. 178.

54. Alidad Mafinezam and Aria Mehrabi, *Iran and Its Place among Nations* (Westport, CT: Praeger, 2008), p. 70.

55. Ibid., pp. 71–72.

56. Sariolghalam, "Iran's Emerging Regional Security Doctrine," p. 181.

57. Ibid., p. 183.

58. Ali R. Abootalebi, "What Went Wrong in Iraq?" in Lesch, *The Middle East and the United States*, pp. 412–433; see p. 431.

59. Lt. General William E. Odom, "The Nuclear Option," *Foreign Policy*, no. 160 (May–June 2007): 51–52.

60. Ali M. Ansari, *Confronting Iran: The Failure of American Foreign Policy and the Next Great Conflict in the Middle East* (New York: Basic Books, 2006), p. 254.

61. Ibid.

62. Mohammed Ali Abtahi, "Iran and International Relations: Impact on Political Stability in the Gulf," in ECSSR, *The Gulf Challenges of the Future*, p.158.

63. Jerrold D. Green, "Iran's Regional Policies: Western Perspectives," in ECSSR, *The Gulf Challenges of the Future*, p. 202.

64. Matt Duss, "Gerson: How Does This Engagement Thing Work?" *National Security*, July 29, 2009; available at http://wonkroom.thinkprogress .org/2009/07/29/gerson-how-does-this-engagement-thing-work; accessed August 14, 2009.

65. Fred Halliday, *The Middle East in International Relations: Power, Politics and Ideology* (New York: Cambridge University Press, 2005), p. 141.

66. Ibid., p. 92.

67. Jubin M. Goodarzi, *Syria and Iran: Diplomatic Alliance and Power Politics in the Middle East* (London: Tauris Academic Studies, 2007), pp. 57–58.

68. Ibid., pp. 290–294.

69. Richard Falk, "International Law and Palestinian Resistance," in Joel Beinin and Rebecca L. Stein, eds., *The Struggle for Sovereignty: Palestine and Israel, 1993–2005*) Palo Alto, CA: Stanford University Press, 2006), pp. 315–323; see esp. p. 315.

70. Ibid., p. 323.

71. Augustus Richard Norton, *Hezbollah: A Short History"* (Princeton, NJ: Princeton University Press, 2007), p. 77.

72. Ibid., p. 151.

73. Ibid., p. 158.

74. Toby Jones, "Saudi Arabia's Not So New Anti-Shi'ism," *Middle East Report* 37, no. 242 (Spring 2007): 29–32; see p. 29.

75. Baker and Hamilton, *The Iraq Study Group Report*, p. 50.

76. Ibid., p. 51.

77. Odom, "The Nuclear Option," pp. 51–52.

78. Ray Takeyh, "Time for Détente with Iran," *Foreign Affairs* 86, no. 2 (March/April 2007): 17–32.

79. Julian Borger, "Iran's Offer of Help to Rebuild Afghanistan Heralds New Age of Diplomacy with the US," *Guardian*, April 1, 2009; available at http://www.guardian.co.uk/world/2009/apr/01/us-iran-afganistan-foreign-pol-icy; accessed May 26, 2009.

80. Ansari, *Confronting Iran*, p. 188.

81. Ibid., p. 191.

82. Ibid., p. 192.

83. Mahmood Monshipouri, "The Islamic Republic at the Crossroad," *Today's Zaman*, June 25, 2009, p. 14.

84. Nicholas Blanford and Scott Peterson, "The Mideast's New Geography," *Christian Science Monitor*, July 5 and 12, 2009, p. 15.

85. Michael Slackman, "In Iran, a Struggle Beyond the Streets," *New York Times*, July 7, 2009; available at http://www.nytimes.com/2009/07/08/world/middleeast/08clerics.html; accessed July 8, 2009.

86. Michael Slackman, "Iran Hosts Regional Summit Meeting," *New York Times*, May 25, 2009, p. A4.

87. Ansari, *Confronting Iran*, pp. 232–242.

88. Tamar Hermann, "Civil Society and NGOs: Building Peace in Israel," in Edy Kaufman, Walid Salem, and Juliette Verhoeven, eds., *Bridging the Divide: Peacebuilding in the Israeli-Palestinian Conflict* (Boulder, CO: Lynne Rienner, 2006), pp. 39–58; see pp. 51–52.

89. Glenn Greenwald, "The Israeli Flotilla Attack: Victimhood, Aggression, and Tribalism," available at http://www.salon.com/news/opinion/glenn_greenwald/index.html; accessed June 3, 2010.

90. Akiva Eldar, "His Majesty King Abdullah's Interview with Haaretz," January 19, 2007; available at http://www.jordanembassyus.org/hmka01192007.htm; accessed June 11, 2008.

91. Mona Harb, "Deconstructing Hizballah and Its Suburb," *Middle East Report* 37, no. 242 (Spring 2007): 12–17; see esp. p. 13.

92. Robert G. Rabil, *Syria, the United States, and the War on Terror in the Middle East* (Westport, CT: Praeger Security International, 2006), pp. 207–208.

93. Raghida Dergham, "The Arab Moderates Locked between Two Options: The US and Iran," *Al-Hayat*, January 18, 2008; available at http://english.daralhayat.com/opinion/OPED/01-2008/Article-20080118-8dfee36c-c0a8-10ed.01ae-8; accessed June 3, 2008.

94. "Lebanon: Lipping Peace," *Panorama: The Gulf Today*, June 6–12, 2008, pp. 34–41; see esp. p. 38.

95. Shibley Telhami, "The Contemporary Middle East: Some Questions, Some Answers," in Karl Yambert, ed., *The Contemporary Middle East* (Boulder, CO: Westview Press, 2006), pp. 257–270; see esp. p. 270.

96. John Hughes, "The Other Critical US Relationship: Turkey," *Christian Science Monitor*, June 28, 2010, p. 32.

97. Ariel Zirulnick, "Turkey Risks Syria's Friendship in Last-Ditch Effort to End Violence," *The Christian Science Monitor*, August 9, 2011, available at http://www.csmonitor.com/World/terrorism-security/2011/0809/Turkey-risks-Syria-s-friendship-in-last-ditch-effort-to-end-violence; accessed on August 22, 2011.

98. Patricia Carley, "Turkey's Role in the Middle East," United States Institute of Peace; available at http://www.usip.org/pubs/peaceworks/pwks1.html; accessed June 6, 2008.

99. F. Stephen Larrabee, "Turkey Rediscovers the Middle East," *Foreign Affairs* 86, no. 4 (July-August 2007).

100. Serdar Poyraz, "Turkish-Iranian Relations: A Wider Perspective," *SETA Policy Brief*, no. 37, November 2009, pp. 1–14; see esp. p. 10.

101. Ibid., p. 13.

102. Ibid.

103. Larrabee, "Turkey Rediscovers the Middle East."

104. Ihsan Dagi, "Islamic Identity and the West: Is Conflict Inevitable?" in Pamela Kilpadi, ed., *Islam and Tolerance in Wider Europe* (New York: Open Society Institute, 2007), pp. 103–111; see esp. p. 109.

105. Ihsan Dagi, *Turkey Between Democracy and Militarism: Post-Kemalist Perspectives* (Ankara: Orion Publications, 2008), pp. 289–294.

106. Deniz Gokalp and Seda Unsar, "From Myth of European Accession to Disillusion: Implications for Religious and Ethnic Politicization in Turkey," *Middle East Journal* 62, no. 1 (Winter 2008): 93–116.

107. Ihsan D. Dagi, "The Justice and Development Party: Identity, Politics, and Human Rights Discourse in the Search for Security and Legitimacy," in M. Hakan Yavuz, ed., *The Emergence of a New Turkey: Democracy and the AK Parti* (Salt Lake City: University of Utah Press, 2006), pp. 88–106; see p. 104.

108. Burhanettin Duran, "JDP and Foreign Policy as an Agent of Transformation," in Yavuz, *The Emergence of a New Turkey*, p. 294.

109. "Olmert Urges Arab Moderates to Unite against Iran," *China Daily,* November 15, 2006; available at http://www.chinadaily.com.cn/world/2006-11/15/content_733711.htm; accessed June 3, 2008.

110. Fulya Ozerkan, "Turkey Patient Peacemaker," *Turkish Daily News*, April 29, 2008; available at http://www.turkishdailynews.com.tr/article.php?enewsid=103139; accessed June 4, 2008.

111. Eduard Soler i Lecha, "Turkey's Potential (and Controversial) Contribution to the Global 'Actorness' of the EU," in Nursin Atesoglu Guney, ed., *Contentious Issues of Security and the Future of Turkey* (Burlington, VT: Ashgate, 2007), pp. 33–50; see esp. p. 43

112. Ibid., p. 44.

113. Ioannis N. Grigoriadis, "Friends No More? The Rise of Anti-American Nationalism in Turkey," *Middle East Journal* 64, no. 1 (Winter 2010): 51–66; see esp. 63–64.

114. Kiliç Bugrat Kanat, "AK Party's Foreign Policy: Is Turkey Turning Away from the West?"*Insight Turkey* 12, no. 1 (2010): 205–225; see esp. p. 222.

115. Grigoriaids, "Friends No More?" pp. 62–65.

116. Ozden Zeynep Oktav, "The Limits of Change: Turkey, Iran, and Syria," in Guney, *Contentious Issues of Security*, p. 93.

117. H. Sonmez Atesoglu, "Mediterranean Fault Line—The Future of Greece and Turkey," in Guney, *Contentious Issues of Security*, p. 154.

118. Scott Peterson, "US-Iran Regional Power Plays Shift," *Christian Science Monitor,* May 30, 2008, pp. 1 and 10; see p. 10.

119. Jonathan Steele, "A War Fated to Fail: America's False Template in Iraq," *World Policy Journal* 25, no. 1 (Spring 2008): 80–88; see 87.

120. Ibid., 88.

121. Bruce Riedel, "The Return of the Knights: Al Qaeda and the Fruits of Middle East Disaster," *Survival* 49, no. 3 (Autumn 2007): 107–120; see 117.

122. For a similar argument, see Shlomo Ben-Ami and Trita Parsi, "The Alternative to an Israeli Attack on Iran," *Christian Science Monitor*, July 2, 2008, p. 9.

123. Daniel Byman, "US Counter-terrorism Options: A Taxonomy," *Survival* 49, no. 3 (Autumn 2007): 121–150; see 144.

124. Ibid., 145.

125. Austin Long, "The Anbar Awakening," *Survival* 50, no. 2 (April–May 2008): 67–94; see 87.

126. Philip H. Gordon, "Winning the Right War," *Survival* 49, no. 4 (Winter 2007–08): 17–46; see esp. 38–39.

127. Andrew Hammond, *What the Arabs Think of America* (Westport, CT: Greenwood World, 2007), pp. 106–107.

128. Ibid., p. 108.

129. William B. Quandt, *Peace Process: American Diplomacy and the Arab-Israeli Conflict since 1967* (Washington, DC: Brookings Institute Press, 2005), p. 426.

130. Ibid., p. 427.

131. Arshin Adib-Moghaddam, *The International Politics of the Persian Gulf: A Cultural Genealogy* (New York: Routledge, 2006), p. 125.

132. Mahmood Sariolghalam, "Understanding Iran: Getting Past Stereotypes and Mythology," *Washington Quarterly* 26, no. 4 (Autumn 2003): 69–82; see 76.

133. Rajan Menon, *The End of Alliances* (New York: Oxford University Press, 2007), p. 65.

134. Ibid., pp. 68–69.

135. Philip H. Gordon, *Winning the Right War: The Path to Security for America and the World* (New York: Times Books, 2007), p. 119.

136. Moises F. Salinas, *Planting Hatred, Sowing Pain: The Psychology of the Israeli-Palestinian Conflict* (Westport, CT: Praeger, 2007), p. 127.

137. Mohamad Bazzi, "The Real Goal at Annapolis," *Christian Science Monitor*, November 27, 2007, p. 9.

138. Gordon, *Winning the Right War*, pp. 120–129.

139. Trita Parsi, *Treacherous Alliance: The Secret Dealings of Israel, Iran, and the United States* (New Haven, CT: Yale University Press, 2007), pp. 276–277.

140. Ibid., p. 277.

141. Ibid., p. 280.

142. Gordon, *Winning the Right War*, p. 129.

143. Yigal Schleifer, "Why Turks No Longer Love the US," *Christian Science Monitor*, November 1, 2007, p. 6.

144. Daniel S. Hamilton, "Tackling Terror: A Transatlantic Agenda," in Daniel S. Hamilton, ed., *Terrorism and International Relations* (Washington, DC: Center for Transatlantic Relations, 2006), pp. 197–220; see p. 219.

145. Joseph S. Nye Jr., "Why 'Soft Power' Matters in Fighting Terrorism," *Washington Post*, March 30, 2004, p. A19.

6

The Critical Importance of Human Rights

The declaration of war—the so-called war on terror—in the aftermath of the 9/11 attacks on the United States has spurred a debate among politicians, diplomats, academics, and the military leadership over how this war should be carried out, how it might be won, and how to most effectively engage in "irregular warfare." The call for rethinking has brought policymakers, practitioners, and academics back to the familiar debate over how to balance respect for law and the safeguarding of society. There is reason to believe that, given the potentially devastating consequences of modern terrorists' methods, human rights values may not be seen as being as important in the face of perceived or real security threats to society. Yet, in the long run, respect for human rights and international law seems to be the most effective way to win this war of ideas.

"If unfettered by prudence and judiciousness," as Rodrigo Labardini, a lawyer in Mexico, so aptly cautions, "democracies may become the societies terrorists accuse them of being."[1] Terrorism has revealed not only the inadequacy of most existing legislation but also the natural tension that exists in the law and social institutions when addressing the issue of national security. In the face of this new threat, democracies may emerge as vulnerable to terrorists if they restrict liberties and fundamentally alter their people's lifestyles. Democracies must show a strong identity with the principle that the struggle to maintain legitimacy is entangled with upholding legality and respect for human dignity. In the words of Labardini: "Instead of deconstructing human rights and the rule of law, their basic principles should serve as guidance in the fight against terrorism. And this must emanate from society itself and be reflected in its legislation, practices, and human rights culture."[2]

The policy question facing the international community is: How best can we reconcile claims to security and human rights? To resist the worst excesses of security, human rights advocates must rely on the integrity of the rule of law, but at the same time they will have to engage those who stress the pursuit of security interests as the paramount goal. It is important to underscore the complexity of and limits to the application of human rights at all times while understanding the particular political dilemmas that they invoke when society is faced with grave threats.[3]

My central goal here is to argue that ignoring international humanitarian law on the grounds of "necessity" in "the war on terror" is unlikely to diminish terrorism or make the world safer over the longer term. There is no shortage of evidence that US strategic interests have historically outweighed the country's commitment to human rights. Some scholars and policymakers assert that national security trumps all other values in international relations and that human rights and security stand in a mutually exclusive relationship. Hence, they argue the need for a cynical repackaging of human rights in the face of new threats. But advocates of the global-community ethos, for whom the nation-state is anathema, raise legitimate concerns about the strengthening of sovereignty at the expense of human rights. The Faustian bargain between liberal proponents of the war in Iraq and US neoconservatives has carried the real risk of discrediting the concept of humanitarian intervention altogether.[4]

Some experts—George Lakoff, for example—have noted that evoking the war frame (i.e., the "war on terror") allowed President Bush to use certain tools against terrorism that undermined civil liberties. The "war" justified torture, military tribunals, and the denial of due process.[5] Implementation of this view revealed both the limits of power and the extent to which antiterrorism measures may compromise fundamental democratic values. Seeking to debunk the narrative that security and human rights are intrinsically irreconcilable, in an attempt to harmonize human rights and security, I argue for redefining security. In place of *national security,* we need *human security.* My general point here is that because human rights and security are not mutually exclusive, there is no need for trade-offs between the two. I also argue that the three principles of *universality, identity,* and *enforceable commitment* must enter the existing debate on human rights and security.

A study has found that reducing privacy rights—that is, civil rights—does not necessarily increase security from terrorism. In fact, reducing traditional privacy protections makes it difficult to assess whether such measures actually worked to prevent terrorist attacks. This empirical difficulty serves the policy interests and strategic bias of executive officials, especially when it leads to a high level of judicial deference to the executive on matters of security policy in times of emergency. Moreover, the absence of a terrorist attack does not rationally or cogently imply effective measures.[6]

To discuss the complexities involved in the campaign against terror, I examine three models of counterterrorism: the security model, the social model, and the legal-moral-diplomatic model. Representing a hard-nosed realism, the security model posits that sacrificing human rights in the interest of security is justified and is the most effective means of countering terrorism. Security mechanisms, including military repression, are the hallmarks of this model. The social model postulates that targeting social policy and development assistance constitute the most effective counterterrorism strategy. In this model, the goal is to create an environment in which civil society organizations and moderate Muslim organizations flourish. The legal-moral-diplomatic model employs a wide variety of instruments, ranging from law enforcement and the justice system to international cooperation, intelligence sharing, and diplomacy. These tools are essential to both a successful response to acts of terrorism as well as the prevention of attacks in the future.

In the sections that follow, I examine each model and its critics while addressing several questions: Are coercive counterterrorist policies effective? Are the Western world's values and interests at variance or compatible in the case of counterterrorism? Are coercive counterterrorist policies legal and ethical? Do they require multilateral support or can they be unilaterally conducted? What are the costs, risks, and benefits of coercive counterterrorist policies? Finally, I discuss an alternative discourse on security, human rights, and international law with a view toward refining the debate.

The Security Model: Return of the Imperial Presidency

The notion of sacrificing human rights in the interest of security, which has roots in both classical realism and neorealism, often overlooks one reality: that the war on terror cannot be won in any conventional way. Moreover, the cost to civil liberties far outweighs the harm done by terrorists. The pursuit of security at the expense of freedom enhances the prospects for more terrorism.[7] The US-led global war on terror has had several negative consequences for human rights throughout the world.

In Latin America, as Sonia Cardenas notes, antiterrorism measures have gone hand in hand with rising militarization. With US support, militaries in the region have increasingly engaged in combating gang violence and controlling crowds during protests. Militaries have also been moved to safeguard oil-rich areas like Chiapas. Support for militarization was manifested, for instance, in the resumption of US military aid to Guatemala in 2005, a country with dismal human rights conditions at the time. More recently, US military aid to the region has almost equaled economic aid. The largest recipient of US military aid outside of the Middle East is still Colombia.[8] In the West, we are in danger of allowing a culture of security rooted in fear and anger to displace a laboriously constructed, though still incomplete, culture of human rights.[9]

After 9/11, the Bush administration took several steps in its announced war on terror that resulted in the justification and tolerance of torture, and in some cases even legalization of it. We saw degrading treatment of prisoners in Abu Ghraib in Iraq, Guantanamo Bay in Cuba, and Bagram Air Force Base in Afghanistan. In fact, the war on terror was used to justify a massive expansion in the jurisdiction of the federal government, especially the executive branch. Yet the fundamental question persisted: Was the abuse of enemy prisoners necessary for the life of a democratic nation? In this section, I argue that torture and mistreatment of enemy prisoners was counterproductive.

The USA Patriot Act widened the use of wiretapping on telephone calls and e-mails, and also authorized the attorney general to detain foreign nationals on mere suspicion, without due process and other related legal protections afforded by the US Constitution. Patriot Act surveillance powers pose a greater challenge to privacy because they are authorized secretly, without a showing of probable cause of a crime. The result may be what some experts describe as a "back door to massive wiretapping."[10] The Patriot Act gave the government wide powers with a serious potential for the abuse of civil rights, especially as this authority has been applied to immigrant suspects detained secretly without charges for long periods of time.[11] The Bush administration justified this marginalization of the rule of law by deliberately confusing counterterrorism and the broader foreign policy agenda of restructuring the political landscape of the Middle East, an agenda unlikely to have generated domestic support unless fused in the public mind with counterterrorism.[12]

As a result, more than 750 alleged al-Qaeda and Taliban suspects were held from January 2002 at the US military base at Guantanamo Bay, without trial, charge, or access to lawyers. The Bush administration argued that inmates held there were not "prisoners of war" with rights under the Geneva Conventions, but "enemy combatants."[13] This view clearly contradicted the plain meaning of the Geneva Conventions of August 12, 1949, which apply to all situations of armed conflict. The writ of habeas corpus has historically been a crucial legal tool for the safeguarding of individual freedom against arbitrary state action. Even illegal or irregular combatants are entitled to certain minimal protections.[14]

The Bush administration condoned the torture and illegal interrogation of prisoners held in Guantanamo Bay in defiance of International Humanitarian Law and the US Constitution. Its interpretive understanding of "mental suffering" rising to the level of torture disregarded the international, legal definition of torture. International humanitarian law, for example, applies during armed conflict and prohibits torture or other mistreatment of captured combatants and detainees regardless of their legal status. Regarding such detainees, Article 17 of the Third Geneva Convention of 1949 states: "No physical or mental torture, nor any other form of coercion, may be inflicted on prisoners of war to secure from them information of any kind whatever. Prisoners of war who refuse to answer may not be threatened, insulted, or exposed to any unpleasant or disadvantageous treatment of any kind."[15] Detained civilians are likewise protected by Article 32 of the Fourth Geneva Convention. The United States has been a party to the 1949 Geneva Conventions since 1955.[16]

The Bush team resumed the use of military commissions to try "enemy combatants," employing highly controversial procedures. In the case of *Hamdan v. Rumsfeld* (2006), the US Supreme Court held that military commissions set up by the Bush administration to try detainees at Guantanamo Bay lacked "the power to proceed" because the structures and procedures of such military commissions violated both the Uniform Code of Military Justice and the four Geneva Conventions of 1949. The court argued that the Bush administration had no authority to set up these particular military commissions without congressional authorization. The US Supreme Court in June 2006 mandated, at a minimum, Geneva Conventions Common Article 3 protections for all prisoners linked to the US war on terror and held at Guantanamo.[17] Common Article 3 establishes certain fundamental rules from which no derogation is permitted. It recognized, among other things, that the application of these rules does not depend on the legal status of the parties to the conflict. It also requires humane treatment for all persons in enemy custody, without any adverse distinction founded on race, color, religion or faith, sex, birth, wealth, or other similar criteria. It specifically prohibits murder, mutilation, torture, and cruel, humiliating, and degrading treatment, as well as the taking of hostages and unfair trial.[18]

The process of "disappearing persons," or turning them into "ghost detainees," went on unabated, as did the policy of "rendering," or secretly transporting, suspects to coercive interrogations in places like Uzbekistan and Egypt.[19] Once a low-profile counterterrorism tool, the practice of rendition has become integral to US intelligence-gathering efforts since the 9/11 attacks. The Obama administration appears reluctant to abandon the Bush administration's assertion of the "state secrets" privilege. The "state-secrets" doctrine allows judges to short-circuit certain litigation when the judge determines that it involves highly sensitive government information, which, if disclosed, would damage US national security.[20]

The case of Maher Arar demonstrates the flaws of such counterterrorism practices. Arar, a telecommunications engineer born in Syria who became a Canadian citizen, was detained at New York's John F. Kennedy Airport by US Immigration and Naturalization officials on September 26, 2002. He was deported to Syria, where he was tortured and detained for virtually a year. He was released on October 5, 2003, following effective Canadian "quiet diplomacy."[21] There is ample evidence that aircraft operated by the CIA and that are presumed to have carried "rendition" prisoners flew through and stopped in at airports in Finland, Germany, Hungary, Iceland, Italy, Poland, Portugal, Ireland, and Spain. Many European governments were reluctant to push Washington on the rendition charges lest their own intelligence agencies' cooperation with CIA operations be revealed.[22]

The transfer of detainees out of the area in which they have been captured is a clear violation of International Humanitarian Law.[23] International law experts argue that terrorist suspects captured on the battlefield must be prosecuted according to the standards of the Uniform Code of Military Justice. Bringing accused terrorists to justice according to the procedures of a court-martial would both protect US security and uphold the nation's values.[24] Common Article 3 of the Geneva Conventions, which ensures the barest minimum standard of forbidding commitment of outrages upon personal dignity, is a matter not just of human rights but, like many laws of war, "good fighting practice."[25]

The bottom line is that denying the application of Common Article 3 to the war on terror has negative consequences. "If we want an act that was committed against an American to be a crime," one observer notes, "it also has to be a crime when it is committed by an American."[26] Absent respect for the Geneva Conventions, it is only a matter of time before other countries will exploit similar tactics to avoid having to give fair treatment to captured suspects. The US image as an international leader, to be looked up to by other nations and to be seen as the "city upon a hill" of the founding fathers, has been irreparably damaged by violations of the laws and customs of war that constitute grave breaches of the Geneva Conventions.

In her illuminating book *The Dark Side* (2008), Jane Mayer reveals the inside story of how the war on terror turned into a war against US ideals and values:

> In the name of protecting national security, the executive branch sanctioned coerced confessions, extrajudicial detention, and other violations of individuals' liberties that had been prohibited since the country's founding. They turned the Justice Department's Office of Legal Counsel into a political instrument, which they used to expand their own executive power at the expense of long-standing checks and balances. When warned that these policies were unlawful and counterproductive, they ignored the experts and made decisions outside of ordinary bureaucratic channels, and often outside of the public's view. Rather than risking the possibility of congressional opposition, they classified vital interpretations of law as top secret. No one knows to this day how many more secret opinions the Bush Justice Department had produced. Far from tempering these policies over time, they marginalized and penalized those who challenged their *idées fixes*. Because the subject matter was shrouded in claims of national security, however, much of the internal dissent remained hidden.[27]

The security strategy provided a rationale for the Bush administration to return to the "unitary executive," shrinking from the laws and court decisions that limited presidential power following the Vietnam War and the Watergate scandal in the 1970s. Administration lawyers reinterpreted the constitutional constraints on presidential power, calling it a new paradigm and asserting that the president, as commander in chief, could take any action he deemed necessary to protect national security and the people's safety without Congress or the courts being involved—that is, denying those branches of government the powers of oversight or restriction.[28] Arguing that, as commander in chief, the president has the authority to decide wartime tactics and strategies, the former deputy assistant attorney general John Yoo (2001–2003) and other advocates of the "unitary executive" theory have maintained that "only the executive branch has the ability to adapt quickly to new emergencies and unforeseen circumstances like 9/11."[29]

Similarly, in an attempt to invoke a reservation and arguing that the UN Convention Against Torture (1984) did not apply to terror suspects, Yoo, in an August 1, 2002, memo to Attorney General Alberto Gonzales, referred to the "amorphous concept of mental pain and suffering"—a concept that, he said, departs from those found in international instruments.[30] Consider, however, the way in which the Convention Against Torture, Article 1, ratified by the United States and 145 other countries, defines the term *torture*:

> Any act by which severe pain or suffering, whether physical or mental, is intentionally inflicted on a person for such purposes as obtaining from him or a third person information or a confession, punishing him for an act he or a third person has committed or is suspected of having committed, or intimidating or coercing him or a third person, or for any reason based on discrimination of any kind, when such pain or suffering is inflicted by or at the instigation of or with the consent or acquiescence of a public official or other person acting in an official capacity.[31]

Furthermore, the language of Article 2 is emphatically clear about the responsibility of state parties to the convention, and it declares "torture" to be one of the very few acts whose prohibition cannot be suspended or curtailed under any circumstances:

1. Each State Party shall take effective legislative, administrative, judicial or other measures to prevent acts of torture in any territory under its jurisdiction.
2. No exceptional circumstances whatsoever, whether a state of war or a threat of war, internal political instability or any other public emergency, may be invoked as a justification of torture.
3. An order from a superior officer or a public authority may not be invoked as a justification of torture.[32]

Yoo's reasoning based on a distinction between political and legal realms was even less compelling: "What the law forbids and what policy makers choose to do are entirely different things."[33] Critics question, on both practical and moral grounds, Yoo's view that Congress cannot pass a constitutional law that forbids torture by any member of the executive branch, as long as the president acts under his authority as commander in chief.[34]

Many experts have argued that the impetus for increasingly harsh methods of interrogation did not arise from the bottom of the chain of command but originated at the top. A close look at the official memoranda, executive directives, and public statements by President Bush and other administrative officials demonstrates that the pressure for collecting actionable intelligence did indeed come from the top of the hierarchy. The Bybee memos of August 2002 (the so-called Golden Shield) laid the legal groundwork for justifying abusive methods and the immunization of interrogation personnel from future prosecution.[35]

President Bush's decision to suspend the Geneva Conventions had far-reaching implications and was interpreted to foster the harsh treatment of detainees. The Schlesinger Report, prepared by an independent panel to review Department of Defense operations in Abu Ghraib, noted that the abuse of detainees in Abu Ghraib prison represented deviant behavior and a failure of military leadership and discipline. The report pointed to both institutional and personal responsibility at higher levels.[36] It concluded that "it is clear that pressure for additional intelligence and the more aggressive methods sanctioned by the Secretary of Defense memorandum resulted in stronger interrogation techniques."[37]

The Obama administration has insisted that fighting terrorism should not be conducted at the expense of US values and ideals. But, thus far, Obama has failed to deliver on his promise to shut down the Guantanamo Bay detention center, a shameful reminder of the US history of human rights abuse and the prevailing colonialist perception of US foreign policy.[38] Similarly, the Afghan war has presented many problems for the US and NATO forces. To deplete the hatred toward the US and give Afghanis room to build sustainable political and economic institutions, President Obama and his generals have contemplated shifting strategies, placing protecting the Afghan people above killing insurgents. One army general put it succinctly: "What we really want is the equivalent of a peaceful takeover, where the Taliban are forced out."[39] Terrorism and the illegal drug trade have flourished in Afghanistan in large part because the lack of a functioning economy has allowed warlords to fill the vacuum.

US officials have announced, for instance, that they are shifting their antipoppy efforts from destroying the opium-producing flowers to encouraging different crops. But, as experts remind us, this is a difficult process, given that poppies are easy to grow and yield four times as much profit per acre as wheat. Thus, farmers need cash crops to substitute for the poppies and newly built roads to get their goods to markets without paying bribes along the way. Even the most competent soldiers in the world cannot successfully monitor every step of such a process.

Karl Eikenberry, a retired army lieutenant general, best captured the complexity of the situation when he was US ambassador to Kabul: "The military can help set the conditions of success. But it is not sufficient for success."[40]

The new tenets of counterinsurgency, adopted by the US military in Iraq, have come to address this difficulty: "Focus on protecting civilians over killing the enemy. Assume greater risk. Use minimum, not maximum force."[41] US detention policies and the abuse of prisoners in both Iraq and Guantanamo Bay have irreparably damaged the image of the United States. Concern about the legality of the CIA's detention and interrogation policies has reached an unprecedented level, despite Bush administration officials having described the prisoner abuses at Abu Ghraib and Guantanamo as the unauthorized actions of ill-trained agents, some of whom have been convicted of crimes.[42]

Yet the Obama administration's approach to terrorism soon became the subject of an intense debate over the fate of many terrorist suspects whom the Bush administration had sent to foreign countries. The Obama administration, for example, continues to employ the practice of relying on foreign governments to hold and interrogate terrorist suspects ("extraordinary rendition"). Human rights advocates, however, have argued that the transfer of detainees from their place of capture to other countries without extradition proceedings could carry enormous risks. It could increase the potential for abuse at the hands of foreign interrogators and could also yield poor intelligence.

Even in cases where extradition proceedings are in place, the inclusion of torture evidence has become problematic. Whereas the prohibition of torture in interrogation and penal procedures is an essential element of US criminal law, in the context of international extradition proceedings, US law does not require the exclusion of evidence elicited through torture. Both the Eighth Amendment, which prevents the use of cruel and unusual punishment, and the Fifth Amendment, which prohibits compulsion of self-incriminating testimony, are predicated on the *jus cogens* prohibition of torture in US law.[43] This uneven treatment and discrepancy in US law has invited controversy. In ratifying the UN Convention Against Torture, the United States declared that substantive articles 1 through 16 would not be self-executing, and opted out of the dispute mechanism in article 30.[44] A compelling case can be made for tightening protections against the admission of coerced evidence. This affords the United States a unique opportunity to restore its moral leadership in an area where its fundamental values have come under question by its own citizens and foreign nations alike. As one legal expert suggests, "the United States should pass implementing legislation for article 15 of the [Convention Against Torture], which would demonstrate its commitment to excluding torture evidence in any proceedings, whether or not the US government was responsible for its elicitation."[45]

President Obama's approach to counterinsurgency in Afghanistan focuses on protecting the population, training local police and army forces, and going after high-value targets inside both Afghanistan and Pakistan. This narrow definition of the mission in Afghanistan, away from democracy promotion and toward specifically disrupting, dismantling, and defeating such terrorist groups and networks as al-Qaeda and its safe havens in Pakistan or Afghanistan, comes with the growing realization that transforming a country plagued by poverty, corruption, tribalism, robust regional identities, and decentralized society into a stable democracy may not be attainable in the near term. The infusion of thirty thousand additional US troops into Afghanistan may not nudge the country toward stability and prosperity. It may in the long term propel the mission toward open-ended nation building.[46] Critics point out that Richard Holbrooke never resisted the surge in Afghanistan. Under his leadership the operation grew to nearly 150,000 troops and $130 billion of annual expenditure—an operation that was still bent on fighting the old demons, protecting "Western credibility," and promoting a "legitimate accountable state."[47] Others argue that the Afghanistan war reveals serious flaws in the way the NATO alliance has operated. This war, they argue, has taken massive US leadership and more than 150,000 troops on the ground. Yet NATO has made little lasting impact and has begun to retreat without a clear victory in sight. As a result, growing divisions within NATO have alarmingly resurfaced.[48]

On balance, the security model or strategy allows leaders to "bend the rules" as they see fit and leaves unanswered the question of when the so-called war on terror will end. Marc D. Falkoff, a lawyer representing a detainee in Camp Echo at Guantanamo Bay, has questioned the government's right to hold detainees in Guantanamo, without charge or trial, for the duration of the war on terrorism. Since this war has no defined end point, this simply means that a detainee could be held in prison—indefinitely, without law or justice.[49] Furthermore, the security strategy seems to condone torture as a matter of public policy, not only legitimizing but also legalizing abuse under the rubric of "enhanced interrogation techniques."

The next sections examine the issues of torture and the privatization of security and the ambiguity of the laws under which security companies and their personnel (e.g., Blackwater) avoid being held accountable for their actions and operations in Iraq.

The Abuse of Enemy Prisoners: Torture

Regulation of the use of torture that has the endorsement of the state has a long history in the Western legal tradition. Torture was formally laid down in accord with Roman canon law. The European nations, from the Middle Ages through the eighteenth century, employed torture as a routine part of the legal process in grave criminal cases.[50] Some democratic countries have used torture even during the second half of the twentieth century, typically in response to what they regarded as imminent threat to national security. One study shows that torture was as common in the twentieth century as it was in the nineteenth, or even more common.[51] Nevertheless, the Bush administration's descent into torture in the name of waging the war on terror caused serious legal and moral rifts within the Western world. The occupation of Iraq produced gruesome images of abused prisoners at Abu Ghraib. Photographs showing US soldiers forcing naked prisoners into compromising positions caused not only a huge embarrassment for the US military operation in Iraq but, more importantly, humiliation and pain in the Muslim world.

The argument regarding the parsing of torture and its legality in the post-9/11 world has fueled more outrage than confusion. The Bush administration's "torture memos," released in April 2009 by the Department of Justice, outlined the methods employed by the Central Intelligence Agency to interrogate terrorism suspects in its custody. They raised serious concerns in many political camps. Numerous questions exist about the utility and effectiveness of torture to extract good information and uncover the truth. Leaving aside the issue of utility, the debate over the definition of torture continues to cause alarm for a civilization that agrees torture is wrong. "Although not all of its signatories have stood by their pledge," Jina Moore writes, "the Convention Against Torture is a mark of, if nothing else, international semantic consensus."[52] The enhanced interrogation techniques—cramped confinement, sleep deprivation, waterboarding—have been defended by the Bush administration on the grounds that such techniques fall short of posing "threat of imminent death" or "long-lasting mental harm."[53]

The decision to define the campaign against terrorism as war, and not as criminal terrorism, also had many grave implications, none more serious than allowing US forces to treat captives as terrorists who had committed war crimes against the United States. These captives were not treated as prisoners of war, but rather came to be known as "illegal enemy combatants"—a designation that was used to justify President Bush's suspension of the Geneva Conventions and the army field manual on interrogation. As a result, the US government adopted abusive methods of extracting confession and information from detainees, rendering torture a tool of public policy.[54] More insidiously, the government sanction of torture encouraged ordinary soldiers to engage in inhumane acts, believing all the while that following orders was a matter of patriotic duty.[55]

Far from averting cruel and degrading treatment, the Bush administration raised the bar for what counts as torture by equating it only with the infliction of lasting pain commensurate with "serious physical injury such as death or organ failure."[56] Some voices inside the liberal establishment even argued that "mental" torture might be permissible in clearly prescribed circumstances. The Bush administration's relegation of human rights to a lower priority demonstrated that compliance with human rights norms was indeed reversible. A similar rationale pointed to a new reality: "Human wrongs—such as torture in the name of anti-terrorism—can cascade throughout global politics just as quickly as human-rights-enhancing norms can be diffused."[57]

Torture (or "enhanced interrogation techniques," as it was often called by the Bush administration) is not scientific, and it is unlikely that interrogators can use torture in a restrained and specifically controlled manner. Organized torture yields false confessions and poor information.[58] Torture has undermined the prospect of good human intelligence.[59] Even if, as one analyst argues, coercive interrogation may at times yield actionable intelligence of high value, it is debatable whether it is worth the trade-offs. Deploying coercive interrogation methods to draw confessions entails a hefty price. It will most likely undermine the moral legitimacy of the detaining authority, weaken its sense of identity and honor, debilitate its efforts to protect its own soldiers when captured and in custody of the enemy, and more critically, brew the resentment and hostility of other people around the world.[60]

Other observers have come out vehemently against torture, arguing that using torture as a tactic in the name of security violates nations' obligations under international law. In fact, one expert points out, international law prohibits torture under any circumstances, including in times of armed conflict, political crisis, or any other national emergency.[61] In 2007, the UN special rapporteur on promoting and protecting human rights noted that the struggle against terror was not a "war" and that counterterrorism policies had to comply with international law, including human rights law and humanitarian law.[62]

Aside from the illegality of the torture, some scholars question the morality of the way in which information leading to actionable intelligence is drawn from detainees. "Torture still violates human rights," Ronald Dworkin notes, "even if information obtained through torture is needed to save American lives."[63] It is important to note, Dworkin continues, that "torture's object is precisely not just to damage but to destroy a human being's power to decide for himself what his loyalty and convictions permit him to do."[64] By the same token, for people in the United States, jailing suspected criminals without charge or trial or jailing people who have not perpetrated a crime but whom the police judge to be dangerous, would violate our view of human dignity.[65]

In the case of *Rasul v. Bush* (2004), the US Supreme Court established that the US court system retains the authority to decide whether foreign nationals—that is, non-US citizens—held in Guantanamo Bay were rightfully imprisoned. The US Supreme Court reversed a district court decision that the judiciary had no jurisdiction whatsoever to handle wrongful imprisonment cases involving foreign nationals held in Guantanamo Bay. The claimant, Shafiq Rasul, a British citizen, was released before the decision was handed down. It is important to remember that the concept of habeas corpus has been a cornerstone of Western democratic principles since 1679.

It has been argued that torture tends to escalate conflict and that it is an ineffective counterinsurgency strategy. Despite anecdotal claims to the contrary, the effectiveness of torture in generating intelligence is doubtful at best. History shows that democracies that have resorted to torture in counterinsurgency—for instance, the French in Algeria—have lost. The British inched toward peaceful solutions in Northern Ireland only after they ended abusive tactics.[66] The tough Israeli response to the first intifada in Palestine, which according to an Israeli inquiry entailed the mistreatment of 85 percent of Palestinian prisoners, appears to have temporarily suppressed one uprising while planting the seeds of wider violence that would occur in the next.[67]

Deporting suspected terrorists—that is, people regarded as a threat to public order or national security—to countries where they are likely to face torture or death is a clear violation of human rights. Scholars of international law advise caution, warning that one can wage war only on another country. Terrorism is a tactic, and terrorists are not soldiers but criminals who must be taken before a court of law.[68] The CIA's destruction of videotapes of al-Qaeda suspects' detention, depicting waterboarding and other harsh interrogation techniques, raises questions about activity at the highest levels of the agency. Withholding evidence being sought in criminal and fact-finding investigations amounts to obstruction of justice. Although no US court has yet ruled on the legality of the Bush administration's interrogation policies, these aggressive methods and tactics are broadly viewed as unlawful. Even within the administration there was strong resistance to such policies. This came to light following a late-night attempt by Alberto Gonzalez, Bush's legal counsel, and White House Chief of Staff Andrew Card to secure a signature from bed-ridden Attorney General Ashcroft in order that such policies could continue even though against the determination of their own Justice Department.

In the case of *Rumsfeld v. Padilla* (2004), the issue of the quality of US democracy for suspects and citizens raised another set of questions. On May 8, 2002, Jose Padilla, a US citizen who had flown from Pakistan to Chicago's O'Hare International Airport, was detained by FBI agents. He was placed under criminal confinement for about a month, and President Bush designated him as an "enemy combatant" liable to indefinite detention in a Charleston, South Carolina, high-security naval brig. Two years later, Padilla's case appeared before the US Supreme Court, which concluded that Padilla's detention was not authorized by Congress. Absent such authorization, the president lacked the power under Article II of the Constitution to detain as an "enemy combatant" a US citizen seized on US soil outside a zone of combat.[69] In the end, the federal judge disregarded the allegation of torture as irrelevant to the question of his criminal guilt. No serious political investigation has been called for and human rights organizations have been relatively quiet in the aftermath of Padilla's release.[70]

The Privatization of Security

Emerging details regarding the abuse of prisoners demonstrate the growing but unregulated role of private contractors and military intelligence officers in the interrogation of detainees in US military custody.[71] One can trace the roots of private security contractors to the late 1980s when the Cold War ended. The authority of private contractors, who are arguably under no legally binding law or jurisdiction and thus not accountable to any institution, has become the subject of intense debate. Some analysts have argued that there are inadequate safeguards governing who can work for these private military firms and for whom these firms can work.[72]

Other analysts note that an important concern in the employment of contractors relates to knowledge of the rules of engagement and armed movements, both of which are crucial to the safety and success of military missions.[73] That is to say, military missions could be compromised by the necessary dissemination of secret information. The Geneva Conventions only stipulate three categories: combatants, noncombatants, and civilians. The ambiguous status of contractors could lead to their being denied prisoner-of-war status, in which case they could be subject to human rights violations, similar to prisoners in Guantanamo Bay. Additionally, the demand for contractors in Iraq led to the employment of personnel who were not always up to the best-practice standards of Western militaries.[74]

These situations have raised many questions about the clientele of private contractors. Military contractors have worked for democratic governments and the United Nations and even promoted causes associated with humanitarian and environmental organizations, but they have also been hired by "dictatorships, rebel groups, drug cartels, and, prior to September 11, 2001, at least two al-Qaeda-linked jihadi groups."[75] The questions of who has jurisdiction over them and who can prosecute them, both internally and externally, remain unanswered. In cases where contractors commit misdeeds, "it is often unclear how, when, where, and which authorities are responsible for investigating, prosecuting, and punishing such crimes."[76]

War outsourcing has created the corporate equivalent of Guantanamo Bay—a virtual rules-free zone in which perpetrators are unlikely to be held accountable for breaking the law. US criticisms of the governments of Uzbekistan, Colombia, and Russia for systematic human rights violations have been significantly muted. In the name of antiterrorism, counterinsurgency, and national security, private contractors, governments, and other perpetrators appear to have evaded the law. A whole host of questions regarding private military firms in war zones must be answered, not the least of which is the question of regulation and inspection.

On June 29, 2006, the US Supreme Court struck down the military commissions at the US Naval Base at Guantanamo Bay and affirmed the protections of Common Article 3 of the Geneva Conventions that ensures fair trial standards and prohibits torture and other inhumane treatment. The US State Department has also expressed concern that pursuing claims involving foreign governments' human rights records can potentially constrain the war on terror. Although this may be the case to some extent, many issues that relate to the war on terror entail human rights in a global perspective.

Increasingly, private contractors' conduct has raised practical and moral questions as to how we should adapt the fight on terror to certain moral standards. "We may need further adaptations to the circumstances of terror," Michael Walzer writes. "But we can still be guided, even in these new circumstances, by our fundamental understanding of when fighting and killing are just and when they are unjust."[77] The most widely reported incident took place on September 16, 2007, when Blackwater security contractors killed seventeen Iraqi civilians. Although initially denying claims of wrongdoing by Blackwater, an FBI-led investigation later showed that fourteen of those deaths were unwarranted and "violated deadly force rules" in effect for security contractors in Iraq. A military review board concluded that all of the killings were unjustified and potentially criminal. Whether the security contractors who killed the Iraqis will be brought to justice, under the War Crimes Act or some other law, remains to be seen.[78]

The key is to determine under what laws security companies should be held accountable. One option is to remove the contractors' immunity from Iraqi law. But it is important to stress, as experts suggest, that the United States would be hesitant to submit contractors to Iraqi courts, which lack many of the legal safeguards of their US counterparts. US military law, the Uniform Code of Military Justice, was expanded in 2006 to apply to military contractors, but there are lingering debates as to how the expanded law should be implemented.[79]

The Social Model: An Alternative Discourse on Security

Targeting social policy and development assistance requires an alternative discourse on security. Since the tragic events of 9/11, human rights concerns have been marginalized in favor of the crackdown on "terror." The war on terror has led to a significantly more ideological vision of security. The move toward a conception of security with more of a personal dimension—that is, human security—has been halted in favor of a renewed emphasis on national security. As during the Cold War, security considerations have come to counter rather than reinforce human rights concerns.[80] However, the new counterinsurgency doctrine emphasizes manpower over firepower—that is, soldiers in Afghanistan must remain among the people and reside in villages for as long as it takes to build bridges and roads.[81]

Historically, the right to security, as a necessary precondition for individuals' well-being and civil rights, has been emphasized by Thomas

Hobbes and John Locke, and the UN Security Council occupied itself little with the rights of individuals during the first forty years of its existence. The nuanced understandings of the relationship between the state and its citizens were profoundly transformed during the decolonization period, but especially in the aftermath of the collapse of Communism, when a large number of new states lacked the capacity to exercise effective sovereignty over their territories and those living within them. The state's ability to fulfill its role as defender and guarantor of its citizens' rights and security has increasingly come into question.[82]

The reconceptualization of security in terms of human security has focused the debate, however tentatively, on the threats to the welfare of human beings caused by poverty, famine, criminality, genocide, ethnic cleansing, human rights abuses, economic threats, environmental threats, and threats to health.[83] In the post–Cold War period, the emergence of several humanitarian crises in northern Iraq, Somalia, Bosnia, Kosovo, Rwanda, and Sudan led the Security Council to regard these crises as "threats to international peace and security" and subject to authorized intervention under Chapter 7 of the UN Charter. This substantial shift in the Security Council's view of security raised the possibility of waiving the principle of nonintervention in Article 2.7, which permitted no interference by the United Nations in matters that were "essentially within the domestic jurisdiction of any State."[84]

This perceived need to qualify state sovereignty in matters of human security has called for a new debate on the age-old problem of reconciling order and justice, as raised by the proponents of the English school of international relations. The notion that the system of sovereign states is not in decline but rather is foundational to international security has for a long time been advocated by the English school. The discourse on order and justice has resurfaced in light of terror and global upheaval in the aftermath of 9/11. Increasingly, however, the consensus has shrunk on the sustainability of the state system in the face of the uncertainty associated with the post–Cold War era. One critical question appears to be: Is the state system our best chance of achieving order in world politics? The demands for reforming the state system, as Hedley Bull concurs, cannot be met without "a radical redistribution of the world's wealth, resources and other amenities of living."[85]

International relations are largely understood to function as a society of sovereign states that are responsible for protecting their citizens from threats associated with (external and internal) physical violence; it is, however, crucial that this society also recognizes conditions under which the principle of humanitarian intervention could be warranted. A growing recognition in the UN Security Council of the principle that "human survival and human rights concerns can trump sovereignty and the rights of states associated therewith" points to such a justification.[86]

The interplay between power and norms, power and morality, and national and international concerns has come to describe the relationship between state sovereignty and human rights in the twenty-first century. Likewise, interstate justice (based on equal state sovereignty) and global justice (what is right or good for the world as a whole) are coming into conflict.[87] Striking a balance between pluralistic visions of the world and solidaristic views of the international society of states is key to reconciling the security and human rights discourses. This balance demands a new thinking involving the changing conception of security.

New humanitarian discourse—on the grounds of justice, not order—such as the war against Iraq has also created new divisions in international society.[88] Significantly, US unilateral policies in the war on terror enjoy much less international support and tend to further undermine the US people's civil liberties at home as well as the US image abroad. Some commentators argue that rather than focusing on defeating and killing Afghanis or Iraqi insurgents, US forces should concentrate on providing human security and opportunity to the Iraqi or Afghani people, thereby undercutting the popular support that insurgents need.[89] It is vitally significant to promote development assistance programs and social policies that reach out to the bulk of ordinary citizens. A generation of young Iraqis is now mired in daily challenges—lack of electricity, concerns about security, and a dearth of jobs for all but the well-connected. This combination, along with a pervasive sense of injustice, is likely to push these young people to extremism or to joining the drug cartels.[90]

The power of humanitarian spirit is well captured by Greg Mortenson and David Oliver Relin in *Three Cups of Tea* (2006). They expose the governments of both Pakistan and Afghanistan for having failed their young generations on a massive scale. *Three Cups of Tea* faces the problems of terrorism and bravely proposes a cure: the building of schools. They see the key to fighting terrorism as being the promotion of education. This approach appears to be far more balanced and effective in countering the spread of madrasses—Islamic religious institutions—in Pakistan and Afghanistan. Their book underlines the significance of providing universal education—a world cure for poverty, disease, and war.[91]

The social model is not without its own complexities. It is not only the lack of economic development but also the local political, ideological, and cultural dynamics that need to be taken into account. Questioning the extent to which the social model might work, some observers call the policy of pacifying insurgents with jobs and money, which is central to the US strategy in Afghanistan, utterly misguided. If there is one thing that motivates the hard-core Taliban or the insurgents in their fight—religious fervor aside—it is vengeance. Almost all the Taliban are ethnic Pashtuns, whose code of conduct, *Pashtunwali,* seeks revenge against those who have inflicted pain and dishonor on their relatives.[92] Moreover, Taliban who are unwilling to continue putting up with violence and killing are unlikely to defect. Once a fighter has quit the insurgents' ranks, there is no going back, not even to his home village. Those who have done so have often been murdered. One would-be-fighter, interviewed by *Newsweek* magazine, said: "I want to die in the jihad, not as a sick old man under a blanket at home."[93]

The Legal-Diplomatic Model: Multilateral and Enforceable Solutions

It has become abundantly clear that a concerted international strategy is needed to counter the global threat of terrorism on a more sustainable basis. Such meaningful multilateralism has come to be seen as the "best principle" of sustainable human security.[94] There is no denying that progress in human rights and the rule of law will help reduce the extent to which terrorists are able to recruit members in the Muslim world. Respect for the rule of law and fundamental freedoms, some experts insist, is a key antidote to the conditions that give rise to terrorism. In contrast, the abuse of basic rights while fighting terrorism can be self-defeating, blurring the distinction between proponents and opponents of the rule of law.[95] Human rights advocates have grown wary of the consequences of the practice of torture in the name of national security, a practice that is difficult to contain once it has been authorized and is bound to further embolden and empower dictatorial regimes around the world.[96]

The proponents of the legal-diplomatic model employ a full range of instruments, from law enforcement and the justice system to international cooperation, intelligence sharing, and diplomacy. These instruments are pivotal to both a successful response to acts of terrorism as well as the prevention of attacks in the future. Central to this model is the premise that fighting terrorism should be a matter for law enforcement or the judiciary, rather than primarily a military matter. Fighting terror, according to this model, is like fighting crime: it is basically a police issue, not a military campaign. A major objection to this approach is the difficulty encountered in getting to the suspects and mustering evidence for a trial. On balance, however, the emphasis on legal solutions comports with the justice and human-rights-based approach (universality), core values and beliefs of the international community (identity), and respect for the rule of law (enforcement commitment).

On the centrality of law enforcement to the protection of human rights, some experts have argued that building functioning public justice systems is fundamental to socioeconomic progress in the developing world. On the local level, they insist, it is crucial to focus on directly enhancing the capacity of the police, prosecutors, social workers, and judges who are supposed to enforce the law on behalf of the poor.[97] There is also the issue of state identity. Human rights scholars note that state identities are constructed not only in relationship to the wider international society but also in connection with regional and cultural communities. To define the interests of countries faced with renewed security threats in terms of the standards shared by communities of like-minded states is the key to human rights identity and promotion.[98] It is in this context that I suggest that reframing the debate in terms of "universality," "identity," and "enforceable commitment" within the legal-diplomatic framework offers several advantages in the effort to combat terrorism, none more important than developing an enforceable and multilateral counterterrorism regime.

If we concede the permissibility of torture and/or other cruel interrogation techniques, especially in the case of the ticking-bomb scenario, we run the risk of normalizing such practices and undermining strong moral and legal inhibitions against them. Justifying torture on special occasions or on consequential grounds—based on a rational moral calculus of costs and benefits—violates the absolute ban on the practice. By carving out an exception, David Luban warns, "the prohibition on torture is weakened, or becomes less enforceable, and the result will be too many cases of unjustified torture."[99]

Another troubling aspect of torture, as experts rightly argue, is that once torture becomes a government practice, it ineluctably spreads, as demonstrated by the evidence from the conduct of such countries as France in Algeria, Argentina under the junta, and Israel before the supreme court banned "physical pressure."[100] Ultimately, the practice of torture will tell us less about the rationale or the morality behind it and more about the identity of the person who resorts to such horrific acts.

Some legal scholars have suggested that the United States and the international community would benefit from adherence to the UN counterterrorism regime, which determines when and under what conditions the use of force is appropriate. Such a regime would counterbalance the tendencies of countries like the United States that rely too much on military tools to address the issues of global terrorism. "International law," Richard Falk asserts, "is flexible enough to allow the United States, and other countries, to meet novel security needs. Beyond this, neither American values nor strategic goals should be construed to validate uses of force that cannot win support in the UN Security Council."[101] Adhering to the legal system of prohibitions on the use of force would prevent the tragic blunders of reckless foreign intervention.

Others have argued that the UN has a comparative advantage in many important global counterterrorism functions. As Eric Rosand points out, these include the ability to serve as a global setter of norms and to assist states in building up their counterterrorism capacities. The UN can also convene experts from around the world, create universal lists of terrorist groups and individuals against whom sanctions might be targeted, and address conditions conducive to the spread of terrorism.[102] Although states will take the lead in combating and preventing terrorism, UN counterterrorism architecture can yield successful results. With a broad-based consensus framework finally in place, Rosand insists, the UN needs further reforms, streamlining, and more funding to function as an appropriately designed intergovernmental body.[103]

To explain the interconnected nature of the components of the security debate, we need to return to the changing notion of security. Prior to 9/11, the evolving meaning of security was leaning toward placing human security and human well-being at the heart of the debate over national security. The concept of security increasingly focused on the needs of the individual. The growing international emphasis on human security and the parallel development of the right to protect the victims of violence were of paramount importance. The progress made toward the universal recognition of an international responsibility to protect the rights of victims of violence or systematic repression, however tentatively, was a great boost to placing human security on the global agenda. The war on terror, which has emphasized a narrow definition of the right to security, has clearly diverted attention from the notion of human security by resurrecting the classic dichotomy between individual liberty and national security.

It may be helpful to engage two components of the security–human rights debate: (1) that it is imperative to establish a hierarchy of human rights in the face of new threats to society, and (2) that it is critical to ground counterterrorism in a functioning legal system. While advocating the establishment of such a hierarchy of human rights, some legal experts have argued that seeking a balance or proportionality between security and human rights is far too crude an approach to do justice to the debate. The focus instead needs to shift to how the structure of human rights can assign proper weights to security considerations.[104]

Others argue that among human rights, nonderogable rights (the right to life, prohibition of torture, prohibition of slavery or servitude, and nonretroactivity of criminal laws and penalties) signify a more fundamental interest of human beings and share the original character of the concept of a "political trump" that is markedly different from the existing, expanded definition of human rights.[105] While supporting nonderogable rights as a hierarchical norm, they argue that such rights can in fact provide a common framework to promote cultural diversity.[106]

Still others note that while most nonderogable rights are of greater importance, some derogable rights (e.g., due process rights) may be of equal importance. The international community as a whole has neither established a uniform list of nonderogable rights nor ranked nonderogable rights higher than derogable rights, on the assumption that they represent higher-order norms. If the realization of a derogable right conflicts with the fulfillment of a nonderogable right, the latter will not necessarily prevail, unless its status as a preemptory norm of general international law is recognized.[107] Similarly, the provision of security in times of crisis is bound to enhance the government's legitimacy, at least in the short run, as security considerations and counterterrorist activities prevail over competing values. From the practical standpoint, the provision of security tends generally to overlap with nonderogable rights, such as the right not to be subjected to slavery and racial discrimination.

The designation of "basic rights" to certain entitlements highlights two potentially perilous slippery slopes. First, the exclusion of some civil liberties (e.g., freedom of thought, conscience, and religion, and due process rights, including the right to a full and fair trial) from the hierarchy of basic rights is likely to open the door to possible—and even irreversible—abuses of human rights in states of emergency.[108] Consider, for example, the debate over what rules should apply to combating terrorism. In this regard, several questions persist: Should questionable interrogation techniques that involve some degree of torture be tolerated? Should detainee-interrogation techniques that obviously go well beyond those sanctioned in either the Uniform Code of Military Justice or in any humanitarian treatment standards set forth in the Geneva Conventions be permitted? Should the military commissions at Guantanamo Bay, which clearly violate international law, be seen as the best way to bring terrorists to justice? Should indefinite preventive detention be regarded as a "necessity" in times of emergency?

An affirmative response to these questions will bring up the matter of reciprocity, which could potentially lead into the trap of disregarding international standards. Once US forces condone actions deemed illegal according to domestic and international laws, these practices will almost automatically become the benchmark for interrogation methods considered suitable for use by both state and nonstate actors.[109] Policymakers must resist the notion that indefinite periods of detention are necessary to ensure the priority of military operations during crises. These violations are unnecessary and such practices clearly undermine the responsibility for law, order, and justice for the benefit of short-term security.

A second tricky course concerns the widely heard position that rights must assume different levels of protection and importance in different situations. Short of exceptional circumstances having to do with the collective security of the nation, such a position leaves the door open for all sorts of abuses. In South Africa, under the system of racial apartheid, for example, the right to education was viewed as central in that it was a facilitative right whose realization was the key to the enjoyment of other rights and its fulfillment a prerequisite to creating the conditions for the attainment of substantive equality and social justice.[110] But in postapartheid South Africa, questions remain about whether the right to education and other related rights should be relegated to a lower level of priority. Similarly, in Iraq immediately after the occupation, US forces placed security considerations above other concerns such as the the basic economic needs of the local population. As a result, a vacuum was created in which insurgents operated and caused further fear and destruction. Nearly a decade after the occupation, security considerations still preempt other values in one fundamental sense: any precipitous withdrawal of US forces in the name of local autonomy and self-determination would doubtless plunge Iraq into a full-scale civil war, with rampant feelings of insecurity for the Iraqi people. Iraqi prime minister Nouri al-Maliki has agreed to a deal with the Obama administration that could lead to several thousand US troops remaining after the December 31, 2011, deadline for withdrawal. Maliki appears to have enough support for the agreement to be passed by parliament, even as the followers of Shiite cleric Muqtada al-Sadr may pose a serious challenge to the accord.[111]

Even assuming that the global threat of terrorism has made the establishment of a hierarchy of human rights inevitable, there remain questions of costs and risks associated with the disastrous precedents that could result from periods of emergency. The creation of a hierarchical relationship may also lead to an unsolvable moral and legal ambiguity concerning the question of why the restriction of certain rights is necessary. There is no clear agreement regarding an exhaustive list of rights. It is unclear precisely which rights might be considered "fundamental" or indeed how a right reaches the status of "basic rights." The lack of generally agreed-upon standards makes it extremely difficult to establish such a hierarchy of rights.[112] Therefore, the extent to which such a hierarchy—when and if constructed—can provide any reliable theoretical and policy guidance remains in dispute.[113]

As to the trade-off thesis, some experts have argued that restricted trade-offs between different values (e.g., security and human rights) are warranted only if they are made in a context of democratic legitimacy that minimizes injustice and arbitrary violations of rights.[114] Others have argued that US officials must be sure that such trade-offs are not made in areas recognized as nonderogable human rights; the trade-offs must be limited to what is essential, applied under exceptional circumstances, and, in some cases, as temporary measures.[115] The problem with these arguments is that governments routinely compromise their stance on human rights promotion, both at home and abroad, in their search for military allies, intelligence cooperation, and political support.

The notion of trade-off is debatable on two grounds: (1) it is based on a false dichotomy between security and liberty; and (2) it leads to the perilous expansion of executive powers in the name of national security. The key to challenging this false dichotomy lies with the legislature, which should limit the purview of executive powers by emphasizing transparency and accountability.[116] To achieve national security at the expense of fundamental rights central to liberal democracy—life, liberty, property, privacy, and free speech—entails colossal costs and risks. In the same vein, the security/human rights dichotomy renders counterterrorism ineffective, in part because it puts the safety of the state at odds with safeguarding civil liberties. This dichotomy, as one expert puts it, overlooks many grave and complex problems. It is entirely conceivable that measures that seemingly violate individual rights may concurrently protect them more effectively. Identity cards and biometric tracking, for instance, may render more efficient and fair the operation of the criminal justice system by clearly establishing that a suspect was or was not present in the course of a crime. Ultimately, such security measures can advance liberty.[117]

To lay counterterrorism infrastructure in legal grounds evokes different reactions. Some legal scholars question the civil libertarian approach and defend the judicial deference approach, arguing that the legal and institutional basis of the case against counterterrorism is wrong. Pointing to the limited ability of lawyers—qua lawyers—to substantially contribute to the process of decisionmaking in emergencies, they argue that deference to the executive during emergencies is both necessary and desirable.[118] When the executive is pressured—or even obligated—to implement controversial methods of protecting its citizens, such as discrimination against aliens, coercive interrogation techniques, or censorship of hate speech, the judiciary should not interfere on constitutional grounds unless under exceptional circumstances. US constitutional law and international law do not provide reasons for courts or legislators to depart from their historical posture of deference to the executive in times of crisis. To be able to respond effectively to international crises, "the president cannot be hemmed in by international treaties and constitutional limitations, as interpreted by judges."[119]

Other legal experts refute the judicial-deference approach, noting, first, that the absence of an agreed-upon definition of terrorism constitutes an obstacle to the practice of counterterrorism. Because terrorism is context-sensitive and case specific, they assert, it is virtually impossible to create the firm legal grounding that will make counterterrorist acts legitimate and publicly acceptable.[120] Second, under antiterrorism laws, the US National Security Agency (NSA) has been given sweeping investigative powers.[121] The priorities given to NSA's counterterrorism practice, however legitimate, raise a myriad of questions about the ways in which those civil liberties we are fighting terrorists to defend can be strengthened. That also means that the task of reconciling civil rights and counterterrorism cannot be left to the uncontrolled discretion of the executive.

What has emerged from these discussions is that it is insufficient to simply adapt to new political realities. A new way of thinking is needed to demonstrate that the commitment to liberty is resilient in the struggle against terrorism. "If terrorism leads us to close down the society," Anthony Lewis writes, "then the terrorists will have won."[122] Proper moral weights must be given to both liberty and security on the premise that the differences between these two values need not be seen as irreconcilable. There is no easy answer to the tensions between security needs and human rights, making uncomfortable choices almost always unavoidable. But to use a security template that invariably sacrifices civil liberties is not only morally debilitating and hazardous but politically imprudent over the longer term.

* * *

In recent years, US policymakers have underscored the importance of the security model, placing emphasis on security at the expense of human rights. The wars in Afghanistan and Iraq are examples both of the security model's implementation and its pitfalls. The social approach deserves more attention, but it has its own drawbacks. The legal-moral-diplomatic model offers a broader and more comprehensive definition of the "war on terror." The use of force in the absence of legitimacy is enormously wasteful of resources and unlikely to achieve desired outcomes in the long run.[123] At the same time, modern terrorist attacks on civilian targets pose serious moral questions.

Although it is true that human rights may not provide a suitable vehicle for handling every political and legal issue,[124] counterterrorism measures taken without regard for democratic principles and the rule of law are likely to produce more terrorism.[125] Furthermore, the war on terror, which has emphasized a narrow definition of the right to security, has clearly diverted attention from the issue of human security by resurrecting the classic debate between individual liberty and national security. Increasingly, US army strategists are convinced that "supporting Afghan and Pakistani governments that can meet the needs of their own people—including security—must be the long-term solution."[126] The challenge in Afghanistan is to recognize that one cannot simply kill or capture one's way out of a complex insurgency.[127]

The Bush administration overlooked a cardinal rule of modern international relations: multilateralism is in fact the best principle of sustainable human security.[128] There is no denying that progress in human rights and the rule of law will help reduce the extent to which terrorists are able to recruit members in the Muslim world. Human rights advocates have grown wary of the consequences of the practice of torture in the name of national security. The practice of torture is difficult to control once it has been authorized—not to mention that such practices would further embolden and empower dictatorial regimes around the world.[129]

The claim that it is all a question of balancing human rights against the public interest has become increasingly controversial. The trade-off hypothesis—between security, on the one hand, and civil-political rights and democratic governance, on the other—has come under critical scrutiny. This is because increases in international terrorist activity do not affect the status of political rights, civil liberty, or democracy one way or another. The trade-off itself may not be required.[130] Some observers even argue that the expansion of civil and political rights has coincided with an increase in the level of both domestic and international terrorist activity.[131] Democracies seem far more resilient than it is generally believed in that they seem capable of contending with the perpetrators of terrorist attacks without the need to curtail liberty.[132]

Similarly, the trade-off hypothesis is far too crude to do justice to the debate. Rather, the focus needs to be on how the structure of human rights can be so strengthened that it could no longer be easily swept aside in the interest of broader security claims. Perhaps one way to achieve this goal is to reframe the debate over human rights around the notions of universality, identity, and enforceable commitment. Without universality, human rights are nothing but hollow rhetoric. The struggle against violent extremism should not change who Westerners are and what values they hold dear. Ratification of international human rights instruments, such the Convention Against Torture, renders them the supreme law of the land, making their enforcement imperative. There can be no double standards in respecting internationally recognized laws of war and human rights. All signatories to human rights instruments and treaties must comply with them, both nationally and internationally. What has emerged most clearly from this study is that such an adaptation to new political realities is merely insufficient. A basic rethinking of policy choices is in order. From both practical and normative standpoints, the creation of an antiterror norm or regime is the good place to start counterterrorism.[133]

While postconflict nation-building and reconstruction offer the most effective opportunity of counterterrorism and counterinsurgency, it is important to bear in mind that the respect for human rights and social justice remain, in the long term, central to a world free from political and ideological conflicts. Ironically, the post-9/11 era has offered a unique moment whereby different countries and groups, both in the Middle East and the West, have simultaneously engaged in human rights discourses that have transformed consciousness and global awareness.[134] Just as eliminating human rights abuses and political violence is crucial to living a dignified life, so is fulfilling the narrative of social justice, equality, and the rule of law in a crowded world in which all countries face the challenge of deterring terrorism.

Notes

1. Rodrigo Labardini, "Emergency Situations," in David P. Forsythe, ed., *Encyclopedia of Human Rights*, vol. 1 (New York: Oxford University Press, 2009), pp. 128–134; see esp. p. 134.

2. Ibid., p. 134.

3. Liora Lazarus and Benjamin J. Goold, "Security and Human Rights: The Search for a Language of Reconciliation," introduction to Benjamin J. Goold and Liora Lazarus, eds., *Security and Human Rights* (Portland, OR: Hart, 2007), pp. 1–24; see p. 12.

4. Jennifer M. Welsh, "The Responsibility to Protect: Securing the Individual in International Society," in Goold and Lazarus, *Security and Human Rights*, p. 374.

5. George Lakoff, "War on Terror, Rest in Peace," AlterNet, August 1. 2005; available at http://www.alternet.org/story/23810/war_on_terror%2C_rest _in_peace/; accessed February 26, 2010.

6. Tiberiu Dargu, "Is There a Trade-off Between Security and Liberty? Executive Bias, Privacy Protections, and Terrorism Prevention," *American Political Science Review* 105, no. 1 (February 2011): 64–78; see esp. 75.

7. Laura K. Donohue, *The Costs of Counterterrorism: Power, Politics, and Liberty* (Cambridge: Cambridge University Press, 2008).

8. Sonia Cardenas, *Human Rights in Latin American: A Politics of Terror and Hope* (Philadelphia: University of Pennsylvania Press, 2010), pp. 196–197.

9. Stephen J. Toope, "Human Rights and the Use of Force After September 11th, 2001," in Daniel J. Sherman and Terry Nardin, eds., *Terror, Culture, Politics: Rethinking 9/11* (Bloomington: Indiana University Press, 2006), pp. 236–258; see p. 239.

10. Laurie Thomas Lee, "Patriot Act Surveillance Powers Violate Privacy," in Jamuna Carroll, ed., *Privacy: Opposing Viewpoints Series* (New York: Thomson Gale, 2006), pp. 21–28; see p. 29.

11. Richard Falk, "Encroaching on the Rule of Law: Post-9/11 Policies Within the United States," in Alison Brysk and Gershon Shafir, eds., *National Insecurity and Human Rights* (Berkeley: University of California Press, 2007), pp. 14–36; see p. 35.

12. Ibid., p. 36.

13. Robert G. Patman, "Globalization, the New US Exceptionalism, and the War on Terror," *Third World Quarterly* 27, no. 6 (2006): 963–986.

14. David P. Forsythe, "The United States: Protecting Human Dignity in an Era of Insecurity," in Brysk and Shafir, *National Insecurity and Human Rights*, pp. 37–55; see pp. 38–39.

15. Kenneth Roth, "An Open Letter to President Bush on the Torture of Al-Qaeda Suspects," *Counterpunch*, December 27, 2002; available at http://www .counterpunch.org/roth1227html; accessed Feb. 28, 2008.

16. Ibid.

17. David P. Forsythe and John Gruhl, "United States: War on Terrorism," in Forsythe, *Encyclopedia of Human Rights*, vol. 5, p. 239.

18. For an illuminating discussions on the Geneva Conventions, see Shadi Mokhtari, *After Abu Ghraib: Exploring Human Rights in America and the Middle East* (New York: Cambridge University Press, 2009), pp. 34–38.

19. Forsythe, "The United States: Protecting Human Dignity in an Era of Insecurity," pp. 43–47.

20. Warren Richey, "Will Obama Keep Some Bush Anti-terror Tactics?" *Christian Science Monitor*, February 13, 2009, p. 4.

21. Howard Adelman, "Canada's Balancing Act: Protecting Human Rights and Countering Terrorist Threats," in Brysk and Shafir, *National Insecurity and Human Rights,* pp. 137–156; see esp. p. 150.

22. Mary Crane, "U.S. Treatment of Terror Suspects and U.S.-EU Relations," *Council on Foreign Relations*, December 6, 2005; available at http://www.cfr.org/publication/9350/; accessed March 7, 2008.

23. Forsythe, "The United States: Protecting Human Dignity in an Era of Insecurity," p. 43.

24. Katherine Newell Bierman, "Military Commissions in Light of the Supreme Court Decision in *Hamdan v. Rumsfeld*," in John T. Rourke, ed., *Taking Sides: Clashing Views in World Politics*, 13th ed. (Dubuque, Iowa: McGraw-Hill, 2008), pp. 327–335; see p. 327.

25. Ibid., p. 329.

26. Ibid., p. 331.

27. Jane Mayer, *The Dark Side: The Inside Story of How the War on Terror Turned into a War on American Ideals* (New York: Doubleday, 2008), p. 328.

28. David P. Forsythe and John Gruhl, "United States War on Terrorism," in Forsythe, *Encyclopedia of Human Rights*, vol. 5, pp. 234–245; see esp. pp. 243–244.

29. John Yoo, *War by Other Means: An Insider's Account of the War on Terror* (New York: Atlantic Monthly Press, 2006), p. 234.

30. Mokhtari, *After Abu Ghraib*, pp. 36 and 47.

31. See the Convention Against Torture and Other Cruel, Inhuman or Degrading Treatment or Punishment, in Center for the Study of Human Rights, *Twenty-Four Human Rights Documents* (New York: Columbia University Press, 1992), pp. 72–80; see esp. p. 72.

32. Ibid., p. 72.

33. Quoted in James P. Pfiffner, *Torture as Public Policy: Restoring U.S. Credibility on the World Stage* (Boulder, CO: Paradigm, 2010), p. 115.

34. Ibid., p. 121.

35. Jay S. Bybee served as the head of the White House Office of Legal Council during 2001–2003. The Bybee torture memo, issued August 1, 2002, is a comprehensive legal justification and guidebook for torture, systematically explaining why a wide range of international legal precedents do not apply to CIA torturers and/or how to fine-tune torture techniques to circumvent existing US and international law. The term "golden shield" refers to the ways that these memos provided specific, detailed instructions on how to carry out torture under a veneer of civilized legality. See also Pfiffner, *Torture as Public Policy*, p. 145.

36. Department of Defense, *The Schlesinger Report: An Investigation of Abu Ghraib* (Washington, DC: Cosimo, 2005), p. 5.

37. Pfiffner, *Torture as Public Policy*, p. 150.

38. Nicolas Mottas and Myrsini Tsakiri. "Closing Guantanamo Bay: President Obama's Failed Promise," July 19, 2011; available at http://la.indymedia.org/news/2011/07/247044.php; accessed on August 23, 2011.

39. Mark Thompson and Aryn Baker, "Starting Anew," *Time*, July 20, 2009, pp. 28–33; see esp. p. 31.

40. Ibid., p. 31.

41. Nathaniel C. Fick and John A. Nagl, "Counterinsurgency Field Manual: Afghanistan Edition," *Foreign Policy*, January–February 2009, pp. 42–47; see esp. p. 43.

42. Jane Mayer, "The Black Sites: A Rare Look Inside the C.I.A.'s Secret Interrogation Program," *New Yorker*, August 13, 2007, pp. 47–57; see p. 49.

43. Meredith Angelson, "Beyond the Myth of 'Good Faith': Torture Evidence in International Extradition Hearings," *Journal of International Law and Politics* 41, no. 3 (Spring 2009): 603–653; see esp. pp. 604–605.

44. Ibid., p. 604.

45. Ibid., pp. 652–653.

46. Malou Innocent and Ted Galen Carpenter, *Escaping the "Graveyard of Empires": A Strategy To Exit Afghanistan* (Washington, DC: Cato Institute, 2009), pp. 1–21; see esp. p. 4.

47. Rory Stewart and Gerald Knaus, *Can Intervention Work?* (New York: W. W. Norton, 2011), p. 89.

48. Kurt Volker, "Afghanistan and Libya point NATO to Five Lessons," *Christian Science Monitor*, August 1, 2011, p. 35.

49. Mark P. Denbeaux and Jonathan Hafez, eds., *The Guantanamo Lawyers: Inside a Prison Outside the Law* (New York: New York University Press, 2009), pp. 155–156.

50. Pfiffner, *Torture as Public Policy*, p. 5.

51. Christopher J. Einolf, "The Fall and Rise of Torture: A Comparative and Historical Analysis," *Sociological Theory* 25, no. 2 (June 2007): 101–121; see esp. 117.

52. Jina Moore, "Defining Torture," *Christian Science Monitor*, May 17, 2009, pp. 17–18; see esp. p. 17.

53. Ibid., p. 18.

54. Pfiffner, *Torture as Public Policy*, pp. 1–3.

55. Ibid., p. 4.

56. Tim Dunne, "The English School," in Tim Dunne, Milja Kurki, and Steve Smith, eds., *International Relations Theories: Discipline and Diversity* (New York: Oxford University Press, 2007), pp. 127–147; p. 144.

57. Ibid.

58. Darius Rejali, *Torture and Democracy* (Princeton, NJ: Princeton University Press, 2007), pp. 478–479.

59. Ibid., p. 518.

60. David P. Forsythe, "The United States: Protecting Human Dignity in an Era of Insecurity," in Brysk and Shafir, *National Insecurity and Human Rights*, pp. 37–55; see p. 55.

61. William J. Aceves, "Terrorism," in Forsythe, *Encyclopedia of Human Rights*, vol. 5, pp. 16–24; see esp. pp. 22–23.

62. Ibid., p. 23.

63. Ronald Dworkin, *Is Democracy Possible Here? Principles for a New Political Debate* (Princeton, NJ: Princeton University Press, 2006), p. 38.

64. Ibid.

65. Ibid., p. 44.

66. Alison Brysk, "Torture Doesn't Work," *Christian Science Monitor*, November 14, 2007, p. 9.

67. Ibid.

68. Darren J. O'Bryne, *Human Rights: An Introduction* (New York: Longman, 2003), p. 154.

69. Aziz Z. Huq, "Democratic Torture: Has Mill's Safeguard Weakened?" *World Policy Journal* 24, no. 4 (Winter–Spring 2007–2008): 99–107; see 99.

70. Ibid.,105.

71. For further details on this, see Mahmood Monshipouri, "Private Military Industry and the Laws of War," in *Human Rights and Human Welfare*, July 2007; available at http://www.du.edu/gsis/hrhw/roundtable/2007/panel-b/07 -2007/monshipouri/2007b.html.

72. P. W. Singer, "Outsourcing War," *Foreign Affairs*, 84, no. 2 (March–April 2005): 119–132; see p. 124.

73. Deborah Avant, "The Privatization of Security: Lessons from Iraq," *Orbis* 50, no. 2 (Spring 2006): 327–342.

74. Ibid.

75. Singer, "Outsourcing War," p. 125.

76. Ibid., p. 127.

77. Michael Walzer, *Thinking Politically: Essays in Political Theory* (New Haven, CT: Yale University Press, 2007), p. 277.

78. David Johnson and John Broder, "F.B.I. Says Guards Killed 14 Iraqis Without Cause," *New York Times*, November 14, 2007.

79. Arthur Bright, "US Soldiers: Blackwater Attacked Fleeing Iraqi Civilians," *Christian Science Monitor*, October 13, 2007; available at http://www .csmonitor.com/2007/1012/p99sol-duts.html; accessed March 7, 2008.

80. Jack Donnelly, *International Human Rights*, 3rd ed. (Boulder, CO: Westview Press, 2007), p. 217.

81. Fick and Nagl, "Counterinsurgency Field Manual," p. 45.

82. S. Neil Macfarlane, "Human Security and the Law of States," in Goold and Lazarus, *Security and Human Rights*, pp. 345–361; see pp. 350–351.

83. Ibid., p. 352.

84. Ibid., pp. 353–358.

85. Hedley Bull, *The Anarchical Society: A Study of Order in World Politics*, 3rd ed. (New York: Columbia University Press, 2002), p. 304.

86. Ibid., p. 359.

87. Robert Jackson and Georg Sorensen, *Introduction to International Relations: Theories and Approaches*, 3rd ed. (New York: Oxford University Press, 2007), p. 145

88. Andrew Linklater, "The English School," in Scott Burchill et al., *Theories of International Relations* (New York: Palgrave-Macmillan, 2005), pp. 84–109.

89. Andrew F. Krepinevich, "How to Win in Iraq," *Foreign Affairs* 84, no. 5 (September–October 2005): 88–89.

90. Jane Arraf, "Iraq's War Generation," *Christian Science Monitor*, March 1, 2010, pp. 26–31.

91. Greg Mortenson and David Oliver Relin, *Three Cups of Tea: One Man's Mission to Promote Peace . . . One School at a Time* (New York: Penguin, 2006).

92. Ron Moreau and Sami Yousafzai, "Turning the Taliban," *Newsweek*, February 22, 2010, pp. 34–35.

93. Ibid., p. 35.

94. Gershon Shafir, Alison Brysk, and Daniel Wehrenfenning, "Human Rights in Hard Times," in Brysk and Shafir, *National Insecurity and Human Rights,* p. 180.

95. Neil Hicks, "The Impact of Counter Terror and the Promotion and Protection of Human Rights: A Global Perspective," in Richard Ashby Wilson, ed., *Human Rights in the 'War on Terror'* (New York: Cambridge University Press, 2005), pp. 209–224; see esp. p. 222.

96. Seth Stern, "Torture Debate," in *Global Issues* (Washington, DC: CQ Press, 2008), pp. 139–163; see esp. pp. 153–159.

97. Gary Haugen and Victor Boutros, "And Justice for All: Enforcing Human Rights for the World's Poor," *Foreign Affairs* 89, no. 3 (May–June 2010): 51–62; see esp. 59.

98. Alison Brysk, *Global Good Samaritans: Human Rights as Foreign Policy* (New York: Oxford University Press, 2009), p. 34.

99. David Luban, "Unthinking the Ticking Bomb," in Charles R. Beitz and Robert E. Goodin, eds., *Global Basic Rights* (New York: Oxford University Press, 2009), pp. 181–206; see esp. p. 198.

100. Ibid., pp. 200–201.

101. Richard Falk, "What Future for the UN Charter System of War Prevention?" *Transnational Foundation for Peace and Future Research*; available at http://www.transnational.org/SAJT/forum/meet/2003/Falk_UNCharter.html; accessed March 14, 2010.

102. Eric Rosand, "The UN Has Vital Roles to Play in Counterterrorism," in Stuart Gottlieb, ed., *Debating Terrorism and Counterterrorism: Conflicting Perspectives on Causes, Contexts, and Responses* (Washington, DC: CQ Press, 2010), pp. 287–303; see esp. p. 291.

103. Ibid., p. 299.

104. Andrew Ashworth, "Security, Terrorism, and the Value of Human Rights," in Goold and Lazarus, *Security and Human Rights,* pp. 203–226; see pp. 212, 213, and 225.

105. Teraya Koji, "Emerging Hierarchy in International Human Rights and Beyond: From the Perspective of Non-derogable Rights," *European Journal of International Law* 12, no. 5 (2001): 917–941.

106. Ibid., 939.

107. Theodor Meron, "On a Hierarchy of International Human Rights," *American Journal of International Law* 80, no. 1 (January 1986): 1–23; see p. 16.

108. The derogation clause under Article 4 of the International Covenant on Civil and Political Rights (ICCPR) has defined this category of rights in states of emergency, when events such as war and natural disasters present fatal and legitimate threats to national existence.

109. David E. Graham, "Treatment and Interrogation of Detained Persons," in Thomas Mck. Sparks and Glenn M. Sulmasy, eds., *International Law Chal-*

lenges: Homeland Security and Combating Terrorism, International Law Studies, vol. 81 (Newport, RI: US Naval War College, 2006), pp. 215–220; see p. 219.

110. Jody Kollapan, who was chairperson of the South African Human Rights Commission, makes this point. See http://www.sahrc.org.za/sahrc_cms /downloads/School%20violence_Hellen%20Suzman%20foundation.pdf; accessed April 16, 2008

111. Jane Arraf, "Iraq Agrees to Start Talking about US Troops, At Least," *Christian Science Monitor,* August 16, 22, 2011, p. 12.

112. Theodor Meron, "On a Hierarchy of International Human Rights," *American Journal of International Law* 80, no. 1 (January 1986): 1–23; see p. 6.

113. Some human rights scholars have argued that all human rights are "basic rights" in a fundamental sense and that realization of human rights cannot be reduced to a narrow list. See Jack Donnelly, *Universal Human Rights in Theory and Practice* (Ithaca, NY: Cornell University Press, 1989), p. 41.

114. Michael Ignatieff, *The Lesser Evil: Political Ethics in an Age of Terror* (Princeton, NJ: Princeton University Press, 2004).

115. Rosemary Foot, *Human Rights and Counter-terrorism in America's Asia Policy*, Adelphi Papers, no. 363 (New York: Oxford University Press, 2004), p. 78.

116. Laura K. Donohue, *The Cost of Counterterrorism: Power, Politics, and Liberty* (Cambridge: Cambridge University Press, 2008), p. 359.

117. Ibid., p. 31.

118. Eric A. Posner and Adrian Vermeule, *Terror in the Balance: Security, Liberty, and the Courts* (New York: Oxford University Press, 2007), p. 273.

119. Ibid., p. 272.

120. David J. Whittaker, *Terrorism: Understanding the Global Threat*, rev. ed. (New York: Pearson Longman, 2007), p. 197.

121. Ibid., p. 198

122. Anthony Lewis, "Security and Liberty: Preserving the Values of Freedom," in Richard C. Leone and Greg Anrig Jr., eds., *The War on Our Freedoms: Civil Liberties in an Age of Terrorism* (New York: Public Affairs, 2003), pp. 47–73; see p. 73.

123. Rosemary Foot, "Human Rights in Conflict," *Survival* 48, no. 3 (Autumn 2006): 109–126; see esp. 121.

124. A. H. Robertson and J. G. Merrills, *Human Rights in the World: An Introduction to the Study of the International Protection of Human Rights*, 4th ed. (New York: Manchester University Press, 1996), p. 342.

125. Louise Richardson, *The Roots of Terrorism* (New York: Routledge, 2006), p. 9.

126. Fick and Nagl, "Counterinsurgency Field Manual," p. 47.

127. "The General's Next War: The *Foreign Policy* Interview with General David H. Petraeus," *Foreign Policy*, January–February 2009, pp. 48–50; see esp. p. 49.

128. Shafir, Brysk, and Wehrenfenning, "Human Rights in Hard Times," p. 180.

129. Seth Stern, "Torture Debate," in *Global Issues* (Washington, DC: CQ Press, 2008), pp. 139–163; see esp. pp. 153–159.

130. Leonard B. Weinberg, William L. Eubank, and Elizabeth A. Francis, "The Cost of Terrorism: The Relationship between International Terrorism and Democratic Governance," *Terrorism and Political Violence* 20, no. 2 (April–June 2008): 257–270; see esp. p. 265.

131. Ibid., p. 266–267.

132. Ibid., p. 267.

133. Michael J. Boyle, "The War on Terror in American Grand Strategy," *International Affairs* 84, no. 2 (March 2008): 191–209; see esp. p. 209.

134. Shadi Mokhtari, *After Abu Ghraib*, pp. 198–199.

7

Immigration Politics
and the Rise of Islamophobia

Infractions of civil rights and liberties are by and large emblematic of times of dire national security crises or national emergencies. Not surprisingly, for example, asylum seekers, refugees, and immigrant groups are more often than not targeted in such times.[1] The September 11 attacks on the United States, the 2004 Madrid bombings, and the 2005 London transit attacks further inflamed the view of Islam as the "enemy," an image informed by centuries of Orientalist thinking. The persistence of this perception at the public level has made it virtually impossible to extricate Western Muslims from the external political enemy.[2]

The September 11 attacks have renewed the debate in the United States over tensions between security, immigration law, and the civil rights of minorities, especially Arab and Muslim communities in the West. At the same time, a related debate is taking place in Europe over the extent to which homegrown violence reflects the failure to incorporate immigrants into European societies. Although the lack of political, legal, and civil rights and laws can be directly linked to the perceived and actual threat of terrorism, there is a broader political movement to curb the growth of multiculturalism.[3]

While the Muslim diaspora condemned the senseless violence, the reactions of Muslims to the 9/11 attacks have been mixed. Some US Muslims have chosen to retreat from social and cultural life, keeping their distance from the ensuing negative fallout. Others, mostly second- and third-generation Muslims, have resented their host societies' poor treatment of Muslim minorities, turning to their religion as a crucial source of identity and culture. Still others have explored the possibility of reconciling Islam and the West by taking a self-critical approach while arguing that the core messages of Islam, such as equality and egalitarianism, have gained support among other religious groups in Europe and the United States. It is difficult to foretell which approach will persevere the most, but it is clear that these dynamics—tension and reconciliation—will be influenced not only by the conflict within Muslim communities over whether to create a "transcultural space" for dialogue between different ethnic and religious groups but also by the various policies of Western governments for the integration and institutionalization of Islam.[4]

The security measures employed by the Bush administration (e.g., extraordinary renditions) have complicated the accommodation of immigrants by the host culture. In Europe, counterterrorism measures have led to discriminatory policies toward Muslim immigrants, especially in the case of nationality or citizenship tests, which tend to undermine the efforts of those Muslims who have sought to bridge their faith and Western values. Counterterrorism policies are likely to reinforce radical tendencies in diaspora communities, further intensifying identity politics and local unrest.

This chapter explains how the so-called war on terror of the post-9/11 period has affected the attitudes and policies toward Muslim immigrants in the United States and Europe. To better understand the impact that counterterrorism measures have had on Muslim immigrants, I begin by examining the reasons behind increasing Islamophobia in Europe and go on to discuss how new legislative initiatives have resulted in contentious immigration policies in both Europe and the United States. I then turn to the issue of how the politics of immigration have led to coercive integration programs, citizenship tests, and Europe's involvement in secret detentions. My focus then shifts to the issue of how the war on terror has negatively affected Muslims in the United States. By applying a comparative analysis, I try to discern similar and different ways in which Muslim immigrants in the West have embraced integration in some countries and rejected assimilation in others. A recurring theme of this chapter is the need to view integration as a national security matter in order to help reshape the debate over the integration issue. In this context, the role of participation and socioeconomic equality of ethnic and cultural minorities is crucial.

The Rising Islamophobia in Europe

Concerns about the radicalization of young Muslims in Europe in recent years, and especially after 9/11, have intensified the fear of the resurgence of homegrown Islamic defiance. The result has been the imposition of more restrictions on civil and political liberties of minority groups, such as Muslims, in Europe. These constraints have intensified previously existing tensions between Muslim communities and their host countries. In parts of Europe, for example, submissive attitudes toward increasing restrictions on civil liberties have grown in response to rising fears of terrorism. If not properly curbed, such tensions have the potential to be highly unsettling for European societies.

Some Muslim immigrants lack political confidence in mainstream institutional processes (police, political parties, and court systems) of their host countries. Instead, they have attempted to address their problems via local networks and solidarity mechanisms. In fact, some experts note, Muslim communities display the lowest ethnic hostility among immigrant communities throughout the Europe and North America. They also have the lowest crime rates.[5] Ethnic identity, however, persists in large part because of the way in which the Muslim diaspora has been received by the media and the larger Western European society. The media bias against the Muslim diaspora has had a direct impact on the spread of social stigmatization and discrimination targeting Muslims in European countries.

Throughout Europe, Islamic radicalism is partially attributed to the disaffected youth of North African origins or to converts. The French Moroccan young man who killed the Dutch filmmaker Theo van Gogh was affiliated with a Muslim group with no proven direct connection to al-Qaeda or other transnational Muslim organizations.[6] In general, racism and de facto inequality in some European countries have expanded the ranks of the discontented. In the post-9/11 era, several factors have contributed to the radicalization of a minority within Muslim communities. These have included a new wave of intolerance toward Muslim immigrants, but there is also widespread economic deprivation and social and cultural stigma. Members of such communities view their segregation in enclaves—poor suburbs (*banlieues*)—as proof of the absence of prospects for a brighter future. In fact, the 2005 French riots had nothing to do with "terror" or with jihad. Rather, as Gilles Kepel notes, the source of the riots lay in France's defective system of integration, which "had failed to offer certain marginalized populations full participation in a vast culture reaching across the Mediterranean to Africa."[7]

It is important to bear in mind that the French government's concern about social unrest in the banlieues partly related to matters of foreign policy. While there is no evidence that the Muslim minority in France has a direct influence on French foreign policy, the presence of five million Muslims does have an indirect impact on diplomacy vis-à-vis the Middle East. This partly explains why President Jacques Chirac disagreed with the US invasion of Iraq in 2003—a stance reflecting his view that foreign policies and domestic policies were part of a continuum.[8] With respect to the legal restrictions placed on wearing the headscarf, or *hijab*, there is no evidence that banning Islamic dress has substantially reduced the risk of Islamic radicalism. To the contrary, such restrictions may well have provoked a backlash that could foster extremism. Enforcing the ban on wearing the headscarf sends a message to Muslim citizens and immigrants that they are welcome in society only as long as they set their differences—clothing, identity, and beliefs—aside.[9]

Similar challenges to multiculturalism in Europe have sparked debate over the extent to which a common national identity can be constructed to facilitate Muslims' integration in the European culture. Equally contentious was the injection of the war on terror into the public discourse, making terrorism integral to understanding international relations and social unrest in Europe. This view reduced Islam to forms of violent extremism and the leading cause of terror and threats to Western hegemony, resulting in increased hostility toward Islamic civilization and Muslim immigrants. It was in this context—part of a growing anti-Muslim atmosphere—that newspapers across Europe reprinted controversial caricatures of the Prophet Muhammad to show support for a Danish newspaper whose cartoons had sparked Muslim outrage throughout the world.[10]

When the *Jylland-Posten* published twelve cartoons depicting the prophet in late September 2005, including one in which he was shown wearing a turban shaped as a bomb with a burning fuse, a strong backlash ensued not only in Denmark but across the globe. There were demonstrations in the Indian-controlled part of Kashmir, death threats against the artists, condemnation from eleven Muslim countries, and a rebuke from the United Nations. The publication of the cartoons provoked a fierce national debate over whether Denmark's liberal and secular laws on freedom of speech permitted too much.[11] When these cartoons were reprinted on February 1, 2006, in France, Germany, Italy, the Netherlands, Spain, and Switzerland, the Muslim world's uproar over perceived insult to the prophet was on display in the streets of Afghanistan, Egypt, Turkey, Pakistan, Iraq, Iran, Indonesia, Malaysia, Lebanon, and the Palestinian territories. The mocking of Muhammad and the reprinting of the cartoon by major European publications were viewed as blasphemous acts by many Muslims, both in the diaspora and the homelands. To Muslims, these images were offensive not only because they portrayed the prophet as a bomb-carrying terrorist; to understand the extent of the Muslim outrage, one must note that Islamic law explicitly prohibits the depiction of the prophet's image in any shape or form, let alone in an offensive manner.

Public debates surrounding the cartoon controversy also revealed that the views of Muslim religious leaders were not fully shared by European Muslims. While religious leaders described the cartoons as evidence of the West's hatred of Islam, European Muslims typically viewed the issue in terms of the need for equal respect for Muslims as European citizens. In fact, most European Muslims rallied around European values by turning to their local judiciaries and the European Court of Human Rights to further support values such as freedom of belief, multiculturalism, and even secularism.[12] Likewise, the French rioters who set cars and public buildings on fire in October 2005 in Clichy-sous-Bois were not contesting the French model of integration but rather seeking its equitable, just, and effective implementation.[13]

It is evident that the policies, rules, attitudes, and regulations of host societies in Europe partly determine the course that Islamism adopts within those societies. The context of the host society shapes not only the relationship between Islamic movements and the host community but also the form of the Islamist rhetoric. There is a widely held view that Islamic associations are undemocratic, but a comparative study of Islamism in Germany and the Netherlands demonstrated that Islamic groups vary greatly in ideology and method. They can become either a counterhegemonic force that jeopardizes the democratic order of the host country or a potential force for democratization of the Islamic community. What role Islamic associations in Europe play is largely influenced by the social, economic, and political structure within which Islamists operate.

Consider, for example, the case of Milli Görüs, one of the most important Islamic movements for the Turkish immigrant community in Europe. Milli Görüs in Germany adopts a strong anti-Western posture and is treated as an "Islamist extremist group" by the German Federal Ministry of the Interior; in the Netherlands, by contrast, Milli Görüs cooperates with the Dutch authorities in promoting the integration of Muslims into Dutch society.[14] While discrimination and exclusion by the host society cause feelings of insecurity, isolation, and thus radicalization within the Muslim community in Germany, inclusive policies in the Netherlands aim at incorporating immigrants into the host society and culminate in a hopeful integrationist Islamist discourse that encompasses democratic ideals. A comparison of the German and Dutch cases reveals that Islamic movements can generate an undemocratic discourse and challenge hegemonic political institutions and practices of the host society in the face of discrimination and exclusion; alternatively they can be a potent force for the democratization of the Islamic community under conditions of justice, tolerance, and equality.[15]

Some experts have rejected the argument that religion drives both Islamic culture and politics. Transnational networks and forces have transformed the views of the younger generation of Muslims, especially those in the diaspora. Such a transformation may be a short-term generational phenomenon. However, if it turns out to be a long-term development, Europeans must search for pragmatic solutions to Islamophobia and discrimination against their Muslim minorities. It may just be the case that second- and third-generation European Muslims seem intent on constructing a new and critical Islam.[16]

On balance, concerns about the place of Islam within the Western public sphere, which is directly linked to the continued influx of immigrants, are certain to result in further backlash against Muslim immigrants—a development that is likely to worsen as fear of an economic recession hovers over the continent. The upshot is that the majority of Muslim immigrants, who are either moderate or identify with moderates, are tainted by the guilt of the minority.[17] A growing number of Europeans have expressed concerns over the welfare system, arguing that the system is overtaxed by non-natives. Approximately 50 percent of immigrants, according to one study, are "caught up in various forms of welfare benefits."[18] In most Western European countries, with the exception of Spain and Portugal, leftist and centrist parties have lost elections because the majority of electorates supported candidates who were marching to the beat of a nationalist, anti-immigrant drum.[19]

In 2006, the UK communities secretary Ruth Kelly launched a study commission to examine whether multiculturalism was causing greater social isolation, extremism, and ethnic divisions. This investigation was provoked by critics who argued that multiculturalism had encouraged Britons to elevate Islamic values over British values. Critics noted that local-government funding had helped segregate communities and that in the absence of a well-promoted majoritarian culture, Islamic radicalism had interposed. In its report, the commission struck down the term *multiculturalism* in favor of *community cohesion*, indicating the Labour Party government's growing anxiety over its earlier approach.[20] Others, such as Sarah Spencer, associate director at the University of Oxford's Center on Migration, Policy, and Society and former deputy chairwoman of the government's Commission for Racial Equality, have noted that rather than multiculturalism causing the separation, the factors that have contributed the most to ethnic segregation have stemmed from mundane socioeconomic conditions such as housing clusters in poor neighborhoods.[21]

The analysis presented above indicates that the struggle for socioeconomic equality and participation does not necessarily imply the promotion of a homogenization of cultures. One can further argue that cultural assimilation in this case is used as a euphemism to allay the larger population's Islamophobic fears. It should be the government's intent to use multiculturalism to preserve minority cultures and social institutions in a way that does not force assimilation onto the dominant ethnicity or culture. There is still a great deal of uncertainty concerning the capacity of European governments and communities to embrace multiculturalism, giving rise to the question over whether socioeconomic integration would necessarily bring about cultural integration. Increasingly, some European leaders have openly castigated multiculturalism in the wake of terrorist attacks in Europe. In his first speech as prime minister of Great Britain, David Cameron criticized "state multiculturalism" as failing to prevent Islamic extremism and the spread of terrorism. "We have failed to provide a vision of society to which Muslims feel they want to belong. We have even tolerated these segregated communities behaving in ways that run counter to our values." According to Cameron, building a stronger sense of national and local identity holds "the key to achieving true cohesion" by allowing people to say "I am a Muslim, I am a Hindu, I am a Christian, but I am a Londoner . . . too."[22]

Immigration Laws in Europe

Reactions to security concerns following 9/11 led to new legislative initiatives to confront terrorism. These initiatives have resulted in contentious immigration policies in Europe and the United States. In recent years, antiterrorism actions of governments on both sides of the Atlantic have been marked by a convergence in the approach of European countries and the United States with regard to border control and immigration, particularly from Muslim-dominated nations. This pattern of convergence has found justification in the need to fight terrorism, while shifting the attention from external threats of terrorism to internal threats emanating from immigrant populations—citizens, legal residents, and illegal aliens.[23]

At the same time, US security fears and measures have played out in Europe, largely affecting preventive strategies adopted by European governments. The United States has since imposed security measures on other countries with which it conducts business. On December 16, 2003, the United States and the European Commission reached an agreement that required air carriers operating to, from, or through the United States to provide US Customs with electronic access to data contained in their automatic reservation and departure control systems.[24] This data program, known as Passenger Name Records, or PNR, aims at creating uniform standards for collecting a wide range of personal data on passengers before they travel and has affected all foreign air carriers serving the United States.

Full compliance with PNR standards may violate fundamental rights and principles of EU law and national constitutions of member states. Concerns regarding the adoption of such standards have spawned debates over civil liberties throughout Europe.[25] To the extent that there is a convergence of EU and US laws and policies on border security, the emergence of a transatlantic immigration policy has increasingly led to a shift from "border control to the maximum surveillance of populations."[26]

Before addressing issues of security, migration, and border control, it is important to bear in mind certain facts. Rising net migration into Europe is increasingly seen as a crucial factor affecting population change. Despite high levels of unemployment in parts of Europe, many vacancies are present in low-skill jobs. Migrants who are particularly well suited for these positions will immigrate with or without permission.[27] A vast majority of migrants do not engage in violent practices or hold values hostile to those of European citizens.[28] In all integration-related programs—employment, education, health, living standards, civic participation, and community relations—migrants are often disproportionately disadvantaged even among second- and third-generation Muslims.[29] In education, migrants are disproportionately underachievers. Poor language skills are a key factor. The same is true of unemployment and underemployment in labor markets. The gap is particularly noticeable for women. With regard to housing, migrants are often among the homeless population, some live in excessively segregated poor neighborhoods, others live in unbearable housing conditions.[30]

Restrictive measures enforced upon immigrants and asylum seekers have provoked a variety of questions about the abuse of civil liberties, including the right to privacy. Government authorities can now access bank accounts, airline data, and postal information. The application of biometric technologies (through digitized fingerprints, facial recognition, and retinal scans) has now become a routine aspect of the larger post-9/11 "securitization of the inside," facilitating the heightened surveillance of ethnic minority populations.[31] The reaction to asylum seekers in Europe reflects the prevailing governmental response to the potential threats that those seeking refuge pose to the welfare state. In the United States, by contrast, asylum seekers are viewed as threats to national security. Despite these divergent perceptions, European and US governments have adopted a similar strategy toward asylum seekers, namely, detention.[32]

In Europe, Jocelyne Cesari notes, the pressure caused by increasing immigrant populations and the gradual erosion of national boundaries through the transnational force of the European Union have led to a nationalist backlash and an essentializing approach toward identity. The Italian right-wing Forza Nuova party states that "Italy is essentially Catholic, implying that Muslims cannot be good citizens or Italians."[33] In 1999, following riots involving immigrant Maghrebis and local youth in Terrassa, Spain, the center-right Popular Party attributed the problem to the immigrants' presence rather than Spanish society's difficulty in coping with them. Increasingly, because of such incidents, the public mood has shifted to a perception of Islam—characterized by what are attributed to being the essentials of the religion and its values—as the root cause of the problem.[34] Nowhere in Europe have such anti-Islamic sentiments become a staple of political discourse more so than in the Netherlands, where Pim Fortuyn openly criticized Islam in inflammatory terms prior to his assassination in 2002. His party has since his death continued to run on a platform of tougher measures against nonassimilating immigrants.[35]

In November 2004, Mohammad Bouyeri, a Moroccan immigrant, assassinated a Dutch filmmaker and critic of radical Islam, Theo van Gogh, sparking a wave of violence by and against Muslim immigrants. The murder of van Gogh was a consequence of the merging of two trends: the call to fight blasphemy and the alignment of young Westernized Muslims with "international jihadism."[36] The murder raised the specter of political assassination as part of the jihadist arsenal in Europe. Bouyeri, an average, second-generation immigrant who graduated from Amsterdam's best high school, was collecting unemployment benefits when he murdered van Gogh.[37] While the Madrid train bombings of March 2004 were committed by Moroccan immigrants, van Gogh's killer and his group were born and raised in Europe.[38] The Dutch General Intelligence and Security Service (AIVD) claimed that radical Islam had become "an autonomous phenomenon," in that even without direct influence or connections from abroad, Dutch youth were embracing militancy. The same attraction applies to angry young Muslims in Brussels, London, Paris, Madrid, and Milan.[39]

The political reactions to such incidents reflect a general trend across Europe in which anti-Muslim and anti-immigrant rhetoric in politics is now commonplace, and laws have expanded the powers of the state to deal more harshly with potential threats associated with Muslim immigrants.[40] In France, the 2001 Law on Everyday Security expanded police powers by permitting officials to stop vehicles, search unoccupied premises, and monitor or record electronic transactions without prior notice as part of antiterrorism investigations. Additionally, the new laws allow the banning of religious groups that threaten democratic order, unrestricted police access to financial records, electronic and postal communications, and most forms of transportation records. In Great Britain in 2001, immediately after 9/11, the House of Commons passed the Anti-Terrorism, Crime, and Security Act, which permitted the indefinite detention of foreign nationals regarded as unsafe and their deportation to their country of origin, even allowing detention in the anticipation of violence, rather than as a response.[41]

There is, however, no evidence that placing further restrictions on immigration and tightening immigration laws would prevent the threat of domestic terrorism.[42] Moreover, some experts question the plausibility of the securitization thesis, arguing that a range of formal and informal norms and practices impede excessively restrictive immigration policies. Among other things, pursuing a strategy of securitization may endanger such pragmatic goals as ensuring a sufficient supply of migrant labor to help sustain economic growth.[43] Whether states link terrorism to migration control is a question of how states can best generate public support and legitimacy.[44]

In the United States, the link between migration control and counterterrorism has led to the government's heavy-handed immigration control tactics, generally considered a tool of social control. This securitization of immigration policies has led to the interrogation, arrest, incarceration, and deportation of many after 9/11. Immigration laws, especially in their internal enforcement guise, have become a government-sanctioned form of social control for minorities, dissidents, and others deemed suspicious or dangerous. Mere technical violations of immigration laws appear to have prompted government action based on noncitizens' national origin, religious beliefs, or political opinions.[45]

Reports released by the Migration Policy Institute on June 25, 2003, demonstrated a pattern of consistent violations of due process, as well as harsh law-enforcement measures directed solely at males from Arab and Muslim countries.[46] Unlike the hijackers, this report claimed, the majority of those exposed to interrogation and detention had significant ties to the United States and roots in their communities. Of the detainees, for whom a great deal of information was available, more than 46 percent had lived in the United States for at least six years. Approximately half had spouses, children, or other family relationships in the United States.[47]

In November 2001, the Bush administration publicly confirmed that neither the location nor the identities of post-9/11 detainees would be disclosed.[48] Such policies clearly exaggerated the threats posed by immigrants and undermined the civil liberties of citizens and noncitizens alike. Consider, for example, the experience of Tarek Mohammed Fayad, an Egyptian dentist who came to the United States in 1998 to pursue higher education. Fayad was arrested in southern California on September 13, 2001, for violating his student visa. During Fayad's first ten days of incarceration, he was not allowed to make any telephone calls. His attorney was unable to determine his location for more than a month. The Bureau of Prisons continued to deny having Fayad in custody, while keeping him in detention at a federal facility in New York.[49] Rather than relying on vigorous and individualized suspicion or intelligence-driven criteria, the government used national origin—that is, targeting specific ethnic groups—as a proxy for evidence of dangerousness.[50] These actions raise serious concerns about racial profiling and discrimination, which have been enunciated and condemned in the UN Convention on the Elimination of All Forms of Racial Discrimination, ratified by the United States in 1994.

Moreover, such policies imply the convergence between immigration and criminal law in the amorphous "war on terror," blurring historical distinctions among "illegal aliens," "criminal aliens," and "terrorists."[51] In this regard, one key question persists: "To what extent is the nation made more secure when its alien population is subject to harsh, criminal punitive sanctions for relatively minor criminal or immigration transgressions?"[52] Many observers have argued that a series of safeguards must be established so that violations of immigration-status requirements, for example, would not serve as a pretext for avoiding due process requirements. Furthermore, the government's effort to hide the identity, number, and whereabouts of its detainees clearly violates the public's right to be informed about government actions.[53]

The immigration reforms and laws in Europe, by contrast, have been driven by increasing hostility toward multiculturalism, resulting from a growing sense that by fueling extremist ideologies and practices, immigrants pose a threat to national identity. The US public discourse in the post-9/11 era appears to have been overshadowed by fears of Islamic radicals infiltrating the United States and perpetrating large-scale acts of terrorism.[54] These contrasting views toward Muslim immigrants in Europe and the United States can be explained in relation to the class, socioeconomic status, attitudes, and community-related engagement of Muslim immigrants.

The story of the Muslim diaspora communities in the United States has been marked by growth and prosperity. A higher percentage of immigrants from Muslim countries have earned graduate degrees than other US residents, and their average salary is estimated to be roughly 20 percent higher.[55] The majority of European Muslim immigrants, by contrast, are low-skilled laborers who have encountered and continue to face serious hurdles to integration into employment, housing, and education sectors. Almost one-fifth of Muslims in Europe are regarded as low-income, leading some analysts to conclude that economic deprivation triggers radicalism. In the United States, by contrast, only 2 percent of Muslims are considered low-income.[56]

Such differences help explain why European communities employ coercive ways of integrating immigrants, including requiring them to take obligatory civic-integration courses. Some experts remind us that the nonselective nature of immigration policies in Europe—unlike those of the classic immigrant nations of Australia and Canada—explains the point of repressive liberalism.[57] Since 9/11, countries such as Belgium, Germany, and the Netherlands—known for their more liberal immigration policies—have begun to tighten their immigration requirements. In 2004, the first immigration law (*Zuwanderungsgesetz*) to be introduced in Germany focused on an active integration policy, restricting new immigration and allowing only temporary immigration for qualified individuals.[58]

Increasingly, security concerns have led to the introduction of nationality laws or citizenship tests in Europe. These tests continue to highlight the tension in pluralistic democratic societies between the right of immigrants to maintain their cultures and the interest of the state to promote national solidarity. Furthermore, these tests also have raised concerns over two sets of contradictory immigration measures, one motivated by demographic pressures (Europeans have one of the lowest birthrates in the world) and the need for low-skilled labor, and the other fueled by the political risks of expanding the pool of immigrants whose cultural and political tendencies may at times conflict with their host societies and cultures. In the following section, I attempt to explain the rationales behind and controversies surrounding nationality laws and tests.

Coercive Integration and Citizenship Tests

Although not completely novel, citizenship or nationality tests and integration courses have triggered debates over the emerging coercive integration policies across Europe, especially after 9/11. The emergence of obligatory civic integration courses and tests for newcomers, some experts note, makes a strong case in favor of policy convergence across Europe. These convergent policies reflect a fundamental shift from an "old" liberalism of nondiscrimination and equal opportunity to a "new" liberalism of power and discipline.[59] The pendulum has swung from cultural recognition—that is, respect for migrants' own language and culture—to the enforcement of the core values of liberalism.[60]

In the migration domain, the formal introduction of citizenship tests has caused substantial controversy. Some see such tests as a knee-jerk, populist reaction to fear of the newcomers.[61] Others view these tests as emblematic of a return to the familiar ideal of the cohesive nation and strong nation building in the wake of the large-scale influx of immigrants into the European Union;[62] the emphasis on language skills as a precondition for acceptance supports this view. The test is indeed "a tool for the state to promote linguistic assimilation and part of renewed attempts to achieve the old ideal of a linguistically cohesive citizenry."[63]

Still others believe that, by taking part in the political life or the civil society of their adopted countries, new citizens will be better equipped to avoid the problems implicit in the ghettoization of immigrant communities.[64] Another closely related discourse, albeit from a different perspective, is that immigrants who become naturalized citizens are likely to become far more integrated into their new country than those who remain noncitizen residents, or "denizens."[65] The written test has the advantage of a pass-fail grading system that ends the power of the individual immigration officer to decide whether an applicant is eligible for citizenship.

Civic integration policies for immigrants originated in the Netherlands in the late 1990s. These policies were a response to the obvious failure of multiculturalism to advance the socioeconomic integration of immigrants and their offspring.[66] Increasingly, but especially after the 2002 assassination of the right-wing populist Dutch politician Pim Fortuyn—who was killed not by a Muslim immigrant but by Volker van der Graaf, an animal rights activist—the coercive dimension of civic integration programs was pushed to the country's political forefront. To become a full-fledged citizen via naturalization in the Netherlands, immigrants are generally required to be adequately integrated. This policy has become a general tenet of the European liberal democracy. Yet at the same time, one expert notes, "the supposedly difference-friendly, multicultural Netherlands is currently urging migrants to accept 'Dutch norms and values' in the context of a policy of civic integration that is only an inch (but still an inch!) away from the cultural assimilation that had once been attributed to the French."[67]

European nationality tests have arguably replaced the vague concept of integration. The increasing presence of immigrant societies has led to the concern that state identity is at risk and that the protection of historical and national heritage is vital to maintaining stability, patriotism, and even security.[68] In April 2003, a four-hour, partially computerized naturalization test was introduced in the Netherlands. The passing of the test required sufficient oral fluency and written skills as well as background knowledge of Dutch society. The 2003 act led to a dramatic drop in applications for naturalization. Compared with 2002, 70 percent fewer applications were filed in 2004.[69]

On April 1, 2007, this naturalization test was abolished. Now, both applicants for Dutch nationality and immigrants applying for permanent residence status must pass the same "integration examination."[70] Evidence has shown that the test clearly disadvantages weaker groups in society—the elderly, the illiterate, or those with little or no education.[71] The decrease in the number of naturalization applications raises the issue of whether this actually was a desired effect of the naturalization policy. What remains unclear is the ultimate purpose of the new policy: Was it intended for the further integration of future citizens or further reduction of the number of foreign naturalizations?[72] It is to the latter that some critics turn; they argue that, as in Germany, the nationality tests are generally used as a tool to control the level and composition of immigration, rather than to establish qualifications for citizenship.[73]

The new immigrants are tested on their tolerance of the Netherlands' open sexual culture and liberal society. Immigrants should know, for instance, that nude sunbathing is legal in some places in the Netherlands. The process of naturalization also involves a DVD ("Coming to the Netherlands") meant to make immigrants ready for life in the "tolerant" Netherlands by showing them images of topless female bathers and gay men kissing.[74] In addition, imams of Dutch mosques must also attend a mandatory course on Dutch law, covering, among other things, the rights of women and freedom of speech. These new citizenship tests are typically accompanied by new requirements for visas, tougher border-control measures, and greater enforcements of regulation pertaining to work permits. These efforts constitute anti-immigration measures.[75]

Further controversy has arisen regarding the 2006 Citizenship Tests Abroad Act, initiated by the then immigration minister Rita Verdonk. The act, also known as "integration from abroad," makes the Dutch integration program one of the most draconian in the European Union. According to the act, foreign nationals wanting to join their families in the Netherlands have to take the nationality tests in their countries of origin. Their knowledge of the Dutch language and culture is evaluated via telephone links at Dutch embassies and consulates. These candidates are required to answer questions set by computer, which they may or may not have knowledge of how to work with. Questions are randomly chosen by a computer from a preexisting database. Human Rights Watch argues that the Turkish and Moroccan communities, who constitute the largest groups of immigrants requesting family reunions, are disproportionately affected by this law.[76]

A counterpoint is offered by observers who argue that the Turkish and Moroccan ethnicities in the Netherlands have a high propensity for in-group marriage. Most second- and third-generation Turks and Moroccans select a marriage partner in their parents' country of origin. Studies have shown that 70 percent of Turkish young people and more than 50 percent of the Moroccans marry a partner from their parents' home country. The offspring of such unions are raised in ethnically closed families, thus preserving the ethnic segregation that characterizes the Turkish and Moroccan communities in the Netherlands.[77] Immigrants from other parts of the world, including Australia, Japan, Canada, New Zealand, South Korea, and the United States, are not required to take the test. Surinamese citizens who can show that they have followed basic schooling in Dutch also are exempt. Human Rights Watch considers the Tests Abroad act blatantly discriminatory, noting that it clearly sends out the message that certain groups are not welcome. This policy is likely to alienate rather than integrate these communities into Dutch society.[78]

In Germany, the integration debate took a coercive turn in the aftermath of the May 2006 events, when "honor killings" in the Turkish immigrant milieu and ethnic violence at a Berlin public school sparked public outrage over integration policies. Responding to the public outrage, German authorities passed fresh requirements for naturalization, including attendance at civic integration courses and language tests.[79] Since 2006, the southern German state of Baden-Württemberg and the state of Hesse have tested prospective citizens on their views on the country's constitution and Western values. The tests appear to have targeted a single social group: Muslims. Baden-Württemberg requires an education course and a thirty-question oral test to determine whether immigrants support issues pertaining to women's rights and religious diversity. Some state officials suggest that the exam may be illegal, stating that one provision allows citizenship to be removed if it is later found that an applicant disguised his or her true religious or puritan tendencies. Question 27 is typical: "Some people consider the Jews responsible for all the evil in the world and even claim they were behind the September 11 attacks in New York. What do you think about such suggestions?" The nationality test in the state of Hesse lists about ten queries aimed at Muslims, including whether a woman should be allowed in public unaccompanied by a male relative.[80] In the context of Germany's population of three million Muslims, the European Assembly of Turkish Academics has denounced the nationality test as "strongly discriminatory and racist."[81] Kerim Arpad, an assembly spokesperson, said it "is shaped by stereotypes and damages integration."[82]

A cursory look at other questions raised in nationality tests illustrates the prevalence of stereotypical images of male Muslim immigrants: "Imagine that your adult son comes to you and says he is homosexual and plans to live with another man. How do you react? Your daughter or sister comes home and says she has been sexually molested. What do you do as father/mother/brother/sister? What do you think if a man in Germany is married to two women at the same time? In Germany you can decide whether to visit a male or female doctor. In certain cases, though, this is not possible: emergencies, shift changes at the hospital. In such cases, would you rather be treated or operated on by a female doctor (male applicants) or a male doctor (female applicants)?"[83]

The interview and the nationality test end by requesting applicants to sign a statement that threatens them with the loss of citizenship should they fail to act according to the results of their attitude test.[84] The questions summarized above clearly contradict both the spirit and legal protections granted by the German constitution; among them the protection against the elimination of citizenship if it results in the citizen becoming stateless. Article 3 of the German constitution states: "No one may be discriminated against or favored due to their ancestry, race, language, place of origin, or their religious or political beliefs."[85]

Since September 1, 2008, prospective German citizens are required to take a new citizenship test, which includes thirty-three questions on politics and democracy, history and responsibility, and man and society, of which applicants must answer at least seventeen correctly. These questions are intended to test the applicants' knowledge and understanding of German society, not to address matters of conscience, as was the case in the German state of Hesse. In addition to passing the new test, prospective citizens must fulfill several other conditions. An applicant needs to have lived in Germany for eight years, possess a sufficient grasp of the German language, have no previous criminal record, earn a secure living, and commit to upholding Germany's constitution.[86] Many of Germany's immigrants—largely from Turkey, Pakistan, Chechnya, and the former Yugoslavia—say that the citizenship test is another barrier for legal permanent residents hoping to become German citizens. Likewise, human rights groups have warned that the new test will simply deter many people from applying for German citizenship in the future.[87] In recent years, the number of applications for German citizenship has fallen. Whereas in 2000, for example, 186,688 people obtained German nationality, only 126,000 did so in 2007.[88]

A similar trend toward restrictive immigration policies has emerged in France. President Nicolas Sarkozy has called for selective immigration that entails, among other things, DNA testing, language exams, and proof of financial independence.[89] A law was passed in France on November 15, 2001, known as the "Everyday Security Law," which increased the power of the police to confront terrorism, but at the same time led to increased harassment of Muslim immigrants.[90]

Both Belgium and Germany have adopted tougher approaches toward asylum seekers by setting tighter requirements in terms of income, language skills, and length of stay. In 2006, the United Kingdom passed the Immigration, Asylum, and Nationality Act, removing several appeal rights for asylum seekers. Similarly, the 2006 Prevention of Terrorism Act, passed in the aftermath of the July 2005 attacks in London, expanded the discretionary powers granted to both the UK Home Office and the police.[91] On balance, it can be argued that in the majority of European countries it has become increasingly difficult for asylum seekers to obtain financial support, employment, long-term security, and citizenship.[92]

Even more radical and negative reactions toward multiculturalism have appeared in European countries. The Vlaams Belang Party in Belgium has viewed immigration as a threat to the Flemish people and culture, warning of the growing threat of Islamic radicalism, as evidenced by the increase in the number of new mosques and state funding for Muslim organizations. The party now insists on the assimilation of Muslim immigrants to Western values, claiming that Islam runs counter to democratic principles and practices and that Muslims must choose between religion and democracy.[93]

In the United Kingdom in 2001, the British Anti-terrorism, Crime, and Security Act greatly increased the power of the police and the military to demand financial, e-mail, postal communication, and transportation records. The introduction of citizenship requirements ("sufficient" language and knowledge of life in the United Kingdom) since April 2007 has blurred the distinction between citizenship as "nationality" and citizenship as "active participation."[94] The proponents of this new policy tend to emphasize more active participation and integration as the basis for permanent residency, rather than the legal status of nationality.[95]

Europe's Role in Rendition and Secret Detentions

The US security measures in the aftermath of 9/11 played out in Europe in several ways, but none more overtly than European governments' involvement in secret detention sites and their severe consequences for constitutional rights of Europeans and the detainees themselves. In response to the rising wave of Islamic terrorism in Europe and the United States following the 9/11 attacks, there emerged an acute sense that Europe and the United States must coordinate their counterterrorism efforts. Achieving that aim, however, carried risks and complexities. The practice of handing over terror suspects to other countries for interrogation—also called extraordinary rendition—has placed the United States and its European allies in a precarious position with respect to the rights and protections enunciated in the Geneva Conventions.

The notion that constitutional rights of detainees must be bypassed to help win the war on terror has generated a great deal of controversy around the world. In addition to controversial issues surrounding the legality and morality of detention, the use of torture and illegal interrogation tactics, which often generate and distribute false information, has proved problematic.[96] Some of the CIA "black sites," secret places where so-called "high value targets" had been disappeared for interrogation, became notorious detention facilities where a variety of harsh interrogation tactics, such as waterboarding, were exercised. These suspects, one expert writes, "were true ghost prisoners, undeclared to the Red Cross, and held, in some cases, for years without any outside communication, even with their families."[97] Some of these sites were located in Eastern Europe, in countries such as Poland and Romania.[98] Ironically, the Eastern European countries, persuaded by the CIA to participate in these illegal transfers involving al-Qaeda captives, were transitional democracies that had embraced the rule of law and individual rights after decades of Soviet domination. The leaders of these countries have been attempting to cleanse their intelligence services of operatives who have either abused their powers in the name of intelligence gathering or have had illicit connections with organized crime.[99]

Some detainees were moved to new black sites in the Middle East and North Africa, later revealed to be in Syria, Morocco, and Egypt. A plethora of declassified and leaked documents revealed that these practices were sanctioned as policy by US authorities at the highest levels. To avoid the issue regarding the legality of such practices—because it is illegal for the government to hold prisoners in such isolation in secret prisons in the United States—the CIA carried them out overseas. Legal experts and intelligence officials have argued that the CIA's internment practices also would be deemed illegal under the laws of several host countries, where detainees have rights to have a lawyer or to seek defense against allegations of wrongdoing.[100]

Many other European countries have worked closely with US agencies in their dealings with European nationals, sometimes in cooperation with European national intelligence and other agencies, in the context of the war on terror. Amnesty International has reported that:

> Police in Bosnia and Herzegovina arrested Mustafa Aït Idir and five other men. An Italian officer aided the abduction of Usama Mostafa Hassan Nasr, usually known as Abu Omar, in Milan. Macedonian officials seized Khaled el-Masri. Swedish police picked up Ahmed Agiza and Mohammed El Zari. Information supplied by German security forces may have led to the arrest of Muhammad Zammar in Morocco, and telegrams sent by UK security forces resulted in the detention of Bisher Al-Rawi and Jamil El-Banna in the Gambia.[101]

All of these detainees were transferred to the custody of another state. Some were transferred from US custody to countries where they faced torture or other ill treatment. Others were transferred to detention centers in Afghanistan or Guantanamo Bay. All were sent to places where due process protections were not in place. Some were victims of enforced disappearance while in US custody. All claim that they have been tortured or otherwise ill treated.[102] Yet to this date, there have been no known criminal investigations of US military officers for authorizing or participating in the illegal transfer of these detainees from occupied territories in violation of the Geneva Conventions or for the illegal rendition of detainees in violation of the Convention Against Torture. The Bush administration ran the program of enforced disappearances of individuals in violation of several treaties as well as customary international law.[103]

The role of European states in renditions and secret detentions, according to Amnesty International, has ranged from active participation to tacit collusion. European agents have turned detained suspects over to US custody without judicial process. They have directly participated in illegal arrests, in one case helping US agents arrest a suspect in Italy before his rendition to Egypt. Europe's airports have been freely used by CIA-operated planes to transport victims of renditions to interrogation facilities and secret incommunicado detention locations around the world. Between 2003 and 2005, Europe was host to secret prisons run by the CIA, where detainees were frequently subjected to torture or other cruel, inhumane, or degrading treatment.[104]

US Muslim Voices Against Extremism and Terrorism

Since 9/11, Arabs and Muslims in the United States have been singled out for particularly egregious treatment as a result of antiterror measures and laws. The push for the enforcement of such laws has been widely construed as targeting young, Muslim males. In fact, one expert notes, Muslims have become the newest US race, subjected to the same type of bigoted treatment that has been historically reserved for people of color such as blacks, Latinos, Asians, and Native Americans.[105] In its 2001 annual report on hate crimes, the FBI identified a more than 1,600 percent increase in reported hate crimes against Arab Americans, Muslims, and Sikhs, who are said to resemble Muslims.[106] Anti-Muslim hate crimes, which surged in the immediate aftermath of September 11, 2001, were followed by a period of relative decline in such crimes in subsequent years. Yet a slew of attacks against Muslims and their religious centers broke out in 2011, apparently inspired by the protests in New York City over the planned Muslim community center and mosque near where the September 11 attacks took place. Leaders of those protests have frequently made hateful statements against Muslims and Islam, with the National Republican Trust Political Action Committee, for example, saying the construction of the center is meant "to celebrate the murder of 3,000 Americans."[107]

Many Muslim Americans today feel that their lives have become markedly more difficult. They feel their businesses, homes, and mosques have come under surveillance. Their reactions to 9/11 have been mixed. While many Muslims took refuge in their faith, growing more devout, others retreated into their private lives.[108] US antiterrorism policy has compelled Muslims—especially Muslim American college youths—to come together and help forge and preserve a unifying identity among different Muslim communities. Other events, such as the ethnic profiling of Muslims by government and law-enforcement officials, have increased cooperation between Muslim Americans of different ethnic backgrounds.[109]

However, the diversity of ethnic, cultural, and theological backgrounds of US Muslims renders it impossible to imagine a single homogenous unit of Muslims in the United States. Second- and third-generation immigrants and native-born Muslims are struggling to bridge their faith with US values and culture. The Muslim role and participation in US politics and culture remains an unresolved issue. In fact, many scholars argue, "the problem of how to live as Muslim in America is just as complicated as that of how to reconcile the diversities among Muslims."[110]

The diversity of Muslims has made their plight more complicated than simply being that of a product of global immigration, African American nationalism, or one minority group's struggle for social justice. Instead, the dynamic of change may dissolve the old identity or create a new social-assimilation scheme.[111] The lasting role of antiterrorism policies in the United States may have compelled or accelerated the cohesion of many Muslim communities toward cooperation with their adopted country.

The USA Patriot Act, passed in October 2001 and renewed in 2006, put into place new surveillance guidelines for US law-enforcement agencies. The Patriot Act was approved with little debate by lawmakers, many of whom later conceded that they had not seriously examined the bill, which greatly expanded the powers of law enforcement to intrude on the daily lives of US citizens and legal residents. Almost immediately, Muslims in the United States became targets of law-enforcement operations in the name of homeland security. Attorney General John Ashcroft directed the FBI to interview five thousand legal immigrants from Muslim countries, even though there was little or no evidence that linked these people to terrorist activity nor to any knowledge that would aid and abet their investigation.[112] Ashcroft also ordered the special registration and fingerprinting of young males from twenty-five countries:

with the exception of North Korea, all were Muslim countries or Middle Eastern Arab countries.[113]

The federal government, according to the Patriot Act, has adopted a series of new powers that include electronic surveillance of phone conversations, bank accounts, Internet records, and even library lending lists. The "sneak-and-peak" provision of the US Patriot Act (section 213) allows law-enforcement agencies to conduct secret searches of a citizen's premises without a valid warrant or even prior notification to the owner. Investigators may enter a citizen's place of residence, take pictures, search and download computer files, and seize items without informing the resident of the search until days, weeks, or even months later.[114] US Muslims, and especially Arab Americans, believe they are unfairly targeted by these new expansions of power. The Council on American-Islamic Relations (CAIR) has observed a steady rise in civil rights abuse cases targeting Muslims since 9/11. In 2004 alone, it received 1,522 reports of abuse.[115] Critical of the media and the federal courts, which were all too complacent in the face of the Bush administration's response to the terrorism threat, some observers noted that "the Patriot Act . . . [is] a loaded gun lying on the table, aimed at the heart of American democracy, ready for the hand of anyone . . . who would fire it."[116]

In July 2003, the Clear Law Enforcement for Criminal Alien Removal Act (CLEAR) gave local police the power to enforce federal immigration laws. The enforcement of the Patriot and CLEAR acts, which led to the creation of a "fortress America," came at the expense of civil rights of many Muslim Americans. According to the seventh annual CAIR report, "government policies after 9/11 have negatively affected 60,000 American Muslims."[117]

Some 54 percent of Muslims, according to the Pew Research Center, indicated that the war on terror singled out Muslims.[118] The social inclusion of US Muslims stands in sharp contrast to what is transpiring in Europe, where Muslims are often economically and socially excluded. Nonetheless, even in a country where Muslims are relatively assimilated, Arab Americans have become targets of widespread discriminatory acts and hate crimes. The USA Patriot Act and other counterterrorism measures have infringed upon the civil liberties of Arab and Muslim immigrants who have been detained in various investigations. Despite the fact that many of accused Muslim detainees have had no connections to terrorists, they have sustained widespread abuse in detention centers. Other efforts by the Department of Justice (DOJ) to combat terrorism, including unleashing a series of high-profile initiatives that explicitly target Arabs and Muslims, have not only resulted in the detention of thousands of people but also facilitated workplace discrimination and fear in the Arab American community.[119]

In the immediate aftermath of 9/11, the DOJ rounded up at least twelve hundred immigrants, the vast majority of whom were of Arab or Muslim background. While refusing to release any information about the detainees, the DOJ charged that the detentions were linked to the 9/11 investigations. In 2002, the DOJ inspector general concluded that the designation of detainees of interest to the 9/11 investigation was "indiscriminate and haphazard," failing to sufficiently distinguish between terrorism suspects and other immigrant detainees.[120] These abuses have harmed the ability of the US government to act as a credible advocate for democratic reforms in the Middle East. Another political fallout from such abuses has been the damage done to the US ability to deal more effectively with the fundamental causes of terrorism.[121]

In response to these US security measures, some Muslims in the United States have turned to a self-critical debate about Islam and their faith. These Muslims, caught in the process of redefining what it means to be a Muslim, have become interested in shifting the terms of the debate away from radicals.[122] For their part, US Muslims are likely to foster the spread of new dynamics of Islamic ideas and identity politics. US Muslims, like their European counterparts, have malleable but distinct identities, woven from multiple narratives. Arguing that the culture of hate, martyrdom, and killing is tearing apart the moral fabric of Muslim societies, one Muslim observer notes, "The biggest victims of hate-filled politics as embodied in the actions of several Muslim militias all over the world are Muslims themselves."[123]

In the case of *Padilla v. Bush*, the tension between protecting individual liberties and national security came to the surface. On May 8, 2002, Jose Padilla, a Muslim US citizen, was arrested in Chicago and transferred to New York. On June 9, 2002, President Bush signed a secret order, designating Padilla as an illegal "enemy combatant," arguing that he was thereby not entitled to trial in civilian courts. Padilla was moved to a naval brig in Charleston, South Carolina, where he remained in military prison for three and half years as an "enemy combatant," held without charge. The Bush administration insisted, in Padilla's case as with other enemy combatants, that these subjects are to be held indefinitely.[124] Padilla's case was eventually moved to a civilian court under pressure from civil liberties groups.

On January 3, 2006, Padilla was transferred to a Miami, Florida, jail to face criminal conspiracy charges. On August 16, 2007, Padilla was found guilty by a federal jury. The final charges against him included conspiracy in the killing of victims in an overseas jihad operation and funding overseas terrorism. He was described in the media as suspected of planning to build and detonate a "dirty bomb" in the United States, though he was not convicted on that charge. On January 22, 2008, Padilla was sentenced by Judge Marcia G. Cooke of the United States District Court for the Southern District of Florida to seventeen years and four months in prison.

In a highly controversial move, the Bush team resumed the use of military commissions to try "enemy combatants." The executive branch's expanding powers were checked by two notable Supreme Court decisions: *Hamdi v. Rumsfeld* in July 2004 and *Hamdan v. Rumsfeld* in June 2006. These cases reveal the limits to the prerogative of the president to authorize unlimited detention of US citizens. In both the Guantanamo case (*Hamdi v. Rumsfeld*) and the *Hamdan* case, the court decided to apply similar standards to noncitizens being held at Guantanamo Bay.[125] The case of *Hamdi v. Rumsfeld* illuminated yet another painful and costly dilemma in which civil liberties of a Muslim US citizen were traded for vague claims by the executive branch involving national security.[126]

Yaser E. Hamdi was captured in Afghanistan and later relocated to the Guantanamo Bay Naval Base, Cuba, and then to the Norfolk naval brig in Norfolk, Virginia, where he was labeled an "enemy combatant." According to government prosecutors and Bush administration officials, Mr. Hamdi had no right to legal counsel. The US Supreme Court decision reversed the dismissal of a habeas corpus petition brought on behalf of Hamdi. The Supreme Court recognized the power of the government to detain unlawful combatants, but ruled that detainees who are US citizens must have the ability to challenge their detention before an impartial judge. On June 29, 2006, the Supreme Court issued a decision, five votes to three, holding that military commissions set up by the Bush administration to try detainees at the Guantanamo Bay lack "the power to proceed" because the structures and procedures of such military commissions violate both the Uniform Code of Military Justice and the four Geneva Conventions of 1949. But more to the point, the court argued that the Bush administration had no authority to set up these particular military commissions without congressional authorization.

Most of the procedural illegalities identified by the Supreme Court in the case of *Hamdan v. Rumsfeld* were related to the Military Commissions Act (MCA) of 2006. Many constitutional problems surrounded the creation of military commissions outside a war zone or war-related occupied territories and absent the context of an actual war. The act justified discrimination on the basis of national origin, denial of equality of treatment, and denial of justice to aliens. Under the act, only an "alien unlawful enemy combatant is subject to trial by military commission."[127] The problem with categorizing enemy combatants as "unlawful" and "lawful" is that, under certain conditions, aliens entitled to prisoner-of-war status under the Geneva law might be mislabeled as "unlawful" enemy combatants. They will thus be subject to trial in a military commission in violation of Article 102 of Geneva prisoner-of-war statutes, which requires trial in the same tribunals using the same procedures as the trials of US service members.[128]

The process of "disappearing persons," or turning them into "ghost detainees," went on unabated, as did the policy of "rendering" suspects to coercive interrogations in places like Uzbekistan and Egypt. Once a low-profile counterterrorism tool, the practice of rendition has become integral to US intelligence-gathering efforts since the 9/11 attacks. The case of Maher Arar demonstrates the flaws of such counterterrorist practices. Arar, a Syrian-born Canadian telecommunications engineer who became a Canadian citizen, was detained at New York's John F. Kennedy Airport by the US Immigration and Naturalization officials on September 26, 2002. He was deported to Syria, where he was tortured and detained for nearly a year. He was released on October 5, 2003, following effective Canadian "quiet diplomacy."[129] There is ample evidence that planes operated by the CIA flew through and stopped in at airports in Finland, Germany, Hungary, Iceland, Italy, Poland, Portugal, and Spain. Many European governments are reluctant to push Washington on the rendition charges, fearing that their own intelligence agencies' cooperation with CIA operations may be revealed.[130]

Similarly, on November 7, 2001, Liban Hussein, a Somalian-born Canadian citizen, was placed on a list of sixty-two people accused by the US government of supporting terrorism. Hussein ran Barakaat North America Inc., a money-transfer business (*hawalas*). The Bush administration claimed that hawalas funneled money from the United States to terrorist organizations, including al-Qaeda. But when the Canadian government could not produce evidence of terrorism, Liban Hussein was cleared of charges.[131] The racialization of citizenship is bound to pose serious challenges to Muslim diaspora communities seeking integration into Western societies.

The growing disaffection among immigrants, aggravated by increasing resentment toward wars in Afghanistan and Iraq, has led to a myriad of security anxieties among Arab and Muslim communities in Europe and the United States. The question of whether security imperatives have compromised democratic principles of Western states has become a deeply divisive one among both the US allies in the West and Muslim immigrants. Furthermore, a steady diet of images of Israeli oppression of Palestinians and US collusion in that oppression has created conditions among the masses that assure the terrorists of sympathy and support.[132]

In sum, the above analysis demonstrates that US policies of cracking down on terrorism in the post-9/11 era—largely in the form of arrests, interrogations, detentions, military commissions, the use of torture, rendition, deportation, and special registration requirements—have specifically targeted South Asian and Middle Eastern Arab/Muslim immigrants in the United States. The cases reviewed in this section suggest that these groups have become targeted as suspected "terrorists" and that anti-Arab/Muslim policies have particularly tainted enforcement measures. For the most part, the fears and warnings about immigrants as national security threats are exaggerated.[133] The Vera Institute of Justice, a nonprofit policy research center based in New York, reported in 2006 that programs such as "special registration," in which more than eighty thousand immigrant men were fingerprinted, photographed, and questioned by the authorities, provided a way to punish even those with minor immigration violations.[134]

* * *

Coming to terms with Muslim immigrants in the West requires a deeper understanding of the rapidly changing face of Europe and the United States—demographically as well as politically. Some skepticism notwithstanding, the majority of Muslims in the United States tend to interpret their experiences in light of the typical US narrative: "a fight for social inclusion successfully waged by other American racial, ethnic, and religious minority groups."[135] In contrast to a mixture of hope and pessimism in the drive toward inclusion in the United States, in Europe the concept of the Muslim enemy has become commonplace in the public discourse—especially among right-wing populist movements. In the anti-Islamic narrative, the central role of Europe and the West is constructed as a community of values opposed not just to the Muslim minorities in the respective European communities but also to the Muslim world as a whole. To many Muslim immigrants, this narrative is distressfully alienating and dangerous.

A broad-based economic integration and civic-political inclusion of immigrants into their host societies is likely to decrease homegrown terrorism in the West. The alternative to militant Islam within the Muslim diaspora of Europe is European Islam. Integrated Muslims would become true European citizens, whereas marginalized Muslims are prone to be mobilized as ethnoreligious minorities for the political objectives of extremist groups.[136] Experts on European Islam and Turkey have pointed out that integration of the EU members' Muslim citizens is crucial to the EU processes and that an exclusion of Turkey on religious and cultural grounds would lead to potentially dire consequences.[137]

The link between security and integration has never been more transparent. Significantly, national security is more contingent on the way in which Muslim Europeans are integrated into their host societies than on how restrictive immigration laws and policies are. Yet, in perilous times, integration policies tend to come under attack. As concern about violent extremism grows in the West, European governments are rethinking their approaches to integration. Recent strictures intended to heighten European security have exposed immigrants and ethnic minorities, especially Muslims, to mistreatment and discrimination. At the same time, some Muslim Americans have been abducted, detained indefinitely, and denied access to courts or lawyers to contest the legality of their detention. Moreover, the convergence of criminal law enforcement and immigration laws underscores the persistent tension between Muslim immigrants and their host countries.

Whereas the negative reactions to Muslim migrants in Europe reflect a grassroots-level discontent with multiculturalism, there is a much higher degree of multicultural tolerance in the United States. Second-generation European Muslims feel socially and economically alienated. Their exclusion tends to foster resentment toward the political and cultural structures of the host countries, making them vulnerable to the recruitment campaigns of extremist Islamic organizations. In the United States, by contrast, such sentiments of alienation and economic deprivation have been minimized in large part because, even though they are only first-generation immigrants, 77 percent are citizens. Due to their diverse backgrounds, Muslims in both Europe and the United States do not form a homogenous group.[138] Yet Muslim Americans enjoy much better socioeconomic conditions because they are not concentrated in pockets of poverty and disaffection. Rather, they benefit from an integrative process and a multicultural environment, even as expressions of racism and Islamophobia have intensified following 9/11.[139]

To many observers, citizenship tests and civic integration programs in Europe represent an effort to prevent migration rather than promote the integration of immigrants and ethnic minorities. A more nuanced focus, rather than the prevailing security-oriented perspectives, is needed to alleviate the situation. Despite the fact that the "Dutch model" has quietly launched civic integration programs into the rest of Europe, linking immigration and border control—with the overarching need to combat terrorism—has failed to generate an enhanced ability to respond to terrorist threats. There are several basic reasons for this. First, Europe still depends on immigrants, as its aging population leaves it no other alternative. Second, European leaders continue to regard integration and security as entirely separate issues, with migration policies largely directed at meeting goals of economic growth and welfare. Third, evidence shows that using border control and restrictive asylum policies as a way to improve internal security have proven utterly ineffective.[140] Finally, numerous domestic measures focused on internal surveillance have failed to identify and isolate radical fringes or groups. In short, the failure to integrate Muslim immigrants has become a major source of insecurity in Europe.[141]

There is a need for socioeconomic reform in Europe that brings material well being and cultural and political inclusion to Muslim immigrants. Western governments should not treat the tensions associated with the war on terror simply as a matter of securitization—that is, an immigration and border control issue. Terrorism, as one expert notes, is a multicausal social phenomenon that has psychological, social, and economic dimensions. Rather than blaming ideologies or religions, we should identify the forces within all ideologies and religions, as well as personal motivations, that drive a minority of adherents to violent extremism.[142] To effectively deal with these issues, it is necessary to support efforts to integrate Muslim immigrants into the socioeconomic fabric of their host societies. Failure to do so will fuel Islamic radicalism and spark social unrest of the sort that broke out in October 2005 in suburbs surrounding Paris, Lyons, and other French cities. There is little doubt that Muslims have become a permanent presence in the West, and even less doubt that they and their host countries together must find a way to negotiate a mutually acceptable future.

Notes

1. This substantially revised chapter is based on my earlier contribution, entitled "The War on Terror and Muslims in the West" in Jocelyne Cesari, ed., *Muslims in the West after 9/11: Religion, Politics and Law* (New York: Routledge, 2010), pp. 45–66.

2. Jocelyne Cesari, *When Islam and Democracy Meet: Muslims in Europe and the United States* (New York: Palgrave, 2004), p. 175.

3. Bryan S. Turner, "New and Old Xenophobia: The Crisis of Liberal Multiculturalism," in Shahram Akbarzadeh and Fethi Mansouri, eds., *Islam and Political Violence: Muslim Diaspora and Radicalism in the West* (London: Tauris Academic Studies, 2007), pp. 65–86; see esp. p. 84.

4. Cesari, *When Islam and Democracy Meet*, p. 181.

5. Sedat Laçiner, Mehmet Özcan, and Ihsan Bal, *European Union with Turkey: The Possible Impact of Turkey's Membership on the European Union* (Ankara: ISRO, 2005), p. 19.

6. Farhad Khosrokhavar, "Terrorism in Europe," in Daniel S. Hamilton, ed., *Terrorism and International Relations* (Washington, DC: Center for Transatlantic Relations, 2006), pp. 23–37; see esp. 27–28.

7. Gilles Kepel, *Beyond Terror and Martyrdom: The Future of the Middle East* (Cambridge: Belknap/Harvard University Press, 2008), p. 256.

8. Jonathan Laurence and Justin Vaisse, *Integrating Islam: Political and Religious Challenges in Contemporary France* (Washington, DC: Brookings Institute Press, 2006), pp. 220–221.

9. Ben Saul, "Wearing Thin: Restrictions on Islamic Headscarves and Other Religious Symbols," in Jane McAdam, ed., *Forced Migration, Human Rights, and Security* (Portland, OR: Hart, 2008), pp. 181–212; see esp. p. 212.

10. Kepel, *Beyond Terror and Martyrdom*, p. 213.

11. Dan Bilefsky, "Denmark Is Unlikely Front in Islam-West Culture War," *New York Times*, January 8, 2006, p. A3.

12. Amel Boubekeur and Samir Amghar, "The Role of Islam in Europe: Multiple Crises?" in Pamela Kilpadi, ed., *Islam and Tolerance in Wider Europe* (New York: Open Society Institute, 2007), pp. 16–20; see esp. pp. 18–19.

13. Ibid., p. 19.

14. Gönül Tol, "What Type of Islamism for Europe? Islamism in Germany and the Netherlands," *Insight Turkey* 11, no. 1 (2009): 133–149; see esp. pp. 133–134.

15. Ibid., 145–147.

16. Peter Mandaville, *Transnational Muslim Politics: Reimaging the Umma* (New York: Routledge, 2004).

17. Jorgen S. Neilsen, "Islam in Europe: Review Article," *Middle East Journal* 62, no. 1 (Winter 2008): 144–148; see esp. p. 145.

18. Handan T. Satiroglu, "The Rise of the Right: Europe's Scary Solution to Immigration," January 29, 2009; available at http://www.alternet.org /immigration/122868/the_rise_of_the_right:_europe's_scary_solution_to _immigration; accessed March 12, 2009.

19. Ibid.

20. Sarah Glazer, "Radical Islam in Europe," in CQ Press, *Global Issues* (Washington, DC: CQ Press, 2009), pp. 81–113; see esp. p. 90.

21. Ibid., p. 91.

22. BBC News, "State Multiculturalism Has Failed, Says David Cameron," *News UK Politics*, February 5, 2011, available at http://www.bbc.co.uk/news /uk-politics-12371994; accessed on August 24, 2011.

23. Martin Schain, "Immigration Policy and Reactions to Terrorism after September 11," in Ariane Chebel d'Appollonia and Simon Reich, eds., *Immigration, Integration, and Security: America and Europe in Comparative Per-*

spective (Pittsburgh: University of Pittsburgh Press, 2008), pp. 111–129; see esp. p. 113.

24. Valsamis Mitsilega, "Borders, Security, and Transatlantic Cooperation in the Twenty-First Century: Identity and Privacy in an Era of Globalized Surveillance," in Terri E. Givens, Gary P. Freeman, and David L. Leal, eds., *Immigration Policy and Security: US, European, and Commonwealth Perspectives* (New York: Routledge, 2009), pp. 148–166; see esp. 152.

25. Ibid., pp. 159–160.

26. Ibid., p. 159.

27. Sarah Spencer, "The Challenge of Integration in Europe," in Demetrios G. Papademetriou, ed., *Europe and Its Immigrants in the Twenty-first Century: A New Deal or a Continuing Dialogue of the Deaf?* (Washington, DC: Migration Policy Institute, 2006), pp. 3–5.

28. Ibid., p. 11.

29. Ibid., p. 21.

30. Ibid., pp. 4–5.

31. Ariane Chebel d'Appollonia and Simon Reich, "Immigration: Tensions, Dilemmas, and Unresolved Questions," in d'Appollonia and Reich, *Immigration, Integration, and Security*, pp. 321–340; see esp. p. 324.

32. Michael Welch and Liza Schuster, "American and British Constructions of Asylum Seekers: Moral Panic, Detention, and Human Rights," in David C. Brotherton and Philip Kretsedemas, eds., *Keeping Out the Other: A Critical Introduction to Immigration Enforcement Today* (New York: Columbia University Press, 2008), pp. 138–158; see esp. 151–152.

33. Jocelyne Cesari, "Securitization of Islam in Europe," in Cesari, *Muslims in the West after 9/11*, pp. 9–27; esp., p. 13.

34. Ibid., p. 13.

35. Ibid., pp. 13–14.

36. Olivier Roy, "A Clash of Cultures or a Debate on Europe's Values?" *ISIM Review* 15 (Spring 2005): 6–7; see p. 6.

37. Robert S. Leiken, "Europe's Angry Muslims," *Foreign Affairs* 84, no. 4 (July–August 2005): 120–135; see esp. pp. 124–125.

38. Ibid., p. 125.

39. Ibid., p. 126.

40. Cesari, "Securitization of Islam in Europe," pp. 14 and 20.

41. Ibid., p. 21.

42. D'Appollonia and Reich, "Immigration: Tensions, Dilemmas, and Unresolved Questions," p. 324.

43. Christina Boswell, "Migration, Security, and Legitimacy," in Terri E. Givens, Gary P. Freeman, and David L. Leal, eds., *Immigration Policy and Security: US, European, and Commonwealth Perspectives* (New York: Routledge, 2009), pp. 93–108; see esp. p. 103.

44. Ibid., p. 105.

45. Daniel Kanstroom, "Immigration Law as Social Control: How Many People Without Rights Does It Take to Make You Feel Secure," in Christopher Mele and Teresa A. Miller, eds., *Civil Penalties, Social Consequences* (New York: Routledge, 2005), pp. 161–184; see esp. p. 165.

46. Migration Policy Institute "New US Report Shows Post-September 11 Immigration Measures Ineffective in Fighting Terrorism," June 26, 2003; avail-

able at www.migrationpolicy.org/pubs/ Americas_Challenge_PressRelease.doc; accessed March 12, 2009.

47. Ibid.

48. Kanstroom, "Immigration Law as Social Control," p. 170.

49. Muzaffar A. Chishti, "Immigration Measures Used in the War on Terrorism Have Harmed Civil Liberties," in Andrea C. Nakaya, ed., *America's Battle Against Terrorism* (New York: Thompson Gale, 2005), pp. 115–121; see esp. pp. 116–117.

50. Ibid., p. 121.

51. Daniel Kanstroom, "Legal Lines in Shifting Sand: Immigration Law and Human Rights in the Wake of September 11th"; available at http://www.bc.edu/schools/lawreviews/meta-elements/journals/; accessed March 12, 2009.

52. This question is attributed to Teresa A. Miller, who is quoted in ibid.

53. Chishti, "Immigration Measures," p. 117.

54. D'Appollonia and Reich, "Immigration: Tensions, Dilemmas, and Unresolved Questions," pp. 335–336.

55. Andrea Elliot, "More Muslims Arrive in US, after 9/11 Dip," *New York Times*, September 10, 2006; available at www.nytimes.com/2006/09/10/nyregion/10muslims.html?_r=3; accessed March 12, 2009.

56. Sarah Glazer, "Radical Islam in Europe," in *Global Issues* (Washington, DC: CQ Press, 2009), pp. 81–113; see esp. p. 88.

57. Christian Joppke, "Beyond National Models: Civic Integration Policies for Immigrants in Western Europe," *West European Politics* 30, no. 1 (January 2007): 1–22; see esp. p. 19.

58. "Immigration," *Euro-Islam.Info*; available at http://www.euro-Islam.info/key-issues/immigration-coming-soon/; accessed March 10, 2009.

59. Christian Joppke, "Transformation of Immigrant Integration: Civic Integration and Antidiscrimination in the Netherlands, France, and Germany," *World Politics* 59 (January 2007): 243–273; see esp. p. 244.

60. Christian Joppke, "Beyond National Models: Civic Integration Policies for Immigrants in Western Europe," *West European Politics*, no. 1 (January 2007): 1–22; see esp. pp. 2–4.

61. Sue Wright, "Citizenship Tests in Europe—Editorial Introduction," *International Journal on Multicultural Societies* 10, no. 1 (2008): 1–9.

62. Ibid., p. 2.

63. Ibid., p. 3.

64. Ibid.

65. Marc Morje Howard, "The Politics of Immigration and Citizenship in Europe," in Carol M. Swain, ed., *Debating Immigration* (Cambridge: Cambridge University Press, 2007), pp. 237–253; see esp. pp. 242–243.

66. Joppke, "Transformation of Immigrant Integration," p. 249.

67. Joppke, "Beyond National Models," p. 2.

68. Ricky van Oers, "From Liberal to Restrictive Citizenship Policies: The Case of the Netherlands," *International Journal of Multicultural Societies* 10, no. 1 (2008): 40–59; see esp. p. 41.

69. Ibid., pp. 49–50.

70. Ibid., p. 41.

71. Ibid., p. 56.

72. Ibid., p. 58.

73. Amitai Etzioni, "Citizenship Tests: A Comparative, Communitarian Perspective," *Political Quarterly* 78, no. 3 (July–September, 2007): 353–363; see esp. p. 353.

74. Deanne Corbett, "Testing the Limits of Tolerance," March 16, 2006; available at http://www.dw-world.de/dw/article/0.2144.1935900.00.html.; accessed March 15, 2009.

75. Etzioni, "Citizenship Tests," p. 356.

76. Sebastian Gottlieb and Laurens Nijzink, "Dutch Citizenship Tests Discriminate," *Human Rights Watch*, May 15, 2008; available at .http://www.rnw.nl/internationaljustice/specials/HumanRights/080515-dutch-immigration-mc; accessed March 17, 2009.

77. Joppke, "Transformation of Immigrant Integration," p. 251.

78. Gottlieb and Nijzink, "Dutch Citizenship Tests Discriminate."

79. Joppke, "Beyond National Models," p. 14.

80. Jeffrey Fleishman, "Some Muslims See German Citizenship Tests as Intrusive," *Los Angeles Times*, April 13, 2006; available at http://dailyuw.com/2006/4/13/some-muslims-see-german-citizenship-tests-as/; accessed March 15, 2009.

81. Kate Connolly, "German to Put Muslims Through Loyalty Test"; *Telegraph.co.uk.*, December 13, 2005; available at http:www.telegraph.co.uk/news/worldnews/Europe/germany/15067; accessed March 15, 2009.

82. Ibid.

83. Ibid.

84. Lena Sokoll, "Germany: Spying and Discrimination Against Muslims," January 18, 2006; available at http://www.wsws.org/articles/2006/germ-j18.shtml.; accessed March 15, 2008.

85. Ibid.

86. "Germany to Introduce Controversial New Citizenship Test," *Spiegel Online International*, June 11, 2008; available at http://www.spiegel.de/international/germany/0,1518,559021,00.html; accessed March 16, 2009.

87. Tristana Moore, "German Citizenship Is Put to Test," BBC News, September 4, 2008; available at http://news.bbc.co.uk/2/hi/europe/7597534.stm; accessed March 16, 2009.

88. "Germany to Introduce Controversial New Citizenship Test," *Spiegel Online International*.

89. "Immigration," *Euro-Islam.Info*.

90. Ibid.

91. Schain, "Immigration Policy and Reactions to Terrorism After September 11," pp. 115–116.

92. "Immigration," *Euro-Islam.Info*.

93. Ibid.

94. Dina Kiwan, "A Journey to Citizenship in the United Kingdom," *International Journal on Multicultural Societies* 10, no. 1 (2008): 60–75; see esp. p. 73.

95. Ibid., pp. 73–74.

96. Darius Rejali, *Torture and Democracy* (Princeton, NJ: Princeton University Press, 2007), pp. 504–508.

97. Stephen Grey, *Ghost Plane: The True Story of the CIA Torture Program* (New York: St. Martin's Press, 2006), p. 224.

98. Stephen Mulvery, "Europe Under 'Rendition' Cloud," BBC News, June 8, 2006; available at http://news.bbc.co.uk/2/hi/europe/5057640.stm; accessed March 8, 2009.

99. Dana Priest, "CIA Holds Terror Suspects in Secret Prisons," *Washington Post*, November 2, 2005, A01; available at http://www.washingtonpost.com /wp-dyn/content/article/2005/11/01/AR2005110101644.html; accessed March 8, 2009.

100. Ibid.

101. Amnesty International, "State of Denial: Europe's Role in US Rendition and Secret Detention," June 24, 2008; available at http://www.amnesty .org/en/library/info/EUR01/003/2008/en; accessed March 8, 2009.

102. Ibid.

103. Jordan J. Paust, *Beyond the Law: The Bush Administration's Unlawful Responses in the 'War' on Terror* (Cambridge: Cambridge University Press, 2007), pp. 32–41.

104. Amnesty International, "State of Denial."

105. Jonathan K. Stubbs, "The Bottom Rung of America's Race Ladder: After the September 11 Catastrophe Are American Muslims Becoming America's New N . . . . .S?" *Journal of Law and Religion* 19 no. 1 (2003–2004): 115–151; see esp. p. 117.

106. Ibid., p. 121.

107. Heidi Beirich, "Wave of Hate Crimes Directed at Muslims Breaks Out," *Hatewatch*, August 26, 2010, available at http://www.splcenter.org/blog /2010/08/26/wave-of-hate-crimes-directed-at-muslims-breaks-out; accessed on August 24, 2011.

108. Andrea Elliot, "Muslims in America: Creating a New Beat," *Nietman Reports*, Summer 2007, pp. 55–56.

109. Fait Muedini, "Muslim American College Youth: Attitudes and Responses Five Years After 9/11," *Muslim World* 99, no. 1 (January 2009): 39–59; see esp. p. 40.

110. Fachrizal Halim, "Pluralism of American Muslims and the Challenge of Assimilation," *Journal of Muslim Minority Affairs* 26, no. 2 (August 2006): 235–244; see esp. p. 235.

111. Ibid., p. 239.

112. Geneive Abdo, *Mecca and Main Street: Muslim Life in America After 9/11* (Oxford: Oxford University Press, 2006), pp. 83–84.

113. Ibid., p. 84.

114. Arsalan Iftikhar, "Presumption of Guilt: September 11 and the American Muslim Community," in David C. Brotherton and Philip Kretsedemas, eds., *Keeping Out the Other: A Critical Introduction to Immigration Enforcement Today* (New York: Columbia University Press, 2008), pp. 108–137; see esp. p. 113.

115. Jenny Cuffe, "US Muslims Alienated by Patriot Act," BBC News; available at http://news.bbc.co.uk/2/hi/programmes/file_on_4/5145970.stm; accessed March 7, 2009.

116. Michael Stern, "Civil Liberties Have Been Compromised by the Patriot Act," in Andrea C. Nakaya, ed., *America's Battle Against Terrorism* (New York: Thompson Gale, 2005): 98–103; see p. 103.

117. Aisha Pena, "Protecting Muslim Civil and Human Rights in America: The Role of Islamic, National, and International Organizations," *Journal of Muslim Minority Affairs* 27, no. 3 (December 2007): 387–400, see esp. p. 388.

118. Jane Lampman, "In Many Ways, US Muslims Are in Mainstream America," *Christian Science Monitor*, May 24, 2007, pp. 2 and 4.

119. James J. Zogby, "The Civil Rights of Arab American Muslims Are Being Violated," in Laura K. Egendorf, ed., *At Issue: Islam in America* (New York: Greenhaven Press, 2006), pp. 46–52; see esp. pp. 48–49.

120. Ibid., p. 49.

121. Ibid., p. 52.

122. James Piscatori, "The Turmoil Within: The Struggle for the Future of the Islamic World, *Foreign Affairs* 81, no. 3 (May–June 2002): 145–150.

123. M. A. Muqtedar Khan, "American Muslims Must Be Less Hypocritical in Their Views Toward the United States and Israel," in Laura K. Egendorf, ed., *At Issue: Islam in America* (New York: Greenhaven Press, 2006), pp. 76–80; see esp. p. 79.

124. Glenn Greenwald, *How Would a Patriot Act? Defending American Values from a President Run Amok* (San Francisco: Working Assets Publishing, 2006), p. 47.

125. Schain, "Immigration Policy and Reactions to Terrorism after September 11," p. 123.

126. Stubbs, "The Bottom Rung of America's Race Ladder," p. 147.

127. Paust, *Beyond the Law*, p. 127.

128. Ibid.

129. Howard Adelman, "Canada's Balancing Act: Protecting Human Rights and Countering Terrorist Threats," in Alison Brysk and Gershon Shafir, eds., *National Insecurity and Human Rights: Democracies Debate Counterterrorism* (Berkeley: University of California Press, 2007), pp. 137–156; see esp. p. 150.

130. Mary Crane, "US Treatment of Terror Suspects and US-EU Relations," *Council on Foreign Relations*, December 6, 2005; available at http://www.cfr.org/publication/9350/; accessed March 7, 2008.

131. Ibid., pp. 86–87.

132. Ian S. Lustick, "The Political Requirements of Victory," *Middle East Policy* 8, no. 4 (December 2001): 14–17; see esp. p. 15.

133. John Tirman, "Immigration and Insecurity: Post-9/11 Fear in the United States," *Audit of the Conventional Wisdom*, MIT Center for International Studies, June 2006, pp. 1–3.

134. Andrea Elliot, "After 9/11, Arab-Americans Fear Police Acts, Study Finds," *New York Times*, June 12, 2006; available at www.nytimes.com/2006/06/12/us/12arabs.html; accessed March 12, 2009.

135. Louise Cainkar, "American Muslims at the Dawn of the Twenty-first Century: Hope and Pessimism in the Drive for Civic and Political Inclusion," in Cesari, *Muslims in the West after 9/11*, pp. 176–197; see esp. p. 193.

136. Bassam Tibi, "Jihadism and Intercivilizational Conflict: Conflicting Images of the Self and the Other," in Shahram Akbarzadeh and Fethi Mansouri,

eds., *Islam and Political Violence: Muslim Diaspora and Radicalism in the West* (London: Tauris Academic Studies, 2007), pp. 39–64; see esp. p. 63.

137. Laçiner, Özcan, and Bal, *European Union with Turkey*, p. 21.

138. Andrea Elliot, "After 9/11, Arab-Americans Fear Police Acts, Study Finds," in ibid.

139. Justin Vaisse, "Muslims in Europe: A Short Introduction," *US-Europe Analysis Series*, Center on the United States and Europe at Brookings (Washington, DC, September 2008), pp. 1–6; see esp. p. 6.

140. D'Appollonia, "Immigration, Security, and Integration in the European Union," in d'Appollonia and Reich, *Immigration, Integration, and Security*, pp. 203–228.

141. D'Appollonia and Reich, "Immigration: Tensions, Dilemmas, and Unresolved Questions," p. 340.

142. Neil Smelser, *The Faces of Terrorism: Social and Psychological Dimensions* (Princeton, NJ: Princeton University Press, 2007).

8

Toward Reframing the Debate

I have argued the need to rectify flaws in counterterrorism policy by examining the possibilities and limits surrounding alternative strategies for combating terrorism. In considering the logic and justifications underlying each policy option and strategy, I have attempted to demonstrate the political, economic, and legal costs, as well as the benefits associated with launching various strategies. By doing so, I seek to recalibrate the balance between security and human rights, which has so often led to the dilemma of whether terrorism should be treated fundamentally as a legal issue or as a national security threat.

But as critical and varied as governments' interests and roles may be in detaining those who pose an immediate threat to their countries, "history and common sense teach us that an unchecked system of detention carries the potential to become a means for oppression and abuse of others who do not present that sort of threat."[1] There is no doubt that, as David P. Forsythe notes, prominent US officials knowingly authorized the severe abuse of various prisoners in Abu Ghraib in Iraq, Guantanamo Bay in Cuba, and Bagram Air Base in Afghanistan, often as part of enforced disappearances or secret detentions, in the face of legal prohibition, even as some lower-level personnel exceeded instructions.[2] Underscoring the significance of the Geneva Conventions and harnessing the rule of law, Forsythe astutely observes that it is an undeniable fact that terror and torture feed off each other and that at present "it is not clear that law can control torture. But if we do not try, we will end up worse off."[3] The protection against terrorist actions involves wide-ranging measures, including, but not limited to, using criminal-law statutes to pursue alleged terrorists, promoting democracy and establishing human rights, altering immigration and border-control policies, sharing intelligence, initiating diplomatic dialogue, and as a last resort intervening militarily.

In this concluding chapter, I review the strategies discussed earlier, with an eye toward reframing the debate on security and human rights. More specifically, I argue that the Western world has a stake in protecting and promoting an international legal system that restrains the right of governments to detain terror suspects without formal charges or trials. Some analysts argue that a policy of restraint in fighting al-Qaeda or similar militant jihadists cannot be sustained and that neither the Geneva Conventions nor the recent US Detainee Treatment Act and Military Commissions Act can provide satisfactory answers to the question of how to conduct a campaign against an enemy who does not respect the internationally recognized conventions of warfare.[4]

Democracy Promotion and Reform

The post–September 11 environment has renewed an old and familiar debate over whether practical considerations such as trade and security concerns should trump the imperatives of human rights. The tension between security concerns and the promotion of democracy is real and poses a significant challenge to a more credible prodemocracy policy. There is a danger, experts argue, of contaminating the altruistic notion of humanitarian intervention with specious and fabricated justifications for invading countries (e.g., Iraq). Many in the non-Western world viewed the US rhetoric of democracy promotion with deep suspicion and marked apprehension, fearing that humanitarian intervention is a deceptive way to conceal hidden and imperial Western agendas.[5] Moreover, as one study has shown, there is no empirical support for the assumptions that either democratic or economically free countries are less likely to experience transnational terrorism.[6] The US antiterrorism policy under the Bush administration, which rested on the premise that terrorism is the product of illiberal political and economic systems, cannot be supported empirically. Instead, issues of physical security of the population, political stability, and possibly religious and demographic parameters appear to be more important predictors of terrorism.[7]

Aside from dubious interventionist doctrines, one key question persists: what to do about friendly—but corrupt and tyrannical—regimes in the Middle East, whose cooperation the United States requires in order to project its power in the region? Although this issue was pervasive yet dormant before the terrorist attacks of September 11, 2001, the reality of the post-9/11 era has brought this urgent question out of hibernation. Thus, the emergence of the paradox: on the one hand, it is widely believed that the advancement of democratic participation and human rights is in fact an essential safeguard against the rise of terrorism in both local and global contexts; on the other hand, the war on terrorism compelled the Bush administration to seek friendlier relations with authoritarian regimes. This is true not only in the Middle East but also in Central Asia, Russia, and potentially Southeast Asia, where security concerns have more often than not overridden domestic and humanitarian politics.

There is ample evidence to suggest that following 9/11, the Bush administration was selective in pushing for human rights in certain countries while seeking closer security cooperation with a wide variety of authoritarian or semi-authoritarian regimes (e.g., Algeria, Bahrain, China, Egypt, Jordan, Kazakhstan, Kuwait, Malaysia, Pakistan, Qatar, Uzbekistan, Yemen, and even Syria).[8] This approach demonstrated the yawning gap between such idealism and the reality of US foreign policy. In the Middle East, both the autocrats of the region and their Islamic political rivals used the burgeoning violence in Iraq to argue the case that democratization was a recipe for disaster, while simultaneously de-emphasizing the sizable risks associated with their own repressive alternatives to democracy that would likely result in further political instability in the region. A pessimistic view still sees the democratic gains in Iraq as being overwhelmed by the continuing violence. Moreover, such a view also holds that the Iraqi government serves as a client state of the United States.[9] This belief is further buttressed by a lack of US credibility in the region, breeding the perception that the promotion of democracy in the Middle East is largely a Western ploy to dominate the region.

In the Middle East, both social structures and informal mechanisms of obtaining resources substantially shape participation in formal political arenas. Although formal political arenas and the institutional structures within them matter, participation therein cannot be adequately understood independently of social identities and informal venues such as tribes, sects, gatherings, and weddings.[10] While some scholars have viewed elections in authoritarian regimes as extremely important, others see them as virtually meaningless. In Egypt, for example, the liberalization programs and so-called democratic reforms under Hosni Mubarak's regime after 2000 were manipulated by his cooptation networks. Such strategies in fact reinforced and stabilized an authoritarian government struggling for longevity, both domestically and internationally.[11] In both

Tunisia and Egypt, a combination of similar factors paved the way for the 2011 uprisings: a sharp rise in food prices, high unemployment rates (especially among the youth), and widespread resentment directed at corrupt and repressive governments. Some analysts have argued that these uprisings are indeed a reaction to IMF and World Bank interventions and neoliberal policies in the region. More specifically, they note that privatization, falling real wages, and the accumulation of wealth in the hands of ruling families and their cronies contributed largely to the popular uprisings.[12]

While it is true that the indigenous political discourse in the past has been largely shaped by Islamic identity and symbolism, and that the modern Middle East has also been a religious Middle East, it is also apt to note that the 2011 uprisings demonstrated that many in the MENA region are driven more by secular economic grievances (i.e., jobs, wages, and economic security) and political grievances (i.e., achieving human dignity and participation in national affairs), than by grand ideological or—even for that matter—Islamic narratives.[13]

Rory Stewart, Ryan Professor at Harvard University who is also the director of the Carr Center for Human Rights, suggests that despite massive Western investment, Afghanistan is close to being a failed state. It is almost impossible for outsiders to reform this kind of system—though many have tried—largely because judges and police are corrupt. Both history and the latest doctrine on counterinsurgency suggest that ultimate victory will require control of Afghanistan's borders, hundreds of thousands of troops, and a much stronger and more legitimate Afghan state, which could take Afghans decades to build. The West does not have the resources to match their ambitions in counterinsurgency, and they never will have the resources.[14] We in the West should play to our strengths, Stewart argues, by committing more development assistance as well as investment in education and health services. We should focus on counterterrorism, not counterinsurgency, and we should prevent al-Qaeda from building new training camps in the country. Likewise, we should not chase the Taliban around rural areas. Transforming a nation of 32 million people, Stewart concludes, is a task not for the West but for the Afghan people themselves. Afghanis have the energy, the pride, and the competence to lead the process. The West does not.[15]

Both formal and informal venues of political participation tend to shore up authoritarian regimes. In Jordan, for instance, elections help sustain the monarchy, while in Palestine elections can provide for fundamental change in the ruling elite.[16] In many Middle Eastern and North African countries, parliaments are used for managing intraelite conflicts, containing the opposition, lobbying for specific interests, and ensuring the stability of the regime (Morocco and Bahrain).[17] Formal institutions in these countries reflect the demands and desires of the elites rather than providing spaces for promoting public interests and defining policies.[18] In certain circumstances, the timing of initiating reforms is crucial. Hence, the question with regard to promoting elections, which are widely regarded as the central feature of international democratization efforts becomes: Exactly *when* will reform foster the best possible chances for democracy in Middle Eastern countries?[19]

Pundits in the Arab media contend that the United States lacks credibility as a promoter of democracy for several reasons. First, US officials are said to have no credibility to call for the respect of either democracy or human rights, given their callous disregard for the rights of Palestinians. Second, a factor frequently mentioned in the Arab press, is the long-standing US support for autocratic Arab regimes that maintain the status quo and supply the United States with cheap oil.[20] Similar negative views, albeit coming from a different perspective, are to be found back home in the United States, where it is sometimes held that for the neoconservatives in the Bush administration expanding US hegemony and support for Israel was at least as, if not more, important as fostering democracy. Both tasks, under the rubric of state building, proved illusory and unworkable.[21]

Forcible Regime Change

In recent decades, the blunt instrument of regime change by military action has become a simple-minded yet ineffective device, as operations in Grenada, Panama, Afghanistan, and Iraq attest. Those four invasions, launched between 1983 and 2003, were dramatic, violent expressions of deep impulses that have powerfully shaped the collective US view of the world. They assert the core belief that the United States has a right, and even an obligation, to overthrow regimes that its government considers to be evil.[22] Yet a century of US "regime change" operations has shown that the United States cannot effectively rule foreign lands.[23] For most of the "regime change" era, the United States did little or nothing to promote democracy in countries whose governments it deposed. In fact, in Iran, Guatemala, and Chile, the United States overthrew democratically elected leaders and left tyrants in their place. In Afghanistan and Iraq, in contrast, the United States devoted its resources to the most ambitious, unrealistic, and futile task of "nation building" it had ever

248 Terrorism, Security, and Human Rights

undertaken.[24] Ultimately, as experts wearily note, such "regime change" operations have attenuated, rather than strengthened, US security, bringing, both to the people of the United States and to the nations whose histories they sought to alter, far more misery than liberation and promised freedom. These interventions have generated numerous militant groups and violent extremist reactions, further emboldening anti-Americanism and creating resentment toward US policies.[25] Similarly, the NATO intervention that provided rebel fighters with the air power to defeat and ultimately force the collapse of Qaddafi's regime in the fall of 2011 is likely to lead to nation-building efforts in postconflict Libya. These efforts carry the risk of generating resentment toward outside interveners—that is, the Western governments—among disparate groups that have forged an alliance (National Transitional Council—NTC) that routed Qaddafi's armed forces. It remains to be seen whether the transitional period will be sustainable given that the members of the NTC have vastly different and complex political and ideological agendas.

No less troubling are the effects of democracy promotion through forcible regime change. While there seems to be a consensus that support for internal democratic movements is the best antidote to terrorism, there is little agreement on how democracy promotion should be executed. This trendy, semi-articulated justification for the invasion of Iraq has come under heavy criticism, both domestically and internationally, especially in light of the fact that the original pretext, weapons of mass destruction, was absurd, given consistent reports by the International Atomic Energy Agency to the contrary. Iraq's linkage to international terrorism was specious and unlikely. More to the point, the Iraqi government was no longer posing a serious menace to its neighbors, having been effectively hampered by the first Gulf war as well as a decade of UN sanctions.[26]

The US unilateral policy to promote its security interests has enjoyed much less international support than domestic. Most countries, Stanley Hoffmann rightfully asserts, were very uneasy about a world in which the United States was the single superpower. While the United States faces many problems that affect other nations as well—including global warming and the depletion of natural resources—it attacks and undermines fundamental global institutions, such as the International Criminal Court, that enjoy near-universal legitimacy. The United States has damaged its own "soft power" irrevocably—the power of influencing others through persuasion and example—by its preemptive attack against Iraq, its prisoner abuses in Abu Ghraib and Guantanamo, and its restrictions on foreigners eager to migrate to the United States.[27] The overwhelming military might of the United States, Hoffmann continues, can serve as a deterrent, but it acts at its peril when it employs its power to destroy nonthreatening cities, people, and regimes. While all this may be true, the soft power of the United States still has tremendous potential to engage in state-building, exert formidable economic development, promote human rights, and work for substantive change around the globe.[28]

Human Rights and Security:
Trade-off or Mutual Constitution?

The contemporary tendency to argue, in the name of national security, for the suspension, limitation, or even legalized abuse of fundamental rights and democratic freedoms is exceedingly problematic. Rather than viewing the choice between the struggle against violent extremism (terrorism) and the protection of civil-political liberties as a trade-off, we must focus on the constitutive role of security and human rights as well as the relationship between international law and national security.

Although no one can offer a definitive answer as to how we can best confront terrorism while simultaneously maintaining our civil liberties, most experts argue that there cannot be a *successful* war on terrorism. Without political counterstrategy, they assert, terrorists will bounce back. The US media and national security establishment overlooked Afghanistan after the Soviet withdrawal, and several US administrations failed to devise a political strategy for filling the remaining power vacuum after Soviet troops withdrew in 1989—failures that helped account for the rise of the Taliban and al-Qaeda. In short, one critic notes, "everyone missed the story" in the lead-up to 9/11.[29]

The elevation of a security threat to a level of "war" has led to a securitization process in which the identification of an existential threat has come to warrant a suspension of the normal rules of politics, allowing policymakers to take extraordinary measures. The framework of "war" and securitization has enhanced the gravity of the threat, contributing to the deepening of conflict. The fact that President Bush brought the war on terror into being, a war of indefinite duration involving an obscure, nonstate enemy that is outside the rules of war, thus gave rise to a range of acts that would not otherwise have been acceptable. The result was the speedy passage of the Patriot Act and the development, as well as the enacting, of new rules of detention and torture that bypassed both the rules of war, as declared in the 1949 Geneva Conventions, and international laws prohibiting torture, as enunciated in the Convention Against Torture.[30] The ensuing surveillance measures and the abrogation of many basic civil liberties in the context of a war of boundless duration proved to be in conflict with the ultimate purpose for which the war was fought, namely, the preservation of a way of life characterized by openness and freedom.[31]

Similarly, this exclusively militarized response to terrorism has resulted in vague and sometimes conflicting definitions and categories. The distinction between insurgency and terrorism, beyond certain tactical differences, has become blurred. Historically, torture was an institution in ancient Greece and the Roman Empire that was used only on slaves, foreigners, and other individuals who did not have full legal personality. In twelfth-century Europe, an inquisitorial process was established to generate evidence or proof for conviction. In serious crimes, given the absence of eyewitnesses, the confession was viewed as the most secure proof, resulting in the introduction of torture into the legal process.[32] In the nineteenth century, the US armed forces and militia used terror in the extermination and ethnic cleansing of American Indians. In the twentieth century, atrocities committed by Nazi Germany in World War II prompted the recognition that governments could no longer treat their own populations inhumanely and that the concept of human rights would delineate the limits to their power. The 1949 Geneva Conventions for the protection of victims of war prohibited torture and various kinds of inhuman treatment. Such acts were deemed "grave breaches"—that is, war crimes.[33] Yet, terror had frequently been used to achieve political goals. Radical and underground Jewish groups, such as the Stern Gang and Irgun, used terror against the British and selected Arabs in an attempt to conquer Palestine. In many countries, including Cyprus, Kenya, Vietnam, Malaya, Burma, and countless other colonial territories, terror became an integral part of violent independence struggles.

Today in the West, however, the term *war on terror* refers primarily to fighting against one network: al-Qaeda.[34] Beyond conceptual clarification, it is important to understand the political and diplomatic factors contributing to terrorism. K. J. Holsti questions the value of those analyses that have focused on psychological, cultural, and economic reasons, arguing that such studies have rarely, if ever, yielded any effective results. Instead, Holsti insists: "One cannot overlook motivation that arises out of strong perceptions of injustice, hypocrisy and double standards. While a more even-handed policy on the Palestine issue would not solve the problem of terrorism, it is certainly a necessary component."[35]

The prevalence of indefinite detention, torture, and other abuses has undermined US credibility as the prime advocate of democracy and human rights. The United States at one point held more than 750 people in detention at Guantanamo Bay. Many others have been held in undisclosed locations abroad, as well as in incommunicado detention in a South Carolina naval brig. Some of the detainees in custody have been subjected to physical and mental pain, while others have been turned over to countries that routinely engage in torture practices, such as Syria and Jordan.[36] Other governments have tried to use this war on terror to annihilate their oppositions. In Colombia, Uzbekistan, Russia, China, and other countries, guerrilla insurgencies, separatist movements, and even nonviolent dissident activities have been stigmatized by governments as terrorists. Such labels have been used to strip the targeted groups of legitimacy and to allow governments to recast their struggles against these groups as counterterrorism.[37]

The guilty verdict delivered against Osama bin Laden's driver Salim Ahmed Hamdan on August 6, 2008, has established a legal precedent with the controversial US military commission system for future trials at Guantanamo Bay. This legal "precedent" will make it easier for prosecutors to convict other suspected war criminals in similar military commission trials. Human rights experts as well as legal analysts challenge the US government's use of material support as a war crime, arguing that Hamdan's role fails to rise to the level of direct participation in war crimes. Hamdan, who has been held in open-ended detention as an unlawful enemy combatant for nearly seven years, has been subjected to a trial shrouded in secrecy and tainted by coercion within a legal process that is fundamentally flawed.[38]

Under human rights laws, states' obligations are twofold: (1) to protect the life and security of any individual within their jurisdiction, and (2) to do so within the bounds of international law. As part of a state obligation to protect individuals within their jurisdiction, all measures must also be taken to combat terrorism within the confines of international law, in particular statutes regarding international human rights, refugee, and humanitarian law. States have an obligation to ensure that all counterterrorism measures comply with human rights norms. The World Summit Outcome (WSO), adopted by the UN General Assembly in 2005, addressed the issue of respect for human rights while countering terrorism and concluded that international cooperation to fight terrorism must be conducted in conformity with international law. This WSO is to include the Charter of the United Nations and relevant international conventions and protocols that specifically pertain to human rights. The General Assembly and the Human Rights Council have emphasized precisely the same concern: that states must ensure that all measures taken to combat terrorism comply with their obligations under international human rights law, refugee law, and international humanitarian law.[39]

The obligation of states to protect individuals residing within their territories raises the question about the "right to security" and whether or not it trumps other rights, such as civil and political rights. If providing security justifies suspension of certain civil-political rights, then the next logical question is precisely how one can discern among issues that purportedly fit under the rubric of "providing security." In situations when disorder and chaos threaten the lives of the people, the maintenance of order (and by extension, security) is an existential requirement for protecting basic human rights. Under such circumstances, this provision of order is in and of itself a rights issue. It should be noted, however, that the right to security must be defined within the nonderogation regime of international law (i.e., the right to life, prohibition against torture, prohibition of slavery or servitude, and nonretroactivity of criminal liability), even as the right to security enjoys primacy under certain circumstances.

US national security leaders have misrepresented the nature of the terrorism issue, writes John Brady Kiesling, a career State Department diplomat. "Their decision for military preemption instead of law and justice violated a fundamental contract between American citizens and their government."[40] Torture, aside from being a shameful and treasonable form of bureaucratic self-promotion, puts US lives in danger, Kiesling argues. Successful counterterrorism thus requires respect for the lives of innocents: "The U.S. war on terrorism," he writes, "is at heart a war to strengthen the rule of law in societies whose citizens are themselves often helpless victims of illegitimate violence."[41] Human rights continue to be everybody's best defense against policies and measures that mitigate the rule of law in the name of security. A growing consensus among analysts, policymakers, and US interrogators holds that the need for greater security must not be articulated at the expense of the rights of others. The struggle against violent extremists ought not to force us to change our identity—that is, who we are.[42] Paradoxically, but understandably, as Shadi Mokhtari so aptly points out, at the same time that post-9/11 developments provided Arabs and Muslims a renewed sense of skepticism toward human rights, they also sparked a new engagement and connection with human rights ideas. Although US human rights abuses at Abu Ghraib were generally perceived as ultimate proof of human rights being nothing more than a tool of US geopolitical ambition, many in the Middle East felt the effects of these abuses, experiencing a profound sense of disempowerment on a very personal level. In their search for a just response to existing double standards in consolidated democracies, many in the Muslim world, including political leaders and media pundits, have turned to and invoked the moral authority and sanction of universalist human rights discourses more directly.[43]

While in the past Middle Easterners have typically used religious or cultural relativist justifications to evade international human rights norms, today many of them seek the universal application of human rights norms as tools for countering international abuses of power.[44] Moreover, in the aftermath of the revelations of Abu Ghraib abuses, a few voices have called for Muslim Arabs to acknowledge their own hypocrisy and double standards—the criticism of US practices while systematic human rights violations were pervasively committed by their own leaders. This could result in what many human rights advocates hope for: the introduction of international norms into the domestic realm through the back door.[45]

Since 9/11, it has become increasingly difficult to defend the trade-off thesis. The tragic events of 9/11 and human rights abuses in its aftermath have offered a unique opportunity to reframe the security–human rights debate in terms of identity, shared meanings, and goals, as well as renewing the commitment to universal standards. It is crucial to remember that human rights violations often have serious security implications. Human rights lawyers, scholars, and activists have consistently argued that the most important word in the Universal Declaration of the Human Rights (UDHR) is *universal*, not the phrase *human rights*. Absent *universality*, we face the possibility of arbitrary enforcement and abuse of norms. The major achievement of the UDHR has been to make human rights something that no government can simply disregard.[46]

The Obama administration can—and should—revive the historical US moral reputation by throwing its weight behind human rights conventions and advancing them as the necessary partner for providing justice in new areas.[47] President Obama's Nobel speech in Oslo affirmed the US government's respect for the Geneva Conventions: "Even as we confront a vicious adversary that abides by no rules, I believe the United States of America must remain a standard bearer in the conduct of war. That is what makes us different from those whom we fight. This is a source of our strength."[48] The Obama administration has abandoned Bush's claim of inherent executive authority and relied instead on an interpretation of Congress's 2001 authorization to use military force against terrorist groups. But both approaches, as the executive director of Human Rights Watch, Kenneth Roth, notes, still permit US soldiers or law-enforcement officials to indefinitely detain suspected terrorists anywhere in the world without regard to the due process standards of the United States or any other country.[49] Moreover, Obama's refusal to terminate the use of military commissions and detention without trial is preserving the spirit of Guantanamo, even after part of the military installation has been shut down.[50]

Failure to live up to acceptable standards will have ominous effects on future US foreign policy and conduct in the campaign against terrorism. The prison at Guantanamo Bay is seen throughout the world as the manifestation of a US attitude bent on treating international rules as well as its own treaty obligations as one-sided, applicable only to other countries. P. Sabin Willet, a partner at the Boston law firm of Bingham McCutchen, writes: "We are committed as a nation to affording all persons fair hearings and due process of law; regardless of religious beliefs, skin color, or national origins and without regard to the nature or seriousness of the crimes of which they are accused. Our actions with regard to the men at Guantanamo Bay have violated and continue to this day to violate these basic American principles."[51]

How to Confront Terrorism: The Internal Debate

It is important to recognize that Islamic militants constitute a tiny minority of the world's one billion-plus Muslims. The "Islamic threat" thus involves small numbers of extremists. This threat feeds on the dysfunctional governmental systems in the Middle East, a perceived sense of humiliation at the hands of the West, and an easy access to technologies of violence.[52] Moreover, the persistence of nondemocratic governments in the Middle East has helped generate resentment against the West to the extent that Western intervention and support has abetted corrupt, autocratic rulers of the region.

Yet for the most part, conflicts within the Muslim world have more to do with specific local conditions than with global aspirations. In Algeria, for example, the Salafist Group for Call and Combat has been engaged in war with the Algerian government since the early 1990s. Islamic opposition forces cannot be viewed solely through the prism of al-Qaeda or anti-American jihad.[53] In fact, experts argue, Osama bin Laden was not, as is generally claimed in the media, the sole mastermind of these attacks; he simply provided these groups with logistical and financial support. The network is not centrally located or fixed; rather, it appears to be a kaleidoscopic web of cells and links that span the globe from camps on the Afghan-Pakistan borderlands to immigrant ghettoes in Europe and the United States. This network is largely disconnected from most Islamic opposition groups in the Middle East, who are embroiled in national struggles to create Islamic states.[54]

Since 9/11, support for al-Qaeda's goals has declined dramatically throughout the Muslim world. According to a poll by the Pew Research Center's Global Attitudes Project, conducted in the months leading up to Osama bin Laden's death, in the six predominantly Muslim nations, bin Laden received his highest level of support among Muslims in the Palestinian territories—although even there only 34 percent said they had confidence in him to do the right thing on the global scene. Minorities of Muslims in Indonesia (26%), Egypt (22%), and Jordan (13%) expressed confidence in bin Laden, while he had almost no support among Turkish (3%) or Lebanese Muslims (1%).[55] The obsession with jihadists' ideologies has diverted attention from the actual Muslim societies and the kind of social change they are undergoing. Frustrated with the extremists, many Muslims embrace modernity and seek practical solutions—not a desire for immortality through death or glorification of martyrdom.[56] The majority of the people in the Middle East, as one expert insists, desire the kind of sociopolitical change that has swept the rest of the world over the past quarter century, even as the war in Iraq escalated and the US agenda of democracy promotion became increasingly discredited.[57] The events of Arab Spring 2011 demonstrated that peaceful democratic change could originate from within the Arab world and that the Tunisians' and Egyptians' aspirations for democratic change were no different from those of other people across the globe. In a country like Egypt, in which nearly 44 percent of the population lives on $2 per day or less, the emergence of such popular uprisings should not have come as a surprise.

An effective campaign against such terrorist acts must therefore focus on internal economic and political reform within these Muslim societies, while at the same time striving to provide channels of meaningful participation from opposing groups. The corrective to Islamic relativists is to integrate mainstream (moderate) Islamists into the political process of their respective countries (as in Jordan). Islamists themselves are increasingly outspoken about the need for democracy and human rights. Perceptions of injustice with regard to a fair resolution of the Palestinian issue, which in the past have motivated political violence in the Middle East, reinforce the militants' position that the national aspirations of the Palestinians, as they are often internationally recognized, can be achieved through armed struggle and armed resistance, rather than diplomacy.

It bears noting that no military or strong-arm model for coping with terror has proved effective in the long term. A trio of experts have pointed out that, in the case of the Palestinians, "suicide attacks have almost always subsided only after the country coping with them has managed to reduce the support for such attacks among the population represented by the organization perpetrating them."[58] The key to reducing terrorism in the Muslim world as elsewhere is state-building—that is, the creation of strong, legitimate, and successful states.

In the context of international relations, an effective multilateral cooperation among the United States, Europe, and the Middle East is the most realistic and effective response to terrorism. This multilateral cooperation would involve coordination and information sharing among all parties. Both the United States and the European Union should encourage Muslim countries to place a high priority on improving socioeconomic and political conditions, with dignity and respect for Muslim countries' limits and capabilities. The acknowledgment of such limitations should not, however, preclude an ongoing dialogue with Muslim authorities on improving their human rights conditions.

Competing visions of reform in the Middle East have thrown the region into an intense debate about change and continuity. Following the secular-nationalists' failure to reform society, the Islamic nationalists have come to see revolution—and subsequently, participation in the political process—as the only effective method to bring about change. Yet the question of the nature of Islamic society and its relationship with *sharia* and the state is still unsettled.[59] The suppression of basic freedoms by authoritarian regimes has not only stifled debates essential for internal reform, it has also given rise to Islamic radicalism. Many studies confirm the assertion that Islamists will be among the beneficiaries of democratization in the short term.[60] Moreover, "some Islamists have proved that they are more committed to democracy than some secular autocrats."[61]

One study argues that Western policymakers must learn to differentiate the Muslim Brotherhood from radical Islamists, engaging the former while taking stock of their strategic interests and capabilities in the Muslim world. The study demonstrates that the members of the Muslim

Brotherhood—in the Middle East and Europe—reject global jihad while embracing elections and other features of democracy. In pursuit of popular authority, the Brotherhood had forged electoral alliances with secularists, nationalists, and liberals.[62] In Europe, Brotherhood-led groups stress the rights of religious minorities. In response to a Danish newspaper that printed cartoons satirizing the Prophet Muhammad in 2006, all European branches of the Brotherhood, though criticizing the cartoons for hurting the feelings of Muslims, officially called for peaceful protest as well as increased cooperation between Muslims and non-Muslims.[63] The Brotherhood-linked organization Union des Organizations Islamiques de France (UOIF) has adopted moderate positions vis-à-vis the stone-throwing, car-burning riots of 2005 in the largely Muslim slums of Paris. Similarly, when French authorities banned the wearing of the headscarf, the position of the UOIF was accommodation. The organization's absence from riots and anti–Iraq War demonstrations, in the European country with the largest Muslim population, surely alleviates some fears of an Islamist takeover of Europe.[64]

In Morocco, for example, under pressure to compromise regarding proposed legislation, most notably the reform of the family code and the anti-terror law, Islamists have demonstrated great ability to adapt to new circumstances.[65] Likewise, in Algeria, there has been no evidence of significant new money and weaponry flowing to the militant group that calls itself al-Qaeda in the Islamic Maghreb, formerly known as the Salafist Group for Preaching and Combat (GSPC). In the coastal city of Oran, the GSPC's tactics have alienated the public, including many desperate, unemployed young men who once looked to the Islamists for inspiration. This is tied to a more general disillusionment with the Islamist movement as the use of al-Qaeda-style suicide attacks, with high civilian casualties, has lost its appeal to the Algerian youth. Barring a sudden infusion of outside funding and resources, experts argue, al-Qaeda in the Islamic Maghreb will have to pursue either its original nationalist goals or its newly acquired role as a key player in the global jihad.[66] Needless to say, al-Qaeda in the Islamic Maghreb wants to impact the direction of the Arab Spring now that violence is fueling the uprisings, and a two-part video series has been released trying to lure new followers to the revolt by jihad.[67] Most Muslims, Islamic movements, and activists desire stable and safe societies, representative governments, and the rule of law, and indeed they are among the most important forces for securing such goals.[68]

Especially in the post-9/11 context, the necessity of dialogue between the Muslim and Western worlds has become more urgent and real.[69] Progressive Muslim reformists have increasingly voiced their concerns about a lack of communication and cross-cultural dialogue. Turkey's Development and Justice Party (AKP) serves as an example: its appeal inside Turkey as well as in the entire Muslim world has dramatically risen. It may be that Islamic reformists are better positioned to strike a synthesis between religious forces and those of modernity. Some scholars of Middle Eastern politics and societies have argued that what shapes the dynamics of change and democratization in the Muslim world is a continued interaction between religion and modernity. "Neither authoritarianism nor an empire's 'war on terror' are ever-lasting: both religion and modernity are."[70] Others have pointed out that Muslims' religious freedom may be greater under secular states than under so-called Islamic regimes, which favor certain sects and interpretations and impose limitations on others. While an Islamic discourse is essential for legitimizing the necessary strategies for shaping the public role of Islam, this discourse cannot be effective or sustainable without the security and stability provided by the secular state.[71]

How to Confront Terrorism: The External Context

Since 9/11, Muslims in the West have been subject to attack, mistreatment, and discrimination, suffering under the so-called "post-9/11 trauma." Recent strictures bent on heightening European security have limited immigration and forced Muslim immigrants onto the fringes of European society. Likewise, many Muslim Americans have been abducted and detained indefinitely; several have been denied access to courts and denied legal representation to contest the validity of their detention or the legality of their treatment. The convergence of criminal and immigration law underscores the persistent tension between Muslim immigrants and their host countries.

There has been a convergence of immigrant integration policies across Europe as a whole, but European countries nevertheless offer a variety of integration processes. Citizenship tests and civic integration programs in Europe have prompted a debate over whether they are intended to help the integration of immigrants and ethnic minorities or prevent migration. The "Dutch model" introduced civic integration programs to Europe.

There is considerable divergence between the integration policies of the EU countries and those of the United States. Public reaction to Muslim migrants in Europe reflects a grassroots-level of discontent with

multiculturalism, whereas there is a higher degree of multicultural tolerance in the United States. In Europe, second-generation Muslims still
feel socially and economically alienated. Their exclusion tends to foster
resentment toward the political and cultural structures of the host countries, making them vulnerable to the recruitment campaigns of extremist
Islamic organizations. In the United States, by contrast, such sentiments
of alienation and economic privation have been minimized. Most US
Muslims are substantially better integrated into society and politics than
are Muslims in Europe. The stimulus toward violent extremism has less
effect among Muslims in the United States.[72] They enjoy much better
socioeconomic conditions than European Muslims, are not concentrated
in pockets of poverty and disaffection, and benefit from an integration
process and the multicultural environment. This has been true even
though, post-9/11, Islamophobia and racism accelerated.[73] Muslims in
the United States do share with European Muslims the characteristic of
not forming a homogenous group. Muslims come from many different
parts of the world and from many different cultural/ethnic traditions.[74]

The creation of a link between immigration-policy/border-control
and security has been counterproductive for several reasons. Europe, for
its part, depends on migrants, as its aging population leaves it no other
alternative for cheap labor. And European leaders and citizens continue
to view the issues of integration and security as entirely separate issues,
with migration policies all too often directed at meeting goals of economic growth and welfare. In any case, evidence indicates that the
methods of border control and restrictive asylum policies as a way to
improve internal security have been useless.[75] Numerous domestic
measures focused on internal surveillance have failed to identify, isolate,
or contain those of the radical fringe holding anti-Western sentiments
among radicals in Europe. For these reasons, the failure of integration
has become a major source of insecurity in Europe.[76]

The issue of national security is connected more to the way in which
Muslim Europeans are integrated into their host societies than to the
practice of restrictive immigration laws and invasive security policies.
The deep and relevant interconnection between security and integration
has never been more apparent. There is an urgent need to promote
socioeconomic reform in Europe that brings material well-being and
cultural inclusion to Muslim immigrants. European governments cannot
defuse the tensions by dealing with the war on terror simply as an immigration and border control situation. To effectively deal with these
issues, it is necessary to support efforts to integrate Muslim immigrants
into the socioeconomic fabric of their host societies. Failure to do so

will fuel Islamic radicalism and spark social unrest of the variety witnessed in late October 2005 in the suburbs surrounding Paris, Lyons, and other French cities.

Aside from condemning senseless violence, the reactions of the Muslim diaspora to the 9/11 attacks have been mixed. Some Muslims have chosen to retreat from social and cultural life, keeping their distance from the ensuing negative fallout. Others—mostly the second- and third-generation Muslims—have resented their host societies' egregious treatment of Muslim minorities, using their religion as a crucial cultural and identity marker. Still others have explored the possibility of reconciliation between Islam and the West by taking a self-critical approach, while also arguing that the core messages of Islam, such as equality and egalitarianism, have gained support among other religious groups in Europe and the United States. Although it is difficult to foretell which approach will persevere, it is clear that these dynamics—tension and reconciliation—will be influenced not only by the conflict within Muslim communities over whether to create a "transcultural space" for dialogue between different ethnic and religious groups, but also by the various policies of Western governments working toward the integration and institutionalization of Islam.[77] There can be no doubt that security and integration are inseparable issues. Given that terrorism in Europe is largely homegrown, counterterrorism measures cannot overlook the deep interconnection between security and integration processes in diaspora communities.

Diplomatic and Legal Tools

There is no one, single way to carry out an effective campaign against violent extremism or terrorism, as I have noted throughout this book. Several studies have identified that military force has rarely been effective in defeating terrorist groups. There is no doubt that Osama bin Laden's killing in Pakistan in May 2011 dealt a critical blow to al-Qaeda's organization—if not its future operations—in the region. It is important to remember, however, that there are two al-Qaeda offshoots that have found sanctuary in the tribal lands of Pakistan's border with Afghanistan: the Haqqani network, which has been responsible for many attacks against soldiers in Afghanistan and suicide bombings there, and Lashkar-e-Taiba, which executed several attacks in Mumbai, India, in November 2008. The presence of these terrorist groups in Pakistan has led to periodical turmoil and a lingering insurgency inside Afghanistan.

Adm. Mike Mullen, chairman of the Joint Chiefs of Staff, in a hearing of the Senate Armed Services Committee on September 22, 2011, directly linked Pakistan's spy agency, Inter-Services Intelligence (ISI), with a truck bomb attack against US targets and assets, as well as the assault on the US embassy in Kabul on September 13, 2011. This view reflected the Obama administration's overall assessment that links exist between the Haqqani network, a group that maintains close ties to the Taliban but often works independently, and some elements within the ISI.[78]

Despite suffering a setback in Iraq, with several senior operatives killed or captured, al-Qaeda has carried out more terrorist attacks after September 11 than it did before.[79] Instead of having a military focus, policing and intelligence cooperation should be the centerpiece of counterterrorism policies. Of the $609 billion in counterterrorism funding authorized by Congress between 2001 and 2007, 90 percent went to military operations. Much of that money could be more effectively spent on law enforcement and intelligence agencies working overseas.[80] The US military must resist being drawn into combat operations in Muslim societies, especially in large numbers, where its presence is likely to increase terrorist recruitment.[81]

Military interventions, especially when conducted in the name of promoting democracy, have rarely, if ever, led to the stability and security of the Middle Eastern region. There is a need to replace the war model with an enhanced law-enforcement strategy in the long term.[82] The British experience in Northern Ireland demonstrates that its military campaign against the Irish Republican Army largely proved ineffective and counterproductive. It was only when the British government began to address the sources of political grievances and to move away from military intervention that a law-enforcement model succeeded in the struggle against the Irish nationalist terror groups.[83]

Guantanamo Bay delivered a severe blow to the moral reputation of the United States, as hundreds of individual were held for years without a fair hearing and were subjected to torture and other abuses. Creating a prison beyond the law "undermined the United States' credibility and security, and diminished its ability to fight terrorism worldwide," as Mark P. Denbeaux and Jonathan Hafetz noted.[84] By the end of the Bush administration, the abuse of law, largely in the form of indefinite detention outside the ordinary judicial system, had become institutionalized.[85] Although the project for global human rights and justice was derailed, it became increasingly clear that campaigning against terrorism and fighting for freedom and social justice were inseparable.

Many in the Middle East see security and justice as different sides of the same coin. Justice for Middle Eastern political groups has consistently been synonymous with addressing the legitimate grievances of the diasporic, imprisoned, and stateless Palestinian populations. Even those who favor a joint or binational solution to the Israeli-Palestinian conflict are troubled by Arial Sharon's vision of unilateral withdrawal from Gaza that would concentrate the Palestinians in segregated enclaves while annexing large areas of the West Bank along the Green Line and the Jordan valley. Sharon's vision, they argue, which is pursued in the hope of neutralizing alternative political plans, such as the roadmap, and to project "terrorism" as the main problem, renders doubtful a workable two-state solution.[86]

Respect for the rule of law, good governance, and human rights are as important as economic reform and growth for the vast majority of the population in the Middle East. US diplomatic or political capital, garnered by its embrace of human rights and democratic ideals, has been recklessly squandered through two hard-fisted invasions and the essential abandonment of the Palestinian issues. The Iraq debacle and domestic economic strains have dramatically weakened the overwhelming power that the United States has previously enjoyed on the global scene. There is a growing and general consensus that the United States needs a new approach in the Middle East. As Stephen M. Walt argues, the United States should use its considerable leverage to bring the Israeli-Palestinian conflict to an end, and this means the creation of a viable and contiguous Palestinian state.[87]

Another factor, the continued occupation of Iraq, fuels a great deal of anti-Americanism and makes it arguably more difficult to effectively control terrorism. The United States should employ nonmilitary tactics to encourage both progressive forces in the Arab and Muslim world and the gradual transformation of Middle East monarchies and dictatorships, instead of simply trying to impose democracy through invasion and occupation.[88] If a legitimate case is to be made for military intervention, the general international consensus seems to hold that multilateral decisions about using force for human protection are preferable to unilateral ones.[89]

Building an Alternative Security Narrative in South Asia

Nearly a decade after the September 11 attacks, the United States finally killed Osama bin Laden, al-Qaeda's founder and nominal figurehead in May 2011. Closing that chapter of the war on terror has raised a myriad of questions about the most effective ways to deal with the problems looming ahead. To be sure, bin Laden's killing will affect US military involvement in Afghanistan and Pakistan. Also at stake is the hugely complicated relationship between the United States and Pakistan, given that the latter is allegedly said to be a sanctuary for terrorists and their network affiliates. The most daunting task for the Obama administration is to avoid any rupture in relations that could endanger the counterterrorism network that it has so painstakingly constructed in Pakistan over the last few years. The question that hangs over any future recalibration of US-Pakistan relations is whether the previous level of cooperation between the two is sustainable, given their different strategic objectives regarding the endgame in Afghanistan.

There can be no doubt that the killing of bin Laden is a major setback for al-Qaeda. This organization with a transnational, decentralized, and ideological terrorist network, however, is likely to continue striking Western targets. Bin Laden and his terror network provided a much-needed alibi for the Bush administration to launch its costly and counterproductive military incursions into Afghanistan and Iraq—wars from which al-Qaeda and its leaders benefited immensely because of the boost it gave them in recruiting foot soldiers. But now his demise could and should open a new dialogue about the way forward.

Perhaps the most crucial question relates to the extent to which Pakistan has been a sanctuary for members of the Taliban and al-Qaeda. If Pakistan's involvement has been extensive, then the center of gravity of terrorism has clearly shifted away from Afghanistan to Pakistan. The United States has provided $20.7 billion in military and development aid to Pakistan since 2002. Slightly more than two-thirds of that aid has gone to military use, the remainder to civilian. The biggest item, at $8.9 billion, is known as "Coalition Support Funds," which are reimbursements for Pakistan's military assistance in the war on terror.[90] According to the US Government Accountability Office, this assistance is vital to help the government of Pakistan overcome the political, economic, and security challenges that pose real threats to its long-term stability.[91]

Yet, as some experts have noted, it is worth asking whether US policy has reached its limits—if, in fact, it is guided more by inertia than strategy. More specifically, they raise the question of why, despite generous US assistance, most Pakistanis do not believe the United States is on their side. Billions in military support, they assert, are unlikely to diminish the deep cynicism toward the US war on terrorism that exists in the Pakistani state, army, and society.[92] Pakistanis such as Aasim Sajjad Akhtar, a political economy professor at Quaid-i-Azam University in

Islamabad, question the extent to which military aid to Pakistan has been effective in the campaign against terror. US assistance to Pakistan, Akhtar notes, has failed to dramatically reduce militancy. If anything, "it has become more acute."[93]

Osama bin Laden lived in a compound near a well-known military academy in Abbottabad, Pakistan, a city not far from Islamabad, and that fact has raised a very real dilemma: Is the Pakistani army and intelligence service incompetent? Or—a more sinister assessment—have they been in cahoots with the terrorists? Both the Pakistani army and intelligence officials deny having had any knowledge of bin Laden's location—a claim impossible to verify or repudiate. Given the multiple centers of power in Pakistan and the complexity of Pakistani politics, US-Pakistan relations remain strained. What accounts for the problematic nature of these relations is the schizophrenic yet symbiotic frame of mind with which they treat each other: There is no trust between them, and yet they cannot abandon each other. Pakistan needs cash and arms from the United States, and Washington needs Islamabad's assistance in bringing some modicum of stability to Afghanistan by creating a reconciliation of sorts with the Taliban. In short, the Obama administration regards its relationship with Pakistan "as too crucial to risk a wholesale break, even if it turned out that past or present Pakistani intelligence officials did know about bin Laden's whereabouts."[94]

It is worth noting that the recent Arab revolts in North Africa and the Middle East have already undermined al-Qaeda's narrative of violent change. The vast majority of the people in the Middle East have chosen, as their means to restore their sense of dignity, the counternarrative of peaceful democratic change, as evidenced by the 2011 uprisings. Victory in the campaign against terror will be attainable only if the United States and the rest of the Western world supports prodemocracy movements and uprisings in the region, rather than supporting despotic regimes under the rubric of "stability" and "security." Support for corrupt, autocratic, and oppressive regimes in the name of a war on terror will almost always foster more and more extremism, forcing the US people to bear the hefty costs of fighting ongoing wars. In the long run, addressing the political and economic grievances of the people in the region is the most effective tool in the counterterrorism arsenal.

Redefining the US strategy to fight terrorism in South Asia requires an alternative narrative that addresses the socioeconomic demands of ordinary people in an attempt to stunt the growth of radicalism and militancy as well as creates tools that could counter the militant groups' religious ideology. The Pakistani state and its traditional political party system have failed to address the social welfare concerns of the majority of the population and promote a moderate religious ideology.[95] Two basic questions persist: What should be the US strategy toward Afghanistan and Pakistan? How important is Pakistan to the stability of Afghanistan if NATO forces withdraw from Afghanistan?

US regional diplomacy, generally known as the "AfPak strategy," is premised on collaboration between Afghanistan and Pakistan. This strategy has proven problematic at best, and it will require bold new ideas. Engaging the Taliban with a view toward integrating them into mainstream Afghanistan politics lies at the heart of AfPak's current strategy. At first glance, this may seem a manageable task given that the Pakistani Inter-Services Intelligence has leverage over the Taliban. But a deeper examination shows that this policy is fraught with complexities and uncertainties. To be sure, Pakistan's role is crucial if this strategy is to work, for Pakistan is in a position either to nudge along or to sabotage the AfPak policy. The government and ISI hold enough political muscle to bring the Taliban to the negotiating table.[96] Nevertheless, the conflicting interests pursued by the parties involved in the AfPak strategy make it difficult to win the confidence of the people and to establish a stable, democratic regime in Afghanistan. Other regional players (India, China, Iran, Russia) that pursue sometimes complementary but at times conflictive policies toward Afghani politics can also play a significant role in such regional diplomacy.[97]

Skepticism regarding the effectiveness of the AfPak strategy has inexorably grown. Three simultaneous crises, Ahmed Rashid argues, complicate the strategy.[98] The first is the failure of Afghanistan's president, Hamid Karzai, to eliminate the corruption within both his central government and the dispersed polities in the provinces. The lack of trust between Karzai and the United States presents a great difficulty for any US plan to stabilize the situation on the ground.

A second problem is that, even if the United States maintains a troop presence in Afghanistan for another five years, the European members of NATO will certainly decline to do so. According to recent polls, 72 percent of British citizens want their troops out of Afghanistan immediately, as do 62 percent of Germans. Polling across Europe, from Spain to Sweden, shows that more than 50 percent of Europeans want their troops to return home.

Thirdly, Afghan Taliban and other militant groups are still able to find sanctuary in Pakistan. The Pakistani military has in the past allowed the Taliban and its allies to direct their campaign against US forces. The inherent contradictions in US-Pakistan relations can be traced back to the Cold War era, when fear of communism led the United States to provide arms and financial support to Pakistan. In its obsession with containing the spread of communism, the United States used Pakistan as a bulwark against China, the Soviet Union, and nonaligned India, and subsequently as a staging ground for assisting the anti-Soviet mujahidin in Afghanistan.[99]

By the 1980s, Pakistan had become a rentier state, exploiting its geostrategic location at the crossroads of Central Asia, the Indian subcontinent, and the Middle East to receive arms and money. US president Ronald Reagan sent more than $3 billion to the Pakistani mujahidin to fight Soviet troops in Afghanistan. During the 1990s, however, US support dwindled in large part because of Pakistan's nuclear proliferation and recognition of the Taliban as the official government of Afghanistan. After 9/11, foreign aid resumed. The Bush administration sent $11 billion to Pakistan, including $8 billion directly to the Pakistani army for "security."[100] Warning against cutting aid to Pakistan, some analysts argue that if the United States "disengaged from its rocky partnership with Pakistan, the Pakistanis would probably ally more closely with China, currently an economic rival to the United States with strategic ambitions in areas of American dominance."[101] The Obama administration, in contrast to its predecessor, has lessened the amount of aid and has committed more of the money to development: the 2009 Kerry-Lugar bill, for instance, earmarked $7.5 billion to development programs over five years. Because of these geostrategic considerations, Washington has rarely, if ever, used its influence in Islamabad to promote democracy.[102]

President George W. Bush considered Pakistan's president Pervez Musharraf (1999 to 2008), to be one of his key allies in the region, despite Musharraf's playing a double game—"supporting Islamist insurgents in his own country while pledging to fight the Taliban in Afghanistan."[103] The Bush administration ignored the issue as long as the Pakistani army went on the offensive against al-Qaeda. Thus far, the Obama administration has set the policy on a different path, pushing Pakistan harder to become more transparent and accountable to internal reform. Yet the Pakistani army has insisted on keeping ties with Islamic insurgents at home accessible because of the perceived, albeit overstated, threat from India.

Pakistan's counterterrorism strategy in Afghanistan, one expert notes, is rife with innate contradictions, caught between a propensity to fight militant forces both at home and in Afghanistan and yet having to partner with some Taliban groups to buttress its future bargaining position.[104] The latter position is grounded in the—not entirely baseless—belief that "the continuation of the fight against terrorist organizations helps Islamabad extract money from Washington."[105] This simply means that it actually benefits the Pakistani state and army to keep the threat of terrorism alive.

Yet, as critics remind us, Washington has vainly tried to get Islamabad on its side in its campaign against the Afghan Taliban. This policy has been counterproductive since the very start, largely because of the continuation of support for the Taliban not only within Pakistan's ISI but also among the Pakistani people at large. "A new US strategy," Anatol Lieven writes, "must recognize that it is essential to ease the pressure on Pakistan, above all by reducing those factors which are increasing radicalization in the country and weakening the status and strength of the Pakistani state and army. This should lead to a *complete* withdrawal of American forces from Afghanistan—as soon as possible."[106] Although views differ on the timing as well as the strategy of US drawdown and its aftermath, it is widely accepted that the United States remains subject to Pakistani leverage as long as it maintains massive combat forces in Afghanistan.[107]

Moreover, the continued presence of US troops in Afghanistan is likely to draw Washington into Afghanistan's deep ethnic, political, and regional differences, leading to more attacks against the Taliban inside Pakistan and spreading further anti-American sentiments there. It is worth noting, Lieven warns, that it is the breakdown of Pakistan, not the outcome of the present war in Afghanistan, that poses the most serious "threat to America and its allies from this part of the Muslim world."[108]

The litmus test of the US policy toward Pakistan, another observer notes, is to pursue a mix of several policies, including containment, diplomacy, and development aid, while avoiding taking on expansive and unrealistic commitments. The toughest challenge will therefore be to strike a proper balance between maintaining a relationship with the Pakistani army and engaging in a de facto proxy competition in Afghanistan. Given this complex strategic situation, which involves the simultaneous convergence and divergence of interests between the United States and Pakistan, the pursuit of a broadly based transformation, counterinsurgency, and harmonization of regional interests in Pakistan and South Asia remains an implausible political project.[109]

There is much evidence to suggest that, with the US plan to withdraw and Pakistan's persisting role as a key regional player, the Pakistani military believes that keeping the Afghan Taliban in reserve as a proxy force gives it "strategic depth" to pursue its interests in Kabul.

Pakistan's army has also supported the Pakistani Taliban—remembering that it was Pakistani Pashtun tribesmen who originally appeared as the "helping hands" for the Afghan Taliban and al-Qaeda in the tribal areas.[110] The Obama administration's promise to prevent neighboring countries from interfering in Afghanistan has thus far failed: Afghanistan's six direct neighbors, Iran, Pakistan, China, Uzbekistan, Tajikistan, and Turkmenistan, and its near neighbors, India, Russia, and Saudi Arabia, will continue to pursue a degree of influence in a post-US Afghanistan. It is Pakistan, however, that holds a firm grip on the Afghani Taliban leadership.[111]

In the meantime, as some keen regional observers point out, negotiations between the Afghan government and the Taliban have become imperative for stability in Afghanistan. But the conditions the West would like to impose on the Taliban can be achieved in the long term only through dialogue. Given the country's weak and decentralized institutions and the numerous predatory neighbors, a power-sharing arrangement with the Taliban is not the best of solutions, but it is the only realistic option if NATO forces pull out.[112] Both the United States and the Karzai administration, as one expert notes, concur on the need to win over Taliban foot soldiers, and they have suggested a common plan and financial scheme in order to do so. But there is still no consensus on trying to engage top Taliban leaders. The Taliban may be too divided, too ideologically motivated, or too manipulated by other regional powers to come together around a peace deal, but talking to them is perhaps the only way that can lead out of this conflict. Both Obama and Karzai share the view that the alternatives to such a scenario are too dreadful to contemplate.[113] For these and many other related reasons, the AfPak strategy continues to be confusing and problematic. Washington's military and diplomatic approaches are in need of an alternative narrative.

Taking the Turkish Option Seriously

On Turkey, the real question for US policymakers is whether Turkey's new regional activism can bolster Western objectives. Given that Turkey's dominant AKP has cultivated good relations with Syria and Iran, US and possible EU pressure for new sanctions aimed at Syria and Iran would contradict Ankara's recent policy of greater engagement with these neighbors. More to the point, with the rising power of China and a marked shift of attention eastward, US engagement in Eurasia and the Middle East may take a different turn. From the Turkish perspective, this could mean that US presence as a regional actor would be less predictable, while additionally, a European role and its active involvement in the region may be desirable. While in the Gulf there may be too much US influence for Turkish taste, in other areas, such as the Balkans or Cyprus, there may be too little US engagement.[114]

In 2006 and 2007, Turkey and Iran cooperated closely in joint military operations against the PKK, the Kurdistan Workers' Party, and its Iranian equivalent, the Party for a Free Life (Partiya Jiyana Azad a Kurdistane—PJAK). Because the United States has reportedly pursued covert operations inside Iran to support minority separatist movements (e.g., the Kurds), this close Turkish-Iranian cooperation has annoyed Washington. Likewise, Ankara's view of Washington's reluctance to target the PKK is a source of continuing irritation to Ankara.[115] In addition to their common interest in preventing the creation of an independent Kurdistan, analysts argue, changes in the international energy market may make Iran's overtures to foreign investors more sanction-proof than they were in the 1990s. The increased demand for oil and natural gas and the expected long-term decline in supplies have led many states to seek future supply lines. The economic growth of India and China has meant that they both are interested in securing energy supplies from Iran.[116]

In July 2007, Ankara and Tehran signed agreements worth $1.5 billion, providing for the joint construction of three 2,000-megawatt thermal power plants, two in Iran and one in Turkey, and several hydroelectric plants in Iran—a total 10,000-megawatt capability. The agreements also provided for upgrading electrical power transmission lines between the two countries.[117]

The agreement runs directly counter to Washington's policy of further isolating Iran because of its uranium-enrichment program. Turkey's pragmatic tack indicates that Ankara has placed its agreement with Iran above other considerations. Turkey has reached a $3 billion agreement with Iran to develop phases 22–24 of the Caspian offshore South Pars project, and potential pipeline projects include twenty-two hundred miles of gas pipelines to transport up to 40 billion cubic meters of gas annually to Europe via Turkey. Many observers in Turkey and Europe argue that rather than pressuring Iran, the time has come for Washington to reconsider the issue of sanctions against Tehran.[118]

These cooperative deals notwithstanding, it is important to remember that Turkey and Iran are also potential competitors for alternative oil and gas transit pipelines from the Caucasus and Central Asia.[119] Using Turkey as an energy route contributes significantly to the energy security of the European Union. The EU already uses the Blue Stream pipeline of Russian gas and the Baku-Ceyhan pipeline. The Nabucco pipeline project, a proposed natural gas pipeline running from Erzurum in Turkey to Baumgarten in Austria, crossing Bulgaria, Romania, and Hungary along the way and thus diversifying natural gas suppliers and delivery routes to Europe, which will be operative by 2012, will carry 31 billion cubic meters of gas to Europe per year.[120] By becoming a Eurasian energy hub, Nabucco will likely become a reliable alternative to Russian gas for the EU.[121]

Turning to the broader scheme of things, the value of Turkey's diplomatic relations with Israel is obvious. Turkey's military cooperation with Israel in the 1990s invited controversy throughout the Middle East, yet it enhanced the country's strategic significance. Between 2000 and 2004, total Israeli arms sales to Turkey exceeded $1 billion.[122] Additionally, in 1998, Turkey, Israel, and the United States conducted joint naval exercises that were to remain open-ended.[123] But the US invasion of Iraq undermined the strategic value of the Turkey-Israel connection, as evidenced by Israeli activities after the war, especially in the northern part of Iraq, where Israel has supported the training of Kurdish guerrilla forces (Peshmerga) and has used the area as a base for anti-Iranian intelligence operations.[124]

On the Kurdish question, it is fair to say that the rise of the AKP in the region—and among the Kurds more generally—demonstrates that the Kurds in Iraq view the PKK as both an irritant for the consolidation of their power and a source of tension for their long-term relationship with the United States. This is so because many among the Kurdish leadership of Iraq deem US support vital for their survival and prosperity in the region. Hence, a strong case can be made for a joint settlement between the PKK and the Turkish state. It is evident that such a settlement would have positive consequences for the entire region.[125]

Increasingly, the AKP has sought a more independent foreign policy that emphasizes good-neighbor relations with all its neighbors and substantive engagement in Middle Eastern issues. This makes the new Turkey an indispensable player for the region's stability.[126] Despite current disagreements, the Turkish-Israeli relationship will most likely endure. The key factor worthy of attention here, however, is that Turkey is the only regional ally of both Israel and Iran that has credibility with most Arab states and Iran.[127]

If history is any guide, there is a desperate need for a novel diplomatic approach. In its purest form, military intervention and occupation has rarely won the support of local people. It is worth remembering that few instances of military intervention have culminated in the creation of stable democratic political systems during occupation or in a postconflict reconstruction period. Only a few countries under military occupation (e.g., Germany and Japan) have served as examples of democratic transition or peaceful transformation over the preceding half-century. It was with heavy economic investment through the Marshall Plan, as well as with policies that were really tailored to allowing self-sufficiency within a free market system, that made such peaceful change possible. Equally contentious has been the so-called "regime change" and "democratic transformation" of the Middle East, as implied in the Bush Doctrine. Underpinning this doctrine is a confluence of premises that have proven not only increasingly naïve, flawed, counterproductive, and out of sync with the region's ethnic, sectarian, and political realities, but also contradictory to conventional US interests in the area.

Some observers dispel the notion that the source of terrorism is religious conviction. They make the case that both privatized and globalized roots of terrorism can be traced to Cold War power politics. By providing a necessary corrective to the way in which Islam is being projected by neoconservative forces in the contemporary West, Mahmood Mamdani questions the widely held assumption that extremist religious tendencies can be equated with political terrorism: "Terrorism is not a necessary effect of religious tendencies, whether fundamentalist or secular. Rather, terrorism is born of a *political* encounter. When it harnesses one or another aspect of tradition and culture, terrorism needs to be understood as a modern political movement at the service of a modern power."[128]

Turning to regional diplomacy in defusing tensions invariably draws attention to a key role that Turkey, Iran, and Syria can play in the region. Turkey's AKP has moved to the center-right band of the political spectrum. AKP represents a public discourse, platform, and social base that are dependent less on a purely Islamic or ideological orientation and more on a globalist, market-oriented, pro-Western, populist foundation. For the AKP, the language of human rights, democracy, and the goal of EU membership have opened an opportunity to build a democratic coalition with modern, secular sectors at home and abroad.[129] Under the AKP, the emphasis of the legitimizing historical reference has shifted to the Ottoman Empire, known for inclusiveness and embracing other Muslim areas of the Middle East. The US invasion of Iraq in 2003 further reinforced this shift in Turkish foreign policy away from the West and toward the region and the wider Muslim world.[130]

At home, however, the AKP's struggles to iron out its differences with secular forces have lingered. Turkey's constitutional court decided on July 30, 2008, not to ban the AKP, which was accused of weakening the nation's secular system. Representing one of the country's most secular foundations, the court imposed financial sanctions on the AKP as a significant warning to reformists' behavior. This controversy had intensified in early 2008 when the AKP attempted to allow Islamic headscarves to be worn at universities. The constitutional court saw that as a violation of the constitution, alleging that such practices posed a direct threat to Turkey's secular principles and foundations. Although in the past many parties have been shuttered for similar violations, this was the first time the threat of closure was directed against a democratically elected ruling party with a considerable parliamentary majority.[131]

Many editorials in the West praised the decision, noting that the no-ban proposal has deepened Turkish democracy, which was once hostage to military and judicial coups. Since the Republic of Turkey was established, the country has experienced three coups (1960, 1971, and 1980). Likewise, Turkish scholars—such as Ihsan Dagi, of the Middle East Technical University—while welcoming the court's verdict, have argued that secularism remains the centerpiece of political debate in Turkey and that the AKP should expedite its evolution into a center-right political identity by pushing for more democratization and EU accession.[132] Middle East experts continue to argue that defeating the AKP on such issues will be very difficult and undemocratic. This is in part because of the AKP's solid economic record alongside Turkish prime minister Erdogan's charismatic leadership and populist message that deeply resonates with a near majority of Turkish people.

No peaceful solution exists that will quickly resolve these tensions other than simply to rely upon the respect for and tolerance of cultural diversity. National reconciliation in Turkey is a two-way street: Islamic symbolism and the identity of voters must be respected; in exchange, the secular principles and foundation upon which modern Turkey was founded must also be respected. Politics in Turkey can reach this equilibrium if the country's leaders display sensitivity to the masses and at the same time govern the country according to the rule of law and human rights standards. Can this equilibrium be successfully managed? The Turkish experience suggests that the only way to curb, if not completely resolve, such tension is to manage the conflict between Islamic modernists and transformational secularists. Both of these groups have come to realize that the freedom of many Turks, and indeed the stability of the country itself, depend now more than ever on finding a resolution to this tension—or an optimal balance. Turkish leaders—secular and Islamic—are heavily burdened with the task of finding such a balance. This may be the key to Turkey's accession to the European Union.

The implications of Turkish success in reconciling its internal differences surely transcend its borders, as the rest of the Muslim world watches the outcome of Turkish politics, feeling both trepidation and hope. Those regimes that are liberalizing their economies and politics are likely to be more receptive to the Turkish experience. The recent "Europeanization" of Turkish foreign policy, which has led to a more balanced approach toward Israel and Arab states, is also likely to increase the receptivity of the Western policymakers, cultural elites, media pundits, and intellectuals to the ongoing transformation process that Turkey has been experiencing.[133]

Some scholars have argued that antidemocratic forces in Turkey are also the most anti-Western. That is why, as one Turkish expert aptly put it, "the fate of democracy in Turkey is closely linked to its relations with the West."[134] With the European Union's unwillingness to admit Turkey as a new member, however, Turkish strategic vision is likely to undergo a profound shift. Since Turkey turned down the US request for use of its military base to invade Iraq, many experts note that this shift is already under way. They argue that Turkey is crafting an independent foreign policy in which its own rational calculus and national interests will take precedence over those of its traditional allies, including the United States. Turkish politicians see Iran as being crucial to this new strategic vision.

Pointing to the emergence of a strategically significant Turko-Persian realm, Alidad Mafinezam and Aria Mehrabi write that "Iran and Turkey are Central Eurasia's most populous and most deeply rooted republics. Their alliance, more than any other, promises to bring stability and development to the region that surrounds them."[135] This growing realm of cooperation is a result of several factors: the rise of development projects (e.g., oil and natural gas, and transit systems of trade with the East and the West) between the two countries; a common stake in the stability and territorial integrity of Iraq; a fear of Kurdish prospects for autonomy; and the increasing possibilities for regional trade. Beyond these factors, the cultural and artistic relations between the two nations have strengthened the notion of a Turko-Persian realm.[136]

Moreover, Turkey's regional role in facilitating Israeli-Syrian negotiations is pivotal for further diplomatic initiatives, with ramifications for the entire region. At the same time, Turkey's open criticism of the Syrian leaders' method of confronting their prodemocracy protesters illustrates that Ankara is unwilling to ignore or tolerate the status quo. As the massacre in Syria seems to have crossed the threshold of acceptability,

Turkey has chosen to shift its position on Syria. Negotiations with Iran could have a stabilizing impact throughout the region. Without security guarantees, experts note, Iranians have plausible fears of attack provoked by either their neighbors or the United States. The guarantees could include nonaggression pacts, removing the US troops stationed near Iran's borders, and a variety of arms-control agreements reminiscent of the later phases of the Cold War between the United States and the Soviet Union. These agreements could also entail the right of all signers of the Nuclear Proliferation Treaty to nuclear energy for civilian uses, a right that can be accompanied by a strict and intrusive inspection regime in those cases where a country insists on enriching nuclear fuel itself.[137]

Prime Minister Erdogan's repeated position that Turkey is willing to play a constructive role in the solution of the Israeli-Palestinian conflict by promoting confidence-building measures has been in keeping with EU interests. Likewise, Turkish soft power was extended to the Palestinians in 2005, when Turkish officials invited Khaled Mershaal, the Syrian-based leader of Hamas, to Turkey. In doing so, Turkey sought to exemplify the importance of democratic engagement.[138] President Shimon Perez of Israel and President Mahmoud Abbas of the Palestinian Authority visited Ankara before the Annapolis Summit in November 2007.[139] The effectiveness of Turkey's soft power, however, should not be exaggerated, as exemplified by the failure to persuade Hamas leaders, following their victory in the Gaza elections in 2006, to recognize Israel and abide by the Oslo accords. This failure of political leverage demonstrated that Turkey's Middle Eastern policy has limited effectiveness. Regardless, Turkey can still play a significant role in defusing tensions. Turkish officials have repeatedly stated that Turkey intends to ease the tension between Iran and the United States over the issue of Iran's nuclear program. Turkey, Deputy Prime Minister Ali Babacan has stressed, has no formal mediation mission; rather its role is "one that is in a sense consolidating and facilitating" the negotiations between Iran and the six major powers—Britain, China, France, Germany, Russia, and the United States.[140]

The perception that Iran's nuclear program threatens Turkey's national security is drastically mistaken. Turkish officials have repeatedly argued that any solution to the issue of the Iranian nuclear program must be found through diplomacy and peaceful means. In this regard, Turkey faces both opportunities and limitations. Mindful of their country's dependence on Iran as a major energy supplier (Iran provides one-fifth of Turkey's natural gas), Turkish authorities display a pragmatic sensitivity to Iran's policy options. But at the same time, they are keenly aware of their goal to join the European Union. Thus Turkish officials attempt to align their country's position on this particular issue with that held by the EU, advocating a negotiated solution while attempting to carve out a mediator role for Ankara.[141]

Turkish officials kept the door of diplomatic negotiations on the Iranian nuclear issue open on June 9, 2010, when the UN Security Council leveled its fourth round of sanctions against Iran's nuclear program. Twelve of the fifteen nations on the council voted for the measures, while Turkey and Brazil voted against it; Lebanon abstained. This new round of sanctions was primarily directed against military purchases, trade, and financial transactions carried out by Iran's Revolutionary Guards, who continue to hold a firm grip on the country's politics and economy. Diplomats from Brazil and Turkey, who had previously negotiated a deal with Iran to send some of its low-enriched uranium to their respective countries in exchange for access to fuel for a medical reactor, criticized the sanctions as derailing a new chance for diplomacy.[142]

Meanwhile, some Turkish experts warned against misunderstanding their country's role in pushing for diplomatic engagement, arguing that while Turkey seeks to stop Iran from developing nuclear weapons, a broader consensus holds that in order to achieve this objective Iran must be kept within the international system and be compelled to be open to the oversight of the International Atomic Energy Agency. Further sanctions on Iran will prove useless, and their futility could then provide a justification for hawkish elements within the Obama administration to push for military strikes against the Iranian nuclear facilities. Turkey is deeply concerned about the possibility of yet another conflict in its neighborhood.[143]

Which Way Forward?

The problems emanating from the US war on terror during the Afghanistan and Iraq wars have compelled the people of the United States to take a fresh look at past policies, especially those that have detoured sharply from liberal society's fundamental values and ideals—those being both civil rights and liberties at home and the Geneva Conventions abroad. These detours have occurred in the interests of security. It is now time to reframe and recast the so-called war on terror and identify the mechanisms by which international terrorism can be confronted, curbed, and prevented. In the years since 9/11, terrorism rhetoric has been employed as a blunt weapon by governments seeking to stifle dissent and avert international scrutiny. It is time, with sober conviction, to return to the path of morality, civil liberty, and governmental accountability.

In general, three "grand narratives" have dominated common understandings of the post-9/11 period. The first is the narrative of the war on terror, which ineluctably leads to policies eschewing or avoiding integration and multiculturalism. These policies tend to create a fertile ground for the growth of radical Islamist political sentiment among Muslim immigrants in Europe and routinely violate the freedoms they are meant to resiliently defend.[144] Scholars and counterterrorism experts have reminded us that fighting terrorism is not a cakewalk, with soldiers greeted by flowers thrown in the streets at their feet; as General Tony Zinni, former commander in chief of US Central Command, and Tony Koltz argue, there is no rosy scenario. Simply fighting a war against terrorists is not enough. The basic tenets of the struggle against terrorism have been fundamentally flawed and require a thorough rethinking.[145]

US and NATO forces in Afghanistan have applied new rules of engagement that better protect civilians. The former Afghanistan theater commander, General Stanley McChrystal, put in place a critical evolution in military tactics and strategy, summarized as: "To save a village, you don't destroy it (a Vietnam War approach). You really have to save it."[146] The new emphasis on civilian protection in the Afghan city of Marjah, where US and NATO forces have fought Taliban insurgents, has accounted for a drastic drop in civilian casualties. Launching a major offensive without turning civilians into enemies is a welcome move toward striking the right balance.[147]

Nevertheless, drone strikes in Afghanistan have come to be viewed by some experts as illegal and destabilizing. UN rapporteur Philip Alston claims that these attacks violate international law, in large part because the secrecy surrounding the program involving such attacks makes it impossible to assess whether the CIA is doing enough to avert the killing of innocent civilians, either through collateral damage or because of faulty intelligence.[148] Not to mention that these policies routinely defy the state-sovereignty measures that the Charter of the United Nations ensconces as inviolable.

There are two aspects to counterinsurgency: strategy and cost. One of the lessons learned in counterinsurgency is that engaging the enemy is important, but the provision for human security of citizens offers the strongest and most optimal antiterrorism strategy. Furthermore, the effectiveness of any counterterrorism and/or counterinsurgency operations, policies, or tactics must be evaluated skeptically through the lens of human security and community cohesion. As I argued in preceding chapters, in most cases torture has produced false and fabricated information, undermined the legal and moral authority of the United States, and provided terrorist groups with a powerful propaganda recruiting tool.

It has been shown that some Taliban members are reconcilable and can be engaged. The manifest value in understanding both the culture and context of the Afghani people is a vital key to effective counterinsurgency operations and the best guarantee of the long-term salience and feasibility of Afghanistan. Harvard professor Rory Stewart, whom I quoted earlier, writes:

> The power of the United States and its allies, and our commitment, knowledge and will, are limited. It is unlikely that we will be able to defeat the Taliban. The ingredients of successful counterinsurgency campaigns in places like Malaya—control of the borders, large numbers of troops in relation to the population, strong support from the majority ethnic groups, a long-term commitment and a credible local government—are lacking in Afghanistan.[149]

Winning the campaign against terror, experts observe, requires eradicating existing enemies while taking pains not to create new adversaries.[150] Lessons from counterterrorism and counterinsurgency operations illustrate that the best strategy launched to defeat terrorists is to concurrently target the enemy and win over the general population. Retaining public support locally is as important as winning the campaign against terror militarily. In the long run, adapting current strategy and tactics toward gathering local support is likely to yield a desirable result. Given the nature of counterinsurgency in Afghanistan, the US and NATO forces cannot prevail without local cooperation. They must adjust accordingly.

It is also important not to lose sight of the fact that wars—even counterinsurgency conflicts—are expensive both in lives and dollars. The effective price tag for counterinsurgency is escalating dramatically. The war in Afghanistan in the 2012 budget year will cost the United States more than any one year of the Iraq operation did. According to the Center for Defense Information, the estimated cost of the wars in Iraq and Afghanistan will reach $1.29 trillion by the end of fiscal year 2011.[151] That is more than the cost of the Vietnam War, adjusting for inflation, or any other US war except World War II, which cost $3.2 trillion in 2007 dollars.[152] Others have put a "moderate-realistic" price tag on the two wars of $5 trillion. By way of comparison: a robust health care safety net for all US citizens would cost less than the two wars. Americans worry about China's growing influence in Africa, but the cost of a month of fighting in Iraq would pay for more than doubling US annual current aid spending on Africa. Ending the war—or even moving rapidly toward winding it down—is likely to yield major economic dividends.[153] If the Afghan war drags on for another four years, it will become the longest war in US history.[154] The new US approach in Afghanistan may be a great start to recasting the definition of the "war on terror." By separating al-Qaeda and Taliban extremists from those who are willing to reject violence, reintegrate, and work to resurrect civil society, community building and legitimacy can be maintained as values of, rather than liabilities to, the cost of this conflict.[155] After more than seven years, NATO efforts have largely failed to pacify or secure Afghanistan. The United States is still battling the Taliban, and al-Qaeda operatives are still plotting from redoubts in Afghanistan and in the mountainous Pakistani border region. The war in Afghanistan is as much fueled by joblessness and poverty as it is by religious zealotry. From both practical and moral standpoints, nation building and reconstruction efforts in the postconflict societies offer the most effective opportunity for a robust counterterrorism. For many, the perceived possibilities for constructive gains and employment for Afghans will be a potent disincentive to take up arms and join terrorist groups. In this sense, fighting poverty is fighting terrorism.

Emphasizing a continued commitment to civilian protection as a major part of this new counterinsurgency strategy has been entirely neglected by many high-ranking generals in the US Army. Some have even argued that the idea of using massive ground troops is passé, outdated, and unnecessary. The logic follows that the United States can simply slash troop strength and rely solely upon precision-weapon systems and space-based intelligence to carry the day. This approach resulted in ineffective and ultimately self-defeating policies in Iraq and Afghanistan by mistakenly targeting friendly groups and factions and turning civilians into enemies. A new mission must be found for the military, perhaps a mission to ensure or enable environment/community security, border patrolling, narcotics enforcement, and public health, to name a few. There is a need for a substantial reconceptualization of strategic thought centered on human rights and personal security. General David H. Petraeus, former commander of US Central Command and current CIA chief, argues that counterinsurgency measures require that soldiers help reestablish institutions and local security forces and assist in rebuilding infrastructure and basic services. Additionally, he notes, they must help facilitate establishing local governance and the rule of law.[156]

The second narrative is the grandiose plan of counterterrorism for democratic transformation in the Middle East. There can be two sides to this narrative. If this narrative means supporting homegrown and peaceful democratic change, it is consistent with a growing realization that the era of Western powers meddling in the Middle East and North Africa is over, as evidenced by the 2011 Arab revolts that demonstrated that Middle Eastern people had an organic capacity to engineer change themselves and needed no external guidance, supervision, or interference. Except for situations that cry for humanitarian interventions, it is important to understand, as one expert reminds us, that the century-old battle to control the Middle East is ending and that no amount of high-tech ordnance and military might can alter the outcome.[157]

If, however, this narrative means imposing democratic transformation from outside, there is little evidence to suggest that it will work. If anything, this approach has proved to be both overly simplistic and fundamentally misguided given the recent history of conflict. Two points merit particular attention: (1) investment in a country's infrastructure, such as schools, hospitals, and electric power and water projects, has proven to be an effective counterterrorism strategy; and (2) as we have learned, transforming even one country like Iraq is a tall order, requiring substantial commitment of both blood and treasure. In the case of Afghanistan, the need for international partnership (NATO, China, and Russia) is as crucial as securing regional security assistance (Pakistan, India, and Iran). As many regional experts have reminded us, Afghanistan is the graveyard of predictions.

The third narrative focuses on economic development and good governance practices. The United States, NATO, and the United Nations must fashion strategies to promote economic development, job creation, advances in education, and social spending. In fact, what the local experts consistently suggest is that some members of the Taliban are not fighting for their religious convictions but for money: "If they had jobs, they would stop fighting."[158]

A crucial element in this strategy will be to strengthen the Afghan government. But several questions arise in this regard: Is a centralized authority possible in a country as disparate as Afghanistan? What about strengthening the loya jirga (Afghanistan's national assembly) and employing some type of loose confederacy for Afghanis? This could put a premium on local control while allowing for some overarching governmental control. It may be that trust and hope in the government would generate psychological security for Afghanis, which would ultimately reduce violence. "We aren't here to win hearts and minds. What we need is to engender hope and faith in the Afghan government," notes Jeremy Brenner, a US State Department adviser based in Jalalabad.[159]

An emphasis on protecting local people over killing terrorists or insurgents is the key to a new strategy of counterterrorism.[160] US soldiers have learned that to deny al-Qaeda a foothold in Afghanistan will require the establishment of a government in which Afghans themselves can trust and invest. Appraising the outlook of winning the war on terror in Afghanistan, Lieutenant Colonel Brett Jenkinson, commander of the US battalion stationed in the Korengal Valley, explained: "We are not going to kill our way out of this war. What we need is a better recruiting pitch for disaffected youth. You cannot build hope with military might. You build it through development and good governance."[161]

Similarly, the US experiences in Vietnam, Cambodia, Lebanon, and Somalia illustrate the risks and benefits of prolonged occupation in conflict-torn countries. The future of Iraq depends, especially after the withdrawal of US forces at the end of 2011, upon forging a broader consensus over a political order that will protect and enhance the living conditions of different sectarian and ethnic groups. Given the fact that Iraq still faces an uncertain and violent environment in 2012, and given that Iraqi leadership has yet to resolve some key political problems and legislative tensions, such as the Kurd-Arab tensions in Kirkuk and elsewhere in the north as well as distribution of national wealth, Prime Minister Nouri al-Maliki has consented to an agreement that allows some US troops to stay past the withdrawal date of December 2011. According to a security agreement between the United States and Iraq made in 2008, US troops have legal immunity within the country only until December 31, 2011. The Obama administration has insisted that remaining US personnel be exempted from any possible future foreign or international prosecution. Given the country's deep divisions, the likely outcome will look more like the sporadically exploding Lebanon than the long-stable Vietnam.[162]

There are no easy answers to the problems of counterterrorism in such circumstances, nor is there a definitive logic or template that can offer the most persuasive explanation for overcoming terrorism or resolving the tensions that caused it. The confrontational approach, adopted by the Bush administration, failed to solve the issue. Instead, it rendered the situation in the Middle East far more volatile than it already was and provoked substantially more uncertainty with regard to the viability of effective counterterrorism policies. The display of military force, intervention, and the practice of torture have also proven to be ineffective policy instruments. They have revealed the perilous limits to the use of force as well as the capacity of the state to effectively guarantee human security and international peace.

The lessons learned from the wars in Afghanistan and Iraq demonstrate that diplomacy, dialogue, law enforcement, and international law may not always provide the most successful, lasting solutions, but that they have a much higher potential to adapt to the complex factors that cause and fuel conflicts in the region. Increasingly, some within the Bush administration came to acknowledge that the most important aspects of the campaign against terrorism were nonmilitary, including good intelligence, interdiction, and the disruption of the financial networks that support terrorism. All of these require cooperation with other nations.[163]

Nevertheless, the question of how to most effectively confront terrorism persists. In the post-9/11 climate of counterterrorism, it is imperative that policymakers, legal professionals, intellectuals, and NGOs move toward refining and reframing the debate over security, human rights, and international law. This requires moving away from standard settings to enforceable commitments. It is clear that abandoning the prohibition of torture and other similar ill-treatment has had a destabilizing impact on the international community's achievements in the past half century, vastly undermining global efforts to maintain the legal and institutional bases necessary for upholding fundamental rights.

As I have argued, the tactics that terrorists employ pose chiefly political and ideological challenges to the West. It is thus incumbent upon policymakers, diplomats, soldiers, and counterterrorism experts to understand that the real fight will be in defeating and destroying the claims and values that terrorists assert. In the end, defeating terrorism requires that its demonic ideology be confronted and exposed. This means that the Western world must offer a more hopeful vision—one that represents empathy, democracy, and construction as opposed to death and destruction.[164]

Some experts have underscored the importance of such a vision by arguing that the means to success in world politics must entail, among other things, soft power. They have noted that the United States won the Cold War not just with its hard power, which effectively deterred Soviet aggression, but also with its soft power—namely, the values and ideas that undermined the Communist regime and Soviet self-confidence from inside.[165]

Perhaps the next biggest challenge for the international community will be to develop the means to guide the civil, political, and economic development of global South nations toward a broad acceptance of the freedoms inherent in the founding documents of all great societies and civilizations. Increasingly, albeit slowly, talk about human rights has permeated local, non-Western cultural contexts, debunking the notion that Muslims' responses to their socioeconomic and political crises are driven by physical welfare needs—not liberty and dignity. A right to life, a protection of human rights, and, at the base of it all, a guarantee of personal security and dignity, are the best means to successfully win the global war of ideas that motivates and sustains the current wave of terrorist violence. Delegitimizing, as well as subverting, the terrorist narrative is far more powerful than foreign invasion, and this goal is most propitiously accomplished through the consistent application of human rights, international law, social justice, civil society, and educational reform. Only a proper and timely mix of the measures and instruments reviewed above can lead to a diminution of the terrorist threat in coming years.

Notes

1. Jean H. Quataert, *Advocating Dignity: Human Rights Mobilizations in Global Politics* (Philadelphia: University of Pennsylvania Press, 2009), p. 290.

2. David P. Forsythe, *The Politics of Prisoner Abuse: The United States and Enemy Prisoners After 9/11* (New York: Cambridge University Press, 2011), p. 24.

3. Ibid., p. 230.

4. Mark Osiel, *The End of Reciprocity: Terror, Torture, and the Law of War* (New York: Cambridge University Press, 2009), pp. 7–11.

5. Thomas G. Weiss, "Using Military Force for Human Protection: What Next?" in Edward Newman, Ramesh Thakur, and John Tireman, eds., *Multilateralism under Challenge? Power, International Order, and Structural Change* (New York: United Nations University Press, 2006), pp. 376–394; see p. 381.

6. James A. Piazza, "Do Democracy and Free Markets Protect Us from Terrorism, *International Politics* 45, no. 1 (January 2008): 72–91; see esp. pp. 83–84.

7. Ibid., p. 84.

8. See "Carothers Replies," in Thomas Carothers, *Critical Mission: Essays on Democracy Promotion* (Washington, DC: Carnegie Endowment for International Peace, 2004), pp. 79–80; see p. 79.

9. Daniel L. Byman and Kenneth M. Pollack, *Things Fall Apart: Containing the Spillover from an Iraqi Civil War* (Washington, DC: Brookings Institution Press, 2007), p. 20.

10. Ellen Lust-Okar, "Taking Political Participation Seriously," in Ellen Lust-Okar and Saloua Zerhouni, eds., *Political Participation in the Middle East* (Boulder, CO: Lynne Rienner, 2008), pp. 1–11; see pp. 9–10.

11. Maye Kassem, "Democratization Reforms as a Means of Stabilizing Authoritarian Rule in Contemporary Egypt," in Dietrich Jung, ed., *Democratization and Development: New Political Strategies for the Middle East* (New York: Palgrave Mcmillan, 2006), pp. 129–150; see p. 148.

12. Bulent Gokay, "Neoliberal Western Policies Led to Uprisings," *Public Service Europe*, March 11, 2011, available at http://www.publicserviceeurope .com/article/99/neoliberal-western-policies-led-to-uprisings; accessed on August 25, 2011.

13. Dietrich Jung, "Democratizing the Middle East: A Means of Ensuring International Security or an End in Itself?" in Jung, *Democratization and Development*, pp. 177–188; see p. 186.

14. Rory Stewart, "How to Save Afghanistan," *Time*, July 28, 2008, pp. 30–34; see p. 33.

15. Ibid., p. 34.

16. Lust-Okar, "Taking Political Participation Seriously," pp. 7–10.

17. Saloua Zerhouni, "Looking Forward," in Lust-Okar and Zerhouni, *Political Participation in the Middle East*, pp. 259–266; see p. 260.

18. Ibid.

19. Ellen Lust-Okar, "Competitive Clientelism in Jordanian Elections," in Lust-Okar and Zerhouni, *Political Participation in the Middle East*, 2008, pp. 75–94; see pp. 76–78.

20. Marina Ottaway, "The Problem of Credibility," in Thomas Carothers and Marina Ottaway, eds., *Uncharted Journey: Promoting Democracy in the Middle East* (Washington, DC: Carnegie Endowment for International Peace, 2005), pp. 173–192; see p. 180.

21. Stanley Hoffmann, *Chaos and Violence: What Globalization, Failed States, and Terrorism Mean for U.S. Foreign Policy* (Lanham, MD: Rowman & Littlefield, 2006), p. 207.

22. Stephen Kinser, *Overthrow: America's Century of Regime Change from Hawaii to Iraq* (New York: Times Books, 2006), pp. 301–302.

23. Ibid., p. 309.

24. Ibid., p. 316.

25. Ibid., pp. 317–322.

26. Jack Donnelly, *International Human Rights*, 3rd ed. (Boulder, CO: Westview Press, 2007), p. 219.

27. Hoffmann, *Chaos and Violence*, p. 205.

28. Ibid., p. 211.

29. Roy Gutman, *How We Missed the Story: Osama bin Laden, the Taliban, and the Hijacking of Afghanistan* (Washington, DC: US Institute of Peace, 2008), pp. 255–262.

30. K. M. Fierke, "Constructivism," in Tim Dunne, Milja Kurki, and Steve Smith, eds., *International Relations Theories: Discipline and Diversity*, 2nd ed. (New York: Oxford University Press, 2010), pp. 177–194; see esp. p. 191.

31. Ibid., p. 193.

32. Nigel S. Rodley, "Torture: International Law," in David P. Forsythe, ed., *Encyclopedia of Human Rights*, vol. 5 (New York: Oxford University Press, 2009), pp. 65–74; see esp. p. 65.

33. Ibid.

34. K. J. Holsti, "Something Old, Something New: Theoretical Perspectives on Contemporary International Peace and Security," in Edward Newman, Ramesh Thakur, and John Tireman, eds., *Multilateralism Under Challenge? Power, International Order, and Structural Change* (New York: United Nations University Press, 2006), pp. 181–206; see pp. 198–199.

35. Ibid., p. 200

36. Joanne Mariner, "Security, Terrorism, and Human Rights," *Counterpunch*, January 20, 2006; available at http://www.counterpunch.org/mariner01202006.html; accessed August 1, 2008.

37. Ibid.

38. Warren Richey, "Tribunals Pass a Test," *Christian Science Monitor*, August 7, 2008, pp. 1 and 10–11; see p. 11.

39. Human Security Report Project, "Human Rights, Terrorism, and Counterterrorism," Office of the United Nations High Commissioner for Human Rights, July 4, 2008; available at http://www.humansecuritygateway.info/showRecord.php?RecordId=25262; accessed August 1, 2008.

40. John Brady Kiesling, *Diplomacy Lessons: Realism for an Unloved Superpower* (Washington, DC: Potomac Books, 2006), p. 191.

41. Ibid., p. 211.

42. See comments made by Matthew Alexander in James P. Pfiffner, *Torture as Public Policy: Restoring U.S. Credibility on the World Stage* (Boulder, CO: Paradigm, 2010), p. 165.

43. Shadi Mokhtari, *After Abu Ghraib: Exploring Human Rights in America and the Middle East* (New York: Cambridge University Press, 2009), pp. 156–157.

44. Ibid., p. 158.

45. Ibid., p. 161.

46. Sarah E. Mendelson, "Dusk or Dawn for the Human Rights Movement?" *Washington Quarterly* 32. no. 2 (April 2009): 103–120; see esp. p. 105.

47. Ibid., pp. 110–111.

48. Quoted in Kenneth Roth, "Empty Promises? Obama's Hesitant Embrace of Human Rights," *Foreign Affairs* 89, no. 2 (March–April 2010): 10–16; see esp. p. 10.

49. Ibid., p. 11.

50. Ibid.

51. P. Sabin Willett, "Who's at Guantanamo Anyway?" in Mark P. Denbeaux and Jonathan Hafetz, eds., *The Guantanamo Lawyers: Inside a Prison Outside the Law* (New York: New York University Press, 2009), pp. 7–12; see esp. p. 12.

52. Fareed Zakaria, *The Post-American World* (New York: W. W. Norton, 2008), p. 10.

53. Ibid., pp. 12–13.

54. Steve Niva, "Fight the Roots of Terrorism," Common Dreams.org, September 21, 2001; available at http://www.commondreams.org/views01/0921-06.htm; accessed February 23, 2010.

55. Pew Research Center Publications, May 2, 2011, available at http://pewresearch.org/pubs/1977/poll-osama-bin-laden-death-confidence-muslim-publics-al-qaeda-favorability; accessed on August 25, 2011.

56. Zakaria, *The Post-American World*, pp. 14–15.

57. Robin Wright, "Support for Bin Laden, Violence Down Among Muslims, Poll Says," *Washington Post*, July 15, 2005, p. 18.

58. Ami Pedahzur, Arie Perliger, and Alexander Bialsky, "Explaining Suicide Terrorism," in Christopher Ankersen and Michael O'Leary, eds., *Understanding Global Terror* (London: Polity, 2007), pp. 37–56; see esp. p. 56.

59. Louay Safi, *Tensions and Transitions in the Muslim World* (Lanham, MD: University Press of America, 2003), pp. 85–86.

60. Moataz A. Fattah, *Democratic Values in the Muslim World* (Boulder, CO: Lynne Rienner, 2006), p. 127.

61. Ibid., p. 138.

62. Robert S. Leiken and Steven Brooke, "The Moderate Muslim Brotherhood," *Foreign Affairs* 86, no. 2 (March–April 2007): 107–121; see pp. 108–110.

63. Ibid., pp. 117–118.

64. Ibid., pp. 118–119.

65. Saloua Zerhouni, "The Moroccan Parliament," in Lust-Okar and Zerhouni, *Political Participation in the Middle East*, pp. 217–237; see p. 227.

66. Peter Kenyon, "Terror Group Entrenched in Algeria," NPR, August 14, 2008; available at http://www.npr.org/templates/story/story.php?storyId=93583141; accessed August 14, 2008.

67. Available at http://weaselzippers.us/2011/08/15/al-qaeda-in-the-islamic-maghreb-urges-arab-spring-jihad, August 15, 2011; accessed on August 25, 2011.

68. John L. Esposito, "Terrorism and the Rise of Political Islam," in Louise Richardson, ed., *The Roots of Terrorism* (New York: Routledge, 2006), pp. 145–158; see p. 157.

69. Marc Lynch, "Dialogue in an Age of Terror," in M. A. Muqtedar Khan, ed., *Islamic Democratic Discourse: Theory, Debates, and Philosophical Perspectives* (Lanham, MD: Lexington Books, 2006), pp. 193–225; see p. 219.

70. Mehran Kamrava, "Reformist Islam in Comparative Perspective," introduction to Mehran Kamrava, ed., *The New Voices of Islam: Rethinking Politics and Modernity: A Reader* (Berkeley: University of California Press, 2006), pp. 1–27; see p. 25.

71. Abdullahi Ahmed An-Na'im, *Islam and the Secular State: Negotiating the Future of Shari'a* (Cambridge, MA: Harvard University Press, 2008), p. 44.

72. Ian S. Lustick, *Trapped in the War on Terror* (Philadelphia: University of Pennsylvania Press, 2006), p. 140.

73. Justin Vaisse, "Muslims in Europe: A Short Introduction," *US-Europe Analysis Series*, Center on the United States and Europe at Brookings, Washington, DC, September 2008, pp. 1–6; see esp. p. 6.

74. Ibid.

75. Ariane Chebel d'Appollonia, "Immigration, Security, and Integration in the European Union," in Ariane Chebel d'Appollonia and Simon Reich, eds., *Immigration, Integration, and Security: America and Europe in Comparative Perspective* (Pittsburgh: University of Pittsburgh Press, 2008), pp. 203–228.

76. Ariane Chebel d'Appollonia and Simon Reich, "Immigration: Tensions, Dilemmas, and Unresolved Questions," in d'Appollonia and Reich, *Immigration, Integration, and Security*, p. 340.

77. Jocelyne Cesari, *When Islam and Democracy Meet: Muslims in Europe and in the United States* (New York: Palgrave Macmillan, 2004), p. 181.

78. Elisabeth Bumiller and Jane Perlez, "Pakistan's Spy Agency Is Tied to Attacks on U.S. Embassy," *New York Times*, September 22, 2011, available at http://www.nytimes.com/2011/09/23/world/asia/mullen-asserts-pakistani-role -in-attack-on-us-embassy.html?ref=corrections, accessed September 27, 2011.

79. Seth G. Jones and Martin C. Libicki, "Stop the 'War' on Terror," *Christian Science Monitor*, August 6, 2008, p. 9.

80. Ibid.

81. Ibid.

82. Richard Ashby Wilson, "Human Rights in the War on Terror," in Richard Ashby Wilson, ed., *Human Rights in the War on Terror* (New York: Cambridge University Press, 2005), pp. 1–36; see p. 30.

83. Ibid., p. 33.

84. Mark P. Denbeaux and Jonathan Hafetz, eds., *The Guantanamo Lawyers: Inside the Prison Outside the Law* (New York: New York University Press, 2009), p. 4.

85. Ibid.

86. Asad Ghanem, "Israel and the 'Danger of Demography,'" in Jamil Hilal, ed., *Where Now for Palestine: The Demise of the Two-State Solution* (London: Zed Books, 2007), pp. 48–74; see p. 54.

87. Stephen M. Walt, *Taming American Power: The Global Response to U.S. Primacy* (New York: W. W. Norton, 2005), pp. 236–237.

88. Ibid.

89. Weiss, "Using Military Force for Human Protection," p. 390.

90. Ben Arnold and Issam Ahmed, "Should U.S. Cut Aid to Pakistan?" *Christian Science Monitor*, May 30, 2011, p. 10.

91. *Economic Times*, "Post9/11, Pak has received USD18bn in US aid," February 18, 2011; available at http://webcache.googleusercontent.com/search ?q=cache:PukbJP8c1AMJ:articles.economictimes.indiatimes.com /2011-02-18/news/28615703_1_civilian-assistance-terror-attacks-staff-admiral -mikemullen+U.S.+foreign+aid+to+Pakistan+since+9/11&cd=7&hl=en&ct =clnk&gl=us&client=firefox-a&source=www.google.com; accessed May 5, 2011.

92. Craig Cohen and Derek Chollet, "When $10 Billion Is Not Enough: Rethinking U.S. Strategy Toward Pakistan," *Washington Quarterly* 30, no. 2 (Spring 2007): 7–19; see pp. 16–17.

93. Quoted in Ben Arnold and Issam Ahmed, "Should U.S. Cut Aid to Pakistan?" *Christian Science Monitor*, May 30, 2011, p. 10.

94. Helene Cooper and Ismail Khan, "U.S. Demands More from Pakistan in Bin Laden Inquiry," *New York Times*, May 6, 2011; available at http://www .nytimes.com/2011/05/07/world/asia/07policy.html?hp; accessed May 7, 2011.

95. Ayesha Siddiqa, "Pakistan's Counterterrorism Strategy: Separating Friends from Enemies," *Washington Quarterly* 34, no. 1 (Winter 2011): 149–162; see esp. pp. 158–160.

96. M. K. Bhadrakumar, " Natural Law Brings AfPak Crashing," *Asia Times Online*, March 6, 2010; available at http://www.atimes.com/atimes /South_Asia/LC06Df01.html.; accessed June 4, 2010.

97. Debidatta Aurobinda Mahapatra, "The AfPak Strategy and Its Implementation," *Journal of Alternative Perspectives in Social Sciences* 1, no. 3 (2009): 1003–1009.

98. Ahmed Rashid, "America's Fatal Flaws in Afghanistan," *Spiegel Online International,* May 26, 2010; available at http://www.spiegel.de/international /world/0,1518,696662,00.html; accessed June 5, 2010.

99. Ibid.

100. See the review by Christophe Jaffrelot of Philip Oldenburg's *India, Pakistan, and Democracy: Solving the Puzzle of Divergent Paths* (New York: Routledge, 2010), "The Indian-Pakistan Divide: Why India Is Democracy and Pakistan Is Not," *Foreign Affairs* 90, no. 2 (March–April 2011): 140–145; see esp. p. 144.

101. John Hughes, "Don't Dump Pakistan," *Christian Science Monitor*, May 30, 2011, p. 33.

102. Jaffrelot, "The Indian-Pakistan Divide," p. 144.

103. Ibid., p. 145.

104. Siddiqa, "Pakistan's Counterterrorism Strategy," p. 149.

105. Ibid., p. 157.

106. Anatol Lieven, "A Mutiny Grows in Punjab," *National Interest*, no. 112, March–April 2011, pp. 15–23; see esp. p. 21.

107. Paul Staniland, "Caught in the Muddle: America's Pakistan Strategy," *Washington Quarterly*, 34, no. 1 (Winter 2011): 133–148; see esp. p. 134.

108. Anatol Lieven, "A Mutiny Grows in Punjab," p. 23.

109. Staniland, "Caught in the Muddle," pp. 144–146.

110. Rashid, "America's Fatal Flaws in Afghanistan."

111. Ibid.

112. Ibid.

113. Ahmed Rashid, "How Obama Lost Karzai," *Foreign Policy*, no. 185, (March–April 2011): 71–76; see esp. p. 76.

114. Ian O. Lesser, "Turkey, the United States and the Delusion of Geopolitics," *Survival* 48, no. 3 (Autumn 2006), pp. 83–96; see esp. pp. 89–92.

115. Graham E. Fuller, *The New Turkish Republic: Turkey as a Pivotal State in the Muslim World* (Washington, DC: United States Institute of Peace Press, 2006), p. 111.

116. Gitty M. Amini, "Globalization and the State in the Middle East: Iran, Turkey, Israel, and the Palestinians," in Richard N. Rosecrance and Artur A. Stein, eds., *No More States? Globalization, National Self-Determination, and Terrorism* (Lanham, MD: Roman and Littlefield, 2006), p. 116.

117. John C. K. Daly, "Energy Resource Analysis: Turkey-Iran Energy Ties," *UPI.com*, November 30, 2007; available at http://www.upi.com/Energy _Resources/2007/11/30/Analysis_Turkey-Iran_energy_ties/UPI-2595119 6443288; accessed July 2, 2008.

118. Ibid.

119. Lenore G. Martin, "Turkey's Middle East Foreign Policy," in Lenore G. Martin and Dimitris Kerdis, eds., *The Future of Turkish Foreign Policy* (Cam-

bridge, MA: The Belfer Center for Science and International Relations, 2004), pp. 157–190; see esp. p. 172.

120. Alper Fevzi Kara, "Turkey's New Card in EU Diplomacy: Energy," *Journal of Turkish Weekly*, February 25, 2008; available at http://www.turkish weekly.net/comments.php?id=2841; accessed July 2, 2008.

121. Ibid.

122. Fuller, *The New Turkish Republic*, p. 117.

123. Ibid,

124. Ibid., p. 120.

125. Ihsan Dagi, "Why Is It the Right Time to Solve the Kurdish Question?" *Today's Zaman*, May 25, 2009; available at http://www.todayszaman.com /tz-web/yazarDetay.do?haberno=176248; accessed May 25, 2009.

126. Fuller, *The New Turkish Republic*, pp. 173 and 180.

127. Ibid., p. 120.

128. Mahmood Mamdani, *Good Muslim, Bad Muslim: America, the Cold War, and the Roots of Terror* (New York: Pantheon, 2004), pp. 61–62.

129. Ihsan Dagi, "Turkey AKP in Power," *Journal of Democracy* 19, no. 3 (July 2008): 25–30.

130. Gareth Jenkins, *Political Islam in Turkey: Running West, Heading East?* (New York: Palgrave McMillan, 2008), pp. 215–217.

131. BBC News, "Turkey's Ruling Party Escapes Ban," July 30, 2008; available at http://news.bbc.co.uk/1/hi/world/europe/7533414.stm; accessed August 8, 2008.

132. Ihsan Dagi, "Lessons for Government and Opposition," *Today's Zaman*, August 4, 2008; available at http://www.todayszaman.com/tz-web/yazarAd .do?kn=73; accessed August 7, 2008.

133. Ziya Onis, "The Political Economy of Islam and Democracy in Turkey: From the Welfare Party to the AKP," in Dietrich Jung, ed., *Democratization and Development: New Political Strategies for the Middle East* (New York: Palgrave Macmillan, 2006), pp. 103–128; see pp. 124–125.

134. Ihsan Dagi, "The Roots of Anti-Westernism in Turkish Military," *Today's Zaman*, July 21, 2008; available at http://www.todayszaman.com /tz-web/yazarDetay.do?haberno+148028; accessed July 21, 2008.

135. Alidad Mafinezam and Aria Mehrabi, *Iran and Its Place Among Nations* (Westport, CT: Praeger, 2008), p. 58.

136. Ibid., pp. 59–60.

137. Hoffmann, *Chaos and Violence*, pp. 213–214.

138. Phar Kim Beng, "Turkey's Potential as a Soft Power: A Call for Conceptual Clarity," *Insight Turkey* 10, no. 2 (2008): 21–40; see p. 23.

139. Ibid.

140. Fars News Agency, "Turkey Intensifies Efforts to Mediate Between Iran, West," July 22, 2008; available at http://english.farsnews.com/newstext .php?nn=8705011725; accessed August 4, 2008.

141. Yigal Schleifer and Mevluk Katik, "Turkey Confronts Geopolitical Dilemma Concerning Iranian Nuclear Research, *Eurasia Insight*, February 14, 2006; available at http://www.eurasianet.org/departments/insight/articles /eav021406.shtml; accessed April 20, 2009.

142. See "UN Approves New Sanctions to Deter Iran," *New York Times*, June 9, 2010; available at http://www.nytimes.com/2010/06/10/world/middleeast /10sanctions.html; accessed June 14, 2010.

143. Ihsan Dagi, "If Not Doomed to Misunderstand Turkey on Iran," *Today's Zaman*, June 14, 2010; available athttp://ihsandagi.blogspot.com/2010/06 /if-not-doomed-to-misunderstand-turkey.html; accessed June 14, 2010.

144. Gilles Kepel, *Beyond Terror and Martyrdom: The Future of the Middle East* (Cambridge, MA: Belknap Press, 2008).

145. Toni Zinni and Tony Koltz, *Leading the Charge: Leadership Lessons from the Battlefield to the Boardroom* (New York: Palgrave Macmillan, 2009).

146. Sarah Holewinski and James Morin, "It's Not Civilians vs. Soldiers," *Christian Science Monitor*, March 15, 2010, p. 34.

147. Ibid.

148. David S. Cloud, "UN Report Faults Prolific Use of Drone Strikes by U.S.," *Los Angeles Times*, June 3, 2010; available at http://www.latimes .com/news/nationworld/world/la-fg-cia-drones-20100603,0,6430644.story; accessed June 3, 2010.

149. Rory Stewart, "The Irresistible Illusion," *London Review of Books* 31, no. 13 (July 9, 2009): 3–6.

150. Rohan Gunaratna, "Ideology in Terrorism and Counter Terrorism," in Anne Aldis and Graeme P. Herd, eds., *The Ideological War on Terror: World-wide Strategies for Counter-terrorism* (New York: Routledge, 2007), pp. 21–34; see esp. p. 33.

151. See "Estimated War-Related Costs: Iraq and Afghanistan," available at http://www.infoplease.com/ipa/A0933935.html; accessed on August 25, 2011.

152. David R. Francis writes in the *Christian Science Monitor*, September 13, 2009, p. 32.

153. Linda Bilmes and Joseph Stiglitz, *The Three Trillion Dollar War: The True Cost of the Iraq Conflict* (New York: W. W. Norton, 2008).

154. David R. Francis, "Afghanistan Will Cost US More than Iraq," *Christian Science Monitor*, September 13, 2009, p. 32.

155. Noah Bialostozky, "Retire 'War on Terror,'" *Christian Science Monitor*, April, 19, 2009, p. 26.

156. "General David Petraeus: New Commander of U.S. CENTCOM Turns His Attention to the Counterinsurgency in Afghanistan," *Canadian-American Strategic Review*; available at http://www.casr.ca/ft-us-troops-afghanistan -petraeus-1.htm; accessed June 2, 2011.

157. Andrew J. Bacevich, "The Last Act in the Middle East," *Newsweek*, April 11, 2011, pp. 48–49.

158. Aryn Baker, "The Longest War," *Time*, April 20, 2009, pp. 24–29; see esp. pp. 27–29.

159. Ibid., p. 28.

160. Mark Thompson and Aryn Baker, "Starting Anew," *Time*, July 20, 2009, pp. 28–33.

161. Aryn Baker and Loi Kolay, "The Longest War," *Time*, April 8, 2009; available at http://www.time.com/time/world/article/0,8599,1890243,00.html; accessed February 26, 2010.

162. Ibid., p. 8.

163. Stephen Zunes, *Tinderbox: U.S. Foreign Policy and the Roots of Terrorism* (Monroe, ME: Common Courage Press, 2003), p. 222.

164. Michael Chertoff, "Ideology of Terrorism: Radicalism Revisited," *Brown Journal of World Affairs* 15, no. 1 (Fall–Winter 2008): 11–20; see esp. p. 19.

165. Joseph S. Nye, "Soft Power: The Means to Success in World Politics," Foreign Policy Association address, May 10, 2010; available at http://www.fpa.org/topics_info2414/topics_info_show.htm?doc_id=225504; accessed June 17, 2010.

Bibliography

Abdo, Geneive. *Mecca and Main Street: Muslim Life in America after 9/11.* Oxford: Oxford University Press, 2006.

Adib-Moghaddam, Arshin. *The International Politics of the Persian Gulf: A Cultural Genealogy.* New York: Routledge, 2006.

Ajami, Fuad. "The Autumn of the Autocracy." *Foreign Affairs* 84, no. 3 (May–June 2005): 20–35.

———. "Demise of the Dictators." *Newsweek*, February 14, 2011, pp. 18–27.

Ajluni, Salem "Report: The Palestinian Economy and the Second Intifada." *Journal of Palestinian Studies* 32, no. 3 (Spring 2003): 64–73.

Akbarzadeh, Shahram, and Fethi Mansouri, eds. *Islam and Political Violence: Muslim Diaspora and Radicalism in the West.* London: Tauris Academic Studies, 2007.

Aldis, Anne, and Graeme P. Herd, eds. *The Ideological War on Terror: Worldwide Strategies for Counter-terrorism.* New York: Routledge, 2007.

Altunisik, Meliha Benli. "The Possibilities and Limits of Turkey's Soft Power in the Middle East." *Insight Turkey* 10, no. 2 (2008): 41–54.

Angelson, Meredith. "Beyond the Myth of 'Good Faith': Torture Evidence in International Extradition Hearings." *Journal of International Law and Politics*, New York University 41, no. 3 (Spring 2009): 603–653.

An-Na'im, Abdullahi Ahmed, *Islam and the Secular State: Negotiating the Future of Shari'a.* Cambridge: Harvard University Press, 2008.

Ansari, Ali M. *Confronting Iran: The Failure of American Foreign Policy and the Next Great Conflict in the Middle East.* New York: Basic Books, 2006.

Armstrong, Karen. "Ghosts of Our Past." In Thomas J. Badey, ed. *Violence and Terrorism 05/06*, 8th ed. Dubuque, IA: Mc-Graw-Hill/Dushkin, 2005, pp. 14–17.

Art, Robert J., and Louise Richardson, eds. *Democracy and Counterterrorism: Lessons from the Past*, Washington, DC: US Institute for Peace, 2007.

Avant, Deborah. "The Privatization of Security: Lessons from Iraq." *Orbis* 50, no. 2 (Spring 2006): 327–342.

Baker, James A. III, and Lee H. Hamilton, co-chairs, *The Iraq Study Group Report: The Way Forward—A New Approach.* New York: Vintage Books, 2006.

291

Baroud, Ramzy. *The Second Palestinian Intifada: A Chronicle of a People's Strug-gle.* London: Pluto Press, 2006.

Baxter, Kylie, and Shahram Akbarzadeh. *U.S. Foreign Policy in the Middle East: The Roots of Anti-Americanism.* New York: Routledge, 2008.

Beinin, Joel, and Rebecca L. Stein, eds. *The Struggle for Sovereignty: Palestine and Israel, 1993–2005.* Palo Alto, CA: Stanford University Press, 2006.

Beitz, Charles R., and Robert E. Goodin, eds. *Global Basic Rights.* New York: Oxford University Press, 2009.

Bellin, Eva. "The Iraqi Intervention and Democracy in Comparative Historical Perspective." *Political Science Quarterly* 119, no. 4 (Winter 2004–2005): 595–608.

Bill, James A., and Robert Springborg. *Politics in the Middle East,* 5th ed. New York: Longman, 2000.

Billitteri, Thomas J. "Afghanistan Dilemma." In *Global Issues: Selections from CQ Researcher.* Washington, DC: CQ Press, 2011, pp. 1–24.

Bilmes, Linda, and Joseph Stiglitz. *The Three Trillion Dollar War: The True Cost of the Iraq Conflict.* New York: W. W. Norton, 2008.

Booth, Ken. *Theory of World Security.* Cambridge: Cambridge University Press, 2007.

Boyle, Michael J. "Do Counterterrorism and Counterinsurgency Go Together?" *International Affairs* 86, no. 2 (March 2010): 333–353.

———. "The War on Terror in American Grand Strategy." *International Affairs* 84, no. 2 (March 2008): 191–209.

Brysk, Alison. *Global Good Samaritans: Human Rights as Foreign Policy.* New York: Oxford University Press, 2009.

Brzezinski, Zbigniew. "From Hope to Audacity: Appraising Obama's Foreign Pol-icy." *Foreign Affairs* 89, no. 1 (January–February 2010): 16–30.

———. "Hegemonic Quicksand." *National Interest* 74 (Winter 2003–2004): 5–16.

———. *Second Chance: Three Presidents and the Crisis of American Super-power.* New York: Basic Books, 2007.

Bull, Hedley. *The Anarchical Society: A Study of Order in World Politics,* 3rd ed. New York: Columbia University Press, 2002.

Buzan, Barry. "Will the 'Global War on Terrorism' Be the New Cold War?" *Inter-national Relations* 82, no. 6 (November 2006): 1101–1118.

Byman, Daniel L. "Friends Like These: Counterinsurgency and the War on Terror-ism." *International Security* 31, no. 2 (2006): 79–115.

———. "Talking with Insurgents: A Guide for the Perplexed." *Washington Quar-terly* 32, no. 2 (April 2009): 125–137.

———. "Terrorism after the Revolutions: How Secular Uprisings Could Help (or Hurt) Jihadists." *Foreign Affairs* 90, no. 3 (May–June 2011): 48–54.

———. "US Counter-terrorism Options: A Taxonomy, *Survival* 49, no. 3 (Autumn, 2007): 121–150.

———, and Kenneth M. Pollack. *Things Fall Apart: Containing the Spillover from an Iraqi Civil War.* Washington, DC: Brookings Institution Press, 2007.

Cairo Institute for Human Rights Studies. *Bastion of Impunity, Mirage of Reform.* Human Rights in the Arab Region annual report 2009, Cairo, 2009, pp. 178–179.

Cardenas, Sonia. *Human Rights in Latin American: A Politics of Terror and Hope.* Philadelphia: University of Pennsylvania Press, 2010.

Carothers, Thomas. *Critical Mission: Essays on Democracy Promotion.* Washington, DC: Carnegie Endowment for International Peace, 2004.

Carroll, Jamuna, ed. *Privacy: Opposing Viewpoints Series.* New York: Thomson Gale, 2006.

Carter, Jimmy. *Palestine Peace Not Apartheid.* New York: Simon & Schuster, 2006.

Cesari, Jocelyne. *Muslims in the West after 9/11: Religion, Politics, and Law.* New York: Routledge–Taylor & Francis Group, 2010.

———. *When Islam and Democracy Meet: Muslims in Europe and the United States.* New York: Palgrave, 2004.

Chomsky, Noam, and Gilbert Achcar. *Perilous Power: The Middle East and U.S. Foreign Policy: Dialogues on Terror, Democracy, War, and Justice.* Boulder, CO: Paradigm, 2007.

Chertoff, Michael. "Ideology of Terrorism: Radicalism Revisited." *Brown Journal of World Affairs* 15, no. 1 (Fall–Winter 2008): 11–20.

Chossudovsky, Michel. "Who Is Osama Bin Laden?" *Global Dialogue* 3, no. 4 (Autumn 2001): 1–7.

Clarke, Richard A. *Against All Enemies: Inside the War on Terror.* New York: Free Press, 2004.

Cleveland, William L., and Martin A. Bunton. *History of the Modern Middle East,* 4th ed. Boulder, CO: Westview, 2009.

Crotty, William, ed. *Democratic Development and Political Terrorism: The Global Perspective.* Boston: Northeastern University Press, 2005, p. 524.

Dagi, Ihsan. *Turkey between Democracy and Militarism: Post-Kemalist Perspectives.* Ankara, Orion Publications, 2008.

———. "Turkey's AKP in Power." *Journal of Democracy* 19, no. 3 (July 2008): 25–30.

Dawisha, Adeeb. "The Unraveling of Iraq: Ethnosectarian Preferences and State Performance in Historical Perspectives." *Middle East Journal* 62, no. 2 (Spring 2008): 219–230.

De Bellaigue, Christopher. "Think Again: Iran." *Foreign Policy,* no. 148 (May–June 2005): 18–23.

Denbeaux, Mark P., and Jonathan Hafetz, eds. *The Guantanamo Lawyers: Inside a Prison Outside the Law.* New York: New York University Press, 2009.

Diamond, Larry. "The Democratic Rollback: The Resurgence of the Predatory State." *Foreign Affairs* 87, no. 2 (March–April 2008): 36–48.

Donnelly, Jack. *International Human Rights,* 3rd ed. Boulder, CO: Westview, 2007.

Donohue, Laura K. *The Cost of Counterterrorism: Power, Politics, and Liberty.* Cambridge: Cambridge University Press, 2008.

Dworkin, Ronald. *Is Democracy Possible Here? Principles for a New Political Debate.* Princeton, NJ: Princeton University Press, 2006.

Edwards, John. "Reengaging with the World: A Return to Moral Leadership." *Foreign Affairs* 86, no. 5 (September–October 2007): 19–36.

Egendorf, Laura K., ed. *At Issue: Islam in America.* New York: Greenhaven Press, 2006.

Einolf, Christopher J. "The Fall and Rise of Torture: A Comparative and Historical Analysis." *Sociological Theory* 25, no. 2 (June 2007):101–121.

Erlich, Reese. *The Iran Agenda: The Real Story of U.S. Policy and the Middle East Crisis.* Sausalito, CA: PoliPoint Press, 2007.

Esposito, John L. "Terrorism and the Rise of Political Islam." In Louise Richardson, ed. *The Roots of Terrorism.* New York: Routledge, 2006, pp. 145–158.

———, ed. *Political Islam: Revolution, Radicalism, or Reform?* Boulder, CO: Lynne Rienner, 1997.

Etzioni, Amitai. "Citizenship Tests: A Comparative, Communitarian Perspective." *Political Quarterly* 78, no. 3 (July–September 2007): 353–363.

Evans, Gareth. "Responding to Terrorism: A Global Stocktake." In Daniel S. Hamilton, ed. *Terrorism and International Relations.* Washington, DC: Center for Transatalantic Relations, 2006, pp. 147–158.

Fair, C. Christine. "Time for Sober Realism: Renegotiating U.S. Relations with Pakistan." *Washington Quarterly* 32, no. 2 (April 2009): 149–172.

Fattah, Moataz A. *Democratic Values in the Muslim World.* Boulder, CO: Lynne Rienner, 2006.

Fawn, Rick, and Raymond Hinnebusch, eds. *The Iraq War: Causes and Consequences.* Boulder, CO: Lynne Rienner, 2006.

Ferguson, Niall. *Colossus: The Price of America's Empire.* New York: Penguin Press, 2004.

———. "Power." *Foreign Policy*, no. 134 (January–February 2003):18–24.

Fick, Nathaniel C., and John A. Nagl. "Counterinsurgency Field Manual: Afghanistan Edition." *Foreign Policy* 170 (January–February 2009): 42–47.

Fletcher, Laurel E., and Eric Stover. *The Guantanamo Effect: Exposing the Consequences of U.S. Detention and Interrogation Practices.* Berkeley: University of California Press, 2009.

Foot, Rosemary. *Human Rights and Counterterrorism in America's Asia Policy.* Adelphi Papers, no. 363. New York: Oxford University Press, 2004.

———. "Human Rights in Conflict." *Survival* 48, no. 3 (Autumn 2006): 109–126.

Forsythe, David P. *Human Rights in International Relations,* 2nd ed. New York: Cambridge University Press, 2006.

———, ed. *Encyclopedia of Human Rights.* New York: Oxford University Press, 2009.

———. *The Politics of Prisoner Abuse: The United States and Enemy Prisoners After 9/11.* New York: Cambridge University Press, 2011.

———, Patrice C. McMahon, and Andrew Wedeman, eds. *American Foreign Policy in a Globalized World.* New York: Routledge, 2006.

Fuller, Graham E. *The New Turkish Republic: Turkey as a Pivotal State in the Muslim World.* Washington, DC: United States Institute of Peace Press, 2006.

Galbraith, Peter W. *The End of Iraq: How American Incompetence Created a War Without End.* New York: Simon & Schuster, 2006.

Givens, Terri E., Gary P. Freeman, and David L. Leal, eds. *Immigration Policy and Security: U.S., European, and Commonwealth Perspectives.* New York: Routledge, 2009.

Gokalp, Deniz, and Seda Unsar. "From Myth of European Accession to Disillusion: Implications for Religious and Ethnic Politicization in Turkey." *Middle East Journal* 62, no. 1 (Winter 2008): 93–116.

Goodarzi, Jubin M. *Syria and Iran: Diplomatic Alliance and Power Politics in the Middle East*. London: Tauris Academic Studies, 2007.

Goodson, Larry P. *Afghanistan's Endless War: State Failure, Regional Politics, and the Rise of the Taliban*. Seattle: University of Washington Press, 2001.

Goold, Benjamin J., and Liora Lazarus, eds. *Security and Human Rights*. Portland, OR: Hart, 2007.

Gordon, Philip H. *Winning the Right War: The Path to Security for America and the World*. New York: Times Books, 2007.

Gottlieb, Stuart, ed. *Debating Terrorism and Counterterrorism: Conflicting Perspectives on Causes, Contexts, and Responses*. Washington, DC: Congressional Quarterly Press, 2006.

Gould, Carol C. *Globalizing Democracy and Human Rights*. Cambridge: Cambridge University Press, 2004.

Greenwald, Glenn. *How Would a Patriot Act? Defending American Values from a President Run Amok*. San Francisco: Working Assets Publishing, 2006.

Griffiths, Sir Eldon. *Turbulent Iran: Recollections, Revelations, and a Plan for Peace*. Santa Ana, CA: Seven Locks Press, 2006.

Gurtov, Mel. *Global Politics in the Human Interests*, 5th ed. Boulder, CO: Lynne Rienner, 2007.

Gutman, Roy. *How We Missed the Story: Osama bin Laden, the Taliban, and the Hijacking of Afghanistan*. Washington, DC: US Institute of Peace, 2008.

Haass, Richard N. "We're Not Winning. It's Not Worth It: Here Is How to Draw Down in Afghanistan." *Newsweek*, July 26, 2010, pp. 30–35.

Hadda, Yvonne Yazbeck. "Islamist Perceptions of U.S. Policy in the Middle East." In David W. Lesch, ed. *The Middle East and the United States: A Historical and Political Assessment*, 4th ed. Boulder, CO: Westview, 2007, pp. 504–533.

Halim, Fachrizal. "Pluralism of American Muslims and the Challenge of Assimilation." *Journal of Muslim Minority Affairs* 26, no. 2 (August 2006): 235–244.

Hammami, Rema, and Salim Tamari. "The Second Uprising: End of a New Beginning?" *Journal of Palestine Studies* 30, no. 2 (Winter 2001).

Hammond, Andrew. *What the Arabs Think of America*. Westport, CT: Greenwood World, 2007.

Harb, Mona. "Deconstructing Hizballah and Its Suburb." *Middle East Report* 37, no. 242 (Spring 2007): 12–17.

Haugen, Gary, and Victor Boutros. "And Justice for All: Enforcing Human Rights for the World's Poor." *Foreign Affairs* 89, no. 3 (May–June 2010): 51–62.

Haynes, Jeff. *Democracy and Civil Society in The Third World: Politics and New Political Movements*. Cambridge, UK: Polity Press, 1997.

Heazle, Michael, and Iyanatul Islam, eds. *Beyond the Iraq War: The Promises, Pitfalls, and Perils of External Intervention*. Northampton, MA: Edward Elgar, 2006.

Hilal, Jamil, ed. *Where Now for Palestine: The Demise of the Two-State Solution*. London: Zed Books, 2007.

Hocking, Jenny, and Colleen Lewis, eds. *Counter-Terrorism and the Post-Democratic State*. Northampton, MA: Edward Elgar, 2007.

Hoffmann, Stanley. *Chaos and Violence: What Globalization, Failed States, and Terrorism Mean for U.S. Foreign Policy*. Lanham, MD: Rowman & Littlefield, 2006.

————. "The Foreign Policy the US Needs." *New York Review of Books* 53, no. 13, August 10, 2006: 60–64.

Hudson, Michael C. "The United States in the Middle East." In Louise Fawcett, ed. *International Relations of the Middle East*. New York: Oxford University Press, 2005, pp. 283–305.

Hunter, Shireen T., and Huma Malik, eds. *Modernization, Democracy, and Islam*. Westport, CT: Praeger, 2005.

Huq, Aziz Z. "Democratic Torture: Has Mill's Safeguard Weakened?" *World Policy Journal* 24, no. 4 (Winter–Spring 2007–2008): 99–107.

Ignatieff, Michael. *The Lesser Evil: Political Ethics in an Age of Terror*. Princeton, NJ: Princeton University Press, 2004.

Innocent, Malou, and Ted Galen Carpenter. *Escaping the "Graveyard of Empires": A Strategy to Exit Afghanistan*. Washington, DC: Cato Institute, 2009, pp. 1–21.

Jackson, Robert, and Georg Sorensen. *Introduction to International Relations: Theories and Approaches*, 3rd ed. New York: Oxford University Press, 2007.

Jenkins, Gareth. *Political Islam in Turkey: Running West, Heading East?* New York: Palgrave McMillan, 2008.

Jones, Toby. "Saudi Arabia's Not So New Anti–Shi'im." *Middle East Report* 37, no. 242 (Spring 2007): 29–32.

Joppke, Christian. "Beyond National Models: Civic Integration Policies for Immigrants in Western Europe." *West European Politics* 30, no. 1 (January 2007): 1–22.

Jung, Dietrich, ed. *Democratization and Development: New Political Strategies for the Middle East*. New York: Palgrave Macmillan, 2006.

Kamrava, Mehran. *The Modern Middle East: A Political History since the First World War*. Berkeley: University of California Press, 2005.

————, ed. *The New Voices of Islam: Rethinking Politics and Modernity: A Reader*. Berkeley: University of California Press, 2006.

Katzenstein, Peter J., and Robert O. Keohane, eds. *Anti-Americanisms in World Politics*. Ithaca, NY: Cornell University Press, 2007.

Kechichian, Joseph A. *Power and Succession in Arab Monarchies: A Reference Guide*. Boulder, CO: Lynne Rienner, 2008.

Kepel, Gilles. *Beyond Terror and Martyrdom: The Future of the Middle East*. Cambridge: Belknap Press/Harvard University Press, 2008.

Khalidi, Rashid. *Resurrecting Empire: Western Footprints and America's Perilous Path in the Middle East*. Boston: Beacon Press, 2004.

Khan, M. A. Muqtedar, ed. *Islamic Democratic Discourse: Theory, Debates, and Philosophical Perspectives*. Lanham, MD: Lexington Books, 2006.

Kiesling, John Brady. *Diplomacy Lessons: Realism for an Unloved Superpower*. Washington, DC: Potomac Books, 2006.

Kilcullen, David. *Counterinsurgency*. New York: Oxford University Press, 2010.

King, Mary Elizabeth. *A Quiet Revolution: The First Palestinian Intifada and Nonviolent Resistance*. New York: Nation Books, 2007.

Kinzer, Stephen. *Overthrow: America's Century of Regime Change from Hawaii to Iraq*. New York: Times Books, 2006.

Kiras, James D. "Terrorism and Globalization." In John Baylis and Steve Smith, eds. *The Globalization of World Politics: An Introduction to International Relations*, 3rd ed. New York: Oxford University Press, 2005, pp. 479–497.

Kodmani, Bassma. "Clearing the Air in the Middle East." *Current History* 107, no. 709 (May 2008): 201–206.

Koji, Teraya. "Emerging Hierarchy in International Human Rights and Beyond: From the Perspective of Non-derogable Rights." *European Journal of International Law* 12, no. 5 (2001): 917–941.

Krepinevich, Andrew F., Jr. "How to Win in Iraq." *Foreign Affairs* 84, no. 5 (September–October 2005): 87–104.

Kurtzer, Daniel C., and Scott B. Lasensky. *Negotiating Arab-Israeli Peace: The American Leadership in the Middle East.* Washington, DC: US Institute of Peace Press, 2008.

Lahneman, William J., ed. *Military Intervention: Cases in Context for the Twenty-First Century.* New York: Rowman & Littlefield, 2004.

Laurence, Jonathan, and Justin Vaisse. *Integrating Islam: Political and Religious Challenges in Contemporary France.* Washington, DC: Brookings Institution Press, 2006.

Layne, Christopher. "Who Lost Iraq and Why It Matters." *World Policy Journal* 24, no. 3 (Fall 2007): 38–52.

Leiken, Robert S. "Europe's Angry Muslims." *Foreign Affairs* 84, no. 4 (July–August):120–135.

———, and Steven Brooke. "The Moderate Muslim Brotherhood." *Foreign Affairs* 86, no. 2 (March–April 2007): 107–121; see 108–110.

Leone, Richard C., and Greg Anrig Jr. *The War on Our Freedoms: Civil Liberties in an Age of Terrorism.* New York: Public Affairs, 2003.

Lesch, David W. *The Arab-Israeli Conflict: A History.* New York: Oxford University Press, 2008.

———, ed. *The Middle East and the United States: A Historical and Political Assessment*, 4th ed. Boulder, CO: Westview, 2007.

Lesser, Ian O. "Turkey, the United States, and the Delusion of Geopolitics." *Survival* 48, no. 3 (Autumn 2006): 83–96.

Lewis, Bernard. "Freedom and Justice in the Modern Middle East." *Foreign Affairs* 84, no. 3 (May–June 2005): 36–51.

Lindsay, James M., and Ray Takeyh. "After Iran Gets the Bomb." *Foreign Affairs* 89, no. 2 (April–May 2010): 33–49.

Little, Douglas. *American Orientalism: The United States and the Middle East since 1945.* Chapel Hill: University of North Carolina Press, 2002.

Loewenstein, Jennifer. "Notes from the Field: Return to the Ruin That Is Gaza." *Journal of Palestinian Studies* 36, no. 3 (Spring 2007): 23–35.

Lopez, Andrea M. "Engaging or Withdrawing, Winning or Losing? The Contradictions of Counterinsurgency Policy in Afghanistan and Iraq." *Third World Quarterly* 28, no. 2 (2007): 245–260.

Lust-Okar, Ellen, and Saloua Zerhouni, eds. *Political Participation in the Middle East.* Boulder, CO: Lynne Rienner, 2008.

Lustick, Ian S. "The Political Requirements of Victory." *Middle East Policy*, VIII, no. 4 (December 2001): 14–17.

———. *Trapped in the War on Terror.* Philadelphia: University of Pennsylvania Press, 2006.

———, Ivan Eland, Rand Beers, and Edward Luttwak. "Are We Trapped in the War on Terror?" *Middle East Policy* 13, no. 4 (Winter 2006): 1–27.

MacBride, Sean S. C. *Israel in Lebanon: The Report of the International Commission to Enquire into Reported Violations of International Law by Israel During Its Invasion of Lebanon.* London: Ithaca Press, 1983.

Macfarlane, S. Neil. "Human Security and the Law of States." In Bejamin J. Goold and Liora Lazarus, eds. *Security and Human Rights.* Portland, OR: Hart, 2007, pp. 345–361.

Mack, Andrew. "Why Big Nations Lose Small Wars: The Politics of Asymmetric Conflict." *World Politics*, 27, no. 2 (January 1975): 175–200.

Mafinezam, Alidad, and Aria Mehrabi. *Iran and Its Place among Nations.* Westport, CT: Praeger, 2008.

Makovsky, David. "Gaza: Moving Forward by Pulling Back." *Foreign Affairs* 84, no 3 (May–June 2005): 52–62.

Mamdani, Mahmood. *Good Muslim, Bad Muslim: America, the Cold War, and the Roots of Terror.* New York: Pantheon, 2004.

Mandaville, Peter. *Transnational Muslim Politics: Reimaging the Umma.* New York: Routledge, 2004.

Mandelbaum, Michael. "Democracy without America: The Spontaneous Spread of Freedom." *Foreign Affairs* 86, no. 5 (September–October 2007): 119–130.

Martin, Lenore G., and Dimitris Keridis, eds. *The Future of Turkish Foreign Policy.* Cambridge, MA: MIT Press, 2004.

Mayer, Jane. "The Black Sites: A Rare Look Inside the C.I.A.'s Secret Interrogation Program." *New Yorker*, August 13, 2007, pp. 47–57.

———. *The Dark Side: The Inside Story of How the War on Terror Turned into a War on American Ideals.* New York: Doubleday, 2008.

Mearsheimer, John J., and Stephen M. Walt. *The Israel Lobby and U.S. Foreign Policy.* New York: Farrar, Straus & Giroux, 2007.

Menon, Rajan. *The End of Alliances.* New York: Oxford University Press, 2007.

Meron, Theodor. "On a Hierarchy of International Human Rights." *American Journal of International Law* 80, no. 1 (January 1986): 1–23.

Mertus, Julie A. *Bait and Switch: Human Rights and U.S. Foreign Policy.* New York: Routledge, 2004.

Milani, Mohsen M. "Tehran's Take: Understanding Iran's U.S. Policy." *Foreign Affairs* 88, no. 4 (July–August, 2009): 46–62.

Mokhtari, Shadi. *After Abu Ghraib: Exploring Human Rights in America and the Middle East.* New York: Cambridge University Press, 2009.

Monshipouri, Mahmood. *US-Iran Relations: Embracing a New Realism.* 77 Emirates Lecture Series. Emirates Center for Strategic Studies and Research, Abu Dhabi, UAE, 2009.

———. "The Paradoxes of U.S. Foreign Policy in the Middle East." *Middle East Policy* 9, no. 3 (September 2002): 65–84.

———. "The PLO Rivalry with Hamas: The Challenge of Peace, Democratization, and Islamic Radicalism." *Middle East Policy* 4, no. 3 (March 1996): 84–105.

———, and Ali Assareh. "The Islamic Republic and the 'Green Movement': Coming Full Circle." *Middle East Policy* 16, no. 4 (Winter 2009): 27–46.

———, and Thaddeus Zolty. "Shaping the New World Order: America's Post–Gulf War Agenda in the Middle East." *Armed Forces and Society* 19, no. 4 (Summer 1993): 551–577.

Mortenson, Greg, and David Oliver Relin. *Three Cups of Tea: One Man's Mission to Promote Peace . . . One School at a Time*. New York: Penguin, 2006.

Muedini, Fait. "Muslim American College Youth: Attitudes and Responses Five Years after 9/11." *Muslim World*, no. 99 (January 2009): 39–59.

Nakaya, Andrea C., ed. *America's Battle against Terrorism*. New York: Thompson Gale, 2005, pp. 98–103.

Nasr, Vali. *The Shia Revival: How Conflicts within Islam Will Shape the Future.*" New York: W. W. Norton, 2006, p. 179.

———. "When the Shiites Rise." *Foreign Affairs* 85, no. 4 (July–August 2006): 58–74.

Neilsen, Jorgen S. "Islam in Europe: Review Article." *Middle East Journal* 62, no. 1 (Winter 2008): 144–148.

Norton, Augustus Richard. *Hezbollah: A Short History*. Princeton, NJ: Princeton University Press, 2007.

O'Bryne, Darren J. *Human Rights: An Introduction*. New York: Longman, 2003.

Olson, Robert. *Turkey-Iran Relations, 1979–2004: Revolution, Ideology, War, Coups, and Geopolitics*. Costa Mesa, CA: Mazda, 2004.

Osiel, Mark. *The End of Reciprocity: Terror, Torture, and the Law of War*. New York: Cambridge University Press, 2009.

Paerthes, Volker. "America's 'Greater Middle East' and Europe: Key Issues for Dialogue." *Middle East Policy* 11, no. 3 (Fall 2004): 85–97.

Parsi, Trita. *Treacherous Alliance: The Secret Dealings of Israel, Iran, and the United States*. New Haven, CT: Yale University Press, 2007.

Patman, Robert G. "Globalization, the New US Exceptionalism, and the War on Terror." *Third World Quarterly* 27, no. 6 (2006): 963–986.

Paust, Jordan J. *Beyond the Law: The Bush Administration's Unlawful Responses in the "War" on Terror*. Cambridge: Cambridge University Press, 2007.

Pelletiere, Stephen C. *Losing Iraq: Insurgency and Politics*. Westport, CT: Praeger, 2006.

Pena, Aisha. "Protecting Muslim Civil and Human Rights in America: The Role of Islamic, National, and International Organizations." *Journal of Muslim Minority Affairs* 27, no. 3 (December 2007): 387–400.

Pfaff, William. "The Iran National Intelligence Estimate and the Eight-Year Carnival of Lies." *Washington Report on Middle East Affairs* 27, no. 1 (January–February 2008).

Pillar, Paul R. *Terrorism and U.S. Foreign Policy*. Washington, DC: Brookings Institution Press, 2001.

Piscatori, James. "The Turmoil Within: The Struggle for the Future of the Islamic World." *Foreign Affairs* 81, no. 3 (May–June 2002): 145–150.

Pollack, Kenneth, and Ray Takeyh. "Taking on Tehran." *Foreign Affairs* 84, no. 2 (March–April 2005): 20–34.

Posner, Eric A., and Adrian Vermeule. *Terror in the Balance: Security, Liberty, and the Courts*. New York: Oxford University Press, 2007.

Poyraz, Serdar. "Turkish-Iranian Relations: A Wider Perspective." *SETA Policy Brief*, no. 37, November 2009, pp. 1–14.

Pryce-Jones, David. "Green Flags and Brown Shirts." *National Review*, July 6, 2009, pp. 16–17.

Quandt, William B. *Peace Process: American Diplomacy and the Arab-Israeli Conflict since 1967*. Washington, DC: Brookings Institution Press, 2005.

Quataert, Jean H. *Advocating Dignity: Human Rights Mobilizations in Global Politics*. Philadelphia: University of Pennsylvania Press, 2009.

Rabil, Robert G. *Syria, the United States, and the War on Terror in the Middle East*. Westport, CT: Praeger, 2006.

Rachman, Gideon. "Democracy: The Case for Opportunistic Idealism." *Washington Quarterly* 32, no. 1 (Winter 2008–2009): 119–127.

Rashid, Ahmed. "How Obama Lost Karzai." *Foreign Policy*, no.185 (March–April 2011): 71–76.

Rejali, Darius. *Torture and Democracy*. Princeton, NJ: Princeton University Press, 2007.

Ressa, Maria A. *Seeds of Terror: An Eyewitness Account of Al-Qaeda's Newest Center of Operations in Southeast Asia*. New York: Free Press, 2003.

Richardson, Louise. *What Terrorists Want: Understanding the Enemy. Containing the Threat*. New York: Random House, 2006.

———, ed. *The Roots of Terrorism*. New York: Routledge, 2006.

Ricks, Thomas E. *Fiasco: The American Military Adventure in Iraq*. New York: Penguin Press, 2006.

Rigby, Andrew. *Living the Intifada*. London: Zed Books, 1991.

Rogan, Eugene L. "The Emergence of the Middle East into the Modern State System." In Louise Fawcett, ed. *International Relations of the Middle East*. New York: Oxford University Press, 2005, pp. 17–39.

Rosecrance, Richard N., and Arthur A. Stein, eds. *No More States? Globalization, National Self-determination, and Terrorism*. Lanham, MD: Rowman & Littlefield, 2006.

Roth, Kenneth. "Despots Masquerading as Democrats." *Journal of Human Rights Practice* 1, no. 1 (March 2009): 140–155.

———. "Filling the Leadership Void: Where Is the European Union?" In Human Rights Watch, *World Report 2007: Events of 2006*. New York: Human Rights Watch, 2007.

Roy, Olivier. "A Clash of Cultures or a Debate on Europe's Values?" *ISIM Review* 15 (Spring 2005): 6–7.

Rubin, Barnett R. *The Fragmentation of Afghanistan: State Formation and Collapse in the International System*, 2nd ed. New Haven, CT: Yale University Press, 2002.

Safi, Louay. *Tensions and Transitions in the Muslim World*. Lanham, MD: University Press of America, 2003.

Said, Edward W. *From Oslo to Iraq and the Road Map*. New York: Pantheon, 2004.

Salinas, Moises F. *Planting Hatred, Sowing Pain: The Psychology of the Israeli-Palestinian Conflict*. Westport, CT: Praeger, 2007.

Sariolghalam, Mahmood. "Understanding Iran: Getting Past Stereotypes and Mythology." *Washington Quarterly* 26, no. 4 (Autumn 2003): 69–82.

Schleifer, Yigal. "Why Turkey Is Taking a Bolder Role." *Christian Science Monitor*, June 21, 2010, p. 10.

Shalev, Aryeh. *The Intifada: Causes and Effects*. Boulder, CO: Westview, 1991.

Sherman, Daniel J., and Terry Nardin, eds. *Terror, Culture, Politics: Rethinking 9/11*. Bloomington: Indiana University Press, 2006.

Simmons, Beth A. *Mobilizing for Human Rights: International Law in Domestic Politics*. New York: Cambridge University Press, 2009.

Singer, P. W. "Outsourcing War." *Foreign Affairs* 84, no. 2 (March–April 2005): 119–132.

Skidmore, David. "Understanding the Unilateralist Turn in U.S. Foreign Policy." *Foreign Policy Analysis* 1, no. 2 (July 2005): 207–228.

Smelser, Neil. *The Faces of Terrorism: Social and Psychological Dimensions*. Princeton, NJ: Princeton University Press, 2007.

Steele, Jonathan. "A War Fated to Fail: America's False Template in Iraq." *World Policy Journal* 25, no. 1 (Spring 2008): 80–88.

Sterling-Folker, Jennifer, ed. *Making Sense of International Relations Theory*. Boulder, CO: Lynne Rienner, 2006.

Stern, Seth. "Torture Debate." In CQ Press, ed. *Global Issues*. Washington, DC: CQ Press, 2008, pp. 139–163.

Stewart, Rory. "How to Save Afghanistan." *Time*, July 28, 2008, pp. 30–34.

———, and Gerald Knaus. *Can Intervention Work?* New York: W. W. Norton, 2011.

Stohl, Michael S. "Counterterrorism and Repression." In Louise Richardson, ed. *The Roots of Terrorism*. New York: Routledge, 2006, pp. 57–68.

Sturkey, Douglas. *The Limits of American Power: Prosecuting a Middle East Peace*. Northampton, MA: Edward Elgar, 2007.

Sussman, Gary. "The Challenge to the Two-State Solution." *Middle East Report* 34, no. 231 (Summer 2004): 8–15.

Swain, Carol M., ed. *Debating Immigration*. Cambridge: Cambridge University Press, 2007, pp. 237–253.

Takeyh, Ray. "Time for Détente with Iran." *Foreign Affairs* 86, no. 2 (March–April 2007): 17–32.

Talentino, Andrea Kathryn. *Military Intervention after the Cold War: The Evolution of Theory and Practice*. Athens: Ohio University Press, 2005.

Teitelbaum, Joshua. "The Palestinian Liberalization Organization." In Ami Ayalon, ed. *Middle East Contemporary Survey*. Boulder, CO: Westview, 1992, pp. 211–243.

Telhami, Shibley. *Reflections of Hearts and Minds*. Washington, DC: Brookings Institution, 2005.

Telhami, Shibley. *The Stakes; America and the Middle East: The Consequences of Power and the Choice for Peace*. Boulder, CO: Westview, 2002.

Terhalle, Maximilian. "Are the Shia Rising?" *Middle East Policy* 14, no. 2 (Summer 2007): 69–83.

US Army and Marine Corps. *Counterinsurgency Field Manual: U.S. Army*. Field Manual no. 3-24, Marine Corps War-fighting Publication no. 3-33.5. Chicago: University of Chicago Press, 2007.

Walt, Stephen M. *Taming American Power: The Global Response to U.S. Primacy*. New York: W. W. Norton, 2005.

———. "Taming American Power." *Foreign Affairs* 84, no. 5 (September–October 2005): 105–120.

Walzer, Michael. *Thinking Politically: Essays in Political Theory*. New Haven, CT: Yale University Press, 2007.

Weinberg, Leonard B.,William L. Eubank, and Elizabeth A. Francis. "The Cost of Terrorism: The Relationship between International Terrorism and Democratic Governance." *Terrorism and Political Violence* 20, no. 2 (April–June 2008): 257–270.

White, Jenny. "The Ebbing Power of Turkey's Secularist Elite." *Current History* 106, no. 704 (December 2007): 427–433.

Whittaker, David J. *Terrorism: Understanding the Global Threat*, rev. ed. New York: Pearson Longman, 2007.

Wilson, Richard Ashby, ed. *Human Rights in the "War on Terror."* New York: Cambridge University Press, 2005.

Wright, Robin. *Dreams and Shadows: The Future of the Middle East*. New York: Penguin Press, 2008.

Wright, Sue. "Citizenship Tests in Europe—Editorial Introduction." *International Journal on Multicultural Societies* 10, no. 1 (2008): 1–9.

Yildiz, Kerim. *The Kurds in Iraq: Past, Present, and Future*. London: Pluto Press, 2007.

Yoo, John. *War by Other Means: An Insider's Account of the War on Terror*. New York: Atlantic Monthly Press, 2006.

Zakaria, Fareed. "How Democracy Can Work in the Middle East." *Time*, February 3, 2011; available at www.time.com/time/worldrticle/0,8599,2045888-4,00.html; accessed February 14, 2011.

Zarif, Mohammad Javad, and Mustafa Zahrani, eds. *The New International Trends*. Tehran: Office of Political and International Studies, 2005.

Zinni, Toni, and Tony Koltz. *Leading the Charge: Leadership Lessons from the Battlefield to the Boardroom*. New York: Palgrave Macmillan, 2009.

Zogby, James J. "The Civil Rights of Arab American Muslims Are Being Violated." In Laura K. Egendorf, ed. *At Issue: Islam in America*. New York: Greenhaven Press, 2006, pp. 46–52.

Zunes, Stephen. *Tinderbox: U.S. Foreign Policy and the Roots of Terrorism*. Monroe, ME: Common Courage Press, 2003.

Index

Abbas, Mahmoud, 121–122, 138, 274
Abbottabad, 264
Abu Ghraib prison, 8, 36, 97, 104, 116, 158, 179, 182,
Afghanistan, 247, 264, 280: Bagram Air Force base, 12, 174, 243; budget year 2012, 277; counterinsurgency in, 27, 246; government of, 27; invasion of, 46; mainstream politics, 265; military intervention, 59–60; military measures, 34–37; NATO troops in, 48; post-9/11 war in, 3; proxy competition in, 267; resurgent Taliban in, 5; six direct neighbors, 268; soldiers in, 187; Taliban in, 27–31; *Three Cups of Tea*, 189; tribal areas, 267; US invasion of, 73–75
Afghan Taliban, 267
AfPak strategy, 10, 265, 268
African National Congress (ANC), 42
Ahmadinejad, Mahmoud, 106, 108, 148–149
Akhtar, Sajjad, 263–264
Al-Assad, Bashar, 147
Albright, Madeline, 136
Al-Khalifa, Hamad ibn Isa, 117
Al-Maliki, Nouri, 11, 40, 80, 194, 280
Al-Qaeda, 6, 21, 41–43, 75, 85, 99, 111, 109, 124, 135–137, 140, 143, 231, 244, 246, 249, 251, 257–258, 261, 264, 267–268, 280; al-Qaeda in Iraq (AQI), 27–28, 35; al-Qaeda captives, 225; al-Qaeda in the Islamic Maghreb, 257; leadership and organization, 28–29; Salafist Group for

Preaching and Combat (GSPC), 257
Al-Sadr, Muqtada, 11, 40
Alston, Philip, 276
Amal, 62
Anbar Salavation Council, 41
Ansari, Ali M., 144
Anti-globalization, 154
Anti-immigrant, 212, 216, 221
Anti-Muslim crimes, 226
Anti-terrorism, 146
Anti-Terrorism, Crime, and Security Act, 216
Arab League. *See* League of Arab States
Arab revolts, 96, 279: 2011 Arab Spring, 255, 257; democratic uprisings, 100; mass uprisings in Tunisia and Egypt, 109–112; popular uprisings, 123; 2011 uprisings, 264
Arafat, Yasser, 67
Arar, Maher, 176, 231
Ashcroft, John, 227
Assad, Bashar Al-, 147
Asylum seekers, 214

Babacan, Ali, 274
Bagram Air Base, 12, 243. *See also* Afghanistan
Baku-Ceyhan pipeline, 270
Bal, Ihsan, 44
Banlieues, 209
Barak, Ehud, 137
Bellin, Eva, 98
Ben Ali, Zine El Abidine, 112
Bin Laden, Osama, 14, 120, 251, 260, 262–264
Black sites, 224

Blackwater, 182, 187
Blasphemy, 215
Bonn Agreement, 147
Boyle, Michael J., 26
Brenner, Jeremy, 280
Brzezinski, Zbigniew, 34, 102
Bush, George W., 2, 77, 138, 229, 266
Bush Doctrine, 9, 97–103, 113, 121
Bybee, Jay S., 179
Byman, Daniel, 157

Cairo Institute for Human Rights
    Studies (CIHRS), 105
Cameron, David, 213
Camp David, 145
Cardinas, Sonia, 174
Carter, Jimmy, 70
Caspian Sea, 59
Central Asia, 59
Cesari, Jocelyne, 215
Chechnya, 23, 38, 223
Chirac, Jacques, 210
Chomsky, Noam, 62
CIA, 17, 34, 67, 107, 120, 182, 231,
    276, 279; CIA officials, 34; CIA and
    British agents, 119; CIA-operated
    planes, 226; detention centers in
    Afghanistan and Guantanamo Bay,
    243, 225, 251; "high value targets,"
    224; interment practices, 225; Joint
    Special Operations Command
    (JSOC), 140; secret incommunicado
    detention locations, 226; secret pris-
    ons run by the CIA, 226, 231
Citizenship test, 208, 219, 259
Clarke, Richard A., 135
Clear Law Enforcement for Criminal
    Alien Removal Act (CLEAR), 228
Clientelism, 104
Coalition Support Fund, 263
Commission for Racial Equality, 213
Common Article 3, 175–176
Community cohesion, 212
Convention Against Torture (CAT), 2,
    32, 178, 181–182, 198, 226, 250
Convention on the Elimination of all
    Forms of Racial Discrimination,
    217
Counterterrorism, 1, 5–6, 9, 13–14, 36,
    38, 191–193, 208, 216, 276, 281;

counterinsurgency and counterter-
    rorism, 25–31, 276–277; counterter-
    rorism arsenal, 264; counterterror-
    ism and immigration control tactics,
    216; counterterrorism measures,
    208; counterterrorism policy, 243;
    rendition and secret detention,
    224–226; tools, 12–13, 18, 34
Criminal Justice, 44

Dagi, Ihsan, 272
Darfur, 23
Davidson, Lawrence, 137
Davutoglu, Ahmet, 153
De-Baathification, 35
Denbeaux, Mark P., 261
Department of Justice (DOJ), 228–229
Diplomacy, 131–163: multilateral
    diplomacy, 159; multilateralism,
    163;
Dworkin, Ronald, 33
Dutch law, 221
Dutch Model, 234, 258

Eikenberry, Karl, 180
Enforcement commitment, 13, 172,
    191, 198
"Enhanced interrogation techniques,"
    11, 181–183. *See also* torture
Erdogan, Recep Tayyip, 83, 274;
    Turkish option and, 269–275
European Islam, 233
Europeanization, 273
European Union (EU), 101–103, 269,
    275
Evans, Gareth, 132
Extraordinary rendition, 180, 208, 224

Falk, Richard, 85
Falkoff, Marc D., 181
Faustian bargain, 172
Fatah, 121
Fayed, Tarek Mohammed, 217
Federal Bureau of Investigation (FBI),
    226–227
Forsythe, David P., 243
Fortuyn, Pim, 215
Forward strategy of freedom, 103

Gaza blockade, 72

Gaza elections, 274
Gender inequality, 101
Geneva Conventions, 4, 175, 183, 186, 224, 230, 244, 250, 275
Geneva prisoner-of-war statutes, 231
Ghettoization, 219
Gobat, Michel, 98
Goldstone Report, 72
Gonzalez, Alberto, 185
Gorbachev, Mikhail, 58
Gordon, Philip H., 158
Green line, 262
Green Movement, 96, 105–109
Guantanamo Bay, 8: Afghanistan and Iraq wars, 73–81; CIA and detention centers, 243, 225, 251; DOJ and CIA, 229–232; human rights abuses, 171–198; military measures, 34–37; reframing the debate, 243–282; torture debate, 31–34; unlawful enemy combatants, 171–198; US invasion of Afghanistan, 73–81; US Strategy, 10. *See also* Abu Ghraib prison
Gulf Cooperation Council (GCC), 66, 133, 142

Haass, Richard N., 80
Hafetz, Jonathan, 261
Hague Conference, 147
Hamas, 69–72, 96, 123, 138, 152
Hamdan v. Rumsfeld, 175, 230
Hamdi v. Rumsfeld, 230
Hamdi, Yaser E., 230
Haqqani network, 260
Hariri, Rafiq, 151
Hariri, Saad, 152
Hate speech, 196
Hate crimes, 226
Hezbollah, 61–63, 121, 123, 145–146, 151–152,
Hijab, 210
Hoffmann, Stanley, 248–249
Holbrooke, Richard, 181
Holocaust, 62
Holsti, K. J., 250
Human rights, 171–198, 253: Anti-terror norm, 198; basic rights, 193, 195; civil liberties, 8; civil society, 22; criminal justice, 13, 18; derogable rights, 193; detainess abuse in

Iraq, 11; due process rights, 193; full and fair trial, 193; humanitarian treatment standards, 193; laws of war and human rights, 198; non-derogable rights, 193; post-conflict nation-building and reconstruction, 198; protections, 31; records, 186; rule of law, 9, 192–198; security and liberty, 195; women's empowerment, 101
Human Rights Council, 252
Human Rights Watch, 254
Human security, 172, 187, 190, 197, 249–254, 276
Human wrongs, 183
Hussein, Saddam, 3, 39, 113, 162

Identity, 13, 114, 172, 191, 198
Ijtihad, 114
"Illegal enemy combatants," 183
Imperial presidency, 173
Integration examination, 220
International Atomic Energy Agency (IAEA), 248, 275
International Criminal Court (ICC), 116, 248
International Criminal Tribunal for the Former Yugoslavia (ICTY), 33
International Humanitarian Law (IHL), 175
Intifada, 56, 64–65, 67–68: first intifada, 63–65; second intifada, 67–73
International Monetary Fund (IMF), 246
Interventionist doctrine, 244
Irish Republican Army (IRA), 26, 38, 42
Iranian Revolutionary Guard, 140
Iraq Study Group (ISG), 139
Iraqi National Alliance (INA), 80
Irregular warfare, 171
Islamabad, 266–267
Islamophobia, 207–234, 259
Israeli Defense Forces (IDF), 62–64
Israeli-Palestinian conflict, 12, 104, 113–114, 134–136, 157, 159, 262
Israeli-Palestinian peace, 113, 119
Israeli-Syrian negotiations, 273

Jenkinson, Brett, 280

Judicial deference approach, 196
Jus cogens, 180
Justice and Development Party (Adalet
ve Kalkinma Partisi—AKP), 101,
115–116, 258, 268, 270–272
Jylland-Posten, 210

Kahan Commission, 61
Karimov, Islam, 95
Karoubi, Mehdi, 107
Karzai, Hamid, 74, 143, 265, 268
Kepel, Gilles, 209
Khalidi, Rashid, 57
Khalifa, Hamad ibn Isa Al-, 117
Khamenei, Ayatollah Ali, 108
Khomeini, Ayatollah Ruhollah, 106,
108
Khouri, Rami George, 63
Kibaki, Mwai, 95
Kilcullen, David, 27
King, Mary Elizabeth, 64
Koltz, Tony, 276
Kurdistan Regional Government
(KRG), 156
Kurdish-Arab tensions, 280
Kurdish Workers' Party (PKK),
153–154, 156, 269–270

Labardini, Rodrigo, 171
Landau Commission, 65
Lashkar-e-Taiba, 260
Lausanne Treaty, 44
League of Arab States, 82, 133, 152
Lebanonized, 151
Lewis, Anthony, 196
Lieven, Anatol, 267
Likud Party, 137
Loya jirga, 147, 279
Luban, David, 191

Mafinezam, Alidad, 273
Maliki, Nouri Al-, 11, 40, 80, 194, 280
Mamdani, Mahmood, 271
Marshall Plan, 271
Mayer, Jane, 177
McChrystal, Stanley, 276
Mearsheimer, John, 134
Mehrabi, Aria, 273
Meshaal, Khaled, 155, 274
Migration Policy Institute (MPI), 217

Military intervention, 55–88
Military Commission Act (MCA), 230,
244
Moderate Arab bloc, 150–152
Mokhtari, Shadi, 252
Moore, Jina, 182
Mortenson, Greg, 189
Mossadeq, Mohammad, 57–58, 106,
119
Moussavi, Mir-Hossein, 105–107, 111,
148
Mubarak, Hosni, 21–23, 70, 95, 109,
119, 151, 245
Mugabe, Robert, 95
Mujahidin, 17, 120, 266
Mullen, Mike, 78–79, 261
Multiculturalism, 210–213, 218–219,
223, 233, 276
Musharraf, Pervez, 95, 266
Muslim Brotherhood, 86
Muslim diaspora, 207–209: anti-
Arab/Muslim policies, 232; anti-
Islamic narrative, 232; civic inte-
gration courses, 222; civic-political
inclusion and integration programs,
232–233; economic integration and
militant Islam, 232; ethnic minorities, 233; ethnic violence, 221;
Everyday Security Law, 223;
European Muslims, 233; finger-
print and immigration violations,
232; first-generation and second-
generation immigrants, 233;
Flemish people and culture, 223;
German constitution, 222–223;
homegrown terrorism in the West,
232; honor killings, 221;
Immigration, Asylum, and
Nationality Act, 223; immigrants,
218–220, 232–234; immigrants in
the United States, 232; integration
debate, 221; language tests, 222;
male and female applicants, 222;
Muslim Americans, 233; Muslim
communities in Europe, 231
Muslim enemy, 232; Muslim immigrants, 102; "nationality" and
"active participation," 224; stereotypes, 222; UK Home Office, 223
Mutual constitution, 249

Nacos, Brigitte L., 45
Nasr, Vali, 41, 78
National Intelligence Estimate (NIE),
    141
Nationality Laws, 218
Nationality Tests, 220
National Security Agency (NSA), 196
National Transition Council (NTC), 83,
    248
Neoconservatives, 114, 122
Non-derogation, 252
Non-Proliferation Treaty (NPT), 37,
    150
Nye, Joseph, 163

Obama, Barak, 10, 46, 48, 75, 111–112,
    124
Obama doctrine, 110–112
Oliver Relin, David, 189
Orientalism, 107, 123
Osiraq strike, 143
Oslo Accords, 136–137, 274
Ottoman Empire, 56–57

Padilla, Jose, 185, 229
Padilla v. Bush, 229
Pakistan: Inter-Services Intelligence
    (ISI), 120, 261, 265; military assis-
    tance, 263; Pakistani army, 266;
    Pakistan's counterterrorism strategy,
    266; Pakistani intelligence officials,
    264; Pakistani state, 264; US-
    Pakistan relations, 263–265
Palestine Liberation Organization
    (PLO), 60–64, 68
Passenger Name Records (PNR), 214
Partiya Jiyana Azad a Kurdistane
    (PJAK—Party for a Free Life), 269
Patrimonialism, 104
Perez, Shimon, 274
Persian Gulf, 100, 112, 114, 116, 160
Petraeus, David H., 278
Political Islam, 99, 101
Political liberalization, 103
Private military firms (PMFs), 186
Privatization, 246
Putin, Vladimir, 95

Qaddafi, Muammar, 81, 83–84
Qaeda, al-, 6, 21, 41–43, 75, 85, 99,

111, 109, 124, 135–137, 140, 143,
    231, 244, 246, 249, 251, 257–258,
    261, 264, 267–268, 280; al-Qaeda in
    Iraq (AQI), 27–28, 35; al-Qaeda
    captives, 225; al-Qaeda in the
    Islamic Maghreb, 257; leadership
    and organization, 28–29; Salafist
    Group for Preaching and Combat
    (GSPC), 257
Quandt, William B., 131, 159
Quartet, 135, 138

Rasul v. Bush, 184
Rendition, 224–226
Resistance bloc, 145–150
Responsibility to Protect, 81–82
Reza Shah, 58
Rice, Condoleezza, 33, 103, 119
Richards, Alan, 99
Rogue states, 5
Roth, Kenneth, 254
Rumsfeld v. Padilla, 185

Sadr, Muqtada Al-, 11, 40
Salafi groups, 114, 144
Sarkozy, Nicolas, 223
Securitization, 43, 215–216, 234, 249
Sharon, Ariel, 69, 135, 137, 262
Shiite crescent, 78
Shwe, Than, 95
Siniora, Fouad, 121
Six-Day War, 58
Social networking, 123
Soft power, 43
Special registration, 232
State-secrets doctrine, 176
Stewart, Rory, 246, 277
Strategic depth, 267
Sub-Saharan Africa, 104
Suleiman, Michel, 121, 152
Supreme Council for the Islamic
    Revolution in Iraq (ISCIRI), 40
Supreme Court, 175, 186

Taliban, 18, 73–75, 140, 246, 249, 264,
    266, 268
Tarhanli, Turgut, 44
Telhami, Shibley, 47, 114
Terrorism: anti-terror cooperation, 29;
    campaign against, 47, 255; chal-

lenge of deterring, 198; criminal justice system, 195; fighting poverty, 278; global war of ideas, 282; homegrown, 232; London transit attacks, 207; Madrid bombings, 207; multicausal social phenomenon, 234; roots of, 11, 18–22; September 11 attacks, 31, 207; strategies to counter, 3; war or crime, 163. *See also* "War on Terror"
Torture, 31–33, 183, 191, 226, 232, 249–250, 252, 281
Torture memos, 182
Trade-off, 15, 171–198, 249
Transcultural space, 208
Transnational networks, 212
Transnational terrorism, 244
Turkey: AKP and Hamas-controlled government, 155; anti-terror law, 44; integration in the EU, 233; Justice and Development Party (AKP), 149; Turkey connection, 153–157; visit of Hamas delegation, 155
Turkish-Iranian cooperation, 269
Turkish-Israeli relationship, 270
Turko-Persian realm, 273

Uniform Code of Military Justice, 176, 187, 193
Unilateralism, 133
Unitary executive, 177
Universal Declaration of Human Rights, 253
Universality, 13, 172, 191, 198, 253

UN Resolution 242, 137
US anti-terrorism policy, 244
USA Patriot Act, 4, 174, 227–228, 249
US Central Command, 278
US Detainee Treatment Act, 244

Van Gogh, Theo, 215
Velayate-e faqih, 108
Vera Institute of Justice, 232

Wahhabi, 114
Walzer, Michael, 187
Walt, Stephen M., 80, 134, 262
War crimes, 250
"War on terror," 5, 110, 138, 192, 249, 259, 263, 275–276, 278; and human rights, 171–198; immigration politics and Islamophobia, 207; introduction, 1–14; reframing the debate, 243–282; terrorism, security, and human rights, 17–48;
West, Darrell, 108
World Bank, 246
World Summit Outcome (WSO), 251–252
Wright, Robin, 35, 107

Yoo, John, 177–178

Zelikow, Philip, 33
Zenawi, Meles, 95
Zinni, Tony, 276
Zionist policies, 113

About the Book

Scholars and policymakers disagree on the most effective way to counter transnational terrorism, generating debate on a range of questions: Do military interventions increase or decrease the recruitment capability of transnational terrorists? Should we privilege diplomacy over military force in the campaign against terror? Can counterterrorist measures be applied without violating human rights? More fundamentally, is it possible to effectively wage a war against terrorism? Grappling with these questions, Mahmood Monshipouri reviews alternative strategies for combating terrorism and makes the case for the continued relevance of international law and diplomacy as measures for severing its roots in the Middle East and elsewhere.

Monshipouri underlines the need to redefine security to include the protection of human rights. In that context, he examines the limits of the use of force, torture, and externally imposed democratization and focuses on the conditions under which alternative counterterrorism tools can be viable. While acknowledging that there is no easy remedy to the tensions between security needs and human rights, he makes a compelling argument that the pursuit of a security template that sacrifices civil liberties is not only morally debilitating, but also politically imprudent.

Mahmood Monshipouri is associate professor of international relations at San Francisco State University. His publications include *Muslims in Global Politics: Identities, Interests, and Human Rights* and *Islamism, Secularism, and Human Rights in the Middle East.*